Essays in Animal Behaviour

Essays in Animal Behaviour
Celebrating 50 Years
of *Animal Behaviour*

Edited by

Jeffrey R. Lucas
Leigh W. Simmons

AMSTERDAM • BOSTON • HEIDELBERG • LONDON
NEW YORK • OXFORD • PARIS • SAN DIEGO
SAN FRANCISCO • SINGAPORE • SYDNEY • TOKYO
Academic Press is an imprint of Elsevier

Elsevier Academic Press
30 Corporate Drive, Suite 400, Burlington, MA 01803, USA
525 B Street, Suite 1900, San Diego, California 92101-4495, USA
84 Theobald's Road, London WC1X 8RR, UK

This book is printed on acid-free paper. ∞

Library of Congress Cataloging-in-Publication Data
Essays in animal behaviour : celebrating 50 years of animal behaviour / edited by Jeffrey
    R. Lucas, Leigh W. Simmons.
       p. cm.
    ISBN-13: 978-0-12-369499-7 (alk. paper)
    ISBN-10: 0-12-369499-X (alk. paper)
    1. Animal behavior. I. Lucas, Jeffrey R. II. Simmons, Leigh W., 1960- III. Animal behaviour.
    QL751.E65 2005
591.5—dc22   2005052079

British Library Cataloguing in Publication Data
A catalogue record for this book is available from the British Library

ISBN 13: 978-0-12-369499-7
ISBN 10: 0-12-369499-X

For all information on all Elsevier Academic Press publications visit our Web site at
www.books.elsevier.com

Printed in the United States of America

05   06   07   08   09   10   9   8   7   6   5   4   3   2   1

Credits

Contents

Section III _____

PROXIMATE MECHANISMS

Section IV _____

DEVELOPMENT

Section V _____

ADAPTATION

Section VI

ANIMAL WELFARE

Contributors

John Alcock, (Chapter 2) Department of Biology, Arizona State University, Tempe, Arizona 85287 United States

Jeanne Altmann, (Chapter 4) Institute of Primate Research, National Museums of Kenya, Department of Conservation Biology, Chicago Zoological Society, Department of Ecology and Evolutionary Biology, Princeton University, Princeton, New Jersey 08544 United States

Stuart A. Altmann, (Chapter 4) Department of Ecology and Evolutionary Biology, Princeton University, Princeton, New Jersey 08544 United States

Malte Andersson, (Chapter 15) Department of Zoology, University of Gothenburg, Göteborg SE 405 30 Sweden

Stevan J. Arnold, (Chapter 5) Department of Zoology, Oregon State University, Corvallis, Oregon 97331 United States

Andrew I. Barnes, (Chapter 9) Department of Biology, University College London, London WC1E 6BT United Kingdom

Patrick Bateson, (Chapter 10) Sub-Department of Animal Behaviour, University of Cambridge, Cambridge CB3 8AA United Kingdom

Marian Stamp Dawkins, (Chapter 20) Department of Zoology, University of Oxford, Oxford OX1 3PS United Kingdom

Bennett G. Galef, Jr., (Chapter 11) Department of Psychology, McMaster University, Hamilton, Ontario L8S 4K1 Canada

Patricia Adair Gowaty, (Chapter 14) Institute of Ecology, University of Georgia, Athens, Georgia 30602 United States

Michael D. Greenfield, (Chapter 17) Department of Ecology and Evolutionary Biology, University of Kansas, Lawrence, Kansas 66045 United States

Felicity A. Huntingford, (Chapter 6) Fish Biology Group, Division of Environmental & Evolutionary Biology, Institute of Biomedical & Life Sciences, University of Glasgow, Glasgow G12 8QQ Scotland

Andrew P. King, (Chapter 13) Department of Psychology, Indiana University, Bloomington, Indiana 47405 United States

Jeffrey R. Lucas, (Chapter 1) Department of Biological Sciences, Purdue University, West Lafayette, Indiana 47907 United States

Geoff A. Parker, (Chapter 3) Population and Evolutionary Biology Research Group, School of Biological Sciences, University of Liverpool, Liverpool L69 7ZB United Kingdom

Linda Partridge, (Chapter 9) Department of Biology, University College London, London WC1E 6BT United Kingdom

Gene E. Robinson, (Chapter 7) Department of Entomology and Neuroscience Program, University of Illinois at Urbana-Champaign, Urbana, Illinois 61801 United States

Leigh W. Simmons, (Chapter 1) School of Animal Biology, The University of Western Australia, Nedlands WA 6009 Australia

P. J. B. Slater, (Chapter 18) School of Biology, University of St. Andrews, St. Andrews, Fife KY16 9TS United Kingdom

Judy Stamps, (Chapter 12) Evolution and Ecology, University of California at Davis, Davis, California 95616 United States

Meredith J. West, (Chapter 13) Department of Psychology, Indiana University, Bloomington, Indiana 47405 United States

David J. White, (Chapter 13) Department of Psychology, University of Pennsylvania, Philadelphia, Pennsylvania 19104 United States

Roswitha Wiltschko, (Chapter 19) Fachbereich Biologie und Informatik der J. W. Goethe-Universität, Frankfurt am Main, Zoologie D-60323 Germany

Wolfgang Wiltschko, (Chapter 19) Fachbereich Biologie und Informatik der J. W. Goethe-Universität, Frankfurt am Main, Zoologie D-60323 Germany

John C. Wingfield, (Chapter 8) Department of Zoology, University of Washington, Seattle, Washington 98195 United States

Amotz Zahavi, (Chapter 16) Institute for Nature Conservation Research, Tel-Aviv University, Tel-Aviv 69978 Israel

1

Fifty Years of Animal Behaviour

Jeffrey R. Lucas
Department of Biological Sciences
Purdue University

Leigh W. Simmons
School of Animal Biology
The University of Western Australia

The year 2003 marked the 50th anniversary of the publication of *Animal Behaviour*. The journal first appeared in 1953 as the *British Journal of Animal Behaviour*, a quarterly publication replacing the old *Bulletin* of the founding body of the Association for the Study of Animal Behaviour (ASAB), the Institute for the Study of Animal Behaviour. The brainchild of William H. Thorpe and the product of then ASAB treasurer James Fisher's labour, the *British Journal of Animal Behaviour* provided a flagship for the growing ASAB. Five years after its launch, increasing contact between British and North American researchers resulted in the renaming of the journal to *Animal Behaviour,* which became the joint publication of the ASAB and the Animal Behavior and Sociobiology Section of the Ecological Society of America, the founding body of the Animal Behaviour Society.

To mark the 50th anniversary of *Animal Behaviour*, we asked a group of prominent behaviourists to write essays relevant to their fields to be published in the journal. This book is an outgrowth of those initial essays. With some (but not all) constraints on space relaxed, we solicited seven more essays from an additional seven prominent animal behaviourists. With these additional essays, we were able to expand our coverage of sexual selection and animal communication, the two most published fields in *Animal Behaviour* in recent years. We were also able to add a chapter on molecular genetics, one on the acquisition of information under social settings, one on animal welfare, and an additional chapter on the history of our discipline by Geoff Parker, someone who has been extraordinarily influential in generating that history. The result is a series of essays that we feel is entertaining, thought provoking, and in some cases, capable of promoting new research efforts in our field that will start us on the next 50 years.

It is important for any field to be both retrospective and prospective: where have we been, where are we now, and where are we going? These essays provide a glimpse of the study of behaviour looking in all directions. History and future aside, it is simply interesting to get this information from the perspective of the behaviourists who have helped shape both the past and the future. The authors have done and will do just this.

This book starts with five essays on the history of animal behaviour. John Alcock is the author of one of the most widely published textbooks on behaviour (*Animal Behaviour*), now in its 8th edition. John looks back at how the coverage of behaviour in leading textbooks has changed over the last 50 years. Geoff Parker describes landmark papers as an index of how our field has changed. Stuart and Jeanne Altmann discuss how field studies have changed, and Stevan Arnold discusses the importance of natural history. Finally, Felicity Huntingford takes a "partial, ignorant and prejudiced" view of the history of behavioural studies by focusing on stickleback research. Sticklebacks have been a model organism in behavioural research, dating back to the early landmark studies on sticklebacks by Niko Tinbergen himself, making this view worth considering.

The next set of three essays covers proximate mechanisms of behaviour. Gene Robinson covers molecular genetic approaches to the study of social behaviour. As Robinson shows, this is an exploding field with the capacity to change the way we think about behaviour. Similarly, John Wingfield discusses hormonal aspects of the physiological and behavioural responses to "capricious environments." Finally, Andrew Barnes and Linda Partridge discuss how an understanding of proximate mechanisms of reproduction can influence life-history theory. This essay underscores one of the more exciting aspects of behaviour: multiple approaches (here, proximate and ultimate causation) give us a richer understanding of behaviour.

The third set of essays covers the development of behaviour, as Judy Stamps calls it, "Tinbergen's fourth question." If these essays are any guide, Tinbergen's fourth question has a bright future. Some of this future is firmly grounded in the past, as Patrick Bateson shows with his discussion of imprinting and environmental "triggers" of development, and as Bennett (Jeff) Galef shows with his discussion of the acquisition of information in both social and nonsocial settings. Some of this future is reflective of a missed opportunity. Judy Stamps discusses the "norm of reaction approach," something missing in our first five decades. Judy shows that this approach can give us some insight into stable variation between individuals with predictable suites of correlated traits. West, King, and White are the strongest advocates of this view, suggesting that our neglect of the developmental component of behaviour can give us a biased understanding of behaviour.

The fourth set of essays is about the adaptive significance of behaviour. As Patricia Gowaty illustrates, our understanding of the adaptive significance of mating behaviour, and specifically about extra-pair paternity, has gone through decade-long swings. This underscores the importance of history in our literature. It is important to understand what the prevailing paradigm was when a paper was written in order to understand the context within which that paper was written. The issue of sexual selection, per se, is taken up by Malte Andersson and Amotz Zahavi. Malte discusses condition-dependent signals and argues that our understanding of these signals is aided by explicit mathematical models. In contrast, Amotz Zahavi, the author of the "handicap principle," wonders why such analytical approaches are so necessary. Michael Greenfield looks at signals more broadly, from the perspective of the relative honesty of the signal. His essay provides an interesting link to Stamps and West and colleagues because he argues that we need a better understanding of how reaction norms (i.e., environment-dependent phenotypes) influence the evolution of signals. Peter Slater tackles the history of the study of bird song. Although this essay focuses on the function of song, Slater illustrates that mechanisms (especially genetic) and the development of song have a rich history. He ends his essay with key questions for future research. The final essay in this section is on avian navigation by Roswitha and Wolfgang Wiltschko. Here, the Wiltschkos describe the enormous strides we have made in the study of navigation and where current research should focus.

These essays end with Marian Dawkins's history of behaviour and animal welfare. This is a reasonable capstone for our essays, in part because animal welfare is a central issue in the way that almost all behaviourists conduct their science. It is a reasonable capstone because, even here, we need to know about the development and the proximal mechanisms of behaviour, in addition to its evolutionary aspects, to address animal welfare problems with any reasonable degree of clarity.

The history of any field is a good place to look for its future. This is brilliantly illustrated in this diverse set of essays. In these essays, younger students of animal behaviour will get a unique glimpse of their own field. Established students of animal behaviour will get a personalized exposé of our changing and challenging field. Enjoy!

2

A Textbook History of Animal Behaviour

John Alcock
Department of Biology
Arizona State University

Abstract

The history of animal behaviour research over the last 50 years has been marked by a decline in traditional ethology and an increase in the prominence of behavioural ecology. Here I examine these changes in the discipline of animal behaviour during the past 50 years as reflected in specialized behaviour textbooks and introductory textbooks for general biology courses. Prior to 1975, all the behaviour texts devoted far more coverage to ethological research on the proximate causes of behaviour than to research on the adaptive value of behavioural traits. After 1975, ultimate questions about adaptation received much more attention than they had previously. The change took place because of events in the mid-1960s, including W. D. Hamilton's solution to the evolutionary puzzle of altruism and the group selection debate involving V. C. Wynne-Edwards, G. C. Williams and D. Lack. The effect of these events was to encourage researchers to use sound adaptationist theory untainted by species-benefit thinking. The theory helped identify many new questions about the adaptive value of behavioural traits, stimulating workers to give as much weight to these issues as had previously been devoted to research into the physiology and development of behaviour. Although pure ethological research appeared to decline after 1975, in fact the major proximate concerns of ethology were simply taken on by cell biologists and neurophysiologists who used tools not available to the classic ethologist. The result was the development of neuroethology, which has flourished over the years. However, classic (pre-1975) ethological research still receives considerable coverage in many introductory biology textbooks, possibly because of the weight given these studies by W. T. Keeton in his influential textbook. None the less, ever since the 1980s, most biology textbooks have also discussed some of the fruits of adaptationist theory, especially Hamilton's explanation for altruism, thereby providing a more balanced treatment of proximate and ultimate issues than was once the case.

A textbook tells us something about the nature of a discipline. Admittedly the statement may be biased or unbalanced by the quirks, unusual background or special interests of the author. But still a textbook does provide a snapshot, blurry or otherwise, during the year or two that the text was being written (or revised). Here I examine the history of the field of animal behaviour as reflected primarily in textbook treatments of the subject. These textbooks illustrate some of the major changes that have taken place in our discipline over the last 50 years. I shall examine some, but not all, of the specialized behaviour textbooks as well as sampling several general biology texts that devote a chapter or two to animal behaviour inasmuch as these books introduce a large undergraduate audience to the discipline. My focus will be on the approach to animal behaviour taken by academic biologists and so I will say little about comparative and physiological psychology, two subdisciplines that are not now well represented in *Animal Behaviour* or the other major biological journals of the field, including *Behavioral Ecology and Sociobiology*, *Behavioral Ecology*, *Behaviour* and *Ethology*.

Ethology and the Early Textbooks

Because the ethologists Konrad Lorenz and Niko Tinbergen founded the modern biological approach to behaviour, the starting point for my survey will be Tinbergen's textbook *The Study of Instinct* (Tinbergen 1951). In his book, Tinbergen laid out his famous four main questions about behaviour, which can be paraphrased as follows: how do physiological mechanisms control behaviour, how do these mechanisms develop within individuals, what is the adaptive value of a behavioural trait, and how did the trait originate and become modified over evolutionary time? Tinbergen's four-part scheme is still highly relevant and useful. His system can be easily accommodated within the proximate–ultimate dichotomy that Mayr (1961) argued was central to biology. Tinbergen's first two questions about the physiology and development of behaviour belong to the proximate category, whereas questions about adaptive value and evolutionary origin fall in the complementary ultimate group.

Although Tinbergen's four questions deal with both proximate and ultimate aspects of behaviour, the pioneering ethologists devoted more effort and made more important contributions to understanding the proximate causes of behaviour, especially with respect to instincts. The extra investment in proximate studies can be seen in Tinbergen's (1951) book. There he quickly disposes of the distinctive descriptive element of ethology, the construction of ethograms. He then outlines what was known by 1950 about the developmental and physiological causes of selected behaviour patterns, with special emphasis on the relation between sign stimuli and innate responses. His coverage of these matters consumes roughly 135 pages (the total number of pages in the five chapters that deal primarily with proximate questions about behaviour, such as Chapter II on 'Behaviour as a reaction to external stimuli'). Tinbergen examines evolutionary aspects of animal behaviour in just two chapters, one on adaptive behaviour and the other reviewing the factors affecting the evolutionary history of behaviour. These two chapters total only 60 pages and included among these are six pages that deal with the ethological study of man, a section given over almost exclusively to proximate analyses of human instincts. Thus, Tinbergen gave even greater emphasis to proximate research than is indicated by simply comparing the total page counts from the two sets of chapters.

The emphasis on the proximate component of behavioural research (physiology and development) continued in the textbooks that followed into the early 1970s (Fig. 2-1). In addition, other important reviews such as Peter Marler and W. J. Hamilton's *Mechanisms of Animal Behavior* (1966) also

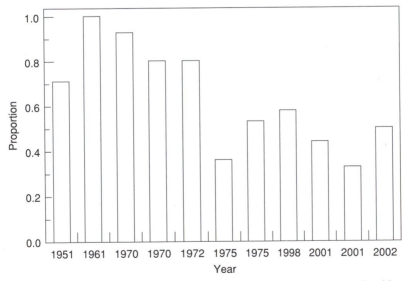

Figure 2-1 The change over the years in the proportion of chapters dealing primarily with proximate causes in selected behavioural textbooks, beginning with Tinbergen (1951), then Dethier & Stellar (1961), Hinde (1970), Eibl-Eibesfeldt (1970), Manning (1972), Brown (1975), Alcock (1975), Manning & Dawkins (1998), Goodenough *et al.* (2001), Alcock (2001) and Drickamer *et al.* (2002). (All introductory chapters and any others that cover both proximate and ultimate matters were considered to contribute equally to the proximate and ultimate tally when calculating an overall proportion of chapters devoted to proximate issues.)

focused primarily on proximate aspects of behaviour. Indeed, the authors state explicitly that they omitted behavioural ecology on the grounds that the topic 'seemed to demand quite a different treatment' (page vii in Marler & Hamilton 1966). In fact, *Mechanisms* did raise evolutionary issues from time to time as in a discussion of the functional advantages and disadvantages of acoustical versus visual signalling systems. Nevertheless, Marler & Hamilton's book was primarily about proximate causes. The fact that they could write more than 700 pages on this subject says something about the quantity of proximate behavioural research that had been done by 1966.

That ethology was strongly allied with proximate matters, especially the developmental and neural control of instinctive behaviours, can also be seen in James Gould's (1982) *Ethology*, which was written at a time when the traditional ethological approach had become somewhat overshadowed by the growing body of research in behavioural ecology. Gould mounted a spirited defence of the instinct concept while summarizing much research on the proximate causes of behaviour in 23 chapters (388 pages). Evolutionary issues were covered much more briefly in 8 chapters (154 pages), and in fact some of the material in these chapters actually dealt with descriptive or proximate aspects of behaviour.

Why did all of the early (and some of the later) ethologically oriented textbooks give more weight to the proximate as opposed to the evolutionary aspects of behaviour? I suggest it was because ethologists published more important papers on proximate matters than on ultimate ones, thanks to their novel and productive theory of instincts. Ethological theory argued that behaviour patterns were traits that could be inherited and then activated by simple sensory cues in the environment. Papers based on this theory dominate the edited collection, *Foundations of Animal Behavior* (Houck & Drickamer 1996), which contains articles deemed classics by a panel of behavioural biologists. The book contains three sections given over to proximate issues, a total of 24 papers, all published before 1974, whereas the key evolutionary articles fill just one section of eight papers. Likewise, when the Nobel Committee honoured Lorenz, Tinbergen and von Frisch in 1973, the award was given in physiology for discoveries about the 'organization and elicitation of individual and social behaviour patterns', in other words, for ethological discoveries about the proximate causes of behaviour.

Instinct theory attracted interest in part because it went against the then prevailing psychological–behaviourist view, exemplified by Skinnerian conditioning theory. Although the debate about the ethological perspective was often spirited (see Lehrman 1953 versus Lorenz 1965) and continued into the 1970s and 1980s, with the ethological position defended by Eibl-Eibesfeldt (1975) and Gould (1982), the controversy about instinct as opposed to learning (nature versus nurture) helped focus attention on the proximate causes of behaviour.

Ethology and Group Selection

If we accept the notion that theory directs research, as some of us do (e.g. Brown 1994), then ethologists had a broad-ranging, productive and controversial theory with which to explore key elements of the proximate causation of behaviour. True, some ethologists also used evolutionary theory when studying the origins and history of complex traits, especially the courtship displays of ducks, gulls and other animals. This ultimate topic is outlined clearly in the books of Tinbergen (1951), Eibl-Eibesfeldt (1970) and Manning (1972). But most early ethologists did not make much use of the component of modern evolutionary theory that deals with adaptation. These persons, like so many biologists prior to the 1970s, did not recognize the distinction between what came to be called group selection theory versus the theory of natural selection acting among individuals (Williams 1966). Lorenz, for example, assumed that selection in favour of group-benefiting traits was commonplace; his book on *On Aggression* explains many aspects of animal conflicts in terms of their supposed species-preserving functions (Lorenz 1966). Tinbergen was less emphatically group selectionist but he too stated that '. . . fighting, while potentially fatal to certain individuals, is generally advantageous to the species as a whole' (page 175 in Tinbergen 1951), a claim he made within a section of his book entitled 'Activities advantageous to the group'. Tinbergen continued to offer group selectionist explanations for social behaviour into the 1960s (Davies 1991). The idea that individuals would act for the benefit of their species persisted even later as in Scott's (1972) *Animal Behavior*, where he accepts several group benefit hypotheses, writing that 'the functions of agonistic behavior tend to evolve in ways which promote the survival of the group' (page 285 in Scott 1972).

During the period when most ethologists accepted the notion that many social attributes had evolved for the benefit of the species as a whole, they were not able to appreciate that apparent self-sacrificing characteristics are puzzling and demand attention. The key to studying behavioural adaptation required an understanding of the incompatibility of selection at the level of the individual versus selection at the level of the group. Brown (1994) argues that V. C. Wynne-Edwards (1962) inadvertently provided the major stimulus for a revived interest in adaptation by laying out a theory of group selection and then interpreting a host of social phenomena in light of this theory. Although some biologists had promptly criticized group selection theory in technical papers (e.g. Brown 1964; Crook 1964), the books by G. C. Williams (1966) and David Lack (1966) convinced a large audience of the problems in logic that group selection theory entailed.

The salutary effect of the combined efforts of Wynne-Edwards, Lack and Williams was to refocus attention on the nature of adaptation and its evolutionary basis. Obviously, selectionist thinking had not disappeared from biology in the mid-20th century as witness, for example, Lack's (1954) analysis of clutch size in birds, Mayr's (1963) discussion of the role of selection in speciation, and Hamilton's (1964) explanation of altruism via inclusive fitness theory. I suspect, however, that many behavioural biologists only became aware of the differences between selection at the level of the group versus the individual (or gene) around 1966 because of the controversy surrounding Wynne-Edwards's view of social evolution. I know that my own education about levels of selection required that my undergraduate advisor, Lincoln Brower, convince me of the logical defects in Wynne-Edwardsian group selection theory, a task that required some time and patience on his part.

Once many researchers understood that selection at the level of the individual (or gene) was likely to be more powerful than selection for group-benefiting attributes, then investigators could begin to re-examine traits that previously might have been casually dismissed as more or less obviously adaptive in the sense of helping the species avoid extinction. In other words, the careful application of natural selection theory after the group selection controversy had been resolved was a powerful stimulus for the exploration of behavioural adaptation (Brown 1994). The results included unusually important papers on territoriality (Brown & Orians 1970; Fretwell & Lucas 1970), mating systems (Orians 1969; Trivers 1972), behavioural responses to sperm competition (Parker 1970) and reciprocity (Trivers 1971), all written between 1969 and 1972.

The Second Wave of Textbooks

The revival of interest in adaptation and the surge of research on the subject eventually influenced textbooks in behaviour. Jerram Brown's *The Evolution of Behavior* and my *Animal Behavior: an Evolutionary Approach* were both published in 1975. Brown and I wrote our books in part because of dissatisfaction with the incomplete treatment of evolutionary issues in the texts available at that time. As suggested by their titles, both books dealt at length with the adaptive aspects of behaviour. The preface to Brown's book begins: 'This is a book about behaviour written with the central, unifying theme of *biological evolution*' (page xv in Brown 1975; emphasis by the author). The second sentence in my preface reads, 'My objective through the book is to suggest how one might approach the genetics, physiology, ecology and history of behaviour from an evolutionary perspective' (page v in Alcock 1975). Both books included summaries of Williams's analysis of group- versus individual-level selection. Both also reported Hamilton's solution to the problem of altruism, a topic that only becomes truly interesting in the appropriate theoretical context. In addition, both books discussed sexual selection at length, a theory that only became widely used after a few evolutionary biologists, notably Orians (1969), Parker (1970) and Trivers (1972), reminded others that members of the same species often have a significant effect on the genetic success of their fellows.

Beginning in the 1970s and carrying on to the present, the use of Darwinian natural selection theory resulted in an outpouring of research on the adaptive value of various behavioural traits ranging from foraging decisions to sexual tactics, all of which have been scrutinized in terms of how they might contribute to the ability of individuals to leave copies of their genes to future generations. An even more productive application of this approach occurred because of several factors. First, Williams provided the impetus for rigour with his demonstration that 'adaptation is a special and onerous concept that should be used only where it is really necessary' (page 4 in Williams 1966). Subsequently the furore surrounding Wilson's (1975) *Sociobiology* probably supplied additional motivation for cautious use of the adaptationist approach. The controversy arising from *Sociobiology* (Segerstråle 2000) and from Gould & Lewontin's (1979) contentious critique of the 'adaptationist programme' stimulated strong responses over the years, as illustrated by Brown (1982) and Queller (1995). These debates heightened the visibility of studies of adaptation in behaviour, thereby perhaps drawing new researchers into this area. Finally, concerns about how to test adaptationist hypotheses as effectively as possible generated new ways to use the comparative method in the 1980s, which were summarized by Brooks & McLennan (1991) and Harvey & Pagel (1991).

The overall effect of the increased rigour and breadth of the adaptationist approach is evident in all modern behavioural textbooks, which have increased the proportion of space devoted to adaptive aspects of animal behaviour relative to the proximate components (Fig. 2-1). This major change in textbook coverage reflects the success the adaptationist programme had in helping researchers look at behaviour in a new way.

Have Proximate Questions about Behaviour Been Neglected in Recent Decades?

There is little doubt that the rise in behavioural ecology and sociobiology coincided with a decline in the number of researchers who labelled themselves ethologists. Milner (1990) has suggested that biologists began abandoning ethology because of the links between the discipline and several ultimately discredited popular books, especially *On Aggression* by Konrad Lorenz (1966) and *The Naked Ape* by Desmond Morris (1967). These books, however, appeared just as the conceptual foundation was being laid for the revived interest in behavioural adaptation, so the decline in traditional ethology could have stemmed in part from a renewed interest in adaptation. Indeed, Marian Dawkins (1989) argued that a rush to study the adaptive function of behaviour resulted in the unfortunate abandonment of ethological work on proximate issues in the 1980s. Bateson & Klopfer (1989) also deplored the post-1970 changes, which they attributed largely to the influence of E. O. Wilson's (1975) *Sociobiology: the New Synthesis*. Although not a textbook, *Sociobiology* offered a monumental review of social behavioural research and some clear statements about how the field of animal behaviour would develop between 1975 and 2000, statements that proved to be correct (Mealey 2000). Among other things Wilson predicted (Fig. 2-2) that ethology would become less and less dominant within behavioural research. Bateson & Klopfer suggest that Wilson's view steered graduate students into sociobiology and behavioural ecology rather than ethology, generating a self-fulfilling prophecy.

There seems little doubt that the expansion of behavioural ecology and sociobiology meant that fewer researchers were being trained to tackle proximate questions from a traditional ethological perspective. Goodenough and her colleagues go so far as to support the view that 'for a time almost *all* research in animal behaviour was done under the banner of sociobiology' (page 31 in Goodenough *et al.* 2001). This claim, however, is a major overstatement, given the growth over the years in neuroethology, the discipline that integrates the ethological knowledge of real world problems confronting a species with the physiologist's ability to explore the adaptive sensory and motor mechanisms that enable animals to solve ecological problems (Brown & Hunsperger 1963). The utility of integrating evolutionary biology with neurophysiology was illustrated by both Brown (1975) and Gould (1982), whose textbooks reviewed the findings of a large number of neuroethologists, whether they used the label or not.

Even though proximate research in behaviour was not abandoned after 1975, adaptationist questions clearly attracted more attention in the post-1975 era than in the preceding years. But one can argue that the extra attention was required to correct the gap or imbalance created by earlier neglect of one of Tinbergen's four fundamental questions, namely, what is the function of behaviour? Functional issues needed fuller investigation to create a complete understanding of behaviour. These studies were eventually undertaken by population biologists, adaptationists, or selectionists. Whatever one chooses to call these researchers, they began to use evolutionary theory as a guide to their work well before the publication of *Sociobiology* (Brown 1994), providing the material that Richard Dawkins (1976) reviewed in *The Selfish Gene*.

Moreover, Wilson and other advocates of Darwinian theory did not claim that a discipline with an ultimate perspective (sociobiology) should (or could) replace one with a heavy proximate orientation (ethology). Instead, as

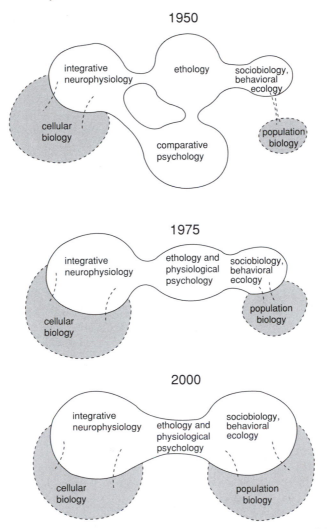

Figure 2-2 E. O. Wilson's diagrammatic representation of possible changes in the field of animal behaviour from 1950 to 2000. (Figure 1–2 from Wilson 1975; reprinted with permission from the Belknap Press, Harvard University, Cambridge, Massachusetts, U.S.A.)

Wilson's diagrams indicated, correctly as it turns out, the proximate study of social behaviour required the involvement of cellular biologists and integrative neurophysiologists. These researchers have stepped forward over the past several decades to explore 'ethological' subjects with analytical tools unavailable to the early ethologists. They ensured that the proximate mechanisms of behaviour were not ignored in the 1970s and 1980s. To confirm this point, one need only check Brown's (1975) textbook, much of which covers topics in neuroethology, as well as the lengthy bibliographies in the specialized modern textbooks devoted exclusively to the proximate causes of behaviour (e.g. Camhi 1984; Simmons & Young 1999; Carew 2000; Nelson 2000; Matthews 2001).

As a result of the work of neuroethologists, broadly defined, the major ethological issues, the developmental basis of instincts and their sensory control, have been dealt with in detail. The instinct–learning controversy has largely evaporated with the general acceptance of the point that both genes and environment interact during every phase of behavioural development. As a result, one cannot justifiably divide behavioural traits into those whose development depends on genetic information versus those whose development requires environmental input. Instead, instincts occur because gene–environment interactions lead to the development of feature detectors, central pattern generators, and the like; these mechanisms generate stereotypical, adaptive responses to biologically relevant stimuli. Learning occurs because different gene–environment interactions lead to the development of different kinds of neural systems whose circuitry can be changed by selected experiences, thereby modifying the behavioural repertoire of the individual. With most persons agreed on these matters, a major impetus and focus for 'pure' ethological research has been removed.

Therefore, the apparent decline and almost disappearance of traditional ethology in recent decades was not caused by the wilful hijacking by E. O. Wilson of the research agenda of a generation of behavioural biologists. Instead, the major revival of selection theory, already underway when it was advertised by Wilson in his highly conspicuous and valuable book, enabled a growing number of adaptationist researchers to compensate for years of relative neglect of behavioural ecology. In the meantime, the contributions that ethology had made on the proximate front made possible still more sophisticated reductionist analyses of the developmental and physiological mechanisms underlying biologically relevant behaviour patterns. The success of this endeavour is exemplified in the findings of persons interested in how some birds learn their songs (Konishi 1985; Catchpole & Slater 1995). The persons who conducted this research rarely called themselves ethologists even though they continued to explore the issues in physiology and development that ethologists had identified as central to a full understanding of the causes of behaviour. The recent textbooks in our field simply reflect the changes that have taken place over the last 25 years as our discipline has grown richer theoretically and researchers have become better able to identify the cellular and molecular bases of behaviour, thanks to improved technology and training.

The Treatment of Animal Behaviour in Introductory Biology Textbooks

To what extent has the evolution of the field of animal behaviour been mirrored in introductory biology textbooks? A great many undergraduates in the 1960s and 1970s were introduced to general biology through William Keeton's *Biological Science*, a highly successful textbook and one that went through many editions. I still have my copy of the first edition (Keeton 1967), which is as good a place as any to begin a survey of introductory textbook treatments of animal behaviour, all the more so because Keeton was an accomplished behavioural biologist who devoted nearly 50 pages to the discipline in his book. The chapter on behaviour covers material on proximate causes from an ethological perspective, including ethological terminology as in Keeton's analysis of releasers and the differences between instinct and learning (presented under the nature–nurture controversy). In addition, the chapter deals heavily with purely descriptive matters, such as a catalogue of the kinds of learned behaviours that can be found in the animal kingdom (habituation, trial and error learning, insight learning and so on) as well as a comparative approach to communication focused on the different modalities involved (visual, olfactory and acoustical senses). In addition, not surprisingly given Keeton's own research on the proximate mechanisms of bird orientation and migration, the chapter also deals with the physiology of navigation. Evolutionary issues arise very occasionally, particularly in the context of the historical sequence of events leading to the communication displays exhibited by modern species. The adaptive functions of behaviour, however, are almost completely ignored, in keeping with the focus of ethology at the time.

Ethological terminology and proximate causation of behaviour took centre stage in many textbooks that followed (Fig. 2-3), perhaps because the authors were influenced by Keeton or some other similar text, as sometimes happens (Burk 1973), in part because few biology textbook authors have full command of all the myriad fields within biology (Baker 1973). The willingness of authors to follow the lead of others may have been particularly pronounced with respect to animal behaviour because few textbook writers other than Keeton have been behavioural researchers. One early exception was *Biology: the Behavioral View* (Suthers & Gallant 1973), which attempted, successfully in my view, to use behaviour as a central organizing theme with which to integrate the diverse disciplines in biology. Although written only a few years after Keeton's book, Suthers & Gallant devoted much more space to behavioural adaptation than did Keeton. They went so far as to discuss possible adaptive features of human behaviour, a topic that Keeton did not deal with and that still does not receive coverage in most modern texts.

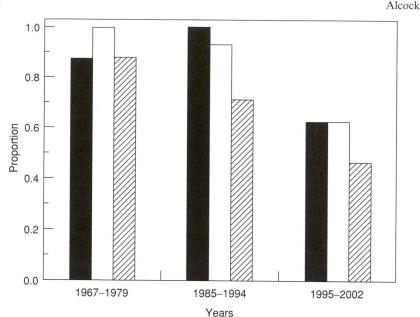

Figure 2-3 The proportion of introductory biology text books from three periods (1967–1979, *N* = 8; 1985–1994, *N* = 14; and 1995–2002, *N* = 13) in which three topics were presented: ethological terms (■), types of learning (□), and communication modalities (▨). The text books surveyed by date were Keeton (1967), Clark (1973), Ebert *et al.* (1973), Suthers & Gallant (1973), Davis & Solomon (1974), Ford & Monroe (1974), Kimball (1974), Baker & Allen (1979), Mader (1985), Davis & Solomon (1986), Keeton *et al.* (1986), Campbell (1987), Mader (1987), Arms & Camp (1988), Brum & McKane (1989), Postlethwait & Hopson (1989), Hopson & Wessells (1990), Wallace (1990), Lewis (1992), Mix *et al.* (1992), Chiras (1993), Campbell *et al.* (1994), Avila (1995), Alters (1996), Mix *et al.* (1996), Sutton (1998), Solomon *et al.* (1999), Cain *et al.* (2000), Pruitt *et al.* (2000), Purves *et al.* (2001), Tobin & Duscheck (2001), Audeskirk *et al.* (2002), Freeman (2002), Krogh (2002) and Lewis *et al.* (2002).

Suthers & Gallant's book, it is safe to say, did not have the influence that Keeton's had on textbook writers, judging from the consistency with which the Keeton model appears over and over in textbooks from the 1970s onward. Classic ethological terms, such as fixed action pattern and sign stimulus, were defined in almost all textbooks prior to 1995 (Fig. 2-3). Even after 1995, the famous ethological experiments typically appear but sometimes without mention of the specialized jargon of the field (Cain *et al.* 2000; Audeskirk *et al.* 2002). Given that little work has been done on fixed action patterns per se for decades, the willingness of most general textbook authors to devote some part of the few pages available for behavioural issues to ethological terminology must reflect the power of tradition.

Even more striking evidence for phylogenetic inertia in the introductory textbook culture comes from the high proportion of authors who have included in their chapter on behaviour a list of the types of learning, ranging from habituation to trial and error learning to insight learning (often illustrated by reference to a captive chimpanzee stacking boxes in order to access an otherwise unreachable banana). Only in the last few years have some authors been willing to drop this holdover from the days of comparative psychology (Fig. 2-3), in order to use the pages for more current material.

Keeton may also have provided the model for inclusion of a descriptive list of communication modalities, which appears in a majority of the textbooks I surveyed until the most recent batch (Fig. 2-3). A fondness for lists of this sort may reflect the perception of authors that their goal is to provide batteries of facts and terms to be memorized by the student reader. In recent years, however, some textbook authors have done more than merely describe the different kinds of communication signals. Thus, for example, Freeman (2002) uses alarm calling to examine the evolutionary costs and benefits of a signal rather than to illustrate a communication system that happens to make use of the acoustical channel.

Freeman deals with alarm calls in a section entitled 'Kin Selection and the Evolution of Cooperation'. The concept of kin selection was not mentioned in any of the eight introductory textbooks I examined dated from 1967 to 1979, but after 1985, almost all the sampled textbooks (23 of 27) discussed the matter. The now nearly universal coverage of kin selection and Hamilton's solution to the evolution of altruism is an indicator of the new focus on behavioural adaptation. In addition, most recent textbooks also outline the fitness consequences of territoriality and dominance hierarchies. Although it took time for the adaptationist approach to enter the general domain, once in place, almost all authors have either recognized the conceptual importance of this issue or else have been persuaded to include it on the grounds that all their competitors discuss the subject.

In contrast, no consensus exists on whether to present an example of an adaptive human behaviour. Although 17 of 27 textbooks published since 1985 refer to human sociobiology, invariably at the very end of a chapter on behaviour, the subject is usually dropped after a paragraph or two. The message of these brief entries is generally that evolutionary approaches to human behaviour are controversial and of uncertain value. Only seven texts describe in modest detail an actual study on the possible adaptive value of a human behaviour or its underlying psychological mechanism.

Perhaps it is not surprising that an adaptationist approach to human behaviour rarely receives much of a hearing given the controversy that has surrounded the subdiscipline (Segerstråle 2000) and the rarity with which human sociobiology is covered even in behaviour textbooks. In another sense, however, it is odd that biology textbook authors have not tackled the subject positively, given the interest that students have in their own social behaviour.

Although the omission of human sociobiology is unfortunate, in my opinion, at least current introductory textbooks now discuss the behaviour of nonhuman animals in a much more balanced and complete fashion than they did just a few decades ago. Thus, behavioural coverage in these books mirrors that in specialized behaviour textbooks, which in turn reflects the general agreement among researchers that all four of Tinbergen's questions about behaviour deserve detailed exploration, a research goal that requires, among other things, an understanding and use of a powerful theory suited for each question. Instinct theory provided what was needed for productive exploration of the hereditary physiological mechanisms underlying many behaviour patterns. The 'rediscovery' of natural selection theory supplied the basis for an equally productive approach to the question of behavioural adaptation. As a result, readers of today's textbooks on animal behaviour and introductory biology have a chance to learn more about a fascinating subject that has come fully into its own.

Acknowledgments

Thanks to Jeffrey Lucas, Sandra Meyer, Ron Rutowski and Leigh Simmons for comments that helped improve an earlier draft. Jerram Brown kindly provided much useful information and helpful perspectives as well.

References

Alcock, J. 1975. *Animal Behavior: an Evolutionary Approach.* Sunderland, Massachusetts: Sinauer.
Alcock, J. 2001. *Animal Behavior: an Evolutionary Approach.* 7th edn. Sunderland, Massachusetts: Sinauer.
Alters, S. 1996. *Biology, Understanding Life.* St. Louis, Missouri: Mosby.
Arms, K. & Camp, P. S. 1988. *Biology: a Journey into Life.* Philadelphia: W. B. Saunders.
Audeskirk, T., Audeskirk, G. & Byers, B. E. 2002. *Biology, Life On Earth.* Upper Saddle River, New Jersey: Prentice Hall.
Avila, V. L. 1995. *Biology: Investigating Life on Earth.* Boston: Jones Bartlett.
Baker, J. J. W. 1973. Kaibab deer incident: long-persisting myth: in reply. *BioScience,* **23,** 275–276.
Baker, J. J. W. & Allen, G. E. 1979. *A Course in Biology.* Reading, Massachusetts: Addison-Wesley.
Bateson, P. P. G. & Klopfer, P. H. 1989. Preface. *Perspectives in Ethology,* **8,** v–viii.
Brooks, D. R. & McLennan, D. A. 1991. *Phylogeny, Ecology and Behavior: a Research Program in Comparative Biology.* Chicago: University of Chicago Press.
Brown, J. L. 1964. The evolution of diversity in avian territorial systems. *Wilson Bulletin,* **76,** 160–169.
Brown, J. L. 1975. *The Evolution of Behavior.* New York: W. W. Norton.
Brown, J. L. 1982. The adaptationist program. *Science,* **217,** 885–886.

Brown, J. L. 1994. Historical patterns in the study of avian social-behavior. *Condor,* **96,** 232–243.

Brown, J. L. & Hunsperger, R. W. 1963. Neuroethology and the motivation of agonistic behaviour. *Animal Behaviour,* **11,** 439–448.

Brown, J. L. & Orians, G. H. 1970. Spacing patterns in mobile animals. *Annual Review of Ecology and Systematics,* **1,** 239–262.

Brum, G. D. & McKane, L. K. 1989. *Biology: Exploring Life.* New York: J. Wiley.

Burk, C. J. 1973. Kaibab deer incident: long-persisting myth. *BioScience,* **23,** 113–114.

Cain, M. L., Damman, H., Lue, R. A. & Yoon, C. K. 2000. *Discover Biology.* 2nd edn. Sunderland, Massachusetts: Sinauer.

Camhi, J. M. 1984. *Neuroethology.* Sunderland, Massachusetts: Sinauer.

Campbell, N. A. 1987. *Biology.* Menlo Park, California: Benjamin/Cummings.

Campbell, N. A., Mitchell, L. C. & Reece, J. B. 1994. *Biology: Concepts and Connections.* Redwood City, California: Benjamin/Cummings.

Carew, T. J. 2000. *Behavioral Neurobiology: the Cellular Organization of Behavior.* Sunderland, Massachusetts: Sinauer.

Catchpole, C. K. & Slater, P. J. B. 1995. *Bird Song, Biological Themes and Variations.* Cambridge: Cambridge University Press.

Chiras, D. D. 1993. *Biology: the Web of Life.* Minneapolis, Minnesota: West.

Clark, M. E. 1973. *Contemporary Biology.* Philadelphia: W. B. Saunders.

Crook, J. H. 1964. The evolution of social organization and visual communication in the weaver birds (Ploceinae). *Behaviour Supplement,* **10,** 1–178.

Davies, N. B. 1991. Studying behavioural adaptations. In: *The Tinbergen Legacy* (Ed. by M. S. Dawkins, T. R. Halliday & R. Dawkins), pp. 18–30. London: Chapman & Hall.

Davis, P. W. & Solomon, E. P. 1974. *The World of Biology: Life, Society, Ecosphere.* New York: McGraw-Hill.

Davis, W. P. & Solomon, E. P. 1986. *The World of Biology.* Philadelphia: Saunders.

Dawkins, M. S. 1989. The future of ethology: how many legs are we standing on? *Perspectives in Ethology,* **8,** 47–54.

Dawkins, R. 1976. *The Selfish Gene.* New York: Oxford University Press.

Dethier, V. G. & Stellar, E. 1961. *Animal Behavior.* Englewood Cliffs, New Jersey: Prentice Hall.

Drickamer, L. C., Vessey, S. H. & Jakob, E. M. 2002. *Animal Behavior: Mechanisms, Ecology, Evolution.* 5th edn. New York: McGraw-Hill.

Ebert, J. D., Loewry, A. G., Miller, R. S. & Schneiderman, H. H. 1973. *Biology.* New York: Holt, Rinehart & Winston.

Eibl-Eibesfeldt, I. 1970. *Ethology: the Biology of Behavior.* New York: Holt, Rinehart & Winston.

Eibl-Eibesfeldt, I. 1975. *Ethology: the Biology of Behavior.* 2nd edn. New York: Holt, Rinehart & Winston.

Ford, J. M. & Monroe, J. E. 1974. *Living Systems: Principles and Relationships.* 2nd edn. San Francisco: Canfield Press.

Freeman, S. 2002. *Biological Science.* Upper Saddle River, New Jersey: Prentice Hall.

Fretwell, S. D. & Lucas, H. K., Jr. 1970. On territorial behavior and other factors influencing habitat distribution in birds. I. Theoretical development. *Acta Biotheoretica,* **19,** 16–36.

Goodenough, J., McGuire, B. & Wallace, R. A. 2001. *Perspectives on Animal Behavior.* 2nd edn. New York: J. Wiley.

Gould, J. L. 1982. *Ethology, The Mechanisms and Evolution of Behavior.* New York: W. W. Norton.

Gould, S. J. & Lewontin, R. C. 1979. The spandrels of San Marco and the Panglossian paradigm: a critique of the adaptationist programme. *Proceedings of the Royal Society of London, Series B,* **205,** 581–598.

Hamilton, W. D. 1964. The genetical theory of social behaviour, I, II. *Journal of Theoretical Biology,* **7,** 1–52.

Harvey, P. H. & Pagel, M. D. 1991. *The Comparative Method in Evolutionary Biology.* London: Oxford University Press.

Hinde, R. A. 1970. *Animal Behaviour: a Synthesis of Ethology and Comparative Psychology.* 2nd edn. New York: McGraw-Hill.

Hopson, J. L. & Wessells, N. K. 1990. *Essentials of Biology.* New York: McGraw-Hill.

Houck, L. D. & Drickamer, L. C. 1996. *Foundations of Animal Behavior: Classic Papers with Commentaries.* Chicago: University of Chicago Press.

Keeton, W. T. 1967. *Biological Science.* New York: W. W. Norton.

Keeton, W. T., Gould, J. L. & Gould, C. G. 1986. *Biological Science.* 4th edn. New York: W. W. Norton.

Kimball, J. W. 1974. *Biology.* 3rd edn. Reading, Massachusetts: Addison-Wesley.

Konishi, M. 1985. Bird song: from behavior to neuron. *Annual Review of Neuroscience,* 8, 125–170.

Krogh, D. 2002. *Biology, A Guide to the Natural World.* Upper Saddle River, New Jersey: Prentice Hall.

Lack, D. 1954. *The Natural Regulation of Animal Numbers.* Oxford: Clarendon.

Lack, D. 1966. *Population Studies of Birds.* Oxford: Clarendon.

Lehrman, D. S. 1953. A critique of Konrad Lorenz's theory of instinctive behavior. *Quarterly Review of Biology,* **28,** 337–363.

Lewis, R. 1992. *Life.* Dubuque, Iowa: W. C. Brown.

Lewis, R., Gaffin, D., Hoefnagels, M. & Parker, B. 2002. *Life.* 4th edn. New York: McGraw-Hill.

Lorenz, K. Z. 1965. *Evolution and Modification of Behavior.* Chicago: University of Chicago Press.

Lorenz, K. Z. 1966. *On Aggression.* New York: Harcourt, Brace & World.

Mader, S. S. 1985. *Biology: Evolution, Diversity and the Environment.* Dubuque, Iowa: W. C. Brown.

Mader, S. S. 1987. *Biology: Evolution, Diversity, and the Environment.* 2nd edn. Dubuque, Iowa: W. C. Brown.

Manning, A. 1972. *An Introduction to Animal Behaviour.* 2nd edn. Reading, Massachusetts: Addison-Wesley.

Manning, A. & Dawkins, M. S. 1998. *An Introduction to Animal Behaviour.* 3rd edn. Cambridge: Cambridge University Press.

Marler, P. & Hamilton, W. J. 1966. Mechanisms of Animal Behavior. New York: J. Wiley.

Matthews, G. G. 2001. *Neurobiology: Molecules, Cells, and Systems.* 2nd edn. Malden, Massachusetts: Blackwell Science.

Mayr, E. 1961. Cause and effect in biology. *Science,* **134,** 1501–1506.

Mayr, E. 1963. *Animal Species and Evolution.* Cambridge, Massachusetts: Harvard University Press.

Mealey, L. 2000. What? Me worry? The status of ethology in the year 2000. *Human Ethology Bulletin,* **15,** 2–8.

Milner, R. 1990. *The Encyclopedia of Evolution.* New York: H. Holt.

Mix, M. C., Farber, P. & King, K. I. 1992. *Biology: the Network of Life.* New York: Harper Collins.

Mix, M. C., Farber, P. & King, K. I. 1996. *Biology: the Network of Life.* 2nd edn. New York: HarperCollins.

Morris, D. 1967. *The Naked Ape.* New York: McGraw-Hill.

Nelson, R. J. 2000. *An Introduction to Behavioral Endocrinology.* Sunderland, Massachusetts: Sinauer.

Orians, G. H. 1969. On the evolution of mating systems in birds and mammals. *American Naturalist,* **103,** 589–603.

Parker, G. A. 1970. Sperm competition and its evolutionary consequences in the insects. *Biological Reviews,* **45,** 526–567.

Postlethwait, J. H. & Hopson, J. L. 1989. *The Nature of Life*. New York: Random House.

Pruitt, N. L., Underwood, L. S. & Surver, W. 2000. *BioInquiry, Making Connections in Biology*. New York: J. Wiley.

Purves, W. K., Sadava, D., Orians, G. H. & Heller, H. C. 2001. *Life: the Science of Biology*. 6th edn. Sunderland, Massachusetts: Sinauer.

Queller, D. C. 1995. The spaniels of St Marx and the Panglossian paradox, a critique of a rhetorical programme. *Quarterly Review of Biology*, **70**, 485–489.

Scott, J. P. 1972. *Animal Behavior*. 2nd edn. Chicago: University of Chicago Press.

Segerstråle, U. 2000. *Defenders of the Truth: the Battle for Science in the Sociobiology Debate and Beyond*. New York: Oxford University Press.

Simmons, P. & Young, D. 1999. *Nerve Cells and Animal Behaviour*. Cambridge: Cambridge University Press.

Solomon, E. P., Berg, L. R. & Martin, D. W. 1999. *Biology*. 5th edn. Fort Worth, Texas: Saunders.

Suthers, R. A. & Gallant, R. A. 1973. *Biology: the Behavioral View*. Lexington, Massachusetts: Xerox College.

Sutton, J. 1998. *Biology*. London: Macmillan.

Tinbergen, N. 1951. *The Study of Instinct*. New York: Oxford University Press.

Tobin, A. J. & Duscheck, J. 2001. *Asking About Life*. Orlando, Florida: Harcourt College.

Trivers, R. L. 1971. The evolution of reciprocal altruism. *Quarterly Review of Biology*, **46**, 35–57.

Trivers, R. L. 1972. Parental investment and sexual selection. In: *Sexual Selection and the Descent of Man* (Ed. by B. Campbell), pp. 136–179. Chicago: Aldine.

Wallace, R. A. 1990. *Biology: the World of Life*. 5th edn. Glenview, Illinois: Scott, Foresman/Little, Brown.

Williams, G. C. 1966. *Adaptation and Natural Selection*. Princeton, New Jersey: Princeton University Press.

Wilson, E. O. 1975. *Sociobiology: the New Synthesis*. Cambridge, Massachusetts: Harvard University Press.

Wynne-Edwards, V. C. 1962. *Animal Dispersion in Relation to Social Behaviour*. Edinburgh: Oliver & Boyd.

3

Behavioural Ecology: Natural History as Science

Geoff A. Parker
Population and Evolutionary Biology Research Group
School of Biological Sciences
University of Liverpool

Abstract

Behavioural ecology emerged from ethology, ecology, and population genetics as the result of a scientific revolution in the late 1960s and the 1970s; this could be seen as the coming of age of natural history as science. With the aid of a straw poll from 25 practising behavioural ecologists, I attempt to review the main components of this revolution in terms of the history of its main subdisciplines and to identify the scientists perceived as having the major influences.

Introduction

This essay is a perspective on the events in the late 1960s and 1970s that led natural history to blossom into a formal science. Although I have obtained views from other behavioural ecologists, it is necessarily a personal overview. Others will see it differently—but I have tried to present a balanced account, with informed postgraduates and post-docs as intended readers. This essay is for them. The difficulty has been to decide what to leave out.

In the beginning—let's start with ethology, the science of animal behaviour as consolidated by the three Nobel laureates, Tinbergen, Lorenz, and von Frisch. It was in the context of ethology that the major animal behaviour journals began: *Zeitschrift für Tierpsychologie* (1937; *Ethology* from 1986), *Behaviour* (1947), and *Animal Behaviour* (1958; starting as the *British Journal for Animal Behaviour* in 1953), which serves the two societies, the Association for the Study of Animal Behaviour (Europe based), and the Animal Behavior Society (North America based). Ethology had (and still has) a wide remit: to understand animal behaviour in terms of its causation, development, and evolution (in the sense of phylogeny) as well as function (adaptive significance). This last area (i.e., understanding the selective forces that have shaped behaviour) exploded in the 1970s, leading to the formation of a new discipline: behavioural ecology (or sociobiology). To cope with this surge, new journals began: *Behavioral Ecology and Sociobiology* (1976), *Ethology and Sociobiology* (1979; *Evolution and Human Behavior* from 1997), and *Behavioral Ecology* (1990), after the founding of the International Society for Behavioral Ecology in 1986. The older journals continue to flourish, publishing increasing numbers of articles on behavioural ecology as well as all other aspects of animal behaviour.

Much has been written about sociobiology, its implications for human nature, and the controversy after the publication of Wilson's (1975) *Sociobiology: The New Synthesis* (e.g., Segerstråle 2000). Unfortunately, this political controversy obscured what was being achieved in the 1970s: a revolution in the way we study and understand animal behaviour. I shall avoid the politics and concentrate on the science (see also Alcock 2001a).

The distinction between natural history and biology is blurred: though its exact remit is debatable (Arnold 2003; Greene 2005), natural history represents a suite of activities, ranging from hobbyist interests in wildlife and nature to subsets of biological science related to evolution, ecology, behaviour, phylogeny, and taxonomy. The best naturalists had always been scientists in the sense of research inquiry. But perhaps the most explicit melding of natural history and biology is the area of behavioural and evolutionary ecology. These disciplines represent the scientific coming-of-age of the best traditions of natural history; this essay celebrates the scientific revolution associated with their genesis.

What's in a Name?

Many would see the first announcement of this revolution as the publication of Wilson's monograph. The term "sociobiology" is still used, but possibly because it lays stress on social behaviour, many have preferred "behavioural ecology," which more naturally includes all aspects of behavioural adaptation. The distinction between behavioural ecology and sociobiology was never clear, and many see them as synonyms or, at most, that sociobiology is a subset of behavioural ecology. In the late 1970s, sociobiology was used much more, and I spent a year in 1978–1979 in a research group in King's College, Cambridge, on their sociobiology (not behavioural ecology) project. After Wilson's book, and the resulting political clamour, there was a push in the States towards its impact on human behaviour. For whatever reason, Wilson himself was driven in this direction (his 1979 book *On Human Nature* won a Pulitzer Prize). In contrast, Krebs and Davies defined the field more widely in their highly influential edited volumes *Behavioural Ecology: An Evolutionary Approach* (1978, 1984, 1991, 1997) and their student text *An Introduction to Behavioural Ecology* (first edition 1981).

There was perhaps a degree of North American–European rivalry involved here. One colleague, an anonymous respondent for the straw poll used in the section *The Influences and the Influencers*, remarked that:

> *[B]ehavioral ecology arose largely as a tactical alternative to sociobiology in the mid-70s. . . . whatever we call this field it was (and largely still is) a US/UK mixed-marriage. . . . John Krebs spearhead[ed] a hostile takeover of E. O. Wilson's "new synthesis" almost before the paint could dry, successfully usurping and greatly improving the emerging field we now perceive.*

The terms probably had some reflection on the interests of the protagonists. Wilson is a world authority on ants, a notably social group of insects, and sociobiology must have seemed an ideal emphasis. Much of Krebs's early interests lay in food foraging, for which the term sociobiology must have seemed less than ideal. But influences are a complex fusion: Krebs began foraging work in Canada under the influence of Charnov, who, at the time, was Orians's student; Orians began his career in the late 1950s, supervised by Lack at Oxford!

The boundary between evolutionary and behavioural ecology is muddy. One respondent for the section *The Influences and the Influencers* saw behavioural ecology as a subdiscipline of evolutionary ecology; others saw them as related disciplines, one dealing with behaviour and the other with growth, timing of maturity, sex allocation, and so on. Thus, foraging and mate searching are typically seen as behavioural ecology and life-history strategy as evolutionary ecology, but in reality, the distinction is blurred. The evolution of switches from juvenile to adult or from one strategy to another during growth cannot be understood without consideration of the behaviour and fitness options associated with each life-history stage.

The terms behavioural ecology and evolutionary ecology are themselves perhaps less than ideal—both have much less to do with classical ecology than with evolution and adaptive value, something that ecology (which typically seeks to explain population numbers, succession, community and ecosystem structure, distribution, and energy flow) has never really espoused. For instance, classical ecology sought to explain distributions among habitats at a proximate level, in terms of tolerance of features such as temperature and salinity. Behavioural ecology sought ultimate explanations, in terms of selective forces shaping the decisions about *where* to search for food or mates. There was also a difference in practical approach: classical ecologists typically ventured into the field to obtain samples for lab analysis. Early behavioural ecologists, like naturalists, tended to do most of their work in the field. They often still do, but most now use more lab technology than formerly.

Ideally, a term was needed that would describe the study of the ecological aspects of strategic adaptation in all aspects of behaviour and in the allocation of expenditures by individuals. To my knowledge, no simple general term exists for this, and our "scientific natural history" has become known as behavioural–evolutionary ecology. Most of us are more than happy that the Krebs and Davies texts have led the revolution, defined the field, and guided its development to maturity.

So What Was the Revolution?

In a very real sense, Darwin was the founder of the discipline. Behavioural ecology can be seen as a return to Darwinian principles after most researchers in behaviour and ecology had abandoned them for decades. The revolution resulted from increased awareness of selection mechanisms, application of predictive Darwinian models, and an understanding of inherent underlying conflicts of interests.

Tinbergen's (1963) celebrated "four questions" had made ethologists aware of the different types of explanations for biological features, one of which concerned why it is favoured by selection. This was to be the new dimension: interpreting behaviour in terms of underlying evolutionary mechanisms. Ethology bequeathed little grounding in what was needed here, and in retrospect ecological–evolutionary biologists such as Lack, Crook, MacArthur, Williams, and Orians were pioneers of the 1960s. Population genetics offered rigorous, but strategically simple genetic models; their expansion to complex multilocus and multiallele cases often became problematic. Behavioural ecologists needed more strategic richness to cope with phenotypic problems in behaviour or resource allocation; a merger was impossible and so phenotype modellers threw out diploid genetics, implicitly or explicitly assuming haploidy or asexuality (now often called the "phenotypic gambit"; Grafen 1984). Population geneticists involved in the attack on sociobiology used this simplification as part of their armoury. Critiques were also levied against the concepts of optimality, and another line of attack branded the "adaptationist programme" as "Panglossian" (e.g., Gould & Lewontin 1979), in the sense that every feature is seen as a perfect adaptation (see Segerstråle 2000). It is true that behavioural ecologists necessarily start by *assuming* adaptation because their mission is to understand the nature of the selective forces that have shaped a given character. But they also assume that there are trade-offs and other nonadaptive constraints on adaptation. Insight is achieved by correctly deducing what is adaptation and what is constraint.

Individual Selection and the Selfish Gene

Two stages stand out in ethology's metamorphosis into behavioural ecology. The first was the attack on implicit or explicit assumptions that the unit of selection is the group or species. Despite believing that they were following Darwinian principles, most ethologists and ecologists in the 1960s typically explained function in terms of "advantage to the species." This verbal shorthand was misguided, leading to error if individual and group (or species) interests differ. In his book *Animal Dispersion in Relation to Social Behaviour*, Wynne-Edwards (1962) argued that social displays were "epideictic" mechanisms evolved to convey information about population density, predicting that reproduction should be reduced at high density to avoid population crashes through overexploitation. Seeing that a non-Darwinian mechanism was required (variants that switched off reproduction could hardly be favoured by natural selection; Darwin had similarly agonised over sterile castes in social insects), he invoked the group as the unit of selection, and thus made group selection explicit for explanations of behaviour (the original concept was due to Carr Saunders, 1922).

A groundswell of rebellion began, crystallised by Williams's seminal book *Adaptation and Natural Selection* (1966a), restating Darwinian principles and stressing that an advantage must be sought at the level of the individual ("individual selection") or the gene. This rebellion had many instigators—the avian ecologist David Lack was notable in the United Kingdom. Wynne-Edwards's proposition had been opposed from the start by such people as Maynard Smith (1964), who analysed the difficulties faced by a gene causing its bearer to act against its own (Darwinian) interests, but in the interests of the group as a whole. Crook pioneered the study of social organisation in an ecological context in weaver birds (1964) and in primates (Crook & Gartlan 1965). One respondent for *The Influences and the Influencers* wrote:

George Williams' 1966 book dealing with Wynne-Edwards' 1962 group selection tome . . .
like Crook's argument that ecology might be a stronger determinant of social structure than
phylogeny, had an enormous effect on those of us entering animal behavior. It focused atten-
tion on the individual, on conflict and competition, and set the scene well for papers that fol-
lowed pursuing the individual selection line of thinking.

Another respondent pointed out that Williams's book had actually been written before he read Wynne-Edwards's (1962): it was in response to Emerson considering a termite colony as an individual and was extensively reworked to counter Wynne-Edwards.

"Advantage to the species" is still seen or heard today, mostly through naïvety as a prerevolution legacy. It is still defended by those who argue, in view of the relentless extinctions of animal species over geological time, that the species is the unit of selection (see Segerstråle 2000), but few behavioural ecologists see it as a mechanism that shapes phenotypic adaptation.

The three great pioneers of population genetics, Fisher, Haldane, and Wright, were clearly aware of the distinction between group and individual selection. Group selection now has a more rigorous framework than it had in the 1960s and 1970s: it can be argued to work under some conditions (e.g., D. S. Wilson 1980). The general consensus, implicit or explicit, is that Darwinian selection should be the first line of enquiry for understanding adaptation unless there are special reasons for not doing so (e.g., strong group, kin, or reciprocity effects, which require expanded notions of fitness). Dawkins (1976) stressed that the unit of selection is strictly the gene, rather than the individual, an issue that has attracted considerable debate (Segerstråle 2000). His "selfish gene" metaphor has nevertheless had much force in promoting the philosophy of behavioural ecology, and the typical assumption of the phenotypic gambit (Grafen 1984) has some equivalence to Dawkins's premise.

Conflicts of Interest

The second step was the growing awareness of the underlying conflicts of evolutionary interest between individuals. By now, this is seen more explicitly as conflicts at the genetic level within and between genomes. For many adaptations, particularly those that involve conflicts of interest, the fitness "payoff" to a given individual depends not only on its own strategy, but also on the strategies played by individuals with which it interacts or competes. For analysing such situations, Maynard Smith and Price (1973) borrowed ideas from game theory in mathematics (von Neumann & Morgenstern 1944) to produce the crucial concept of the evolutionarily stable strategy (ESS), which, when played by most of the population, cannot be invaded by any rare alternative strategy. In terms of game theory, an ESS is a "best reply" to itself.

Thus, ESS philosophy seeks to explain a current evolutionary state but not evolutionary dynamics that may lead to it. There are two formal stability conditions for a strategy to be an ESS, such that rare individuals deviating from the ESS population cannot invade (Maynard Smith & Price 1973; Maynard Smith 1982). Game theorists later identified the first ESS condition as a Nash equilibrium in game theory (Nash 1951).

ESS theory had several rather specific precursors. Examples are the sex ratio (Fisher 1930) and its distortion from unity (Hamilton 1967), animal distributions (Orians 1966; Fretwell & Lucas 1969; Parker 1970a), and contest behaviour (Maynard Smith & Price 1973; Maynard Smith 1974; Parker 1974). Trivers (1971) explicitly referred to the Prisoner's dilemma, a much-analysed scenario in game theory, while discussing reciprocal altruism, and his seminal papers on parental investment (1972) and parent–offspring conflict (1974) stressed that payoffs depended on the behaviour of other family members in a way that very few had previously envisaged.

Game theory has probably been more successful in its application to evolutionary biology than in its original contexts (economics and the social sciences). Evolutionary game theory has continued to develop since its inception. ESS is a stability concept. A strategy may satisfy Maynard Smith's conditions but may never converge to the ESS: one needs to ensure that a population deviating slightly from the ESS will actually converge back to it rather than spin away chaotically, cycle, or move towards a different equilibrium. One ideally now requires additional extra conditions for convergence, ensuring that an ESS is also *continuously stable* (Eshel 1983).

Associated with ESS is the concept of optimality. Optimality models make assumptions about selective forces and biological constraints (such as known trade-offs). The possible strategies (plausible possibilities that might be generated by mutation) and their "fitness payoffs" are defined. The optimal solution is that which maximises Darwinian (or inclusive) fitness. There may be more than one local optimum. ESS is simply competitive optimisation: one seeks a strategy that when played by most of the population is stable against invasion by rare mutant strategies (Maynard Smith 1982). Optimisation, without this frequency dependence, is used widely for some problems, such as life histories (Stearns 1976) and foraging behaviour (Stephens & Krebs 1986). David McFarland and his coworkers in Oxford pioneered the application of state-dependent optimisation to motivational decision making in the 1970s (e.g., Sibly & McFarland 1976; MacFarland & Houston 1981). This "state–space" approach was analytical, though explicit solutions were not always possible. It developed into the more accessible, computer-based, dynamic programming approach that has by now been applied to many problems in behavioural ecology (Houston & McNamara 1985; Mangel & Clark 1988). One major change was that numeric solution of dynamic programming equations allowed the incorporation of stochastic effects. Dynamic programming techniques have more recently been developed to solve state-dependent ESS problems or "dynamic games" (Houston & McNamara 1999; Clark & Mangel 2000).

ESS–optimality models are best seen not as tests of whether animals behave optimally but as a means of testing our insight into the moulding of an adaptation (Parker & Maynard Smith 1990). A fit between model predictions and empirical observations indicates that we may have correctly identified the selective forces and the biological constraints against which they are operating. Models have typically two functions. General models make simple assumptions and generate wide-ranging conclusions (e.g., what forms of solution might be possible). Specific models make quantitative predictions for a given species, are usually more complex, and have parameters specifically relating to that species.

The value of formal modelling has been that assumptions about selection, constraints, and underlying conflicts could be used to make testable predictions. Behavioural ecology's triumph has been to allow much more rigorous evaluation of how behaviour is shaped by selection.

The Influences and the Influencers

In an attempt to get a balanced view of the major influences, I e-mailed 31 well-known behavioural ecologists, most (but not all) between 50 and 60 years of age. Each was asked to list: (1) the 12 papers (not books) that have had the biggest influence on behavioural ecology's development (series such as Hamilton's two 1964 papers counted as one paper), and (2) the 10 people who have most influenced behavioural ecology. I explained that although many of the authorities in the two lists would overlap, (2) gave an opportunity to include, say, the author of a highly influential book, or body of research papers, none of which individually may qualify for (1). Self-citations were not allowed in either list. Any part of evolutionary biology or ecology was eligible for inclusion if it had had an impact on behavioural ecology. I received 25 responses (5 U.S.A., 16 U.K., 4 elsewhere) for list (1) and 22 (3 U.S.A., 15 U.K., 4 elsewhere) for list (2).

Obviously, this could never be a rigorous exercise; it is flawed in several ways. Selections were made from my e-mail list, which imposed immediate bias, though I attempted a spread across gender, continents, and areas of interest. Both lists would probably have had more bias towards U.S. nominations if there had been more U.S. respondents. There was an understandable and expected tendency for respondents to nominate preferentially within their own areas. I did not define a time period (e.g., post-1950): several respondents mentioned that legendary names, such as Darwin, Fisher, Haldane, Lack, and Bateman, should be included but were omitted because they were considered too early. Finally, my request inevitably put respondents in an embarrassing position: nominations to myself must be heavily discounted. What began as a simple, ingenuous attempt to strive for balance and fairness quickly became an absorbing exercise in data analysis, only a part of which is given here.

With these caveats in mind, there is nevertheless considerable uniformity in opinions about influencers and influential papers; 35 influencers and 70 influential papers were nominated. I took a vote score as the number of nominations for a person or paper divided by n (the number of respondents), or n-1 if the respondent was a candidate.

For influencers, 11 names had a vote score greater than 0.4 (9 or more votes): after this the score dropped below 0.2 (Fig. 3-1A). Table 3-1 shows

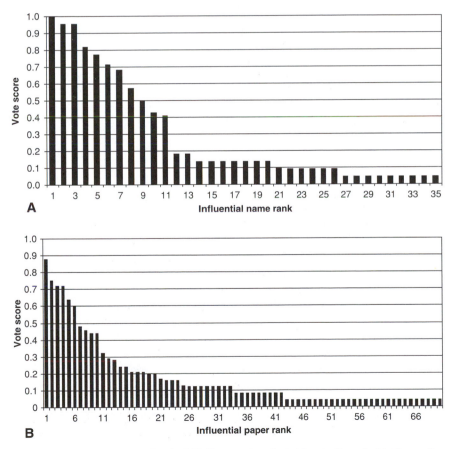

Figure 3-1 A, The vote scores for the 35 influencers nominated (see text), ranked in descending order. **B,** The vote scores for the 70 influential papers nominated (see text), in descending order.
Continued

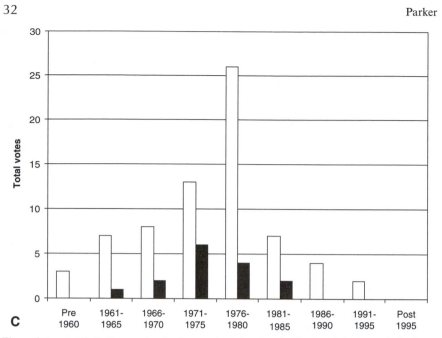

Figure 3-1—cont'd C, Summed votes for nominated papers in blocks of 5-year periods. Open histograms = all papers; black histograms = votes for top 12 papers.

the top 10 influencers by vote score (relegating myself to an arbitrary 11th place), with three other measures for each influencer: (1) the number of their papers nominated, (2) the summed votes for their nominated papers, and (3) a "textbook score" (sum of total first-author references listed, or number of pages on which that author is listed in the index, for eight texts in the general areas of animal behaviour or behavioural ecology; see Table 3-1). Each influencer's rank (out of 35) is shown in brackets. It is notable that influencers are a mix of theorists and empiricists. Whereas theorists (e.g., Hamilton, Trivers, and Maynard Smith) were ranked higher in paper nominations, empiricists (e.g., Krebs, Davies, and Clutton-Brock) ranked higher in the textbook score (the top textbook scorer [83] was S. T. Emlen). Names in Table 3-1 account for 77% of total votes; the remaining 24 names each gained between 1 and 4 votes.

For influential papers, the distribution of scores (Fig. 3-1B) showed a typical decay curve with a maximum of 0.88 for Hamilton (1964), to 27 papers each with just one vote. Fifteen papers were nominated by about a quarter of the respondents or more (gaining a score of 0.24 or more), representing 62% of the total votes. The remaining 54 nominated papers gained between 1 (28 papers) and 5 (5 papers) votes each. In the spirit of the original request, Table 3-2 lists the top 12 papers (two had a score of 0.24, counting as tied at

Table 3-1 Nominations for top 10 influencers

	Influential name	Vote score	Number of nominated papers	Summed votes for nominated papers	Text book score
1	J. R. Krebs	1.00	3 (6=)	6 (8)	81 (2)
2	J. Maynard Smith	0.96	6 (3)	34 (4)	71 (6)
3	W. D. Hamilton	0.82	7 (2)	60 (1)	61 (8)
4	R. L. Trivers	0.77	5 (4=)	59 (2)	45 (12)
5	N. B. Davies	0.71	2 (8=)	2 (19=)	79 (3)
6	E. O. Wilson	0.68	0	0	41 (14)
7	E. L. Charnov	0.57	5 (4=)	20 (5)	35 (15)
8	R. Dawkins	0.50	2 (8=)	4 (12)	58 (10)
9	T. H. Clutton-Brock	0.43	1 (11=)	1 (21=)	73 (5)
10	G. C. Williams	0.31	2 (8=)	4 (11)	23 (22)
	[G. A. Parker]	0.95	8 (1)	44 (3)	76 (4)

Rank (out of the 35 nominations) for measures other than vote score is given in parenthesis. Text book scores were derived from: counting indexed page citations—Dugatkin (2004), Krebs & Davies (1991); counting first author references—Alcock (2001b), Barnard (2004), Goodenough, McGuire & Wallace (2001), Krebs & Davies (1997), McFarland (1999), Manning & Dawkins (1998).

12th), after deleting two of my own (relegated arbitrarily to 14th and 15th places in Table 3-2). Table 3-2 also includes ISI cumulative citations for each paper.

The 70 nominated papers showed a marked peak in the second half of the 1970s: after this the fall-off is steep, and no nominations are later than 1992 (Fig. 3-1C). In contrast, the 12 most influential papers (see Table 3-2) peaked in the first half of the 1970s. The results may be sensitive to the respondents' age distribution, though there was no obvious tendency for younger respondents to nominate more recent papers. The distribution (see Fig. 3-1C) concurs with the genesis of behavioural ecology in the 1970s.

Papers nominated as most influential tend to be theoretical; no purely empirical works are included in Table 3-2. Reviews tended to be excluded, exceptions being Trivers (1971 *Q. Rev. Biol.*) and Parker (1970b *Biol. Rev.*); arguably these both proposed new ideas rather than just syntheses.

The survey generated a basis for the following brief outline of the areas that were most influential in the development of behavioural ecology. All nominated papers are mentioned. The superscripts before each citation give the number of votes for that paper (e.g., Hamilton ([22]1964) indicates that 22 out of 25 respondents included this in their list of the 12 most influential papers).

Table 3-2 Papers nominated most influential

	Influential paper	Subject area	Vote score	ISI citations
1	Hamilton (1964) *J. Theor. Biol.*	Altruism—inclusive fitness	0.88	4451
2	Trivers (1971) *Q. Rev. Biol.*	Altruism—reciprocal	0.72	1594
3	Trivers (1972) chapter in *Sexual Selection and the Descent of Man*	Sexual selection— parental investment	0.72	4090
4	Maynard Smith and Price (1973) *Nature*	Fighting and ESS	0.64	1008
5	Trivers (1974) *Amer. Zool.*	Parent-offspring conflict	0.60	1135
6	Hamilton & Zuk (1982) *Science*	Sex and sexual selection—role of parasites	0.48	1210
7	Charnov (1976) *Theor. Pop. Biol.*	Optimal foraging— marginal value theorem	0.46	1267
8	Emlen & Oring (1977) *Science*	Sexual selection— mating systems	0.44	2078
9	Hamilton (1967) *Science*	Sex ratio	0.40	1272
10	Zahavi (1975) *J. Theor. Biol.*	Handicaps and signals	0.32	958
11	Axelrod & Hamilton (1981) *Science*	Altruism—reciprocal, cooperation	0.28	1082
12=	Hamilton (1971) *J. Theor. Biol.*	Grouping—selfish herd theory	0.24	1128
12=	Maynard Smith (1977) *Anim. Behav.*	Parental investment	0.24	448
	[Parker (1970) *Biol. Rev.*]	Sexual selection— sperm competition	0.75	1127
	[Parker (1974) *J. Theor. Biol.*]	Fighting and assessment	0.29	648

Cumulative ISI citations were counted at the end of January 2005.

The Areas

A few areas (e.g., kin recognition and fluctuating asymmetry) were not nominated by respondents. Surprisingly, mainstream life-history theory (e.g., Stearns[1]1976) was not perceived as having had a major influence in behavioural ecology despite often being well cited as judged by ISI, presumably being seen by respondents as evolutionary ecology.

Altruism, Sociality, and Cooperation

Hamilton's ([22]1964) remarkable insights into the evolution of altruism and sociality through relatedness have justifiably become legendary and are subject of interest outside the field of behavioural ecology. Hamilton's proposition to replace Darwinian (i.e., "self's") fitness with inclusive fitness is now famous: his equation $rb > c$ (Hamilton's Rule) was to become the $E = mc^2$ of behavioural ecology. Grafen (2004) presents a sensitive and penetrating account of Hamilton's life and Segerstråle (2005), a comprehensive biography. A fascinating autobiographical account is found in *Narrow Roads of Gene Land* (Hamilton 1996, 2001, 2004).

In addition to being a top influencer (see Table 3-1), Hamilton produced several seminal papers (see Table 3-2). The [22]1964 papers in the *Journal of Theoretical Biology* (preceded by a note in *American Naturalist* in [1]1963) attracted the highest vote score and had the highest ISI citation of the entire survey (see Table 3-2). The idea for this work was stimulated by his contact with Fisher (and with Fisher's pioneering 1930 book) as a student at Cambridge and became (at his own proposal) the subject of his postgraduate research at the London School of Economics. Haldane was then at University College, London, and had earlier published verbal statements relating to kin selection (cited by Hamilton [1]1963). Maynard Smith (then also at University College) had similar interests: the now ubiquitous term "kin selection" derived from a paper by Maynard Smith ([3]1964). Hamilton ([22]1964 and elsewhere) used the term "inclusive fitness."

Hamilton's proposition that selection maximises an individual's inclusive fitness has been one of the most studied principles in behavioural ecology; kin-selected altruism enjoys a vast literature. It initially received only gradual attention, mainly in relation to the evolution of sociality in the Hymenoptera due to the high coefficient of relatedness between sisters under haplodiploidy. Later, and probably due to its attention from Wilson (1975), a torrent of research in social behaviour in diverse groups meant that it became hailed as a major triumph. Sherman's ([2]1977) important early study showed that individuals were more likely to perform alarm calls if close relatives were nearby. Hamiltonian principles are now routinely used in all analyses of behaviour involving kin.

Although kin selection was still gaining momentum, Robert Trivers (a top influencer, see Table 3-1; producer of several major papers, see Table 3-2) had begun work on reciprocal altruism, an alternative mechanism for the evolution of altruistic behaviour (Trivers [18]1971). His proposal that individuals that interact repeatedly can achieve an overall gain by cooperation was not opposed to kin selection but an alternative mechanism that may apply when beneficiary and donor are unrelated. This idea has also attracted much attention; most notably, Axelrod and Hamilton ([7]1981, see Table 3-2) proposed the simple "tit-for-tat" rule of thumb for reciprocal interactions. One of the first claims for reciprocal altruism in nature concerned consortships of the same two males guarding receptive female olive baboons (Packer 1977): at a given consortship, one tended to guard against rivals while one mated; roles were reversed in other consortships. Reciprocal food sharing in vampire bats (Wilkinson 1984) remains a convincing example.

Optimal Foraging

The study of food foraging was one of the first topics to be developed. Prerevolution pioneers were MacArthur and Pianka ([3]1966), Emlen (1966), and Schoener (1969, [2]1971). Eric Charnov (a top influencer, see Table 3-1) quickly became the leading theorist of the early phase. He had worked on optimal foraging as his doctorate of philosophy topic under the supervision of Gordon Orians. Charnov has generated many original and fundamental insights, particularly in sex allocation (1982) and life-history theory (1993), and most notably (for behavioural ecology), he was the originator of the Marginal Value Theorem, a citation classic (Charnov [11]1976a, see Table 3-2). Parker and Stuart ([1]1976) developed the same theorem independently, but Charnov's paper has received almost eight times the number of citations. Charnov gave the principle a name (from economics) and framed it in terms of food foraging, which was at that time one of the areas of greatest movement. Parker and Stuart's paper, though general, was set in terms of mate searching and was more diffuse, including a model of competitive foraging. Charnov ([5]1976b) also developed and tested optimal diet models and coauthored an early review of optimal foraging (Pyke et al. [1]1977). He had a major influence on John Krebs (also a top influencer, see Table 3-1), with whom he collaborated at that time (Krebs et al. [2]1974).

Most early foraging models assumed gain rate maximisation. Only later did predation risk become seen as an important parameter: Milinski and Heller ([1]1978) were first to show that sticklebacks shift their foraging behaviour to balance feeding benefits against predation risk. "Risk-minimisation" models typically asked a different question: should foragers avoid variance in gains to reduce their risk of starvation? They are an alternative to gain maximisation (see Stephens & Krebs 1986).

A possible reason for the early boom in optimal foraging was that simple experiments (sometimes adapted from operant psychology) were easily set up (most animals eat more readily than they mate or give alarm calls), generating results that could be compared *quantitatively* with theoretical predictions. The psychology link may have been one impetus for the statistical sophistication in behavioural ecology. John Krebs did much to establish behavioural ecology as a rigorous discipline by pioneering the meticulous empirical testing of models in optimal foraging. He achieved the highest of all scores as an influencer (nominated by all respondents): his name has become synonymous with behavioural ecology and his role as a top influencer relates both to his research and to the classic Krebs and Davies text and edited volumes.

An early hope of MacArthur and Schoener was that optimal foraging theory would help in the understanding of broader ecological questions about community structure. This remains unfulfilled. But there have been many triumphs (see Stephens & Krebs 1986): optimal diet models and Marginal Value Theorem have found hundreds of uses and continue to do so.

Animal Contests and Evolutionarily Stable Strategy

Darwin had seen the evolution of horns, antlers, and so on, in terms of male–male competition for females (intrasexual selection). Later, in the ethology era, implicit group selection arguments repeatedly proposed that contests should be settled without undue harm to contestants.

The beginnings of contest models and ESS theory were intimately entwined. John Maynard Smith and George Price realised that a logic for contest rules remained unformulated. Their paper (Maynard Smith & Price [16]1973) centred on "symmetric contests" (i.e., between identical opponents), and is usually cited as the origin of the ESS concept. My own interest in contests came from observing struggles between male dung flies for females but was stimulated by the same question: how should individual fitness be maximised in a contest? It centred on asymmetries between opponents: (1) in "resource holding potential" (RHP; roughly equivalent to fighting ability), and (2) in the value of the contested resource (Parker [7]1974). Although not deduced by ESS logic (the manuscript was completed before the Maynard Smith and Price paper), it proposed a rule for asymmetric contests that was later vindicated by ESS analysis (Hammerstein & Parker 1982). Simultaneously, Maynard Smith ([4]1974, [2]1976) showed that a purely arbitrary asymmetry (i.e., unrelated to RHP or to resource value) could be used to settle contests. I first met John Maynard Smith in 1974, and our subsequent collaboration (Maynard Smith & Parker [3]1976) concerned the role of payoff–related asymmetries and became an ISI citation classic. John was one of the most delightful of people, but I was so fearful of his intellectual abilities that I cannot claim to have contributed much directly to this paper. One credit I could perhaps take relates to proposing the "information acquired during a contest" model, which John (rarely for him) decided to approach by simulation rather than analysis. Later, Enquist and Leimar (1983) took this idea much further in their "sequential assessment game"; it has much greater biological reality than earlier models.

Animal fighting had long been the subject of empirical research, but the ESS models quickly spawned studies that were interpreted within the new framework. A notable early example was Nick Davies's ([1]1978) study of territoriality in speckled wood butterflies, where an arbitrary asymmetry (prior residence) appeared to be used to settle contests conventionally (i.e., without escalation or damage to either contestant). Though the arbitrary asymmetry rule may not explain why residents win in the butterflies (Stutt & Willmer 1998), Davies's study was nevertheless very influential in stimulating a combination of experiments and game theory in field studies of animal contests.

Though contest behaviour still attracts both theoretical and detailed empirical research (e.g., Elwood & Briffa 2001), it is now less popular. Its greatest contribution to behaviour ecology probably relates to its role in the development of ESS.

Sexual Selection

A third of all nominated papers related to sexual selection; the three decades of behavioural ecology have probably seen more research in this field than any other.

Darwin's first brief account of sexual selection is in *The Origin of Species* (1859); he formulated the principles extensively later in *The Descent of Man and Selection in Relation to Sex* (1871). Many earlier papers supported his ideas (e.g., Richards 1927). However, probably due to Huxley's (1938) influence, it lost ground to the ubiquitous impact of implicit group selectionism. To comply with "advantage to the species," male–male combat was seen as an adaptation to purge weakness from the population (stronger males fathered progeny that survived predation, thus "the species" benefited). Thus, Huxley, although accepting that males competed for females, denigrated intrasexual selection as an explanation and entirely dismissed Darwin's second mechanism, intersexual selection (female choice). From 1930 to 1970, sexual selection received little support. Notably, Bateman's ([3]1948) seminal paper stood against the tide: it was to become very influential later, but at the time was largely ignored, especially by ethologists and ecologists.

Against this background, the early 1970s saw dramatic changes that reasserted sexual selection as a powerful adaptive explanation. Bob Trivers's paper ([18]1972) had a huge influence: it has been cited almost as often as Hamilton's 1964 classic (see Table 3-2). My own field studies of dung flies began in 1965, supervised by the late Howard Hinton, a leading entomologist. Robin Baker (then a fellow postgraduate studying butterfly migration) and I had settled on what would later be termed individual selection as the logic for adaptive interpretation (I first encountered Williams's book in Liverpool around 1970). Perhaps fortunately, Hinton did not read my thesis.

Though liked and admired by his postgraduates, he supervised by example but did not delve deeply into what they actually did. I recall a conversation where he criticised my intrasexual selection interpretation of mate guarding by male dung flies, urging me to seek advantages to the female and the off-spring. My Ph.D. thesis, completed in 1968 and published in 1970–1974, was an attempt to vindicate intrasexual selection (see Parker 2001). I calculated expected gain rates (fertilised eggs per minute) to males, adopting various strategies to predict the male's optimal: (1) copula duration, (2) locality to search for females, (3) locality for copulation (dung or surrounding grass), and (4) strategy for guarding or not guarding his female after copulation. Most calculations were early ESS analyses—they depended on the current strategy played in the population. The predictions matched the field observations and perhaps provided the first detailed quantitative evidence that intrasexual selection shapes adaptation (see Parker [5]1978 for a summary). They also generated my interests in sperm competition (Parker [18]1970b), animal fighting (Parker [7]1974), animal distributions (Parker [5]1978), and sexual conflict (Parker [4]1979).

By the late 1970s, intrasexual selection had regained widespread acceptance as an explanation of much of male combat and competitive searching. The notion that it could also shape postcopulatory adaptations to reduce sperm (interejaculate) competition (Parker [18]1970b, see Table 3-2) took longer to attract interest. Bob Smith, a sperm competition pioneer (1979), organised a symposium at the 1980 Annual Meeting of American Society of Naturalists and the Society for Study of Evolution in Tucson, Arizona, which generated the first edited volume on sperm competition (Smith 1984). Interest subsequently soared; now there are six research books, a fascinating popular science book (Birkhead 2000), and a best-seller (Baker 1996).

It was quickly appreciated that female choice for direct benefits (Orians [5]1969; Verner & Willson 1966; Thornhill 1983) posed less difficulty than when benefits are purely genetic. For the latter, R. A. Fisher (1930) had formulated a theory, leading to his celebrated "runaway" process, and his last Ph.D. student, Peter O'Donald, had modelled the population genetics of female choice (see 1982 for summary). Zahavi ([8]1975) saw male ornaments as handicaps, arguing that females should choose handicapped males, because they must carry "good genes" for condition (having survived the costs). This notion attracted considerable controversy until Grafen ([3]1990) claimed it to be vindicated in his pioneering work on biological signalling. Lande ([2]1981) pointed out that Fisher's runaway depended on genetic covariance between the female preference and the preferred character and discovered his famous line of equilibrium between the magnitude of the male ornament and that of the female preference. His work catalysed a wave of interest, and new theoretical developments followed swiftly (e.g., Kirkpatrick 1982, Pomiankowski *et al.* [1]1991, Iwasa and Pomiankowski [1]1991). The renewed interest in intersexual selection stimulated an important conference (the "porno-Dahlem"; Bradbury & Andersson 1987).

A problem is that additive genetic variance associated with the male trait should diminish through selection by female choice, unless recurrent mutation is very high. Hamilton and Zuk ([12]1982, see Table 3-2) suggested that genetic cycles in host resistance and parasite virulence could sustain heritable variation in fitness, allowing continued selection for female choice if male ornaments reflect male condition (and hence true fitness). They found a correlation between brightness of ornaments and reduced parasite burdens (Hamilton & Zuk [12]1982). Some tests (e.g., Møller [1]1990) and proposed mechanisms (e.g., Folstad & Karter [1]1992) for the Hamilton and Zuk theory are persuasive. Additional ways to avoid the problem of diminishing genetic variance have been proposed more recently (Pomiankowski & Møller 1995; Rowe and Houle 1996).

The 1980s developments in female choice were not purely theoretical. Partridge ([1]1980) showed that *Drosophila* females allowed to choose their mate produced larvae with higher competitive ability than females randomly allocated a mate, suggesting female choice of "good genes" (though male–male competition could not be ruled out). Andersson's ([3]1982) beautiful field experiment showed that female widow birds prefer males with long tails, suggesting that the tail had evolved through female choice. Bateson ([1]1982) found that both sexes of Japanese quail preferred cousins when offered siblings, cousins, or unrelated individuals as potential mates and proposed that mate choice had evolved to generate "optimal outbreeding."

Interest in the cause of sexual selection began with Darwin (1871), who argued that it arose from the gamete size difference between males and females (anisogamy). Parker and colleagues ([5]1972) showed how anisogamy could arise by disruptive selection on an isogamous, externally fertilising, marine ancestor. Trivers ([18]1972) proposed that sexual selection was fuelled by sex differences in parental investment (PI = the cost of an offspring to the parent measured in terms of lost future offspring), allowing role reversal if male care sufficiently exceeds female care. Gwynne and Simmons (1990) induced role reversals experimentally in a bush cricket, and Simmons (1992) confirmed that these followed reversals in relative PI. Clutton-Brock and Vincent (1991) proposed that the intensity and direction of sexual selection related to potential rates of reproduction of the two sexes. In a classic, highly cited paper, Emlen and Oring ([11]1977, see Table 3-2) outlined how ecology and mating systems shape the "operational sex ratio" (OSR) and proposed that OSR determined the intensity of sexual selection. Bateman ([3]1948) had argued that sexual selection arises out of a higher variance in male than female fitness, using

Drosophila as a demonstration. Sutherland (1985) pointed out that although variance in reproductive success indicates a potential for sexual selection, it does not actually demonstrate it: Bateman's result could be explained by chance due to sex differences arising from the OSR.

The definitive synthesis of sexual selection by Malte Anderson (1994) relates mainly to precopulatory adaptations; any deficit in terms of postcopulatory adaptations is redressed by the several books on sperm competition and the two books by Eberhard (1985, 1996), developing the idea that females may operate various forms of sperm selection ("cryptic female choice") over acceptance or use of given ejaculates, generating a suite of postcopulatory adaptations arising through intersexual selection.

Sexual Conflict

The "battle of the sexes"—long a concept of human life—was nevertheless slow to invade evolutionary biology. Trivers ([18]1972) described conflict between the sexes over parental investment in his classic model of mate desertion. My dung fly work (Parker 1970a, [5]1978), examined the different fitness interests of male and female, and stimulated a series of general sexual conflict models (Parker [4]1979) in work completed in 1976 but that languished long in press. I stressed that male behaviour may often serve male interests but be deleterious to females. One model analysed when it is favourable or unfavourable for a female to mate with a male with a mating advantage trait that reduces her own immediate reproductive success (see also Andrés & Morrow 2003). Another, a male–female arms race game, generated "unresolvable evolutionary chases" between the sexes. Something rather similar has recently been proposed as "chase away" by Holland and Rice (1998). Charnov (1979) developed ideas of sexual conflict for hermaphrodites and applied it to some features of plant reproduction (e.g., double fertilisation in angiosperms).

Sexual conflict has been studied empirically in many species. One of the earliest studies was that of Downhower and Armitage (1971) on conflict over the mating system in yellow-bellied marmots. A powerful example occurs in *Drosophila*, where males ejaculate an agent in the seminal fluid that increases male success in sperm competition but reduces the female's longevity (Chapman *et al.* 1995). Other notable studies concern infanticide and rape in langurs (Hrdy 1977), mate guarding in water striders (Arnqvist 1989), and dunnock mating systems (Davies 1992). Sexual conflict is currently one of the fastest moving areas in behavioural ecology, and remains controversial (e.g., Eberhard 2004). An excellent new monograph by Arnqvist and Rowe (2005) defines the field and marks the maturation of sexual conflict as a discipline.

Sex Ratio and Sex Allocation

Many great triumphs in understanding adaptation have occurred in the area of sex ratio and sex allocation (Charnov 1982). The relatively low number of nominations in this area by respondents probably relates to its perception as evolutionary ecology. Fisher solved the unity sex ratio problem in a cryptic verbal account in his famous 1930 monograph. In a paper far ahead of its time, Shaw and Mohler (1953) formulated Fisher's argument game theoretically and showed that the ESS (as it would later become called) was the unity ratio (see also Shaw 1958). Similarly, Hamilton's classic paper ([1]1967, see Table 3-2) used game theory to find "unbeatable strategies" (a precursor of ESS) that deviated from unity. He examined intragenomic conflict (the ESS ratio depended on whether sex-determining genes were on sex chromosomes or autosomes) and population-biased sex ratios. For example, if matings are between progeny of N females (local mate competition), then under autosomal sex determination at low N the sex ratio will be female-biased. Such skews occur in parasitoid wasps. Trivers and Willard ([3]1973) first proposed the notion of individual-based sex ratio "decisions," arguing that if offspring size or condition, or both, is more important to one sex than the other, the offspring's sex should depend on the mother's condition. There have been many investigations of this idea, some giving remarkable support (e.g., Burley [1]1986; Clutton-Brock et al. 1986).

Eric Charnov (see Table 3-1) has been highly influential in sex allocation theory, especially in showing how sex ratio decisions should be tuned to the local environment (e.g., Charnov & Bull 1977). Decisions in specific conditions should relate to the distribution of conditions across the breeding population, an idea supported by data on parasitoid wasps (Charnov et al. 1981). He also made seminal advances in modelling hermaphroditic systems (e.g., Charnov 1979a). His highly cited monograph (Charnov 1982) reviewing the evidence for prediction–observation concurrence in sex allocation studies by the early 1980s is a remarkable testament to the force of Darwinian selection.

Life-History Switches and Alternative Strategies

Life-history strategy also received relatively few nominations: the most attractive areas related to reproduction and sexual selection (Hamilton [1]1967; Trivers & Hare [5]1976; Trivers & Willard [3]1973; Williams [2]1966b; Burley [1]1986; Charnov [1]1979b), though two concerned senescence (Williams [2]1957; Hamilton [1]1966).

The most commonly cited area has been alternative mating strategies (or tactics), where males show more than one mating pattern, often associated with their phenotype. Typically, males play opportunistic "sneak" strategies when smaller, switching to "guarder" when larger and able to defend females or territories. The pioneering study was that of Alcock and colleagues ([1]1977) in the bee *Centris pallida*, where adult male size varies greatly due to larval nutrition.

Environmentally determined alternative strategies whose frequencies are not moderated by selection, and hence may differ in fitness, were termed "best of a bad job" strategies (Maynard Smith 1982). Commonly, fitness of alternative strategies is frequency-dependent. Gadgil (1972) proposed that sexual selection might generate polymorphism with fitness of two male morphs equalised at their ESS frequencies. Evidence soon followed for equal fitness of the two male morphs (fighting, winged) in fig wasps (Hamilton 1979) and for the two alternative male life histories in bluegill sunfish (Gross and Charnov 1980).

Alternative strategies need not be restricted to male mating behaviour. Brockmann and colleagues (1979) showed the two strategies for gaining a burrow (digging and entering) shown by female digger wasps were frequency-dependent and had similar fitnesses. Barnard and Sibly's (1981) "producer–scrounger" concept was an early general formulation of alternative strategies maintained by frequency-dependence.

If payoffs are frequency-dependent, and phenotypes show continuous variation (e.g., size), selection should generate an ESS switch point (e.g., switch size) at which it pays to change from one strategy to another. This idea had its origin in Ghiselin's (1969) "size advantage" hypothesis for sequential hermaphroditism—individuals should first occupy the sex where size increases fitness less, so that size benefits occur where it counts most (see Warner *et al.* 1975). The ESS rules (West-Eberhard 1979; Charnov *et al.* 1978; Parker 1982, 1984; Repka & Gross 1995) are that: (1) the switch point phenotype must have equal fitness in the two strategies that it separates, and (2) no phenotype must be able to profit by switching to any alternative strategy. These rules apply generally to continuous phenotypes, (e.g., strategies may be alternative patches in a habitat) (Parker & Sutherland 1985). Charnov and colleagues (1978) first provided evidence that age of sex change in a pandalid shrimp fits this "equal fitness at the switch point" principle.

It was quickly realised that alternative male mating strategies were ubiquitous and diverse (Dunbar 1983); several such strategies may occur in just one species (Taborsky 1994). By now a large literature exists.

Biological Signals

Zahavi's ([8]1975) handicap idea (see the section *Sexual Selection*) was highly controversial until supported theoretically (Pomiankowski 1987; Grafen [3]1990). The papers by Dawkins and Krebs ([3]1978) and Krebs and Dawkins

([3]1984) were probably more attractive to behavioural ecologists at the time. Nevertheless, the Zahavi controversy stimulated interest in the evolution of biological signals. Enquist (1985) first brought game theory and signalling together, but it was Grafen ([3]1990a, b) who incisively defined biological signalling as an area. Grafen's model requires that signals be costly, which is why it appears to vindicate Zahavi. One respondent wrote, "This paper not only reinstated Zahavi's idea, it finally brought animal communication, game theory, and sexual selection together."

So much depends on the interpretation of Zahavi's ([8]1975) writing that Grafen could possibly (in my view) have avoided stressing Zahavi's paper; Grafen's model is a continuous strategy game involving female preference and costly male advertisement, where increasing advertisement yields increasing benefits. Godfray (1991) applied Grafen's model to interpret offspring begging as an honest signal of need; an alternative is that begging represents scramble competition among offspring (Macnair & Parker [1]1979).

Recent discussion has centred on whether signals must always be costly. Maynard Smith's (1991) discrete strategy "Sir Philip Sidney game" shows that for a cost-free signal to be reliable, signaller and receiver must place the possible outcomes of the interaction in the same rank order of preference. Animal signals and communication are the subjects of several books and reviews, the most recent being that of Maynard Smith and Harper (2003) stressing the diversity of ways signal reliability might be maintained, depending on the system.

Animal Distributions

Habitat choice and spatial distribution have arguably been the developments of greatest importance to mainstream ecologists. Fretwell and Lucas ([4]1969; Fretwell 1972) deduced the evolution of distributions in patchy habitats, under various assumptions about territoriality or its absence. The "ideal free" distribution (unconstrained animals distribute such that no individual can profit by moving elsewhere) later became a much-studied concept (Milinski 1979 was the first direct test).

Others had foreshadowed Fretwell's visionary insights, but less generally. I developed my own version (the "equilibrium position") of "ideal free" in my Ph.D. thesis (1968) to explain the distribution of male dung flies (Parker 1970a, [5]1978). Orians's ([5]1969) "polygyny threshold" model (see also Verner & Willson 1966) predicted how successive females should settle when faced with a choice of male territories. One respondent wrote:

> [Orians's model] was for me the first clear example of how good theoretical models were useful in our field. . . . [Fretwell's] notion of ideal free settlement was critical at the time it came out by providing some feasible mechanisms for how Crook-type processes might arise

by simply mapping animals down on heterogeneous landscapes. It built on Orians's [model], but also generalized it.

The concept developed in many ways (see Tregenza 1995). Sutherland (1983) showed how "ideal free" applies under interference competition, and Sutherland and Parker (1985; Parker & Sutherland 1986) investigated effects of competitive asymmetries between individuals.

Comparative Approach

Major advances in comparative analysis techniques accompanied the behavioural ecology revolution. Traditional ethology had tended to focus on phylogenetic constraints on behaviour. John Crook pioneered a comparative approach that stressed ecological influences. He sought correlations across species and between types of social behaviour and ecological variables, first in his weaver bird monograph ([1]1964) and later in overviews of avian ([1]1965) and primate (Crook & Gartlan [2]1966) social organisation. Crook's approach was soon extended to avian breeding biology (Lack 1968) and antelope social organisation (Jarman [1]1974).

A seminal development came when Clutton-Brock and Harvey ([1]1977) measured adaptations and ecological variables on a continuous scale and applied multivariate statistics to seek correlations. Initially, each species was used as a data point, which posed problems: methods quickly developed using contrasts between independent evolutionary events as data (pioneers were Ridley 1983, for discrete comparisons; Felsenstein 1985, for continuous characters). By 1990, comparative methods had become powerful tools for studying biological adaptations (Harvey & Pagel 1991; Harvey & Purvis 1991) and are now used extensively.

Predation, Flocking, and Vigilance

With typical originality, Hamilton ([6]1971) proposed flocking to be the result of each individual's reducing its "domain of danger" to predators by moving closer to others ("selfish herd" theory). For a flock of size N, individual risk dilutes to $1/N$.

Lazarus (1978) argued that an individual's domain of danger is reflected by its vigilance against predators. Competition may reduce food intake: flocking and vigilance soon became seen as resulting from trade-offs between feeding and predation. Caraco and colleagues ([1]1980) demonstrated that both flock size and vigilance increase in the presence of a predator. Vigilance was seen as a second advantage in flocking—in addition to Hamilton's dilution effect, "many eyes" reduced the predator's chance of success. Bertram (1980) showed that although individual vigilance levels decreased with flock size, the summed vigilance does increase, supporting "many eyes" predictions, and numerous subsequent studies have shown similar trends. But theoretically, the ESS vigilance per individual declines so steeply with flock size that the summed vigilance generally also declines (Parker & Hammerstein 1985). Counter to "many eyes" predictions, predators should be more successful with bigger flocks, leaving Hamilton's dilution effect the main reason for aggregation. This theoretical prediction is counter to observations and remains something of a mystery, unless the effective flock is smaller than the total flock.

Alexander's seminal paper ([4]1974) built on Hamilton ([6]1971) by stimulating a more general approach to the advantages and disadvantages of group living and reinforcing the interpretation that sociality requires a net benefit to the individual rather than to the group.

Mating Systems, Reproductive Skew, and Social Groups

Sexual selection, ecological constraints, and patterns of dispersion of the sexes all interact and thus influence the structure of the mating system (Emlen & Oring [11]1977; Clutton-Brock 1989; Davies 1992). Given that males and females will be under selection to maximise their own interests, there can be considerable sexual conflict over the mating system (Davies 1992). Early landmarks were Orians's ([5]1969) study of New World blackbirds and Bradbury and Vehrencamp's ([1]1977) study of bats.

Alexander's ([4]1974) analysis of individual costs–benefits of social grouping acted as a catalyst for many new developments. In social breeders, dominance and priority over access to resources leads to reproductive skew: the reproductive success differential between dominants and subordinates. The first skew model was developed by Sandy Vehrencamp ([1]1983) to analyse, in relation to group size, how much bias a dominant can enforce before it pays a subordinate to leave to breed independently. Her model spawned a series of skew models, and its basic approach is still applied for understanding dynamics within groups. Social breeding now represents a huge area in behavioural ecology.

Intrafamilial Conflict

Lack ([1]1947) applied a pioneering optimality approach to the problem of clutch size: the optimal clutch size maximised the product of offspring number and fitness, implicitly assuming that selection maximises the caring parent's fitness. Hamilton's inclusive fitness classic ([22]1964) had hinted that parent and offspring interests were not identical. But it was Trivers's revolutionary paper on parent–offspring conflict ([15]1974, see Table 3-2) that laid bare the notion of the family as a harmonious unit. Trivers predicted that in sexually reproducing species, a current offspring gains by receiving more PI than is optimal for the parent to give. He later (Trivers & Hare [5]1976) showed that investment in progeny in social insects matched offspring interests, rather than those of queens. In contrast, Alexander's widely cited paper on evolution of social behaviour ([4]1974) developed the idea of "parental manipulation," (i.e., that parents can manipulate offspring into the outcome best for the parent), supporting Lack's ([1]1947) original emphasis. Such an outcome is likely in some instances; for example, hatching asynchrony in birds is something that parents determine long before offspring can exert any influence. (It is set by the start of incubation.)

Alexander's (1974) paper also disputed the theoretical basis of parent–offspring conflict, something he later retracted (Alexander 1979) after an analysis by Blick (1977). Mark Macnair and I (Parker & Macnair [1]1978; Macnair & Parker [1]1978) applied a combination of population genetics and ESS approaches, confirming that Trivers was correct and examining the effect of different mating systems and types of conflict. Haig (1992) extended our approach to allow for genomic imprinting, suggesting that the conflict was not only between mother and offspring, but between the genes (determining how much PI the offspring takes) inherited from the male and female parents. O'Connor ([1]1978) showed that in birds, where death of offspring is common if food is scarce, there are three different thresholds (reflecting the different interests of the players) as food supply diminishes: (1) one for fratricide (now generally called siblicide), (2) one for infanticide, (3) and one for suicide.

Since 1980, much empirical and theoretical work has been directed towards intrafamilial conflict. The family is now perceived as a cauldron of conflict, with each of the players having different interests: resolution must satisfy sexual conflict, parent–offspring conflict, and sib-competition simultaneously (see Mock & Parker 1997 for review).

The Future

Mercifully, the political feuds about human nature and criticisms that the adaptationist approach was "Panglossian" (Gould & Lewontin [1]1979) proved to be only diversions that obscured what was happening: the explosion of one of Tinbergen's ([3]1963) celebrated "four questions" (see Alcock 2001a).

I write this essay exactly 40 years after starting work in behavioural ecology. My travel with this obsession has been immense fun: my only sadness is that I shall not see how our understanding will have developed after the next

40 years. I might like to conclude that behavioural ecology has now matured, is now safe, secure, and forever will be so. I would probably be wrong. The generation of ethologists working before the behavioural ecology revolution probably felt secure about ethology. Perhaps ethology did not actually die, but rather was revolutionised by concepts from population biology and economics. If the ethologists could be criticised, it is only for taking their eyes off the Darwinian ball—and if this was refocused by Williams, Maynard Smith, Hamilton, Trivers, and others, they may have argued that it was difficult to be an expert in behaviour and evolutionary biology at the same time. But it all felt more like a revolution than a gentle, gradual metamorphosis. Sooner or later, behavioural ecology may be similarly assaulted. The future in science is about as predictable as the stock markets.

At the moment, I see the main changes as involving technology. Advances in molecular biology such as fingerprinting (Jeffries et al. [1]1985) have revolutionised how we can study paternity (the first application being that of Burke et al. [2]1989), sperm competition, kinship, and so on. Modern comparative methods and computer technology have revolutionised how we can analyse comparative or other data. These advances have extended existing insights rather than changed the philosophy: we are still integrating the conceptual advances from the revolution. Deeper understanding of mechanisms is eroding the view of the animal as a "black box," a necessary approach of the 1970s. By this more broadly zoological approach (genes to physiology to behaviour), the constraints underlying each suite of adaptations are gradually becoming better understood. With deeper understanding of constraints, we can develop more realistic evolutionary models and predictions for the adaptations.

Revolution or gradual changes are not the only possibilities. My bet is that each area of behavioural ecology will each become a discipline in its own right, with coverage spanning the molecular to the evolutionary. That is the current trend: natural historians are simply becoming much more enlightened.

Finally, to the new colleagues for whom this essay might serve a purpose, I sincerely wish you as much joy from behavioural ecology as it has given me. Science is about seeing questions and discovering how to answer them. Hopefully, your generation will not only be able to answer some of the questions we failed to answer but will also see some of the questions we failed to see.

Acknowledgments

I am grateful to Leigh Simmons for inviting me to do this chapter and to Ian Harvey for lending me several of his books. I am deeply indebted to the

25 anonymous respondents for taking time to reply, sometimes at length. Without your help, it would all have been a much less interesting exercise.

References

Alcock, J. 2001a. *The Triumph of Sociobiology*. New York: Oxford University Press.

Alcock, J. 2001b. *Animal Behavior, an Evolutionary Approach*, 7th edn. Sunderland, Massachusetts: Sinauer.

Alcock, J., Jones, C. E., Buchmann, S. L. 1977. Male mating strategies in the bee *Centris pallida* Fox (*Anthophoridae-Hymenoptera*). *American Naturalist*, **111**, 145–155.

Alexander, R. D. 1974. The evolution of social behaviour. *Annual Review of Ecology and Systematics*, **5**, 325–383.

Alexander, R. D. 1979. *Darwinism and Human Affairs*. London: Pitman.

Andersson, M. 1982. Female choice selects for extreme tail length in a widowbird. *Nature*, **299**, 818–820.

Andersson, M. 1994. *Sexual Selection*. Princeton, New Jersey: Princeton University Press.

Andrés, J. A. & Morrow, E. H. 2003. The origin of interlocus sexual conflict: is sex linkage important? *Journal of Evolutionary Biology*, **16**, 219–223.

Arnqvist, G. 1989. Multiple mating in a water strider: mutual benefits or intersexual selection? *Animal Behaviour*, **38**, 749–756.

Arnqvist, G. & Rowe L. 2005. *Sexual Conflict*. Princeton, New Jersey: Princeton University Press.

Axelrod, R. & Hamilton, W.D. 1981. The evolution of cooperation. *Science*, **211**, 1390–1396.

Baker, R. R. 1996. *Sperm Wars: The Science of Sex*. London: Fourth Estate.

Barnard, C. J. 2004. *Animal Behaviour: Mechanism, Development, Function and Evolution*. Harlow: Pearson Educational.

Barnard, C. J. & Sibly, R. M. 1981. Producers and scroungers: a general model and its application to captive flocks of house sparrows. *Animal Behaviour*, **29**, 543–550.

Bateman, A. J. 1948. Intrasexual selection in *Drosophila*. *Heredity*, **2**, 349–368.

Bateson, P. 1982. Preferences for cousins in Japanese quail. *Nature*, **295**, 236–237.

Bertram, B. C. R. 1980. Vigilance and group size in ostriches. *Animal Behaviour*, **28**, 278–286.

Birkhead, T. R. 2000. *Promiscuity and Evolutionary History of Sperm Competition and Sexual Conflict*. London: Faber & Faber.

Blick, J. E. 1977. Selection for traits which lower individual reproduction. *Journal of Theoretical Biology*, **67**, 597–601.

Bradbury, J. W. & Andersson, M. B. (eds.) 1987. *Sexual Selection: Testing the Alternatives*. New York: Wiley Interscience.

Bradbury, J. W. & Vehrencamp, S. L. 1977. Social organization and foraging in *Emballonurid* bats. 3. Mating systems. *Behavioral Ecology and Sociobiology*, **2**, 1–17.

Brockmann, H. J., Grafen, A. & Dawkins, R. 1979. Evolutionarily stable nesting strategy in a digger wasp. *Journal of Theoretical Biology*, **77**, 473–496.

Burke, T., Davies, N. B., Bruford, M. W. & Hatchwell, B. J. 1989. Parental care and mating behavior of polyandrous dunnocks, *Prunella modularis*, related to paternity by DNA fingerprinting. *Nature*, **338**, 249–251.

Burley, N. 1986. Sex ratio manipulation in color-banded populations of zebra finches. *Evolution*, **40**, 1191–1206.

Caraco, T., Martindale, S. & Pulliam, H. R. 1980. Avian flocking in the presence of a predator. *Nature*, **285**, 400–401

Carr-Saunders, A. M. 1922. *The Population Problem: a Study in Human Evolution*. Oxford: Clarendon Press.

Chapman, T., Liddle, L. F., Kalb, J. M., Wolfner, M. F. & Partridge, L. 1995. Cost of mating in *Drosophila* females is mediated by male accessory gland products. *Nature,* **373,** 241–244.

Charnov, E. L. 1976a. Optimal foraging: the marginal value theorem. *Theoretical Population Biology,* **9,** 129–136.

Charnov, E. L. 1976b. Optimal foraging: attack strategy of a mantid. *American Naturalist,* **110,** 141–151.

Charnov, E. L. 1979a. Simultaneous hermaphroditism and sexual selection. *Proceedings of the National Academy of Sciences of the USA,* **76,** 2480–2484.

Charnov, E. L. 1979b. Natural selection and sex change in Pandalid shrimp—test of a life history theory. *American Naturalist,* **113,** 715–734.

Charnov, E. L. 1982. *The Theory of Sex Allocation.* Princeton, New Jersey: Princeton University Press.

Charnov, E. L. & Bull, J. J. 1977. When is sex environmentally determined? *Nature,* **266,** 828–830.

Charnov, E. L., Gotshall, D. & Robinson, J. 1978. Sex ratio: adaptive response to population fluctuations in *Pandalid* shrimp. *Science,* **200,** 204–206.

Charnov, E. L., Los-den Hartogh, R. L., Jones, W. T. & van den Assem, J. 1981. Sex ratio evolution in a variable environment. *Nature,* **289,** 27–33.

Clark C. W. & Mangel, M. 2000. *Dynamic State Variable Models in Ecology.* Oxford: Oxford University Press.

Clutton-Brock, T. H. 1989. Mammalian mating systems. *Proceedings of the Royal Society of London, Series B,* **236,** 339–372.

Clutton-Brock, T. H., Albon, S. D. & Guinness, F. E. 1986. Great expectations: maternal dominance, sex ratios and offspring reproductive success in red deer. *Animal Behaviour,* **34,** 460–471.

Clutton-Brock, T. H. & Harvey, P. H. 1977. Primate ecology and social organization. *Journal of Zoology,* **183,** 1–39.

Clutton-Brock, T. H. & Vincent, A. C. J. 1991. Sexual selection and the potential reproductive rates of males and females. *Nature,* **351,** 487–489.

Crook, J. C. 1964. The evolution of social organisation and visual communication in weaver birds (*Ploceidae*). *Behaviour Supplements,* **10,** 1–178.

Crook, J. C. 1965. The adaptive significance of avian social organisation. *Symposia of the Zoological Society of London,* **14,** 181–218.

Crook, J. H. & Gartlan, J. S. 1966. Evolution of primate societies. *Nature,* **210,** 1200–1203.

Darwin, C. 1871. *The Descent of Man and Selection in Relation to Sex.* London: Murray.

Davies, N. B. 1978. Territorial defence in the speckled wood butterfly (*Pararge aegeria*)—the resident always wins. *Animal Behaviour,* **26,** 138–147.

Davies, N. B. 1992. *Dunnock Behaviour and Social Evolution.* Oxford: Oxford University Press.

Dawkins, R. 1976. *The Selfish Gene.* Oxford: Oxford University Press.

Dawkins, R. & Krebs, J. R. 1978. Animal signals: information or manipulation? In: *Behavioural Ecology: an Evolutionary Approach,* 1st edn. (Ed. by J. R. Krebs & N. B. Davies), pp. 282–309. Oxford: Blackwells.

Dawkins, R. & Krebs, J. R. 1979. Arms races between and within species. *Proceedings of the Royal Society of London, Series B,* **205,** 489–511.

Downhower, J. F. & Armitage, K. 1971. The yellow-bellied marmot and the evolution of polygamy. *American Naturalist,* **105,** 355–370.

Dugatkin, L. A. 2004. *Principles of Animal Behavior.* New York: Norton.

Dunbar, R. I. M. 1983. Intraspecific variations in mating srategy. In: *Perspectives in Ethology,* Vol. 5 (Ed. by P. P. G. Bateson & P. H. Klopfer), pp. 384–431. New York: Plenum Press.

Eberhard, W. G. 1985. *Sexual Selection and Animal Genitalia.* Cambridge, Massachusetts: Harvard University Press.

Eberhard, W. G. 1996. *Female Control: Sexual Selection by Cryptic Female Choice.* Princeton, New Jersey: Princeton University Press.

Eberhard, W. G. 2004. Male–female conflict and genitalia: failure to confirm predictions in insects and spiders. *Biological Reviews,* **79,** 121–186.

Elwood, R. W. & Briffa, M. 2001. Information gathering and communication during agonistic encounters: a case study of hermit crabs. *Advances in the Study of Animal Behaviour,* **30,** 53–97.

Emlen, J. M. 1966. The role of time and energy in food preference. *American Naturalist,* **101,** 385–389.

Emlen, S. T. & Oring, L. W. 1977. Ecology, sexual selection, and the evolution of mating systems. *Science,* **197,** 215–223.

Enquist, M. 1985. Communication during aggressive interactions with particular reference to variation in choice of behaviour. *Animal Behaviour,* **33,** 1152–1161.

Enquist, M. & Leimar, O. 1983. Decision rules and assessment of relative strength. *Journal of Theoretical Biology,* **102,** 387–410.

Eshel, I. 1983. Evolutionary and continuous stability. *Journal of Theoretical Biology,* **103,** 99–112.

Felsenstein, J. 1985. Phylogenies and the comparative method. *American Naturalist,* **125,** 1–15.

Fisher, R. A. 1930. *The Genetical Theory of Natural Selection.* Oxford: Clarendon Press.

Folstad, I. & Karter, A. J. 1992. Parasites, bright males, and the immunocompetence handicap. *American Naturalist,* **139,** 603–622.

Fretwell, S. D. 1972. *Populations in a Seasonal Environment.* Princeton, New Jersey: Princeton University Press.

Fretwell, S. D. & Lucas, H. L. 1969. On territorial behaviour and other factors influencing habitat distribution in birds. *Acta Biotheoretica,* **19,** 16–36.

Gadgil, M. 1972. Male dimorphism as a consequence of sexual selection. *American Naturalist,* **102,** 574–580.

Ghiselin, M. T. 1969. The evolution of hermaphroditism among animals. *Quarterly Review of Biology,* **44,** 189–208.

Godfray, H. J. C. 1991. The signalling of need by offspring to their parents. *Nature,* **353,** 328–330.

Goodenough, J., McGuire, B. & Wallace, R. 2001. *Perspectives on Animal Behavior,* 2nd edn. New York: Wiley.

Gould, S. J. & Lewontin, R. D. 1979. The spandrels of San Marco and the Panglossian paradigm: a critique of the adaptationist programme. *Proceedings of the Royal Society of London, Series B,* **205,** 581–598.

Grafen, A. 1984. Natural selection, kin selection and group selection. In: *Behavioural Ecology: an Evolutionary Approach,* 2nd edn. (Ed. by J. R. Krebs & N. B. Davies), pp. 62–84. Oxford: Blackwells.

Grafen, A. 1990. Biological signals as handicaps. *Journal of Theoretical Biology,* **144,** 517–546.

Grafen, A. 2004. *William Donald Hamilton: Biographical Memoirs of Fellows of the Royal Society,* **50,** 109–132.

Gross, M. R. & Charnov, E. L. 1980. Alternative male life histories in bluegill sunfish. *Proceedings of the National Academy of Sciences of the USA,* **77,** 6937–6940.

Gwynne, D. T. & Simmons, L. W. 1990. Experimental manipulation of courtship roles in an insect. *Nature,* **346,** 172–174.

Haig, D. 1992. Genomic imprinting and the theory of parent–offspring conflict. *Seminars in Developmental Biology,* **3,** 153–160.

Hamilton, W. D. 1963. The evolution of altruistic behavior. *American Naturalist,* **97,** 354–356.

Hamilton, W. D. 1964. The genetical evolution of social behaviour. I, II. *Journal of Theoretical Biology,* **7,** 52.

Hamilton, W. D. 1966. The moulding of senescence by natural selection. *Journal of Theoretical Biology,* **12,** 12–45

Hamilton, W. D. 1967. Extraordinary sex ratios. *Science,* **156,** 477–488.

Hamilton, W. D. 1971. Geometry for the selfish herd. *Journal of Theoretical Biology,* **31,** 295–311.

Hamilton, W. D. 1979. Wingless and fighting males in fig wasps and other insects. In: *Sexual Selection and Reproductive Competition in Insects* (Ed. by M. S. Blum & N. A. Blum), pp. 167–220. London: Academic Press.

Hamilton, W. D. 1996. *Narrow Roads of Gene Land: The Collected Papers of W. D. Hamilton. Volume I: Evolution of Social Behaviour.* Oxford: Oxford University Press.

Hamilton, W. D. 2001. *Narrow Roads of Gene Land: The Collected Papers of W. D. Hamilton. Volume II: The Evolution of Sex.* Oxford: Oxford University Press.

Hamilton, W. D. 2004. *Narrow Roads of Gene Land: The Collected Papers of W. D. Hamilton. Volume III: The Final Years* (with essays by co-authors, Ed. by M. Ridley). Oxford: Oxford University Press.

Hamilton, W. D. & Zuk, M. 1982. Heritable true fitness and bright birds: a role for parasites? *Science,* **218,** 384–387.

Hammerstein, P. & Parker, G. A. 1982. The asymmetric war of attrition. *Journal of Theoretical Biology,* **96,** 647–682.

Harvey, P. H. & Pagel, M. D. 1991. *The Comparative Method in Evolutionary Biology.* Oxford: Oxford University Press.

Harvey, P. H. & Purvis, A. 1991. Comparative methods for explaining adaptations. *Nature,* **351,** 619–624.

Holland, B. & Rice, W. R. 1998. Chase-away sexual selection: antagonistic seduction versus resistance. *Evolution,* **52,** 1–7.

Houston, A. I. & McNamara, J. M. 1985. The choice of two prey types that minimises the risk of starvation. *Behavioral Ecology and Sociobiology,* **17,** 135–141.

Houston A. I. & McNamara J. M. 1999. *Models of Adaptive Behaviour.* Cambridge: Cambridge University Press.

Hrdy, S. B. 1977. *The Langurs of Abu: Female and Male Strategies of Reproduction.* Cambridge, Massachusetts: Harvard University Press.

Huxley, J. S. 1938. The present standing of the theory of sexual selection. In: *Evolution* (Ed. by G. De Beer). Oxford: Oxford University Press.

*Iwasa, Y. & Pomiankowski, A. 1991. The evolution of costly mate preferences. 2. The handicap principle. *Evolution,* **45,** 1431–1442. *[Vote also includes Pomiankowski, Iwasa & Nee (1991).]

Jeffreys, A. J., Wilson, V. & Thein, S. L. 1985. Hypervariable minisatellite regions in human DNA. *Nature,* **314,** 67–73.

Kirkpatrick, M. 1982. Sexual selection and the evolution of female choice. *Evolution,* **36,** 1–12.

Krebs, J. R. & Davies, N. B. (eds.) 1978 (1st edn.); 1984 (2nd edn.); 1991 (3rd edn.); 1997 (4th edn.). *Behavioural Ecology: an Evolutionary Approach.* Oxford: Blackwell.

Krebs, J. R. & Davies, N. B. 1981 (1st edn.); 1993 (3rd edn.). *An Introduction to Behavioural Ecology.* Oxford: Blackwell.

Krebs, J. R. & Dawkins, R. 1984. Animal signals: mind-reading and manipulation. In: *Behavioural Ecology: an Evolutionary Approach,* 2nd edn. (Ed. by J. R. Krebs & N. B. Davies), pp. 380–402. Oxford: Blackwell.

Krebs, J. R., Ryan, J. C. & Charnov, E. L. Hunting by expectation or optimal foraging? A study of patch use by chickadees. *Animal Behaviour,* **22,** 953–964.

Lack, D. 1947. The significance of clutch size. *Ibis,* **89,** 302–352.

Lande, R. 1981. Models of speciation by sexual selection on polygenic traits. *Proceedings of the National Academy of Sciences of the USA,* **78,** 3721–3725.

Lazarus, J. 1978. Vigilance, flock size and domain of danger size in the white-fronted goose. *Wildfowl,* **29,** 135–145.

MacArthur, R. H. & Pianka, E. R. 1966. On optimal use of a patchy environment. *American Naturalist*, **100**, 603–609.

*Macnair, M. R. & Parker, G. A. 1978. Models of parent-offspring conflict. I. Promiscuity. *Animal Behaviour*, **26**, 111–122. *[Vote includes all papers in this series.]

Mangel, M. & Clark, C. W. 1988. *Dynamic Modeling in Behavioral Ecology*. Princeton, New Jersey: Princeton University Press.

Manning, A. & Dawkins, M. S. 1998. *An Introduction to Animal Behaviour*, 5th edn. Cambridge: Cambridge University Press.

Maynard Smith, J. 1964. Group selection and kin selection. *Nature*, **201**, 1145–1147.

Maynard Smith, J. 1974. The theory of games and the evolution of animal conflicts. *Journal of Theoretical Biology*, **47**, 209–221.

Maynard Smith, J. 1976. Evolution and the theory of games. *American Scientist*, **64**, 41–45.

Maynard Smith, J. 1977. Parental investment—a prospective analysis. *Animal Behaviour*, **25**, 1–9.

Maynard Smith, J. 1982. *Evolution and the Theory of Games*. Cambridge: Cambridge University Press.

Maynard Smith, J. 1991. Honest signalling: the Philip Sidney game. *Animal Behaviour*, **42**, 1034–1035.

Maynard Smith, J. & Harper, D. 2003. *Animal Signals*. Oxford: Oxford University Press.

Maynard Smith, J. & Parker, G. A. 1976. The logic of asymmetric contests. *Animal Behaviour*, **24**, 159–175.

Maynard Smith, J. & Price, G. R. 1973. The logic of animal conflicts. *Nature*, **246**, 15–18.

McFarland, D. J. 1999. *Animal Behaviour*, 3rd edn. Harlow: Longman.

McFarland, D. J. & Houston, A. I. 1981. *Quantitative Ethology: The State Space Approach*. London: Pitman.

Milinski, M. 1979. An evolutionarily stable feeding strategy in sticklebacks. *Zeitschrift für Tierpsychologie*, **51**, 36–40.

Milinski, M. & Heller, R. 1978. Influence of a predator on optimal foraging behavior of sticklebacks (*Gasterosteus aculeatus* L.). *Nature*, **275**, 642–644.

Mock, D. W. & Parker, G. A. 1997. *The Evolution of Sibling Rivalry*. Oxford: Oxford University Press.

Møller, A. P. 1990. Effects of a hematophagous mite on the barn swallow (*Hirudino rustica*)—a test of the Hamilton and Zuk hypothesis. *Evolution*, **44**, 771–784.

Nash, J. F. 1951. Non-cooperative games. *Annals of Mathematics*, **54**, 286–295.

O'Connor, R. J. 1978. Brood reduction in birds: selection for infanticide, fratricide, and suicide. *Animal Behaviour*, **26**, 79–96.

O'Donald, P. 1980. *Genetic Models of Sexual Selection*. Cambridge: Cambridge University Press.

Orians, G. H. 1969. On the evolution of mating systems in birds and mammals. *American Naturalist*, **103**, 589–603.

Packer, C. 1977. Reciprocal altruism in *Papio anubis*. *Nature*, **265**, 441–443.

*Parker, G. A. 1970a. The reproductive behaviour and the nature of sexual selection in *Scatophaga stercoraria* L. (Diptera: Scatophagidae). II The fertilization rate and the spatial and temporal relationships of each sex around the site of mating and oviposition. *Journal of Animal Ecology*, **39**, 205–228. *[Vote also includes other papers in this series together with Parker (1978).]

Parker, G. A. 1970b. Sperm competition and its evolutionary consequences in the insects. *Biological Reviews*, **45**, 525–567.

Parker, G. A. 1974. Assessment strategy and the evolution of fighting behaviour. *Journal of Theoretical Biology*, **47**, 223–243.

*Parker, G. A. 1978. Searching for mates. In: *Behavioural Ecology: an Evolutionary Approach*, 1st edn. (Ed. by J. R. Krebs & N. B. Davies), pp. 214–244. Oxford: Blackwells. *[Vote includes this paper together with series of Parker (1970a).]

Parker, G. A. 1979. Sexual selection and sexual conflict. In: *Sexual Selection and Reproductive Competition in Insects* (Ed. by M. S. Blum and N. A. Blum), pp. 123–166. London: Academic Press.

Parker, G. A. 1982. Phenotype-limited evolutionarily stable strategies. In: *Current Problems in Sociobiology* (Ed. by King's College Sociobiology Group), pp. 173–201. Cambridge: Cambridge University Press.

Parker, G. A. 1984. The producer/scrounger model and its relevance to sexuality. In: *Producers and Scroungers: Strategies of Exploitation and Parasitism* (Ed. by C. J. Barnard), pp. 127–153. London: Croom Helm.

Parker, G. A. 2001. Golden flies, sunlit meadows: a tribute to the yellow dung fly. In: *Model Systems in Behavioural Ecology: Integrating Conceptual, Theoretical, and Empirical Approaches* (Ed. by L. A. Dugatkin), pp. 3–26. Princeton, New Jersey: Princeton University Press.

Parker, G. A., Baker, R. R. & Smith, V. G. F. 1972. The origin and evolution of gamete dimorphism and the male–female phenomenon. *Journal of Theoretical Biology*, **36**, 529–553.

Parker, G. A. & Hammerstein, P. 1985. Game theory and animal behaviour. In: *Evolution: Essays in Honour of John Maynard Smith* (Ed. by P. J. Greenwood, P. H. Harvey & M. Slatkin), pp. 73–94. Cambridge: Cambridge University Press.

*Parker, G. A. & Macnair, M. R. 1978. Models of parent–offspring conflict. I. Monogamy. *Animal Behaviour*, **26**, 97–110. *[Vote includes all papers in this series.]

Parker, G. A. & Maynard Smith, J. 1990. Optimality theory in evolutionary biology. *Nature*, **348**, 27–33.

Parker, G. A. & Stuart, R. A. 1976. Animal behaviour as a strategy optimizer: evolution of resource assessment strategies and optimal emigration thresholds. *American Naturalist*, **110**, 1055–1076.

Parker, G. A. & Sutherland, W. J. 1986. Ideal free distributions when individuals differ in competitive ability: phenotype-limited ideal free models. *Animal Behaviour*, **34**, 1222–1242.

Partridge, L. 1980. Mate choice increases a component of offspring fitness in fruit flies. *Nature*, **283**, 290–291.

Pomiankowski, A. 1987. Sexual selection: the handicap principle does work—sometimes. *Proceedings of the Royal Society of London, Series B*, **231**, 123–145.

*Pomiankowski, A., Iwasa, Y. & Nee, S. 1991. The evolution of costly mate preferences. 1. Fisher and biased mutation. *Evolution*, **45**, 1422–1430. *[Vote also includes Iwasa & Pomiankowski (1991).]

Pomiankowski, A. & Møller, A. P. 1995. A resolution of the lek paradox. *Proceedings of the Royal Society of London, Series B*, **260**, 21–29.

Pyke, G. H., Pulliam, H. R. & Charnov, E. L. 1977. Optimal foraging—selective review of theory and tests. *Quarterly Review of Biology*, **52**, 137–154.

Repka, J. & Gross, M. R. 1995. The evolutionarily stable strategy under individual condition and tactic frequency. *Journal of Theoretical Biology*, **176**, 27–31.

Richards, O. W. 1927. Sexual selection and related problems in the insects. *Biological Reviews*, **2**, 298–364.

Ridley, M. 1983. *The Explanation of Organic Diversity: the Comparative Method and Adaptations for Mating.* Oxford: Oxford University Press.

Rowe, L. & Houle, D. 1996. The lek paradox and the capture of genetic variance by condition dependent traits. *Proceedings of the Royal Society of London, Series B*, **263**, 1415–1421.

Schoener, T. W. 1971. Theory of feeding strategies. *Annual Review of Ecology and Systematics*, **2**, 369–404.

Segerstråle, U. 2000. *Defenders of the Truth: the Battle for Science in the Sociobiology Debate and Beyond.* Oxford: Oxford University Press.

Segerstråle, U. In press. *Nature's Oracle: an Intellectual Biography of the Evolutionist W. D. Hamilton.* Oxford: Oxford University Press.

Shaw, R. F. 1958. The theoretical genetics of the sex ratio. *Genetics,* **93,** 149–163.

Shaw, R. F. & Mohler, J. D. 1953. The selective advantage of the sex ratio. *American Naturalist,* **87,** 337–342.

Sherman, P. W. 1977. Nepotism and the evolution of alarm calls. *Science,* **197,** 1246–1253.

Sibly, R. & McFarland, D. 1976. On the fitness of behavior sequences. *American Naturalist,* **110,** 601–617.

Simmons, L. W. 1992. Quantification of role reversal in relative parental investment in a bushcricket. *Nature,* **358,** 61–63.

Smith, R. L. 1979. Repeated copulation and sperm precedence: paternity assurance for a male brooding water bug. *Science,* **205,** 1029–1031.

Smith, R. L. (ed.) 1984. *Sperm Competition and the Evolution of Animal Mating Systems.* London: Academic Press.

Stearns, S. C. 1976. Life history tactics—a review of the ideas. *Quarterly Review of Biology,* **51,** 3–47.

Stephens, D. W. & Krebs, J. R. 1986. *Foraging Theory.* Princeton, New Jersey: Princeton University Press.

Stutt, A. D. & Willmer, P. 1998. Territorial defence in speckled wood butterflies: do the hottest males always win? *Animal Behaviour,* **55,** 1341–1347.

Sutherland, W. J. 1983. Aggregation and the "ideal free" distribution. *Journal of Animal Ecology,* **52,** 821–828.

Sutherland, W. J. 1985. Chance can produce a sex difference in variance in mating success and explain Bateman's data. *Animal Behaviour,* **33,** 1349–1352.

Sutherland, W. J. & Parker, G. A. Distribution of unequal competitors. In: *Behavioural Ecology: the Ecological Consequences of Adaptive Behaviour* (Ed. by R. M. Sibly & R. H. Smith), pp. 255–273. Oxford: Blackwell.

Taborsky, M. 1994. Sneakers, satellites, and helpers: parasitic and cooperative behavior in fish reproduction. *Advances in the Study of Behavior,* **23,** 1–100.

Thornhill, R. 1983. Cryptic female choice and its implications in the scorpionfly *Harpobittacus nigriceps. American Naturalist,* **122,** 765–788.

Tinbergen, N. 1963. On aims and methods of ethology. *Zeitschrift für Tierpsychologie,* **20,** 410–433.

Tregenza, T. 1995. Building on the ideal free distribution. *Advances in Ecological Research,* **26,** 253–302.

Trivers, R. L. 1971. The evolution of reciprocal altruism. *Quarterly Review of Biology,* **46,** 249–264.

Trivers, R. L. 1972. Parental investment and sexual selection. In: *Sexual Selection and the Descent of Man 1871–1971* (Ed. by B. Campbell), pp. 136–172. Chicago: Aldine-Atherton.

Trivers, R. L. 1974. Parent–offspring conflict. *American Zoologist,* **14,** 249–264.

Trivers, R. L. & Hare, H. 1976. Haplodiploidy and the evolution of the social insects. *Science,* **191,** 249–263.

Trivers, R. L. & Willard, D. E. 1973. Natural selection of parental ability to vary the sex ratio of offspring. *Science,* **179,** 90–92.

Vehrencamp, S. L. 1983. A model for the evolution of despotic versus egalitarian societies. *Animal Behaviour,* **31,** 667–682.

Verner, J. & Willson, M. F. 1966. The influence of habitats on mating systems of North American passerine birds. *Ecology,* **47,** 143–147.

von Neumann, J. & Morgenstern, O. 1944. *Theory of Games and Economic Behavior.* Princeton, New Jersey: Princeton University Press.

Warner, R. R., Robertson, D. R. & Leigh, E. G. 1975. Sex change and sexual selection. *Science,* **190,** 633–638.

West-Eberhard, M. J. 1979. Sexual selection, social competition and evolution. *Proceedings of the American Philosophical Society,* **123,** 222–234.

Wilkinson, G. S. 1984. Reciprocal food sharing in vampire bats. *Nature,* **308,** 181–184.

Williams, G. C. 1957. Pleiotropy, natural selection and the evolution of senescence. *Evolution,* **11,** 398–411.

Williams, G. C. 1966a. *Adaptation and Natural Selection.* Princeton, New Jersey: Princeton University Press.

Williams, G. C. 1966b. Natural selection costs of reproduction and a refinement of Lack's principle. *American Naturalist,* **100,** 687–690.

Wilson, D. S. 1980. *The Natural Selection of Populations and Communities.* Menlo Park, California: Benjamin Cummins.

Wilson, E. O. 1975. *Sociobiology: the New Synthesis.* Cambridge, Massachusetts: Belknap Press.

Wilson, E. O. 1979. *On Human Nature.* New York: Bantam Books.

Wynne-Edwards, V. C. 1962. *Animal Dispersion in Relation to Social Behaviour.* Edinburgh: Oliver & Boyd.

Zahavi, A. 1975. Mate selection—a selection for a handicap. *Journal of Theoretical Biology,* **53,** 205–214.

4

The Transformation of Behaviour Field Studies

Stuart A. Altmann
Department of Ecology and Evolutionary Biology
Princeton University

Jeanne Altmann
Department of Ecology and Evolutionary Biology
Princeton University
Institute of Primate Research
National Museums of Kenya
Department of Conservation Biology
Chicago Zoological Society

Abstract

As areas of science mature, they pass through three broadly overlapping stages of development, characterised respectively by description, explanation, and synthesis. Field research on animal behaviour is making the transition from an area with a preponderance of purely descriptive studies to one that also includes the development and testing of verifiable hypotheses about the structure, causes, and consequences of behaviour. We survey several reasons for this transformation of behaviour field studies and some of the major trends that characterise it, including: (1) patterns discerned in our cumulative knowledge of natural history; (2) increased support for behaviour field studies; (3) interfaces with related areas of science; (4) the development of observational sampling methods and other aspects of data sampling and analysis; (5) the development of models of behaviour's adaptive functions and life history consequences; (6) long-term field sites, which make possible complete life histories, increased attention to individual differences, and intergenerational studies of behaviour; and (7) the development of techniques for remote tracking of animals and for noninvasive, hands-off sampling of a range of behavioural, physiological, genetic, and environmental phenomena.

From Description to Explanation

The study of animal behaviour in the wild is currently in the midst of a major transition. In the half century that the journal *Animal Behaviour* has been published, field studies of behaviour have been moving from studies devoted almost entirely to descriptive natural history to a new stage that also includes development and testing of explanations for the causes and consequences of behaviour.

This transformation is not unique to animal behaviour. As each field of science matures, it passes through three broadly overlapping stages of development, characterised respectively by description, explanation, and synthesis (cf. Wold 1956). In the initial descriptive approach, the wonders of the natural world are revealed and patterns are discerned. Research is based on observation, description, correlation, and classification, and on assessing collective characteristics and demarcating classes of phenomena. Explanations, when offered at this initial state in a science's development, are typically developed post hoc, and treatment of quantitative data, when available, rarely goes beyond descriptive statistics. To this day, these are the characteristics of most field studies of behaviour.

As areas of science shift from description to explanation, the focus shifts from asking "What?" to asking "Why?" and in some form or other the answer involves an element of causal inference. Tinbergen (1951, 1972) reminded us not only to describe behaviour but also to investigate its evolution, its functional consequences, and its causation, including external stimuli, internal mechanisms, and development.

Although some explanations are proposed in the descriptive phase of research, those in the second phase characteristically are models, that is, they are explanations sufficiently explicit to be tested against empirical research: they can be confirmed or falsified. A common misconception is that models of behaviour will displace descriptive studies. To the contrary, both the development and testing of models place a premium on good information about the natural world, on the quality and quantity of behavioural records.

In the final, synthetic stage, theories for disparate phenomena become special cases of more general theories.

Why Now?

Why is an accelerating transformation to testable explanations of naturalistic behaviour taking place at this time? We suggest several reasons. First, cumulative knowledge of natural history has repeatedly turned up patterns of behaviour that, along with their exceptions, cry out for explanation. For example, decades of field studies revealed that over 90% of bird species pairbond "monogamously" (Lack 1968). Why the consistency—and why the exceptions? In attempts to answer, several models of mating systems have been proposed and tested (e.g., Orians 1969; S. Altmann *et al.* 1977; Lenington 1980; Vehrencamp & Bradbury 1984; Krebs & Davies 1993).

Second, the study of naturalistic behaviour is surrounded by numerous relevant fields of science, many of which are relatively mature. In formulating and testing explanations of behaviour, we shamelessly borrow from ecology, demography, and selection theory, from molecular genetics, functional anatomy, physiology, and nutritional sciences, from the physical, mathematical, and social sciences. Other sciences not only provide us with a wealth of concepts and techniques, they stimulate integration of behaviour with processes at other levels of organisation, both higher and lower, including genetics, physiology, and life history processes.

Several developments in engineering and research design (more about this follows) are now greatly facilitating the gathering and analysis of field data that previously could be obtained and analysed only labouriously or not at all. Recent conceptual and laboratory developments, which we survey later, have greatly facilitated important areas of research.

Finally, the transformation has been accelerated by increased support for field studies during the last half-century, particularly in the decades after World War II. This support included increased research funding, development of long-term field sites, creation at various institutions of faculty positions earmarked for animal behaviour research, and increases in the numbers of scientific societies and journals devoted to naturalistic behaviour studies.

In our own field research on primate behaviour, we have witnessed and participated in many aspects of the transformation of behaviour field research. Although for illustrations we draw inordinately on our own experiences, the changes that we describe have been part of a much more widespread research trend, involving many people and, to varying degrees, many other taxa.

Towards an Animal's Eye View: Individual Identification, Systematic Sampling, and Terminology

Animal behaviour research, like history as it was taught during the 1950s, has undergone a major transition from telling the story of a society by describing a few of the most conspicuous individuals performing their most spectacular acts, to a story of all individuals all of the time. In history class and textbooks, it was kings and queens, war and intrigue, and perhaps a dash of sex. For animal behaviour, it often wasn't much different, the emphasis in this case being on sex and aggression: warring ants, raping ducks, dominant male primates that were controlling, leading, and protecting the masses while obtaining sexual access to the females.

In the 1970s and 1980s, a major shift began to occur that is still underway today. Many factors have contributed to the development of a much more comprehensive and realistic picture of animal behaviour, but three stand out—individual identification, systematic sampling methods, and a growing recognition of the biases that result from ageism, sexism, and their attendant terminology.

Not surprisingly perhaps, the drive to understand individual variability, and, therefore, the effort to identify individuals, received particular impetus from researchers studying nonhuman primates, a mammalian order for which the importance of individuality is difficult to ignore. Although one might have expected individual recognition to be enthusiastically and rapidly embraced by any student of behavioural evolution, because intraspecific variability is so central to natural selection, study of individual primates and attention to individual differences was initially considered by some to be irrelevant or somewhat unscientific. Nonetheless, students investigating a range of research questions in a diversity of species from ants to swans to zebras soon developed observational or minimally intrusive identification techniques and revealed hitherto unappreciated interindividual variability and individual plasticity in behaviour. (Even in social insects, "much of the variability in behaviour not connected to caste and age polyethism must be attributable to individual differences in experience": Wilson 1971.) The resulting explosion of possibilities for testing a range of evolutionary and mechanistic hypotheses will be ongoing for many decades to come.

Second, the rapid adoption of systematic sampling methods in field research and the associated concept of nonexperimental design also had a major role in development of less biased and deeper studies of animal behaviour. A study of the relationships between observational sampling methods and the types of research questions for which each is appropriate (J. Altmann 1974) apparently filled a widespread need in behavioural research: that study has been cited more than 3000 times. (See also Rogosa and Ghandour [1991] for statistical properties of these sampling methods.) Quantitative data on differences among individuals, at various life stages, and in a diversity of contexts became a reality when systematic sampling was combined with individual recognition and with the earlier insistence on rigour in ethograms. The promise of such data then demanded better testable hypotheses, more rigorous analyses, and appropriate statistical techniques. These needs remain, particularly in terms of statistical developments.

At the same time, collection and use of the data that could now be imagined under field conditions cried out for techniques of data collection that were faster and easier to analyse than is possible with the classical stopwatch combined with pencil and paper or tape recorder. At first, a few intrepid souls carried electronic data collection devices weighing 5 kg or more, ones that were vulnerable to dust, rain, and dropping when one was chased by an elephant, and a range of other calamities. Only 20 years later, we take for granted hand-held electronic data loggers, in which, at the push of a button or two, one records an event and the time of its occurrence, all in computer-compatible form. At the end of the day, back at one's base camp, the data are transferred electronically into a computer that can be powered by solar cells. Summary statistics can quickly be generated, so that one can check on, say, sample sizes. The arduous, time-consuming, and error-prone task of transcribing dictated data or computerising paper-and-pencil data is eliminated.

A third major contributor to a less biased and more holistic picture of animal behaviour has to do with challenging the ageism and sexism that have been common in animal behaviour research and related fields of evolution and behavioural ecology (Hrdy &Williams 1983) and that have resulted from choices of topics and measures, use of loaded and biased terminology, and ways of interpreting findings. This transition also began approximately 20 to 25 years ago with challenges to loaded and biased terminology (e.g., Gowaty 1982), with attention to selection during juvenile life stages (e.g., Hrdy & Williams 1983), and with a shift in research focus from primarily males to both sexes and to the contrasting forces shaping the two sexes (e.g., Hrdy 1977, 1999; J. Altmann 1980, 1997; Fedigan 1982; Wasser 1983). Subsequently, research on sexual selection broadened from a primary focus on male competition and a secondary one on female choice to one that is finally beginning to consider the potential of male choice and female competition and that is extending the study of female choice through recognition of what Randy Thornhill (1983) termed "cryptic female choice." However important cryptic female choice turns out to be (Eberhard & Cordero 1995; Eberhard 1996), it does now seem ludicrous that for so long, a female role was ignored in so-called sperm competition, even though such competition was usually being conducted within the bodies of females! The transformation is still underway, with both behavioural plasticity and ontogeny receiving much-deserved renewed attention (e.g., West & King 1988; King *et al.* 1996; West-Eberhard 2003).

Life History and Intergenerational Studies of Behaviour

As animal behaviour studies increasingly encompassed immature and ageing individuals—not just those in their reproductive prime—and females as well as males, consideration of complete life histories became possible (Merila & Sheldon 2000; Grant & Grant 2000). Yet, research on different life stages remains primarily that: the same individuals have only rarely been followed through time, even for short-lived species. Even when longitudinal data might have been obtained, as in long-term bird-banding studies, the study of individual-based life histories lagged behind other topics. Perhaps inertia had a role in this delay. Perhaps, too, people have not appreciated the extent of covariances among life stages, cohort effects, and the importance of early experience on adult functioning, although these have long been recognised within studies of human life histories, and a focus on these issues is routine in human demography and sociology (Manton *et al.* 1992; Seeman *et al.* 2002). Landmark longitudinal studies of human populations remain rare but significant. At the same time, quantitative genetic approaches (see Lande 1982; Arnold 1985; Halliday & Arnold 1987; Arnold & Duvall 1994) and matrix models (e.g., Stearns 1992; Caswell 2001) have been greatly developed and are being applied to studies of behavioural ecology and evolution (McDonald & Caswell 1993; Alberts & Altmann 2003).

Nonetheless, challenges remain to obtaining appropriate lifetime demographic and behavioural data. One practical challenge is associated with some of the very life-history variants we seek to understand. The widespread presence of dispersal and the sex-biased nature of dispersal of many species often have posed seemingly insurmountable obstacles to obtaining lifetime behavioural and life-history data even in long-term field studies. Nonetheless, hindrances were circumvented in three particularly rich and well-known studies, those of scrub jays (Woolfenden & Fitzpatrick 1984), Darwin's finches (Grant 1986; Grant & Grant 2002), and red deer (Clutton-Brock *et al.* 1982; Kruuk *et al.* 2000).

Techniques for Remote and Indirect Behaviour Monitoring

Advances in remote tracking of radio-tagged animals are beginning to contribute immeasurably to enabling one to locate animals that otherwise would have been very difficult or impossible to find and also to providing indirect evidence of behaviour that occurs in our absence: such as automated tracking of deer by Yagi antennas, studies of marine animals for whom attached measuring devices record and store a month of data on location, level of activity, and physiological information for later collection, radio-collared elephants, or long-distance migrating birds that are tracked and whose physiology is monitored by radio tracking from vehicles or from airplanes, or now by satellites (Bevan *et al.* 1994; Guyton *et al.* 1995; Block *et al.* 1998; Lutcavage *et al.* 1999; Butler *et al.* 2000; Block *et al.* 2001; Boehlert *et al.* 2001; Beck *et al.* 2002; Cochran & Wikelski 2005).

Within this decade, we are likely to have far greater capacity for remote tracking. For example, in a project dubbed Zebranet (Schultz 2002), wild animals will carry radio tags that can "talk" to each other. Thus, when two tagged animals interact or are near each other, the logged information from each will be transferred to the other, and as a tagged lion eats a tagged zebra, all the stored information about the activities of the prey and all other tagged zebras that it has been near will be transferred to the lion's tag. On Barro Colorado Island, Panama, arrays of directional antennas on seven towers now enable radio-tagged animals to be located almost anywhere on the island (Larkin *et al.* 1996; Wikelski 2002), and the ICARUS initiative (ICARUS 2002) will make possible the tracking of intercontinental songbird migrations.

Similarly, in the tradition of Muybridge's (1887) early trip-camera studies of locomotion, animal-activated sound recorders and still or video cameras have been used to great advantage in recent decades to record behaviour in the absence of an observer (Frith *et al.* 1996), revealing unknown or poorly documented aspects of behaviour and enabling hypothesis testing where only rare case studies would otherwise be available.

Analysis of isotopes in faeces can reveal the trophic levels of animals and the proportions of browse versus graze that herbivores consume (Tieszen 1991). Microscopic analysis of plant residues in herbivore faeces can, labouriously, reveal their diet (Stewart & Stewart 1970). Of course, technical developments have also benefited studies of observable animals, greatly improving the quality and scope of field data. Locations, once recorded on labouriously drawn maps, can now be obtained with sub-metre accuracy almost anywhere in the world from satellite information by way of hand-held instruments, using the Global Positioning System (GPS). The speed of a running or flying animal can be measured precisely by instruments that use Doppler-effect phase shift (Tong 2002). For measuring distances, hand-held, laser-based rangefinders have an accuracy of one part per thousand. Some come with a built-in electronic compass. One can foresee an offshoot of these in which the laser beam is pointed in turn at each animal in a group, and the instrument records the group's geometry, that is, the spatial deployment of the individuals relative to each other. Although precision heat-sensing devices are not yet within the price range for most field use, West and Packer (2002) used a borrowed one to great advantage in a study of body heat of lions that differed in mane color.

For recording animal sounds, parabolic reflectors, which need to be large for sounds of low frequencies or low intensities, have been replaced by "shotgun" microphones, which are far more compact and thus less intrusive as well as more manageable. For many years, portable Nagra recorders have made possible high-quality field recordings of animal sounds, and sound spectrographs have provided the means of analysing their temporal, frequency, and amplitude components. Repositories and distributors such as the MacCauley Library of Natural History Sounds at Cornell University have greatly expanded and also increasingly serve as a source of information about equipment and software for acoustics analysis. Like other research areas, field studies benefit from the World Wide Web's ability to facilitate locating, obtaining, and distributing information.

Perhaps the one major piece of field equipment that has had only minor improvements in the last half-century is the field vehicle: still too uncomfortable, too fragile, and too expensive.

Techniques for Behaviour-Friendly Physiological Studies

Just as remote tracking and recording provide clues and indirect measures or traces of behaviour that we are unable to observe directly, other methodological developments are enabling the testing of hypotheses about causes and consequences of behaviour in undisturbed natural populations—hypothesis testing that was previously impossible for many species, particularly without intolerable disturbance. One such area is field measurement of physiological variables, including indicators of body condition (Knott 1998), energy expenditure (Schoeller 1988), and steroid concentrations (Sapolsky 1993; Soma & Wingfield 2001; Wingfield et al. 2001). The landmark physiological studies such as those of Sapolsky and Wingfield required blood sampling, which is still needed for many physiological variables, (e.g., energy expenditure and total body fat, measured through doubly-labeled water) (Schoeller 1988).

For some species or for repeated sampling of individuals, trapping or darting to obtain blood samples is not always desirable, feasible, or in some cases legal. Thanks to emerging methods for completely noninvasive, hands-off sampling, through use of urine or faeces, we can obtain a greatly enhanced window into an individual's physiology, throughout its lifetime. For some species and habitats, urine sampling is possible, increasing the range of hormones that can be measured (Andelman et al. 1985; van Schaik et al. 1991; Robbins and Czekala 1997). For others, only faeces are feasible, thereby restricting the range to steroid hormones, but enhancing the ability to obtain measures that are integrated over time (Brockman & Whitten 1996; Whitten & Russell 1996; Savage *et al.* 1997; Whitten *et al.* 1998). Initial studies using urine or faeces have included a range of mammals, including mongooses, wild dogs, wolves, elephants, and primates (Monfort *et al.* 1998; Creel *et al.* 2002, and earlier citations). As validation extends to more species, conditions, and hormones, the potential is enormous. Although noninvasive hormone sampling has thus far been implemented primarily in mammal species, recent documentation of variability among avian species in timing of the stress response to capture (e.g., Romero & Romero 2002) may be one of several factors that will favour application of these techniques to avian and other taxa.

Research Design and Statistical Analysis

In this section, we touch briefly on a few topics that are of particular relevance to the ongoing transformation of behaviour field studies.

Research Design

All too often, students of naturalistic behaviour have returned from the field and discovered that their samples are too small to provide adequate answers to some of their questions, yet are unnecessarily large for others. Or samples, however large, may not be appropriate for the questions being asked. Fortunately, statistical research design is increasingly being used in planning and midcourse evaluation of observational field studies of behaviour and the literature on this topic is growing (e.g., Wold 1956; Cochran 1983; Manly *et al.* 1993; Martin & Bateson 1993; Lehner 1996; Bart *et al.* 1999). A related development is a growing number of experiments on behaviour carried out in the field. Typically, the most illuminating of these abide by Tinbergen's admonition (1951) to observe the animals' full range of behaviour first, then experiment later, so that the most appropriate experiments can be designed. Outstanding examples include field experiments by Bachmann and Kummer (1980), von Frisch's classical experiments on bees, and Tinbergen's own research. A growing number of acoustical playback experiments are revealing a wide variety of social, perceptual, and ecological phenomena (e.g., Cheney 1990; McComb *et al.* 1993; Cheney *et al.* 1995; Rendall *et al.* 1998; McComb *et al.* 2000; Mougeot & Bretagnolle 2000; Semple & McComb 2000; Fischer *et al.* 2001; Lewis *et al.* 2001; Wilson & Vehrencamp 2001; Charrier *et al.* 2002).

Sample Distribution Biases

Field samples may be biased with regard to group size (Sharman & Dunbar 1982), to particular behaviours, to age- or sex-classes, time of day, and so on. Some of these biases are unconscious. Some may result from preconceived ideas. Others result inevitably from field conditions. In the latter case, when estimating actual values, the observed values need to be adjusted for differences in sample sizes (e.g., Why do white sheep eat more than black ones? Because there are more of them!). In some situations, special techniques need to be developed, as we have done, for example, to calculate mean descent time of baboons from sleeping trees (Wagner & S. Altmann 1973), and time spent in various quadrants of their home range (S. Altmann & J. Altmann 1970).

Rates of Behaviour

A common question: how often does this behaviour occur? Because the answer usually depends on the span of time involved, many questions about frequencies of behaviour are actually questions about rates, that is, frequencies per unit of time. Rates can be estimated in four ways: (1) from samples of the numbers of events in a fixed amount of time, (2) from samples of the amounts of time for a fixed number of events, (3) from samples of the number of events per unit of time where both time and number are random variables (e.g., bite rates during feeding bouts), and (4) from samples of the inverses of interevent intervals. Not surprisingly, each of these methods requires its own type of statistical analysis, but we do not know of any general survey of this topic. For the Poisson rate process, statistical methods are available (Cox & Lewis 1966). However, a Poisson model is inappropriate for many types of behaviour, particularly ones that are durable (Rogosa & Ghandour 1991). Recent statistical analyses of some other rate processes (e.g., Gardner *et al.* 1995; Susko *et al.* 2002) may be useful to students of behaviour.

Mathematical demography, including survival analysis, has produced some very useful tools for analysing behavioural field data. Here we consider two. In each case, the beginnings of intervals of behaviour (bouts) may be thought of as their births, the terminations, as their deaths.

Bout Durations and Censored Data

A common problem in field studies of behaviour is that the observer's view of the subjects is often interrupted by intervening foliage or other material, not because the animal is reacting to the observer, but just because its movements inadvertently interpose view-blocking objects. Even on short-grass savannah, where we work, such interruptions are a problem; in tropical rain forests, they are often daunting. Consider an observer's focal sample data for a study on bout lengths of various activities. Although many bouts may have been observed and timed from beginning to end, for others the actual duration is not known because intervening material blocked the observer's view of the bouts' terminations or of their onsets. Fortunately, the statistical properties of such "censored" data under various conditions have been the subjects of numerous studies (e.g., Kaplan & Meier 1958; Mantel 1966; Breslow 1970; Meier 1975). Statistical methods for estimating mean bout lengths and other distribution properties from censored data are now available and can be applied to field samples of behaviour (Bressers *et al.* 1991; S. Altmann 1998). Such techniques are now standard components of major statistical packages such as SAS/STAT (SAS® Institute 1990).

Event Distributions during Bouts

Similarly, demographic analysis can be used to study the temporal distribution of events during intervals of behaviour. For example, in the sampling of patch foraging to test hypotheses about patterns of resource depression (Charnov *et al.* 1976), the consumption of each food item in a foraging bout is comparable to a birth during the interval's (the mother's) lifetime, and our task is that of estimating age-specific birth rates (S. Altmann & J. Shopland, unpublished data).

Adaptations

In recent years, the concept of adaptations has been changing in ways that are directly relevant to field studies of behaviour. Statements about the adaptive significance of traits, behavioural or otherwise, are being regarded not merely as plausible, post hoc explanations (Gould & Lewontin 1979), but as testable hypotheses. The question underlying virtually all such testable hypotheses is this: under given conditions, how would a well-adapted animal of this species behave? For behaviour, if the answer to this question is sufficiently explicit, then perforce we know, for any given pair of individuals, which one has behaviour that is better adapted to the circumstance. By an adaptation we mean a phenotypic variant that, within the environment considered, results in greater fitness relative to a specified set of competing variants (cf. West-Eberhard 1992; Reeve & Sherman 1993).

Two separate but intimately related approaches are used to answer the earlier question about the adaptive significance of traits: by testing hypotheses relating to a trait's short-term (functional) consequences, or by testing hypotheses relating to its long-term (fitness) consequences. Over the last half-century, testable models relating to functional consequences of behaviour have been developed for various aspects of every major form of behaviour: territoriality, mate choice, parental care, foraging, and so on. Such models about functional consequences of behaviour predominate over studies that focus on behaviour's fitness consequences. This preponderance is well illustrated by research on foraging behaviour, the type of naturalistic behaviour that has produced the greatest number of explicit models and tests thereof (Pyke 1984; Stephens & Krebs 1986; Kramer 2001).

At the heart of function-based models are behaviour's short-term consequences, variations of which can be ordered along an axis of better versus worse. For example, because energy is vital to all biological activities, higher-energy diets are assumed to be better. In biology, the ultimate criterion of being better is biological fitness. For that reason, functional consequences are ordered better to worse by their (presumed) fitness consequences, and so are sometimes referred to as "fitness surrogates." Those individuals that behave so as to maximise the functional consequences of their behaviour (or minimise it, as appropriate) are assumed to be better off. (The more energy that is available for an animal's activities, the higher should be its fitness.)

However, the benefits that accrue from any behaviour also entail costs. "There's no such thing as a free lunch" (Friedman 1975). These costs are constraints or limiting factors (Liebig 1840; Blackman 1905; Shelford 1911): they limit the extent to which functional consequences of behaviour can be maximised (or minimised), and so, the function is said to be optimised. Optimality theory "has revealed a richness and complexity in the patterns of foraging that could not have been imagined only a few decades ago" (Kramer 2001).

By themselves, function-based models are not able to address the possibility that our identification of a trait's functional consequences is incorrect, that the putative function may be a consequence that does not increase fitness. Yet, crucial in modelling adaptive behaviour is the correct identification of the model's "currency," the functional consequence assumed to be optimised. For example, many foraging models use energy intake rate as the currency, whereas in some animals, protein maximisation (White 1978) or foraging time minimisation (Pyke *et al.* 1977) may be the primary factor limiting fitness. Even if an animal's fitness is energy-limited, the rate at which energy-producing foods are consumed per minute of feeding may be the wrong currency, rather than, say, the amount of energy obtained per day. Maximising the former does not in general maximise the latter (S. Altmann 1998).

In the second approach, the student of behaviour looks for a correlation between a trait (say, a form of behaviour) and biological fitness (as estimated by, say, lifetime reproductive success or other life-history components), in the hope of finding a consistent relationship, a "fitness function," between the trait and fitness. This can lead, in turn, to studies of selection on such traits in natural populations (Endler 1986). However, not all fitness-correlated traits of an organism are interpretable as adaptations. Some may be mere by-products of other adaptations (Gould & Lewontin 1979). To show that the trait in question actually results in greater fitness, we must ask: how does it do so?

An adaptation requires a rationale, a mechanism (Williams 1966). That brings us back to the question of whether we have correctly identified the functional significance of a trait. The most direct way to demonstrate that increased fitness is the result of a trait, not just a spurious correlate of it, is to confirm the two intermediate steps: to show that the trait has particular short-term, functional effects, and that these, in turn, limit fitness by altering life-history processes. Suppose that, by hypothesis, a form of behaviour or other trait has certain short-term effects that supposedly affect fitness. Then, by taking advantage of intraspecific variability, one can test the behaviour's putative adaptive significance by asking whether those individuals whose behaviour has consequences that come closer to the hypothesised functional optimum are the ones whose fitness is higher, or at least (considering equivalent effects) not lower (S. Altmann 1991, 1998). Studies that combine quantitative data on all three—on behaviour, on its functions, and on the fitness-limiting effects of those functions—are labour-intensive. However, they provide a richness of insights that cannot otherwise be obtained, and for that reason, we expect them to become more common.

Of growing importance in behaviour modelling is the use of dynamic optimisation and game theory. This trend results from the ability of such models to incorporate context-dependent changes in behaviour, processes that are ignored in classical "static" optimisation models. In dynamic optimisation (Houston & McNamara 1999; Clark & Mangel 2000), the animal's optimal choice of behaviour at any given time depends on its present condition and the future consequences of its available courses of action. Thus, these models deal with changing trade-offs in trajectories of decisions over time. For example, a great tit cannot defend its territory by singing and patrolling in the treetops while simultaneously foraging on the ground. Should a foraging great tit delay further feeding to shore up its territorial defence? That depends not only on the risk of territory intrusions but also on what the tit has eaten so far: a well-fed tit can afford to make the switch sooner (Ydenberg & Houston 1986). Dynamic optimisation models are currently being applied to diverse forms of behaviour (e.g., Pratt 1999; Weber et al. 1999; Kaesar et al. 2001; Pravosudov & Lucas 2001; Webb et al. 2002).

Game theory (Maynard Smith 1982, 1984) and the related concept of evolutionarily stable strategies (Parker 1984) are particularly suitable for modelling the course of interactions among individuals who are responding to previous behaviour of individuals that are, in turn, responding to them.

Consequently, game theory is particularly useful for modelling interactions among individuals who are adversaries or cooperators—or both. Currently, game theoretic models are being applied to a considerable variety of behaviour, both in humans and in nonhuman animals (e.g., Noë 1990; Ball & Parker 1998; Fryer *et al.* 1999; Giraldeau & Caraco 2000; Godfray & Johnstone 2000; Sirot 2000; Dodson & Schwaab 2001; Renison *et al.* 2002; Richards 2002; Stevens and Stephens 2002; and Maynard Smith *supra*).

Genetic Relatedness and Behaviour

Many questions in behavioural ecology and adaptation require measures of fitness and of genetic relatedness among individuals. A few decades ago, relatedness within natural populations was deduced almost entirely from observations of broad categories of social behaviour. For example, avian social pair-bonding and offspring care by an adult male and female were assumed to indicate monogamy—to cite the example that best represents the revolution initiated by numerous recent advances in molecular genetic techniques and applications (e.g., polymerase chain reaction [PCR], microsatellite developments, and the Human Genome Project). When various "monogamous" species were suddenly found to be not so (e.g., Gowaty & Karlin 1984; Westneat 1987; Gowaty & Bridges 1991), some at first doubted the genetic results. However, with confirmation and with similar findings in many species (Birkhead & Møller 1992), the pendulum soon swung the other way, with many questioning any ability to predict parentage from behaviour. The problem, of course, was not with behaviour but with the level of behaviour that was being recorded by researchers. The nestling's true father must have mated with the mother, but observers did not observe these matings.

If anything, the genetic results of the past decade have reminded us that behaviour must be taken more seriously, not less, and studied with rigour. We cannot count on gross measures several steps removed. For example, even in a "promiscuous" (more accurately, polygynandrous) species, the savannah baboons that we study, we identified conditions in which not only observed mating behaviour but also male dominance status were excellent predictors of paternity distribution (J. Altmann *et al.* 1996). However, we also postulated the conditions—those when "queue-jumping" occurs—under which dominance would not be a good predictor of actual mating behaviour. This hypothesis has received support in recent tests (Alberts *et al.* 2003); genetic investigations are underway in Alberts's laboratory.

One of the results of the growing number of parentage studies in wild populations is the realisation that not only do some offspring have different parents than assumed by observers (and perhaps by the putative parents), but also that females are mating with more than one male and are even seeking these additional matings—the final blow to the Victorian and male-oriented remnants of an earlier era of animal behaviour studies. Not only shouldn't we assume that pair-bonded female birds were being "raped" when they mated with a nonmate, and not only are we forced to recognise that "rape" may occur within pair-bonds, but perhaps what was previously called "rape" outside a pair-bond is an instance of "adultery," paternity confusion, or other aspects of females' control over their own reproduction (Smuts & Smuts 1993; Gowaty 1994, 1997). We are only beginning to elucidate the many ways that females and males affect their potential for offspring production.

In addition, evolutionary geneticists are finally joining with behavioural ecologists in acknowledging the need for studies that cross generations, not stopping with mates obtained, or even with zygotes produced. As evolutionary models and empirical research increasingly include topics such as parental effects (alas, termed "maternal effects"), and as developmental biology at its best begins to elucidate the transformation of genotype to phenotype at all life stages and within the full range of potential contexts, we will come full circle in focusing on the whole individual, in its social and ecological contexts and throughout its life, which is the subject that originally captured the attention of so many of us. We can now do so with the potential to dig much deeper than we could previously and, in the process, we shall find even more exciting uses for the emerging technologies than the particular tasks for which they were developed. We can already provide an example. Genetic analysis can be carried out not only on blood, muscle, or other tissue, as in the earlier studies cited previously, it can also be done on hair or faeces, which can be obtained from undisturbed, wild, but identified individuals (Höss et al. 1992; Inoue & Takenaka 1993; Sugiyama et al. 1993; Morin et al. 1994; Kohn & Wayne 1997). This makes possible both determination of genetic relatedness, and also the study of population genetics and its relation to group processes without compromising behaviour-sensitive investigations (Melnick 1987; Melnick & Goldstein 1988; Morin et al. 1994; Alberts 1999; Smith et al. 2003).

Caveat

Recent and continuing advances in concepts and methods are beginning to transform field research in ways that could hardly be imagined 50 years ago when *Animal Behaviour* began publication. We are able to study not only the behaviour of animals in the wild, but also its causes and its consequences. That doesn't mean that we can do such studies with just our binoculars, a pair of boots, and a beaten-up field vehicle, although we still need these. Many of the tools of modern research on naturalistic behaviour are costly, for both field work and the related laboratory investigation: genotyping and sequencing, sound recording and analysis equipment, physiological assays, and so on. A major and essential challenge to our community for assuring the health of future decades of animal behaviour research will be to convince the sources of funding that such research requires the budgets of modern biology to achieve both the potential of animal behaviour research and of the reductionist fields to which, in exchange for their tools and approaches, it can contribute valuable insights into the significance of lower-level processes. If we keep our eyes on our animals, if we retain what Helen Fox Keller (1983) termed "a feeling for the organism," animal behaviour will never be a field that is tool-driven, but it must become a field that is tool-enabled if we are to answer many of the central questions of behavioural biology.

Acknowledgments

Our thanks to Jeff Lucas, Dan Rubenstein, and an anonymous reviewer for their comments on drafts of this chapter, and to Susan Alberts, Jessica Lynch, Kerri Smith, and Martin Wikelski, who provided relevant references. We gratefully acknowledge the many animal behaviourists who, both formally and informally, have helped shape our rich experiences studying naturalistic behaviour, and the students, collaborators, and animals with whom so many wondrous research experiences have been shared over several decades. Jeanne Altmann appreciates research support from the U.S. National Science Foundation (IBN 9985910).

References

Alberts, S. C. 1999. Paternal kin discrimination in wild baboons. *Proceedings of the Royal Society of London, Series B,* **266,** 1501–1506.

Alberts, S. C. & Altmann, J. 2003. Matrix models for primate life history analysis. In: *Primate Life History and Socioecology* (Ed. by P. Kappeler & M. E. Pereira), pp. 66–102. Chicago: University of Chicago Press.

Alberts, S. C., Watts, H. E. & Altmann, J. 2003. Queuing and queue-jumping: long-term patterns of reproductive skew among male savannah baboons. *Animal Behaviour,* **65,** 821–840.

Altmann, J. 1974. Observational study of behavior: sampling methods. *Behaviour,* **49,** 227–265.

Altmann, J. 1980. *Baboon Mothers and Infants.* Cambridge, Massachusetts: Harvard University Press.

Altmann, J. 1997. Mate choice and intrasexual reproductive competition: contributions to reproduction that go beyond acquiring more mates. In: *Feminism and Evolutionary Biology: Boundaries, Intersections, and Frontiers* (Ed. by P. A. Gowaty), pp. 320–333. New York: Chapman Hall.

Altmann, J., Alberts, S. C., Haines, S. A., Dubach, J., Muruthi, P., Coote, T., Geffen, E., Cheesman, D. J., Mututua, R. S., Saiyalel, S. N., Wayne, R. K., Lacy, R. C. & Bruford, M. W.

1996. Behaviour predicts genetic structure in a wild primate group. *Proceedings of the National Academy of Sciences of the United States of America,* **93,** 5797–5801.

Altmann, S. A. 1991. Diets of yearling primates (*Papio cynocephalus*) predict lifetime fitness. *Proceedings of the National Academy of Sciences of the United States of America,* **88,** 420–423.

Altmann, S. A. 1998. *Foraging for Survival: Yearling Baboons in Africa.* Chicago: University of Chicago Press.

Altmann, S. A. & Altmann, J. 1970. *Baboon Ecology: African Field Research.* Chicago: University of Chicago Press.

Altmann, S. A., Wagner, S. S. & Lenington, S. 1977. Two models for the evolution of polygyny. *Behavioural Ecology & Sociobiology,* **2,** 397–410.

Andelman, S. J., Else, J. G., Hearn, J. P. & Hodges, J. K. 1985. The noninvasive monitoring of reproductive events in wild vervet monkeys (*Cercopithecus aethiops*) using urinary pregnane-diol-3-alpha-glucuronide and its correlation with behavioural observations. *Journal of Zoology,* **A205,** 467–477.

Arnold, S. J. 1985. Quantitative genetic models of sexual selection. *Experientia,* **41,** 1296–1310.

Arnold, S. J. & Duvall, D. 1994. Animal mating systems: a synthesis based on selection theory. *American Naturalist,* **143,** 317–348.

Bachmann, C. & Kummer, H. 1980. Male assessment of female choice in hamadryas baboons. *Behavioural Ecology & Sociobiology,* **6,** 315–321.

Ball, M. A. & Parker, G. A. 1998. Sperm competition games: a general approach to risk assessment. *Journal of Theoretical Biology,* **194,** 251–262.

Bart, J., Fligner, M. A. & Notz, W. I. 1999. *Sampling and Statistical Methods for Behavioural Ecologists,* p. 352. Cambridge: Cambridge University Press.

Beck, C. A., McMillan, J. I. & Bowen, W. D. 2002. An algorithm to improve geolocation positions using sea surface temperature and diving depth. *Marine Mammal Science,* **18,** 940–951.

Bevan, R. M., Woakes, A. J., Butler, P. J. & Boyd, I. L. 1994. The use of heart rate to estimate oxygen consumption of free-ranging black-browed albatrosses. *Diomedea melanophrys. Journal of Experimental Biology,* **193,** 119–137.

Birkhead, T. R. & Møller, A. P. 1992. *Sperm Competition in Birds: Evolutionary Causes and Consequences.* London: Academic Press.

Blackman, F. F. 1905. Optima and limiting factors. *Annals of Botany,* **19,** 281–295.

Block, B. A., Dewar, H., Blackwell, S. B., Williams, T. D., Prince, E. D., Farwell, C. J., Boustany, A., Teo, S. L. H., Seitz, A., Walli, A. & Fudge, D. 2001. Migratory movements, depth preferences, and thermal biology of Atlantic bluefin tuna. *Nature,* **298,** 1310–1314.

Block, B. A., Dewar, H., Farwell, C. & Prince, E. D. 1998. A new satellite technology for tracking the movements of Atlantic bluefin tuna. *Proceedings of the National Academy of Sciences of the United States of America,* **95,** 9384–9389.

Boehlert, G. W., Costa, D. P., Crocker, D. E., Green, P., O'Brian, T., Levitus, S. & LeBoeuf, B. J. 2001. Autonomous pinniped environmental samplers: using instrumented animals as oceanographic data collectors. *Journal of Atmospheric and Oceanic Technology,* **18,** 1882–1893.

Breslow, N. 1970. A generalized Kruskal-Wallis test for comparing K samples subject to unequal pattern of censorship. *Biometrika,* **57,** 579–594.

Bressers, M., Meelis, E., Haccou, P. & Kruk, M. 1991. When did it really start or stop: the impact of censored observations on the analysis of duration. *Behavioral Processes,* **23,** 1–20.

Brockman, D. K. & Whitten, P. L. 1996. Reproduction in free-ranging *Propithecus verreauxi*: Estrus and the relationship between multiple partner matings and fertilization. *American Journal of Physical Anthropology,* **100,** 57–69.

Butler, P. J., Woakes, A. J., Bevan, R. M. & Stephenson, R. 2000. Heart rate and rate of oxygen consumption during flight of the barnacle goose, *Branta leucopsis. Comparative Biochemistry and Physiology, Part A,* **126,** 379–385.

Caswell, H. 2001. *Matrix Population Models: Construction, Analysis, and Interpretation*. 2nd edn. Sunderland, Massachusetts: Sinauer.

Charnov, E. L., Orians, G. H. & Hyatt, K. 1976. Ecological implications of resource depression. *American Naturalist,* **110,** 247–259.

Charrier, I., Mathevon, N. & Jouventin, P. 2002. How does a fur seal mother recognize the voice of her pup? An experimental study of *Arctocephalus tropicalis. Journal of Experimental Biology,* **205,** 603–612.

Cheney, D. L. 1990. *How Monkeys See the World: Inside the Mind of Another Species*. Chicago: Chicago University Press.

Cheney, D. L., Seyfarth, R. M. & Silk, J. B. 1995. The role of grunts in reconciling opponents and facilitating interactions among adult female baboons. *Animal Behaviour,* **50,** 249–257.

Clark, C. W. & Mangel, M. 2000. *Dynamic State Variables in Ecology: Methods and Applications*. New York: Oxford University Press.

Clutton-Brock, T. H., Guinness, F. E. & Albon, S. D. 1982. *Red Deer: Behavior and Ecology of Two Sexes*. Chicago: University of Chicago Press.

Cochran, W. G. 1983. *Planning and Analysis of Observational Studies*. Chichester: John Wiley.

Cochran, W. W. & Wikelski, M. 2005. Individual migratory tactics of New World *Catharus* thrushes: current knowledge and future tracking options from space. In: *Birds of Two Worlds: the Ecology and Evolution of Migration* (Ed. by R. Greenberg & P. Marra). pp. 274–289. Baltimore, Maryland: Johns Hopkins University Press.

Cox, D. R. & Lewis, P. A. W. 1966. *The Statistical Analysis of Series of Events*. London: Methuen.

Creel, S., Fox, J. E., Hardy, A., Sands, J., Garrott, B. & Peterson, R. O. 2002. Snowmobile activity and glucocorticoid stress responses in wolves and elk. *Conservation Biology,* **16,** 809–814.

Dodson, G. N. & Schwaab, A. T. 2001. Body size, leg autonomy, and prior experience as factors in the fighting success of male crab spiders, *Misumenoides formosipes. Journal of Insect Behavior,* **14,** 841–855.

Eberhard, W. G. 1996. *Female Control: Sexual Selection by Cryptic Female Choice*. Princeton, New Jersey: Princeton University Press.

Eberhard, W. G. & Cordero, C. 1995. Sexual selection by cryptic female choice on male seminal products—A new bridge between sexual selection and reproductive physiology. *Trends in Ecology & Evolution,* **10,** 493–496.

Endler, J. 1986. *Natural Selection in the Wild*. Princeton, New Jersey: Princeton University Press.

Fedigan, L. M. 1982. *Primate Paradigms: Sex Roles and Social Bonds*. Montréal: Eden Press (revised and reprinted 1992, Chicago: University of Chicago Press).

Fischer, J., Metz, M., Cheney, D. L. & Seyfarth, R. M. 2001. Baboon responses to graded bark variants. *Animal Behaviour,* **61,** 925–931.

Friedman, M. 1975. *There's No Such Thing as a Free Lunch*. LaSalle, Illinois: Open Court.

Frith, C. B., Borgia, G. & Frith, D. W. 1996. Courts and courtship behaviour of Archbold's bowerbird (*Archboldia papuensis*) in Papua New Guinea. *IBIS,* **138,** 204–211.

Fryer, T., Cannings, C. & Vickers, G. T. 1999. Sperm competition I: basic model, ESS and dynamics. *Journal of Theoretical Biology,* **196,** 81–100.

Gardner, W. E., Mulvey, E. P. & Shaw, E. C. 1995. Regression-analyses of counts and rates: Poisson, overdispersed Poisson, and negative binomial models. *Psychological Bulletin,* **118,** 392–404.

Giraldeau, L.-A. & Caraco, T. 2000. *Social Foraging Theory*. Princeton, New Jersey: Princeton University Press.

Godfray, H. C. J. & Johnstone, R. A. 2000. Begging and bleating: the evolution of parent–offspring signaling. *Philosophical Transactions of the Royal Society of London, Series B,* **355,** 1581–1591.

Gould, S. J. & Lewontin, R. C. 1979. The spandrels of San Marco and the Panglosian paradigm: a critique of the adaptationist programme. *Proceedings of the Royal Society of London, Series B,* **205,** 581–598.

Gowaty, P. A. 1982. Sexual terms in sociobiology: emotionally evocative and, paradoxically, jargon. *Animal Behaviour,* **30,** 630–631.

Gowaty, P. A. 1994. Architects of sperm competition. *Trends in Ecology & Evolution,* **9,** 160–162.

Gowaty, P. A. 1997. *Feminism and Evolutionary Biology: Boundaries, Intersections, and Frontiers.* New York: Chapman Hall.

Gowaty, P. A. & Bridges, W. 1991. Nestbox availability affects extra-pair fertilization and conspecific nest parasitism in eastern bluebirds, *Sialia sialis. Animal Behaviour,* **41,** 661–675.

Gowaty, P. A. & Karlin, A. A. 1984. Multiple maternity and paternity in single broods of apparently monogamous eastern bluebirds (*Sialia-sialis*). *Behavioral Ecology and Sociobiology,* **15,** 91–95.

Grant, P. R. 1986. *Ecology and Evolution of Darwin's Finches.* Princeton, New Jersey: Princeton University Press.

Grant, P. R. & Grant, B. R. 2000. Nonrandom fitness variation in two populations of Darwin's finches. *Proceeding of the Royal Society of London, Series B,* **267,** 131–138.

Grant, P. R. & Grant, B. R. 2002. Unpredictable evolution in a 30-year study of Darwin's finches. *Science,* **296,** 707–711.

Guyton, G. P., Stanek, K. S., Schneider, R. C., Hochachka, P. W., Hurford, W. E., Zapol D. G., Liggins, G. C. & Zapol, W. M. 1995. Myoglobin saturation in free-diving Weddell seals. *Journal of Applied Physiology,* **79,** 1148–1155.

Halliday, T. & Arnold, S. J. 1987. Multiple mating by females: a perspective from quantitative genetics. *Animal Behaviour,* **35,** 939–941.

Höss, M., Kohn, M. & Paabo, S. 1992. Excrement analysis by PCR. *Nature,* **359,** 199.

Houston, A. I. & McNamara, J. M. 1999. *Models of Adaptive Behaviour: an Approach Based on State.* Cambridge: Cambridge University Press.

Hrdy, S. B. 1977. *The Languages of Abu: Female and Male Strategies of Reproduction.* Cambridge, Massachusetts: Harvard University Press.

Hrdy, S. B. 1999. *Mother Nature: a History of Mothers, Infants and Natural Selection.* New York: Pantheon Books.

Hrdy, S. B. & Williams, G. C. 1983. Behavioral biology and the double standard. In: *Social Behavior of Female Vertebrates* (Ed. by S. K. Wasser), pp. 3–17. New York: Academic Press.

ICARUS. 2002: www.princeton.edu/~tracking/ICARUS_website/index.htm

Inoue, M. & Takenaka, O. 1993. Japanese macaque microsatellite PCR primers for paternity testing. *Primates,* **34,** 37–45.

Kaesar, T., Ney-Nifle, M., Mangel, M. & Swezey, S. 2001. Early oviposition experience affects patch residence time in a foraging parasitoid. *Entomologia Experimentalis Et Applicata,* **98,** 123–132.

Kaplan, E. L. & Meier, P. 1958. Nonparametric estimation from incomplete observations. *Journal of the American Statistical Association,* **53,** 457–481.

Keller, H. F. 1983. *A Feeling for the Organism: the Life Work of Barbara McClintock.* New York: W. H. Freeman.

King, A. P., West, M. J. & Freeberg, T. M. 1996. Social experience affects the process and outcome of vocal ontogeny in two populations of cowbirds. *Journal of Comparative Psychology,* **110,** 276–285.

Knott, C. D. 1998. Changes in orangutan caloric intake, energy balance, and ketones in response to fluctuating fruit availability. *International Journal of Primatology,* **19,** 1061–1079.

Kohn, M. H. & Wayne, R. K. 1997. Facts from feces revisited. *Trends in Ecology & Evolution,* **12,** 223–227.

Kramer, D. L. 2001. Foraging behavior. In: *Evolutionary Ecology* (Ed. by C. W. Fox, D. A. Roff & D. J. Fairbairn), pp. 232–246. Oxford: Oxford University Press.

Krebs, J. R. & Davies, N. B. 1993. *An Introduction to Behavioural Ecology,* 3rd edn. Oxford: Blackwell Science.

Kruuk, L. E. B., Clutton-Brock, T. H., Slate, J., Pemberton, J. M., Brotherstone, S. & Guinness, F. E. 2000. Heritability of fitness in a wild mammal population. *Proceedings of the National Academy of Sciences of the United States of America,* **97,** 698–703.

Lack, D. 1968. *Ecological Adaptations for Breeding in Birds,* p. 409. London: Methuen.

Lande, R. 1982. A quantitative genetic theory of life history evolution. *Ecology,* **63,** 607–615.

Larkin, R. P., Raim, A. & Diehl, R. H. 1996. Performance of a nonrotating direction-finder for automatic radio tracking. *Journal of Field Ornithology,* **67,** 59–71.

Lehner, P. N. 1996. *Handbook of Ethological Methods,* 2nd edn. New York: Cambridge University Press.

Lenington, S. G. 1980. Female choice and polygyny in red-winged blackbirds. *Animal Behaviour,* **28,** 347–361.

Lewis, E. R., Narins, P. M., Cortopassi, K. A., Yamada, W. M., Poinar, E. H., Moore, S. W. & Yu, X. L. 2001. Do male white-lipped frogs use seismic signals for intraspecific communications? *American Zoologist,* **41,** 1185–1199.

Liebig, J. 1840. *Chemistry in Its Application to Agriculture and Physiology.* London: Taylor and Walton.

Manly, B. F. J., McDonald, L. L. & Thomas, D. L. 1993. *Resource Selection by Animals: Statistical Design and Analysis of Field Studies,* p. 177. London: Chapman & Hall.

Mantel, N. 1966. Evaluation of survival data and two new rank order statistics arising in its consideration. *Cancer Chemotherapy Report,* **50,** 163–170.

Manton, K. G., Stallard, E. & Singer, B. 1992. Projecting the future size and health-status of the United States elderly population. *International Journal of Forecasting,* **8,** 433–458.

Martin, P. & Bateson, P. 1993. *Measuring Behaviour: an Introductory Guide,* 2nd edn. Cambridge: Cambridge University Press.

Maynard Smith, J. 1982. *Evolution and the Theory of Games.* Cambridge: Cambridge University Press.

Maynard Smith, J. 1984. Game theory and the evolution of behaviour. *Behavior and Brain Sciences,* **7,** 95–125.

McComb, K., Moss, C., Sayialel, S. & Baker, L. 2000. Unusually extensive networks of focal recognition in African elephants. *Animal Behaviour,* **59,** 1103–1109.

McComb, K., Pusey, A., Packer, C. & Grinnell, J. 1993. Female lions can identify potentially infanticidal males from their roars. *Proceedings of the Royal Society of London, Series B,* **252,** 59–64.

McDonald, D. B. & Caswell, H. 1993. Matrix methods in avian demography. *Current Ornithology,* **10,** 139–185.

Meier, P. 1975. Estimation of a distribution function from incomplete observations. In: *Perspectives in Probability and Statistics* (Ed. by J. Gani), pp. 67–87. Sheffield: Applied Probability Trust.

Melnick, D. J. 1987. The genetic consequences of primate social organization: a review of macaques, baboons and vervet monkeys. *Genetica,* **73,** 117–135.

Melnick, D. J. & Goldstein, S. J. 1988. Are primate social groups random collections of a population's genotypes? *American Journal of Physical Anthropology,* **75,** 250.

Merila, J. & Sheldon, B. C. 2000. Lifetime reproductive success and heritability in nature. *American Naturalist,* **155,** 301–310.

Monfort, S. L., Mashburn, K. L., Brewer, B. A. & Creel, S. R. 1998. Evaluating adrenal activity in African wild dogs (*Lycaon pictus*) by fecal corticosteroid analysis. *Journal of Zoo and Wildlife Medicine,* **29,** 129–133.

Morin, P. A., Moore, J. J., Chakraborty, R., Jin, L., Goodall, J. & Woodruff, D. S. 1994. Kin selection, social structure, gene flow, and the evolution of chimpanzees. *Science*, **265**, 1193–1201.

Mougeot, F. & Bretagnolle, V. 2000. Predation as a cost of sexual communication in nocturnal seabirds: an experimental approach using acoustic signals. *Animal Behaviour*, **60**, 647–656.

Muybridge, E. 1887. *Animal Locomotion: an Electro-Photographic Investigation of Consecutive Phases of Animal Movement, 1872–1885*. Philadelphia: University of Pennsylvania Press.

Noë, R. 1990. A veto game played by baboons—a challenge to the use of the prisoners dilemma as a paradigm for reciprocity and cooperation. *Animal Behaviour*, **39**, 78–90.

Orians, G. H. 1969. On the evolution of mating systems in birds and mammals. *American Naturalist*, **103**, 589–603.

Parker, G. A. 1984. Evolutionarily stable strategies. In: *Behavioural Ecology: an Evolutionary Approach*, 2nd edn. (Ed. by J. R. Krebs & N. B. Davies), pp. 3–61. Sunderland, Massachusetts: Sinauer.

Pratt, S. C. 1999. Optimal timing of comb construction by honeybee (*Apis mellifera*) colonies: a dynamic programming model and experimental tests. *Behavioral Ecology and Sociobiology*, **46**, 30–42.

Pravosudov, V. V. & Lucas, J. R. 2001. Daily patterns of energy storage in food-catching birds under variable daily predation risk: a dynamic state variable model. *Behavioral Ecology and Sociobiology*, **50**, 239–250.

Pyke, G. H. 1984. Optimal foraging theory: a critical review. *Annual Review of Ecological Systems*, **15**, 523–575.

Pyke, G. H., Pulliam, H. R. & Charnov, E. L. 1977. Optimal foraging: a selective review of theory and tests. *Quarterly Review of Biology*, **52**, 137–154.

Reeve, H. K. & Sherman, P. W. 1993. Adaptation and the goals of evolutionary research. *Quarterly Review of Biology*, **68**, 1–32.

Rendall, D., Owren, M. J. & Rodman, P. S. 1998. The role of vocal tract filtering in identity cueing in rhesus monkey (*Macaca mulatta*) vocalizations. *Journal of the Acoustical Society of America*, **103**, 602–614.

Renison, D., Boersma, D. & Martella, M. B. 2002. Winning and losing: causes for variability in outcome of fights in male Magellanic penguins. *Behavioral Ecology*, **13**, 462–466.

Richards, S. A. 2002. Temporal partitioning and aggression among foragers: modeling the effects of stochasticity and individual state. *Behavioral Ecology*, **13**, 427–438.

Robbins, M. M. & Czekala, N. M. 1997. A preliminary investigation of urinary testosterone and cortisol levels in wild male mountain gorillas. *American Journal of Primatology*, **43**, 51–64.

Rogosa, D. & Ghandour, G. 1991. Statistical models for behavioral observation. In: *Journal of Educational Statistics. Special Issue: Behavioral Observations* (Ed. by R. K. Tsutakawa), pp. 157–252. Washington, D.C.: American Educational Research Association.

Romero, L. M. & Romero, R. C. 2002. Corticosterone responses in wild birds: the importance of rapid initial sampling. *Condor*, **104**, 129–135.

Sapolsky, R. 1993. Endocrinology Alfresco: psychoendocrine studies of wild baboons. *Recent Progress in Hormone Research*, **48**, 437–468.

SAS Institute. 1990. *SAS/STAT user's guide*, Version 6. Cary, North Carolina: SAS Institute.

Savage, A., Shideler, S. E., Soto, L. H., Causado, J., Giraldo, L. H., Lasley, B. L. & Snowdon, C. T. 1997. Reproductive events of wild cotton-top tamarins (*Saguinus oedipus*) in Colombia. *American Journal of Primatology*, **43**, 329–337.

Schoeller, D. A. 1988. Measurement of energy expenditure in free-living humans by doubly labeled water. *Journal of Nutrition*, **118**, 1278–1289.

Schultz, S. 2002. Engineers and biologists design wireless devices to unlock secrets of animal kingdom. *Princeton Weekly Bulletin*, **92**, 9: http://www.princeton.edu/pr/pwb/02/1111/

Seeman, T. E., Singer, B. H., Ryff, C. D., Love, G. D. & Levy-Storms, L. 2002. Social relationships, gender, and allostatic load across two age cohorts. *Psychosomatic Medicine,* **64,** 395–406.

Sempe, S. & McComb, K. 2000. Perception of female reproductive state from focal cues in a mammal species. *Proceedings of the Royal Society of London, Series B,* **267,** 707–712.

Sharman, M. & Dunbar, R. I. M. 1982. Observer bias in selection of study group in baboon field studies. *Primates,* **23,** 567–573.

Shelford, V. E. 1911. Physiological animal geography. *Journal of Morphology,* **22,** 551–618.

Sirot, E. 2000. An evolutionarily stable strategy for aggressiveness in feeding groups. *Behavioral Ecology,* **11,** 351–356.

Smith, K., Alberts, S. C. & Altmann, J. 2003. Wild female baboons bias their social behaviour towards paternal half-sisters. *Proceedings of the Royal Society of London, Series B,* **270,** 503–510.

Smuts, B. B. & Smuts, R. W. 1993. Male aggression and sexual coercion of females in nonhuman primates and other mammals: evidence and theoretical implications. *Advances in the Study of Behavior,* **22,** 1–63.

Soma, K. K. & Wingfield, J. C. 2001. Dehydroepiandrosterone in songbird plasma: seasonal regulation and relationship to territorial aggression. *General and Comparative Endocrinology,* **123,** 144–155.

Stearns, S. C. 1992. *The Evolution of Life Histories.* Oxford: Oxford University Press.

Stephens, D. W. & Krebs, J. R. 1986. *Foraging Theory.* Princeton, New Jersey: Princeton University Press.

Stevens, J. R. & Stephens, D. W. 2002. Food sharing: a model of manipulation by harassment. *Behavioral Ecology,* **13,** 393–400.

Stewart, D. R. M. & Stewart, J. 1970. Food preference data by faecal analysis for African plains ungulates. *Zoologica Africana,* **5,** 115–129.

Sugiyama, Y., Kawamoto, S., Takenaka, O., Kumazaki, K. & Miwa, N. 1993. Paternity discrimination and intergroup relationships of chimpanzees at Bossou. *Primates,* **34,** 545–552.

Susko, E., Inagaki, Y., Field, C., Holder, M. E. & Roger, A. J. 2002. Testing for differences in rates-across-sites distributions in phylogenetic subtrees. *Molecular Biology and Evolution,* **19,** 1514–1523.

Thornhill, R. 1983. Cryptic female choice and its implications in the scorpion fly *Harpobatticus nigriceps. American Naturalist,* **122,** 765–788.

Tieszen, L. L. 1991. Natural variation in the carbon isotope values of plants: implications for archeology and paleoecology. *Journal of Archaeological Science,* **18,** 227–248.

Tinbergen, N. 1951. *The Study of Instinct.* Oxford: Clarendon Press.

Tinbergen, N. 1972. *Social Behaviour in Animals.* London: Chapman & Hall.

Tong, J. 2002. Can it clock a nerf ball? *New York Times,* 13 November 2002 [Sect. 3:2].

van Schaik, C. P., van Noordwijk, M. A., van Bragt, T. & Blankenstein, M. A. 1991. A pilot study of the social correlates of levels of urinary cortisol, prolactin and testosterone in wild long-tailed macaques. *Primates,* **32,** 345–356.

Vehrencamp, S. L. & Bradbury, J. W. 1984. Mating systems and ecology. In: *Behavioral Ecology,* 2nd edn. (Ed. by J. R. Krebs & N. B. Davies), pp. 251–278. Sunderland, Massachusetts: Sinauer.

Wagner, S. S. & Altmann, S. A. 1973. What time do the baboons come down from the trees? An estimation problem. *Biometrics,* **29,** 623–625.

Wasser, S. K. 1983. Reproductive competition and cooperation among female yellow baboons. In: *Social Behavior of Female Vertebrates* (Ed. by S. K. Wasser). New York: Academic Press.

Webb, J. N., Szekely, T., Houston, A. I. & McNamara, J. M. 2002. A theoretical analysis of the energetic costs and consequences of parental care decisions. *Philosophical Transactions of the Royal Society of London, Series B,* **357,** 331–340.

Weber, T. P., Houston, A. I. & Ens, B. J. 1999. Consequences of habitat loss at migratory stopover sites: a theoretical investigation. *Journal of Avian Biology,* **30,** 416–426.

West, M. J. & King, A. P. 1988. Female visual displays affect the development of male song in the cowbird. *Nature,* **334,** 244–246.

West, P. M. & Packer, C. 2002. Sexual selection, temperature, and the lion's mane. *Science,* **297,** 1339–1343.

West-Eberhard, M. J. 1992. Adaptation: current usages. In: *Keywords in Evolutionary Biology* (Ed. by E. F. Keller & E. A. Lloyd), pp. 13–18. Cambridge, Massachusetts: Harvard University Press.

West-Eberhard, M. J. 2003. *Developmental Plasticity and the Major Themes of Evolutionary Biology.* Oxford: Oxford University Press.

Westneat, D. F. 1987. Extra-pair fertilizations in a predominantly monogamous bird—genetic evidence. *Animal Behaviour,* **35,** 877–886.

White, T. C. R. 1978. The importance of a relative shortage of food in animal ecology. *Oecologia,* **33,** 71–86.

Whitten, P. L., Brockman, D. K. & Stavisky, R. C. 1998. Recent advances in noninvasive techniques to monitor hormone-behavior interaction. *Yearbook of Physical Anthropology,* **41,** 1–23.

Whitten, P. L. & Russell, E. 1996. Information content of sexual swellings and fecal steroids in sooty mangabeys (*Cercocebus torquatus atys*). *American Journal of Primatology,* **40,** 67–82.

Wikelski, M. C. 2002. www.princeton.edu/~wikelski/research/

Williams, G. C. 1966. *Adaptation and Natural Selection: a Critique of Some Current Evolutionary Thought.* Princeton, New Jersey: Princeton University Press.

Wilson, E. O. 1971. *The Insect Societies.* Cambridge, Massachusetts: Belknap Press.

Wilson, P. L. & Vehrencamp, S. L. 2001. A test of the deceptive mimicry hypothesis in song-sharing song sparrows. *Animal Behaviour,* **62,** 1197–1205.

Wingfield, J. C., Lynn, S. E. & Soma, K. K. 2001. Avoiding the "costs" of testosterone: ecological bases of hormone-behavior interaction. *Brain Behavior and Evolution,* **57,** 239–251.

Wold, H. 1956. Causal inferences from observational data—a review of ends and means. *Journal of the Royal Statistical Society, Series A,* **119,** 28–50.

Woolfenden, G. E. & Fitzpatrick, J. W. 1984. *The Florida Scrub Jay: Demography of a Cooperative-breeding Bird.* Princeton, New Jersey: Princeton University Press.

Ydenberg, R. C. & Houston, A. I. 1986. Optimal tradeoffs between competing behavioral demands in the great tit. *Animal Behaviour,* **34,** 1041–1050.

5

Too Much Natural History, or Too Little?

Stevan J. Arnold
Department of Zoology
Oregon State University

Abstract

A number of commentators have recently expressed concern about the fate of both natural history and naturalists in the modern world. In this essay I examine those concerns from a historical perspective. From this standpoint, I conclude that natural history is alive and well, but its future critically depends upon conceptual infusions from adjacent disciplines. Naturalists are proliferating rather than dying out.

The next time I find myself in a public debate about natural history I am going to follow a colleague's advice. I will keep my mouth shut. I made this resolve last summer in Banff at the annual meeting of the American Society of Naturalists. The Society's President, Peter Grant, convened a symposium on the role of the naturalist in various contemporary contexts (e.g. genomics, biological invasions). During the symposium several participants commented on the need for more natural history information. At the end, when discussion was invited from the floor, the state and fate of natural history was the main topic under debate. The discussion was lively, impassioned, disjointed, engaging and frustrating. I found myself voicing opinions that I instantly regretted. Later, I decided I did not understand natural history or my feelings about it. I went to the library.

Naturalists who worry about the fate of natural history have recently produced a distinctive genre of essays (Bartholomew 1986; Greene & Losos 1988; Greene 1994; Noss 1996; Futuyma 1998). Among the claims in this genre are the notions that naturalists are dying off and that natural history is unappreciated and disappearing. I think these notions are wrong, born of a narrow, nonhistorical view of naturalists and natural history. The view that I favour is that natural history is a vigorous, blossoming enterprise. I arrived at this view by adopting the perspective of historians of science, especially that of Provine (1971), Mayr (1982), Kingsland (1985) and Farber (2000). From a historical perspective, viewing natural history as a lineage that includes descendants, the title of this essay is a trick question, an absurdity.

Natural History Yesterday

Natural history emerged as a discipline in the 18th century as part of the Enlightenment, a philosophical movement in western Europe based on rationalism (Mayr 1982). Farber (2000) identifies the quest to find order in nature as the core of the natural history tradition. From its onset, the tradition sought order in three realms, which today would be called geology, botany and zoology. Carl Linnaeus and Georges Buffon were pivotal figures in the early stages of the discipline. Linnaeus devised a system for organizing the diversity of known plants and animals. Buffon pursued a massive compilation of facts about animals, resulting in a 36-volume encyclopaedia. The immediate effect of work by Linnaeus and Buffon was to stimulate energetic pursuit of discovery, an activity that continues to the present time. For the modern biologist, the early history of 'natural history' conjures up images of students and descendants of Linnaeus and Buffon looking for unknown plants and animals by prowling the jungles of Asia and South America. These romantic images are only part of the picture. Linnaeus and Buffon were consummate organizers of large-scale projects. Furthermore, new species were not sought in a vacuum. Field workers operated in a framework of taxonomic organization and encyclopaedic accretion. This conceptual and organization side of the picture tends to be forgotten, but it is crucial to a full appreciation of contemporary natural history. In the decades from 1750 to the present, the conceptual frame-work for natural history became more detailed and complex. These developments, the most important of which was Darwinism, merely modified a conceptual framework that was present from the onset of the discipline, a framework that sought order in nature.

A sense of natural history's genealogy, from the mid-1700s to the present, can be captured by focusing on the fields that diverged from the ancestral discipline (Farber 2000). Early divisions produced geology, botany and zoology. The later dates at which familiar societies were founded help sketch the tempo of specialization (Table 5-1). A founding date does not represent the

Table 5-1   Founding dates for various societies

Society	Date founded
Linnean Society of London	1788
Zoological Society of London	1826
American Society of Naturalists	1883
Ecological Society of America	1915
Genetics Society of America	1931
Association for the Study of Animal Behaviour	1936
Society for the Study of Evolution	1946
Animal Behavior Society	1964
International Society for Behavioral Ecology	1986

actual birth of a discipline, but it does indicate the date at which critical mass was achieved for a self-conscious movement. Founding dates also roughly correspond to the dates at which specialized courses appeared in university curricula. The transformation of natural history into more specialized societies continues at an accelerated pace. Many modern disciplines derived from natural history reached critical mass during the 20th century. Within the last two decades new societies and journals have appeared that are devoted to such topics as behavioural ecology, molecular ecology, molecular evolution, bioinformatics, genomics and so on. These too are natural history derivatives.

To be sure, viewing natural history as a genealogy neglects the influence of ideas imported from other disciplines. Conflict accompanied the most important conceptual infusions. One of the most important imports was the experimental approach that arose in the early 1800s in physiology (Farber 2000). Allied with medical education, the early physiologists represented a separate tradition from natural history. Experimentation was the hallmark that most cleanly separated the physiologists from the naturalists. Over the next century experimentation merged with the natural history tradition by infusion through a variety of disciplines: embryology, ecology, genetics, evolutionary biology and animal behaviour. These infusions generated tensions that persist to the present day. Some naturalists see experiments as too simplistic; some experimentalists see nonmanipulative analyses as hopelessly ambiguous. Mathematical modelling first produced similar tensions in genetics and later when modelling entered ecology. Stress in ecology between modellers and nonmodellers was intense in the 1930s and again in the 1960s (Kingsland 1985) and can still be detected today (see below). Currently, we are in the midst of a merging of molecular biology with the various disciplines derived from natural history. Molecular biologists struggle to understand Darwinism; animal behaviourists wrestle with the new molecular vocabulary. The marriage is both joyous and contentious.

Natural History Today and Tomorrow

Commentators on the current plight of 'natural history' usually take a narrow view of the naturalist's tradition. Bartholomew (1986, page 326) did take a broad historical view of natural history, but also noted that 'At its most stereotyped, natural history has been, and is, strictly phenomenological'. Greene (1994) adopts this more stereotyped vision when he focuses on descriptive ecology and ethology as the building blocks of natural history. When Noss (1996, page 1) argued that 'The naturalists are dying off and have few heirs', he means individuals who can identify all the inhabitants in a local community and describe their interactions. Futuyma (1998) circulated a questionnaire among graduate and postdoctoral students and obtained revealing answers to the question, 'What is your reaction to someone who says he/she is interested in natural history?' Among the responses: (1) 'You won't get a job', (2) '. . . you must not be a successful academic biologist', (3) 'I most often hear this used to describe the interests of older members of my department. I interpret this to mean they are not very conceptually oriented or maybe not very current.' How can we reconcile these narrow, sometimes pejorative views of 'natural history' with a 250-year-old naturalist's tradition that includes the development of Darwinism and other major concepts as well as the incorporation of experimentation and model building? Why do we take a narrow view of 'natural history'?

As new disciplines split off from natural history, the genealogical trunk kept the original name, but in time the trunk was whittled down to a remnant. It is not surprising that scientists identify with derivatives rather than with the trunk. Each new generation of scientists focuses on new developments in their fields. There is also a premium on adopting the moniker of a newly christened discipline. Beginning in the 1870s many scientists followed T. H. Huxley's lead and called themselves 'biologists' to proclaim their interest in everything from cells to evolution. Henceforth, 'natural history' meant field work and work with collections (Farber 2000). The meaning of the term 'natural history' continues to contract. Today, systematists are not likely to say that their field is natural history, nor are behavioural ecologists. The current trend is to define natural history by what it is not. Within a few decades, in this narrow view, 'natural history' will be a small sliver-like remnant, a vacant scientific profession.

Natural History as a Living Tradition, Rather than a Dying Remnant

Natural history lives today in the bustling enterprises of its descendant disciplines. The bustle is largely due to new concepts that are imported or generated within these disciplines. Collections, life-history facts, and ethograms are products of conceptual pursuits in natural history sensu lato. Collections, in the large sense of specimens and the information associated with them, are hugely important resources; but collections are not the essence of natural history. Great naturalists are remembered for their concepts rather than for their fieldwork and collections. Natural history lives and breathes because of the concepts it has produced and continues to produce. The powerful concepts of the naturalist's tradition, past and present, include: natural order in biological diversity, descent with modification, natural selection, Mendelian inheritance, polygenic inheritance, competitive exclusion, logistic population growth, allopatric speciation, trophic structure, adaptive landscapes, island biogeography, correlated response to selection, inclusive fitness, optimal foraging and sexual selection. All of these are conceptual tools for finding order in nature. They are powerful because they change the way we perceive nature. These concepts, and many others, are the triumphs of natural history, the essence of the discipline and its descendants.

A focus on natural history as a concept-building enterprise changes what we see as natural history and who we see as naturalists. Equations and computer simulation can be powerful weapons in the arsenal of the naturalist. The key is whether these weapons are aimed at issues in the natural world. It follows that some naturalists are theoreticians. You do not have to have dirt under your finger-nails to be a naturalist. The essential requirement is that you follow Linnaeus and Buffon in pursuit of order in nature. I reserve special admiration for naturalists who excel both in the field and at the blackboard (e.g. R. H. MacArthur, W. H. Hamilton, E. O. Wilson), but a naturalist does not have to be biphasic, an expert in both of those realms. Niko Tinbergen and George Schaller are great naturalists because of their special talents at uncovering the lives of free-ranging animals. If we could erase the constraints of time, these naturalists could report directly to Buffon. But now we confront a quandary. If equations and simulations, as well as field experiments and observations from blinds, are all legitimate parts of natural history, why do we hear our colleagues disparage each other's activities? Why are there conflicts within the natural history community, sensu lato? Where does the tension come from?

Past and Current Debates in Historical Perspective

Conflict in scientific communities is a revealing behavioural phenomenon that has attracted the attention of historians of science. Most scientists would like to believe that scientific debates are objective intellectual exercises, divorced from base motivations and emotions. Historical analysis suggests otherwise (Provine 1971; Kingsland 1985; Farber 2000).

Vehemence and intensity in a scientific conflict are indications that something is at stake (Kingsland 1985). Sometimes the stakes are power and resources, or the threat of extinction. Some conflicts in the natural history community are recurrent, as well as intense, another indicator of deep roots. A debate with all of these characteristics concerns the role of modelling in ecology and, more recently, in conservation biology. Reactions in the 1930s to the models of population dynamics produced by Lotka, Volterra, Nicholson and Bailey in the 1920s and 1930s have a familiar ring. The main complaints were that theory had gone far beyond observation and experimentation and that the complexity of nature was not represented in the models (Kingsland 1985). A similar litany of complaints was voiced in the 1960s and 1970s in reaction to models by MacArthur, Wilson and Levins. Most recently, conservation biologists have jousted over the role and importance of models (Noss 1996; Bowen & Bass 1996), using much of the same language. Power, influence and even extinction were at stake in the first two episodes, and may be at stake in the third. In the early days the ranks of the modellers were thin. The fate of a new approach was at stake, and the defenders of modelling came out swinging. These days models are everywhere. It is the defenders of natural history sensu stricto who feel their backs are against the wall. The operative words here are sensu stricto.

I do not think we have to fret about the fate of stand-alone, descriptive natural history. It is not that the 'facts' of natural history aren't important. They are, and we should keep reporting them. My point is that the future of the naturalist's tradition lies in concept development. Observation, discovery, experimentation, models and simulation are all subservient to the task of concept building. All of these tools are valid, legitimate and worthy of our respect. And, just as it seems silly to argue that someone who uses just a hammer is the only true carpenter, history does not support the idea that the field worker armed with just a notebook is the only true naturalist. There are many varieties of naturalist and, so, no real threat of extinction.

Conclusions

Although I will stay on the sidelines at the next debate, I have reached four conclusions by taking a historical perspective on natural history.

(1) Natural history is a vital, proliferating lineage. Worries about the fate of natural history arise when we focus on the small twig that now carries the name 'natural history' rather than on the lineage itself. Viewed as a lineage with all of its branches, natural history is a flourishing enterprise.

(2) The crux of the natural history tradition is the search for order in nature. The goal of the tradition is, and always has been, to formulate concepts that allow us to perceive order in nature. It is the pursuit of the goal, rather than the tools of employment, that defines the tradition and hence the naturalist. The tools of the naturalist are equations and sequencers, as well as binoculars and notebook.

(3) The naturalists are not dying. You may not think you are a naturalist, but you probably are. If your eyes are on the prize of finding order in nature, you are part of a naturalist tradition that stretches back to the 1750s. Look around at your next scientific meeting. Naturalists and their heirs are all around you.

(4) The vitality of the naturalist's tradition depends on new ideas and tools from other disciplines (Wilson 1989). Our future depends on new infusions even though they can produce tension and conflict. We need an inclusive vision of natural history rather than a tussle over the discipline's mantle. Disciplinary coexistence, mutual respect and collaboration serve our own mental health as well as the future of natural history.

Acknowledgments

I thank L. K. Arnold, P. L. Farber, L. D. Houck, M. K. Manier, M. Westphal and A. M. Wood for helpful discussions.

References

Bartholomew, G. A. 1986. The role of natural history in contemporary biology. *BioScience*, **36**, 324–329.

Bowen, B. W. & Bass, A. L. 1996. Are the naturalists dying off? *Conservation Biology*, **10**, 923–924.

Farber, P. L. 2000. *Finding Order in Nature: the Naturalist Tradition from Linnaeus to E. O. Wilson*. Baltimore, Maryland: Johns Hopkins University Press.

Futuyma, D. J. 1998. Wherefore and wither the naturalist? *American Naturalist*, **151**, 1–6.

Greene, H. W. 1994. Systematics and natural history, foundations for understanding and conserving biodiversity. *American Zoologist*, **34**, 48–56.

Greene, H. W. & Losos, J. B. 1988. Systematics, natural history and conservation. *BioScience*, **38**, 458–462.

Kingsland, S. E. 1985. *Modeling Nature: Episodes in the History of Population Ecology*. Chicago: University of Chicago Press.

Mayr, E. 1982. *The Growth of Biological Thought, Diversity, Evolution and Inheritance*. Cambridge, Massachusetts: Belknap Press.

Noss, R. F. 1996. The naturalists are dying off. *Conservation Biology*, **10**, 1–3.

Provine, W. B. 1971. *The Origins of Theoretical Population Genetics*. Chicago: University of Chicago Press.

Wilson, E. O. 1989. The coming pluralization of biology and the stewardship of systematics. *BioScience*, **39**, 242–245.

6

A History of *Animal Behaviour* by a Partial, Ignorant and Prejudiced Ethologist

Felicity A. Huntingford
Fish Biology Group, Division of Environmental & Evolutionary Biology
Institute of Biomedical & Life Sciences
University of Glasgow

Abstract

This essay looks back on the history of *Animal Behaviour* through a compilation of all the papers published in the journal, since it got its present name, that used sticklebacks, the white rat of ethology, as experimental subjects. This stickleback-eye view confirms the role that *Animal Behaviour* has played during its first 50 years in fostering and recording the important developments that have taken place in the discipline. It also speaks to its current flourishing state as a key journal for the dissemination of results in both ethology (in the sense of studies looking at causation, development and evolution as well as function) and behavioural ecology.

When asked to write a commentary for the 50th anniversary of *Animal Behaviour* I planned, ambitiously, to screen all the papers published in the journal during the last half-century, with a view to identifying changes and trends in how behavioural biologists do their work. This proved altogether too daunting a task, so I had to use some sort of filter. In her *History of England by a partial, ignorant and prejudiced historian*, Jane Austen wrote simply to prove that Mary Queen of Scots was a sainted martyr and Elizabeth I of England a monster, using this to decide what to include and what to leave out. Borrowing a leaf from her book, I have omitted from my review all papers that did not use sticklebacks (arguably the perfect fish) as subjects. Since the stickleback is the white rat of ethology, I hoped that the remaining body of work (primary studies using any species of stickleback, omitting commentaries and reviews; Appendix 1) might give a representative picture of what has happened in our discipline.

Clearly there have been many changes, the most obvious being the rapidly accelerating rate of publication: five papers on sticklebacks in the 1960s, 12 in the 1970s, 17 in the 1980s, 37 in the 1990s and five so far this century. The first points to emerge are therefore that an increasing body of high-quality work is being submitted to and published by *Animal Behaviour* and that sticklebacks continue to play their part in generating this work.

As Table 6-1 shows, there has been little change in the broad behavioural topics that this work has addressed. Studies of sex and violence continue to dominate, but there has also been a steady stream of work on foraging and antipredator behaviour in sticklebacks. Looking in more detail, one can see reflections of various specific hot topics that have come and (in some cases) gone: time sharing and the motivational bases of behavioural switches (Cohen & McFarland 1979), group life as an antipredator adaptation (Jakobsen & Johnsen 1988; Ranta *et al.* 1992; Jakobsen *et al.* 1994; Peuhkuri 1997), kin recognition (Smith & Whorisky 1988), manipulation by parasites of host behaviour (Giles 1983; Tierney *et al.* 1993; Barber & Ruxton 1998), tit-for-tat and predator inspection (Kulling & Milinski 1992; Huntingford *et al.* 1994; McLeod & Huntingford 1994), and so on. One can also see the expected broader trends in the kinds of questions that biologists have been asking about behaviour: from an emphasis on causation in the days of ethology, to an emphasis on function in the days of behavioural ecology, to a very productive mixture of these two approaches in more recent publications.

Several interesting strands of accumulating evidence and developing understanding on specific topics are evident. One such strand (strongly linking causal and functional approaches) concerns foraging behaviour. This runs from Thomas's (1974, 1977) demonstration of how simple alterations to search paths contingent on finding food can lead sticklebacks to profitable feeding patches, through work by Milinski & Regelmann (1985) on short-term memory and patch quality and by Hughes and collaborators on the effects of learning and memory on prey profitability (Croy & Hughes 1991a, b) to Hughes's recent elegant studies of the precise nature of spatial memory and how this relates to foraging efficiency (Hughes & Blight 1999, 2000).

Table 6-1 The percentage of papers using sticklebacks as subjects published in *Animal Behaviour* in each decade, classified by broad subject matter

Decade	Aggression	Reproductive behaviour	Foraging	Antipredator behaviour
1950/60s	57	43		
1970s	40	34	13	13
1980s	24	34	12	30
1990s	23	26	23	28
2000s	30	50	20	0

Thanks to Niko Tinbergen, sticklebacks have been famous since the beginning of ethological time for their nuptial coloration and its role as an aggression-eliciting stimulus and for their zig-zag courtship behaviour; two further strands reflect these behaviour patterns. A series of papers published in *Animal Behaviour* has elucidated the controversial topic of red coloration in breeding male three-spined sticklebacks and its relation to aggression. For example, stimulated by failure of several workers to get red dummies to trigger attack, Collias (1990) quantified the responses of individual males to dummies of different colours. He concluded that red coloration elicits fear as well as aggression and that the balance between these determines the response of an individual male to a red dummy. This conclusion was supported by Rowland *et al.* (1995) and Bolyard & Rowland (1996) in studies in which the strongest aggressive response was shown to video images of males of intermediate brightness. This carefully researched extension of Tinbergen's original view of how red coloration works has yet to reach the textbooks.

All the papers on courtship in sticklebacks published in *Animal Behaviour* in the 1960s and 1970s addressed questions about causation, only occasionally making reference to function, as in the case of Wilz's elegant studies of displacement fanning as a means of switching from aggression to courtship (Wilz 1970a, b). From the 1980s onwards, there was a striking switch to a mainly functional perspective in the context of mate choice. The Tinbergen legacy (particularly the use of dummies to elicit courtship in both sexes) has had two beneficial effects in this context. First, from the start people have studied mate choice by males (e.g. Rowland 1982, 1988, 1989, 2000) as well as by females (Sargent 1982; McKinnon 1995; McLennan 1995; Rowland *et al.* 1995; Ahnesjö 1998) and also by the two sexes simultaneously (Kraak & Bakker 1998), using both dummies and video images (Rowland *et al.* 1995). Second, the proximate cues used to assess mate quality (which can be very subtle, Rowland *et al.* 2002) have often been studied alongside functional aspects of mate choice (e.g. Rowland 1982, 1989), providing insights into physiological and morphological factors that generate honest signalling in this context (females, Rowland *et al.* 2002; males, Candolin 1999, 2000).

So the 76 papers on sticklebacks published by *Animal Behaviour* in its 50 years of existence reflect increasing interest in the discipline and the changes in emphasis that are to be expected as a successful discipline matures. However, there are some striking and interesting omissions.

Even though sticklebacks provide one of the classic examples of breeding territoriality, there is almost nothing about the behavioural ecology of territoriality or about perspectives on aggression derived from game theory, exceptions being papers by Stanley & Wootton (1986) and Rowland (1989). This was clearly not the case for other papers being published in *Animal Behaviour* at the time, so the omission seems to be something special to work on sticklebacks.

Except for the seasonality of aggression and territoriality in sticklebacks, these fish are entirely suitable for such studies, so the explanation must lie elsewhere. Perhaps the emphasis on red colour as a sign stimulus in studies of stickleback aggression has hindered studies of other aspects of aggression.

The majority of the papers on sticklebacks published in the 1950s and 1960s were on aspects of the physiology of reproductive behaviour. These include very interesting papers by Hoar (1962), Smith & Hoar (1967) and Wootton (1970) on hormonal control, and by Segaar & Neuwenhuys (1963) on brain mechanisms. After this, the target literature goes completely quiet on the topic until Bell's (2001) paper on the effects of endocrine disruptors on breeding behaviour. From the papers published on sticklebacks in *Animal Behaviour* one could be excused for thinking that the huge advances in neuroethology and behavioural endocrinology of the last few decades had simply not happened. Arguably this is because sticklebacks are too small to be good models for this kind of study. A quick look at papers on other species published in the journal in the last 2 years shows that studies of hormones and behaviour at least are better represented. An interesting methodological perspective is given by Koren *et al.* (2001) on noninvasive measurement of hormone levels in wild mammals using hair. Several studies used manipulation of testosterone levels as a tool to look at the trade-off between sexual and parental behaviour (Nunes *et al.* 2000; Peters 2001; Lynne *et al.* 2002) or at mate choice (Hagelin & Ligon 2001). Others measured concentrations of cortisol (and other steroids) in studies that are concerned with stress and animal welfare, loosely defined (Sloman *et al.* 2001; Maddocks *et al.* 2002; Parker *et al.* 2002). A number of other papers describe studies of the endocrine bases of individual variability in behaviour, either directly (Nunes *et al.* 2000; Hanley & Stamps 2002; Lynne *et al.* 2002; Pfeffer *et al.* 2002) or via maternal hormones in eggs (Whittingham & Schwabl 2002). Just two papers about the nervous system have been published in the last 2 years, one relating neocortex size to social complexity in primates (Kudo & Dunbar 2001) and the other giving an interesting commentary suggesting that diverse adaptations such as sleep, schooling in fish and flocking during flight in birds depend on the brain's inability to process sensory inputs and control movement at the same time as forming and reinforcing long-term memories (Kavanau 2001).

A few of the papers on sticklebacks published in *Animal Behaviour* report the use of deprivation experiments to identify behaviour patterns that are inherited, in the sense that they develop in the absence of specific experience (e.g. Giles 1984). Sticklebacks lend themselves very well to studies involving experimental breeding programmes, as is shown by Bakker's work on selection for aggressiveness and the genetics of mating preferences in three-spined sticklebacks (e.g. Bakker 1993, 1994), and by numerous studies of within-species divergence in the three-spined stickleback species complex (reviewed by McKinnon & Rundle 2002), yet not one of the 76 papers published in *Animal Behaviour* mentions genetics. Again, from these papers, including my own, one would not know that the genetic revolution had occurred during the intervening period. Until recently (Peichel *et al.* 2001), there has been no genome-wide linkage map for sticklebacks, so perhaps concentrating on the white rat of ethology gives a false impression of all the papers published in the journal. Looking once more at the papers published on other species in the last 2 years, there are of course many that used genetics (traditional and molecular) as a tool for measuring relatedness in studies with purely behavioural aims. Over and above this, a few studies published in *Animal Behaviour* in the last 2 years used traditional behavioural genetic techniques to examine the inheritance of various aspects of behaviour (Arathi & Spivak 2001; Ferguson *et al.* 2001; Gariepy *et al.* 2001; Malmkvist & Hansen 2002; Pankiw *et al.* 2002; Reale & Roff 2002). A particularly interesting paper, still using traditional genetic tools, looked at how genes and hormones interact to generate natural variability in behaviour in lizards (King 2002). Equally interesting is a paper by Iguchi *et al.* (2001) who used clonal strains of red-spotted cherry salmon (generated by chromosome manipulations) to examine the inheritance of persistent individual variability in suites of behaviour that have implications for fitness, such as antipredator responses and feeding. These are all important studies, but it would be good to see in the pages of *Animal Behaviour* studies that use the full power of modern molecular tools to examine the genetic mechanisms that generate behavioural variability.

This stickleback-eye view confirms the role that *Animal Behaviour* has played during its first 50 years in fostering and recording the important developments that have taken place in the discipline. It also speaks to its current flourishing state as a key journal for the dissemination of results in both ethology (in the sense of studies looking at causation, development and evolution as well as function) and behavioural ecology. A less partial, ignorant and prejudiced view (acknowledging the existence of study species other than sticklebacks) recognizes the recent appearance of some extremely interesting physiological and genetic studies. An increasingly multidisciplinary interest is both appropriate and very welcome and hopefully we will see more such papers in the journal in future.

References

Arathi, H. S. & Spivak, M. 2001. Influence of colony genotype composition on the performance of hygenic behaviour in the honeybee. *Animal Behaviour,* **62,** 57–66.

Bakker, T. C. M. 1993. Positive genetic correlation between female preference and preferred male ornament in sticklebacks. *Nature,* **363,** 255–257.

Bakker, T. C. M. 1994. Genetic correlations and the control of behaviour, exemplified by aggressiveness in sticklebacks. *Advances in the Study of Behaviour,* **23,** 135–171.

Ferguson, H. J., Cobey, S. & Smith, B. H. 2001. Sensitivity to change in reward is heritable in the honeybee. *Animal Behaviour,* **61,** 527–534.

Gariepy, J.-L., Bauer, D. J. & Cairns, R. B. 2001. Selective breeding for differentiated aggression in mice provides evidence for heterochrony in social behaviours. *Animal Behaviour,* **61,** 933–947.

Hagelin, J. C. & Ligon, J. D. 2001. Female quail prefer testosterone-mediated traits, rather than the ornate plumage of males. *Animal Behaviour,* **61,** 465–476.

Hanley, K. A. & Stamps, J. A. 2001. Does cortisol mediate bidirectional interactions between social behaviour and blood parasites in the juvenile black iguana, *Ctenosaura gimilis? Animal Behaviour,* **63,** 311–332.

Iguchi, K., Matsubara, N. & Hakoyama, H. 2001. Behavioural individuality assessed from two strains of cloned fish. *Animal Behaviour,* **61,** 351–356.

Kavenau, J. L. 2001. Brain-processing limitation and selective pressure for sleep, fish schooling and avian flocking. *Animal Behaviour,* **62,** 1219–1224.

King, R. B. 2002. Family, sex and testosterone effects on garter snake behaviour. *Animal Behaviour,* **64,** 345–359.

Koren, L., Mokady, O., Karaskov, Y., Klein, J., Koren, G. & Geffen, E. A. 2001. Novel method using hair for determining hormonal levels in wildlife. *Animal Behaviour,* **60,** 403–406.

Kudo, H. & Dunbar, R. I. M. 2001. Neocortex size and social network size in primates. *Animal Behaviour,* **62,** 711–722.

Lynne, S. E., Hayward, L. S., Benowitz-Fredericks, Z. M. & Wingfield, J. C. 2002. Behavioural insensitivity to supplementary testosterone during the parental phase in the chestnut-collared longspur *Calcarius ornatus. Animal Behaviour,* **63,** 795–803.

McKinnon, J. S. & Rundle, H. D. 2002. Speciation in nature: the threespine stickleback model systems. *Trends in Ecology and Evolution,* **17,** 480–488.

Maddocks, S. A., Cuthill, I. C., Goldsmith, A. R. & Sherwin, C. M. 2002. Behavioural and physiological effects of absence of ultraviolet wavelengths for chicks. *Animal Behaviour,* **62,** 1013–1019.

Malmkvist, J. & Hansen, S. 2002. Generalization of fear in farm mink, genetically selected for behaviour towards humans. *Animal Behaviour,* **64,** 487–501.

Nunes, S., Fite, J. E. & French, J. A. 2002. Variation in steroid hormones associated with infant care behaviour and experience in male marmosets. *Animal Behaviour,* **60,** 857–865.

Pankiw, T., Tarpy, D. R. & Page, R. E. 2002. Genotype and rearing environment affect honeybee perception and foraging behaviour. *Animal Behaviour,* **64,** 663–672.

Parker, T. H., Knapp, R. & Rosenfield, J. A. 2002. Social mediation of sexually selected ornamentation and steroid hormone levels in male junglefowl. *Animal Behaviour,* **64,** 291–298.

Peichel, C. L., Nereng, K. S., Ohgi, K. A., Cole, B. L. E., Colosimo, P. F., Buerkle, C. A., Schluter, D. & Kingsley, D. M. 2001. The genetic architecture of divergence between threespine stickleback species. *Nature,* **414,** 901–905.

Peters, A. 2001. Testosterone and the trade-off between maternal and paternal effort in extrapair-mating superb fairy wrens. *Animal Behaviour,* **62,** 103–112.

Pfeffer, K., Fritz, J. & Kotrschal, K. 2002. Hormonal correlates of being an innovative greylag goose. *Animal Behaviour,* **63,** 687–695.

Reale, D. & Roff, D. A. 2002. Quantitative genetics of oviposition behaviour and interactions among oviposition traits in the sand cricket. *Animal Behaviour,* **64,** 397–406.

Sloman, K., Taylor, A. C., Metcalfe, N. B. & Gilmour, K. M. 2001. Effects of an environmental perturbation on the social behaviour and physiological function of brown trout. *Animal Behaviour,* **61,** 325–333.

Whittingham, L. A. & Schwabl, H. 2002. Maternal testosterone in tree swallow eggs varies with female aggression. *Animal Behaviour,* **63,** 63–67.

Appendix 1

Table A1 Papers published in *Animal Behaviour* using sticklebacks as experimental subjects

Authors	Date	Title	Volume	Pages
Hoar, W. S.	1962	Hormones and the reproductive behaviour of the male three-spined stickleback.	10	247–266
Segaar, J. & Nieuwenhuys, R.	1963	New etho-physiological experiments with male *Gasterosteus aculeatus*, with anatomical comment.	11	331–344
Tinbergen, N.	1963	The work of the Animal Behaviour Research Group (including an account of experiments by Mike Cullen using anti-anxiety drugs to test the conflict theory of threat displays).	11	207–209
Smith, R. J. F. & Hoar, W. S.	1967	The effects of prolactin and testosterone on the parental behaviour of the male stickleback *Gasterosteus aculeatus*.	15	342–352
Peeke, H. S., Wyers, E. J. & Herz, M. J.	1969	Waning of aggressive response to male models in the three-spines stickleback.	17	224–228
Wilz, K. J.	1970a	Causal and functional analysis of dorsal pricking and nest activity in the courtship of the three-spined stickleback.	18	115–124
Wilz, K. J.	1970b	The disinhibition interpretation of the 'displacement' activities during courtship in the three-spined stickleback.	18	682–687
Wootton, R. J.	1970	Aggression in the early phases of the reproductive cycle of the male three-spined stickleback.	18	740–746
Black, R.	1971	Hatching success in the three-spined stickleback in relation to changes in behaviour during the parental phase.	19	532–541
Wilz, K. J.	1972	Causal relationships between aggression and the sexual and nest behaviours in the three-spined stickleback.	20	335–340
Wootton, R. J.	1974	Changes in the courtship behaviour of female three-spined sticklebacks between spawnings.	22	850–855
Thomas, G.	1974	The influence of encountering a food object on subsequent searching behaviour in *Gasterosteus aculeatus*.	22	941–952
Huntingford, F. A.	1976a	The relationship between anti-predator behaviour and aggression among conspecifics in the three-spined stickle back.	24	245–260

Continued

Appendix 1

Table A1 *Continued*

Authors	Date	Title	Volume	Pages
Huntingford, F. A.	1976b	A comparison of the reaction of sticklebacks in different reproductive condition towards conspecifics and predators.	24	694–697
Huntingford, F. A.	1976	An investigation of the territorial behaviour of the three-spined stickleback using Principal Components Analysis.	24	822–834
Thomas, G.	1977	The influence of eating and rejecting prey items upon feeding and food searching behaviour in *Gasterosteus aculeatus*.	25	52–66
Cohen, S. & McFarland, D.	1979	Time-sharing as a mechanism for the control of behaviour sequences during the courtship of the three-spined stickleback.	27	270–283
Sargent, R. C.	1982	Territory quality, male quality, courtship intrusions and female nest choice in the threespine stickleback.	30	364–374
Huntingford, F. A.	1982	Do inter- and intra-specific aggression vary in relation to predation pressure in sticklebacks.	30	909–916
Rowland, W. J.	1982	Mate choice by male stickleback.	30	1093–1098
Giles, N.	1983	Behavioural effects of the parasite *Schistocephalus solidus* on an intermediate host, the three-spined stickleback.	31	1192–1194
Giles, N.	1984	Development of the overhead fright response in wild and predator naïve three-spined sticklebacks.	32	264–275
Giles, N. & Huntingford, F. A.	1984	Predation risk and inter-population variation in anti-predator behaviour in the three-spined stickleback.	32	545–550
Milinski, M. & Regelmann, K.	1985	Fading short-term memory for patch quality in sticklebacks.	33	678–680
Stanley, B. V. & Wootton, R. J.	1986	Effects of ration and male density on the territoriality and nest building of male three-spined sticklebacks.	34	527–535
Sargent, R. C., Gross, M. R. & Van den Berghe, E. P.	1986	Male mate choice in fishes.	34	545–550
Tulley, J. J. & Huntingford, F. A.	1987	Paternal care and the development of adaptive variation in anti-predator responses in sticklebacks.	35	1570–1572
Rowland, W. J.	1988	Aggression versus courtship in threespine stickleback and the role of habituation to neighbours.	36	348–357

Author	Year	Title	Vol	Pages
Jakobsen, P. J. & Johnsen, G. H.	1988	Size-specific protection against predation by fish in swarming water fleas.	36	986–990
Bakker, T. C. H. & Feuth-de Bruijn, E.	1988	Juvenile territoriality in sticklebacks, *Gasterosteus aculeatus*.	36	1556–1558
Smith, R. S. & Whorisky, F. G.	1988	Multiple clutches: female threespine stickleback lose the ability to recognise their own eggs.	36	1838–1839
Rowland, W. J.	1989	The effects of body size, aggression and nuptial coloration on competition for territories in male threespine sticklebacks.	37	282–289
Rowland, W. J.	1989	The ethological basis of mate choice in male threespine sticklebacks.	38	112–120
Jamieson, I. G. & Colgan, P. W.	1989	Eggs in the nests of males and their effect on male choice in the three-spines stickleback.	38	859–865
Collias, N. E.	1990	Statistical evidence for aggressive response to red by male three-spined sticklebacks.	39	401–403
Croy, M. I. & Hughes, R. N.	1991a	The role of learning and memory in the feeding behaviour of the fifteen-spined stickleback.	41	149–159
Croy, M. I. & Hughes, R. N.	1991b	The influence of hunger on feeding behaviour and on the acquisition of learned foraging skills by the fifteen-spined stickleback.	41	161–170
Whorisky, F. G.	1991	Stickleback distraction displays: sexual or foraging deception against egg cannibalism.	41	989–995
Croy, M. I. & Hughes, R. N.	1991c	Effects of food supply, hunger, danger and competition on choice of foraging location by the fifteen-spined stickleback.	42	131–139
Rowland, W. J., Baube, C. L. & Horan, T. T.	1991	Signalling of sexual receptivity by pigmentation pattern in female sticklebacks.	42	243–249
Kaiser, M. J., Gibson, R. N. & Hughes, R. N.	1992	The effect of prey type on the predatory behaviour of the fifteen-spined stickleback.	43	147–156
Ranta, E., Lindstrom, K. & Peuhkuri, N.	1992	Size matters when three-spined sticklebacks go to school.	43	160–162
Goldschmidt, T, Foster, S. & Sevenster, P	1992	Inter-nest distance and sneaking in the three-spined stickleback.	44	793–795
Kulling, D. & Milinski, M.	1992	Size-dependent predator risk and partner quality in predator inspection of sticklebacks.	44	793–795

Continued

Appendix 1

Table A1 *Continued*

Authors	Date	Title	Volume	Pages
Goldschmidt, T., Bakker, T. C. M. & Feuth-de Bruijn, E.	1993	Selective copying in mate choice of female sticklebacks.	45	541–547
Tierney, J. F., Huntingford, F. A. & Crompton, D. W. T.	1993	The relationship between infectivity of *Schistocephalus solidus* and antipredator behaviour of its intermediate host, the three-spine stickleback.	46	603–605
Defraispoint, M., FitzGerald, G. J. & Guderley, H.	1993	Age-related differences in reproductive tactics in the three-spined stickleback.	46	961–968
Ranta, E.	1993	There is no optimal foraging group size.	46	1032–1035
Waas, J. R. & Colgan, P. W.	1994	Male sticklebacks can distinguish between familiar rivals on the basis of visual cues alone.	47	7–13
Jakobsen, P. J., Birkeland, K. & Johnsen, G. H.	1994	Swarm location in zooplankton as an anti-predator defence mechanism.	47	175–178
Huntingford, F. A., Lazarus, J., Barrie, B. D. & Webb, S.	1994	A dynamic analysis of cooperative predator inspection in sticklebacks	47	413–423
Gill, A. B. & Hart, P. J. B.	1994	Feeding behaviour and prey choice of the threespine stickleback: the interacting effects of prey size and stomach fullness.	47	921–932
McLeod, P. G. & Huntingford, F. A.	1994	Social rank and predator inspection in sticklebacks.	47	1238–1240
Krause, J. & Regeder, R. W.	1994	The mechanism of aggregation behaviour in fish shoals: individuals minimize approach time to neighbours.	48	353–359
Losey, G. S. & Sevenster, P.	1995	Can three-spined sticklebacks learn when to display? Rewarded displays.	49	137–150
Rowland, W. J., Bolyard, K. J., Jenkins, J. J. & Fowler, J.	1995	Video playback experiments on stickleback mate choice: female motivation and attentiveness to male colour cues.	49	1559–1567
McLennan, D. A.	1995	Male mate choice based upon female nuptial coloration in the brook stickleback.	50	213–221
Rowland, W. J., Boylard, K. J. & Halpern, A. D.	1995	The dual effect of stickleback nuptial coloration on rivals: manipulation of a graded signal using video playback.	50	267–272
McKinnon, J. S.	1995	Video mate preferences of female three-spined sticklebacks from populations with divergent male coloration.	50	1645–1655

Author	Year	Title	Vol.	Pages
Mathis, A., Chivers, D. P. & Smith, R. J. F.	1996	Cultural transmission of predator recognition in fish: intraspecific and interspecific learning.	51	185–201
Gill, A. B. & Hart, P. J. B.	1996	Unequal competition between three-spined stickleback encountering sequential prey.	51	689–698
Bolyard, K. J. & Rowland, W. J.	1996	Context-dependent responses to red coloration in sticklebacks.	52	923–927
Baube, C. L.	1997	Manipulations of signalling environment affect male competitive success in three-spined sticklebacks.	53	819–833
Peuhkuri, N.	1997	Size-assortative shoaling in fish: the effect of oddity on foraging behaviour.	54	271–278
Salvanes, A. G. V. & Hart, P. J. B.	1998	Individual variability in state-dependent feeding behaviour in three-spined sticklebacks.	55	1349–1359
Kraak, S. & Bakker, T. C. M.	1998	Mutual mate choice in sticklebacks: attractive males choose big females, which lay big eggs.	56	859–866
Ahnesjö, I.	1998	Female fifteen-spined sticklebacks prefer better fathers.	56	1177–1183
Candolin, U. & Voight, H. R.	1998	Predator-induced nest site preference: safe nests allow courtship in sticklebacks.	56	1205–1211
Barber, I. & Ruxton, G. D.	1998	Temporal prey distribution affects the competitive ability of parasitized sticklebacks.	56	1477–1483
Hughes, R. N. & Blight, C. M.	1999	Algorithmic behaviour and spatial memory are used by two intertidal fish species to solve the radial maze.	58	601–613
Candolin, U.	1999	The relationship between signal quality and physical condition: is sexual signalling honest in the three-spined stickleback?	58	1261–1267
Hughes, R. N. & Blight, C. M.	2000	Two intertidal fish use visual association learning to track the status of food patches in a radial maze.	59	613–621
Rowland, W. J.	2000	Habituation and development of response specificity to a sign stimulus: male preference for female courtship posture in sticklebacks.	60	63–68
Candolin, U.	2000	Increased signalling effort when survival prospects decrease: male–male competition ensures honesty.	60	417–422
Bell, A. M.	2001	Effects of an endocrine disruptor on courtship and aggressive behaviour of male three-spined stickleback.	62	775–780
Rowland, W. J., Grindle, N., Maclaren, R. D. & Granquist, R.	2002	Male preference for a subtle posture cue that signals spawning readiness in female sticklebacks.	63	743–748

7

Genes and Social Behaviour

Gene E. Robinson
Department of Entomology and Neuroscience Program
University of Illinois at Urbana-Champaign

Abstract

Studying the molecular basis of social behaviour requires an integration of molecular biology, genomics, neuroscience, behavioural biology, and evolutionary biology. An eclectic mix of species, displaying varying levels of sociality, is being used for this endeavour. One emerging theme relating to the relationship between genes and social behaviour is that genes involved in solitary behaviour are also used for social behaviour. A second theme is that the genome is highly sensitive to social influence, via social regulation of gene expression. A transcriptomics-based approach is the method of gene discovery most easily used for model social species.

Overview

Life on Earth has undergone several transitions during its history, from the evolution of cells, to multicellular organisms, and then to the organisation of these organisms into societies (Maynard Smith & Szathmáry 1995). There has been significant progress in elucidating the molecular basis of cellular function and development, and there is now a burgeoning interest in doing the same for social life ("sociogenomics"). The goal of sociogenomics is to achieve a comprehensive understanding of social life in molecular terms: how it evolved, how it is governed, and how it influences all aspects of genome structure, genome activity, and organismal function (Robinson 1997, 2002a; Robinson et al. 1997, 2005). What genes and pathways regulate those aspects of development, physiology, and behaviour that influence sociality, and how are they influenced by social life and social evolution? Spectacular progress in molecular biology and genomics and the output of many genome-sequencing projects makes this a most opportune time for this programme of research (Robinson et al. 2005).

One property that distinguishes sociogenomics from allied molecularly and genetically oriented fields, such as neurogenomics, behavioural neuroscience, and behavioural genetics, is a special interest in species that live in a society. There are many types of social behaviours exhibited by species that differ dramatically in their level of sociality. Organisms that live in a society engage in repeated interactions with each other—both cooperative and competitive—in various contexts related to survival and reproduction. A defining feature of animal society is "reciprocal communication of a cooperative nature" (Wilson 1975). In the most structured societies, these kinds of interactions influence most aspects of life. In other societies, individuals might be less communicative or cooperative except for activities related to reproduction, but they display many related behaviours including attraction, aggression, affiliation, attachment, and dominance.

Of particular interest are species that can be studied under natural or naturalistic conditions. These species, which include birds, bees, crustacea, fish, primates, and voles, offer a rich set of behaviours for analysis that should contribute to the development of general principles. Although powerful studies of social behaviour can be performed in the laboratory (Pfaff 1999), there is keen interest in understanding the molecular machinery of social behaviour in natural contexts. Studies conducted under ecologically relevant conditions make it easier to interpret molecular data within a broad framework that integrates mechanistic and evolutionary perspectives (Robinson 1999; Boake et al. 2002; Stearns & Magwene 2003). Other forms of behaviour studied at the molecular level, such as learning and circadian rhythms (Sokolowski 2001; Rankin 2002; Bucan & Abel 2002), have to date focused on some of the traditional model organisms used for genetic analysis: the fruit fly Drosophila melanogaster, nematode Caenorhabditis elegans, and the mouse Mus musculus.

Two traditional forward-genetic paradigms are used to discover genes that influence behaviour (Tully 1996). Seymour Benzer pioneered the approach that involves creating single-gene mutations, screening for specific behavioural abnormalities, and identifying the mutated gene. A second approach, championed by Jerry Hirsch, involves identifying behavioural variants from natural and artificially selected populations and then using them to find the underlying genetic variation. Unfortunately, limitations in our ability to efficiently breed many model social species preclude generation and maintenance of large numbers of mutant lines, although the second approach is being used effectively in a variety of ways (e.g., Osborne *et al.* 1997; Ruppell *et al.* 2004; Insel & Young 2001).

This chapter reviews studies of social behaviour that make use of a new approach based on transcriptomics: measuring changes in the expression of genes that correlate with changes in behaviour. Gene expression is measured in the brains of individuals performing different behaviours, or different forms of the behaviour of interest.

The transcriptomics approach is based on information from sequencing projects and the availability of microarrays and other highly efficient methods of mRNA quantification. Sequence information eliminates the need to tediously clone genes one at a time before experimentation with candidate genes can even begin (Fitzpatrick *et al.* 2005). Microarrays enable unbiased, open-ended gene discovery in species that, unlike model genetic organisms, cannot be used efficiently for traditional forward-genetic approaches. For the first time it is possible to select organisms on the basis of their compelling social biology and develop powerful and efficient programmes of molecular analysis.

The premise of the transcriptomic approach is that differences in transcript abundance reflect a mechanistic link between gene and behaviour. This premise is well supported in this review and elsewhere (Sokolowski 2001; Rankin 2002; Bucan & Abel 2002). However, transcript abundance is not always predictive of protein abundance, and some differences in gene expression are a consequence, not a cause, of a behavioural change. Thus, it is important to go beyond gene expression–behaviour correlations to manipulate transcript abundance or protein activity via RNA interference (RNAi) (Beye *et al.* 2003), viral vectors (Lim *et al.* 2004), or pharmacology. The transcriptomics-based approach is a powerful entrée to gene discovery for model social species.

This chapter focuses on two emerging themes related to the study of genes and social behaviour. First, genes involved in solitary behaviour are also used for social behaviour. Second, the genome is highly sensitive to social influence, with social regulation of gene expression a potent influence on behaviour. The chapter ends with a discussion of prospects and challenges for the study of genes and social behaviour.

Solitary to Social with the Same Genes

Feeding and the Foraging (*for*) Gene

Studies involving cyclic-GMP (cGMP) signalling pathways have revealed strong conservation in the molecular underpinnings of feeding-related behaviours. In *D. melanogaster,* the *foraging* gene (*for*) encodes a cGMP dependent protein kinase (PKG), and naturally occurring allelic variation in this gene results in two genotypes, "sitters" and "rovers" (Osborne *et al.* 1997). Although *D. melanogaster* lives most of its life in solitary fashion, the behavioural variation associated with these allelic differences suggests a parallel to the feeding-related behaviour of the highly social honey bee *Apis mellifera,* which is expressed as part of a complex system of age-related division of labour.

In virtually all species of social insects, age-related division of labour is based on a pattern of behavioural development. Individuals perform tasks in the nest, such as brood care ("nursing") and nest maintenance, when they are young. They then venture outside to collect food and other materials and defend the nest when they get older. In honey bee colonies, adult workers spend the first two to three weeks of adult life working in the hive and the remaining one to three weeks of life mostly as foragers (Robinson 2002b).

"Sitter" flies obtain food in a more circumscribed area and young honey bees feed in the hive; "rover" flies forage over a larger area and older honey bees travel over great distances outside the hive in search of food. However, foragers collect food to fulfil the needs of the colony and not to satisfy personal hunger, unlike flies. The similarities and differences in the fly–bee behavioural comparison motivated us (Ben-Shahar *et al.* 2002) to use *for* as a candidate gene to study the regulation of social foraging. *Amfor,* an ortholog of the *D. melanogaster for* gene, was found to be involved in the regulation of age-at-onset of foraging in honey bees. Levels of *Amfor* mRNA in the brain are higher in foragers than bees working in the hive, and experimentally activating PKG causes precocious foraging.

How does up-regulation of the *for* gene in the bee brain affect the age of onset of foraging? One effect is a PKG-induced increase in positive phototaxis (Ben-Shahar *et al.* 2003). *Amfor* is preferentially expressed in the optic lobe and in a subset of intrinsic neurons in the mushroom bodies that process visual information (Ben-Shahar *et al.* 2002). The mushroom bodies form a region of the insect brain that is involved in multi-modal sensory integration, learning, and memory. Bees live in a dark hive, and an increase in positive phototaxis positions them closer to the hive entrance. There, they apparently are stimulated to forage by exposure to other stimuli, such as successful foragers communicating by means of the dance language (von Frisch 1967).

cGMP signalling also affects feeding arousal in other species. For example, in *Caenorhabtitis elegans* genotypic differences in the *for* orthologue *egl-4* (*egg-laying defective-4*) are implicated in differences in food-dependent locomotion. Allelic variants of the *egl-4* gene affect the proportion of time that the animals spend "roaming" or "dwelling," due to effects on sensory neurons involved in locomotion and olfaction (Fujiwara *et al.* 2002). Mutations that decrease PKG signalling lead to an increase in roaming, suggesting that this behaviour is PKG-dependent, but that it is regulated differently than in flies and bees. As in *C. elegans,* foragers in colonies of the harvester ant *Pogonomyrmex barbatus* have lower levels of *for* expression in the brain than do individuals that work inside the nest (Ingram *et al.* 2005).

These findings suggest the existence of pathways that are highly conserved but evolutionarily labile enough to be involved with different manifestations of the same general behaviour across diverse species. The *for* gene might be part of such a pathway for feeding-related behaviour. Phylogenetic analysis supports the link between variation in *for* and variation in feeding-related behaviour in eukaryotes (Fitzpatrick & Sokolowski 2004).

The possible existence of such pathways is also important from a strategic perspective because it suggests that molecular insights from simpler (e.g., solitary) forms of behaviour can be used to generate candidate genes for more highly derived patterns of social behaviour. This idea is supported by additional fly–bee studies of another gene, *malvolio* (*mvl*), which encodes a manganese transporter expressed in neurons. A mutation at this locus in *D. melanogaster* causes a loss of responsiveness to sucrose, and this deficit is eliminated by treatment with manganese (Orgad *et al.* 1998). In honey bees, the situation resembles what is seen for the *for* gene: brain levels of *Ammvl* mRNA are higher in foragers than in bees working in the hive, and manganese treatment not only increases sucrose responsiveness but also causes an earlier onset of foraging (Ben-Shahar *et al.* 2004). These results suggest that some genes that influence feeding behaviour in *D. melanogaster* also have been used in social evolution to regulate division of labour in insect societies.

Feeding and Neuropeptide Y

Neuropeptide Y (NPY) is another molecule that appears to be involved in a well-conserved pathway for feeding-related behaviours. This neuropeptide has been studied intensively in the vertebrate hypothalamus for its involvement in regulating appetite (Schneider & Watts 2002). In *D. melanogaster,* neuropeptide F, an ortholog of NPY, influences several feeding-related behaviours including food aversion, hypermobility, and cooperative burrowing (Wu *et al.* 2003). In *C. elegans,* a naturally occurring variation in *npr-1,* a gene encoding a putative receptor for an NPY-like molecule, causes the following variation in feeding behaviour (de Bono & Bargmann 1998): some strains of nematodes feed alone on bacterial "lawns," whereas others aggregate while feeding. The behavioural differences are caused by a single amino acid difference in *npr-1.*

Aggregated feeding in *C. elegans* can be induced by stressful conditions, such as crowding and high concentrations of oxygen (Gray *et al.* 2004), but is inhibited by high NPY-like signalling in several neural circuits. In addition, nociceptive (pain-receptive) pathways promote *C. elegans* aggregation (de Bono *et al.* 2002). This result is consistent with an insight from behavioural ecology studies that show that group formation is often triggered by adverse conditions (Sokowloski 2002). Thus, *C. elegans* can be used to explore further the relationships between "pain," stress, and sociality. It is not clear whether *C. elegans* engage in the kinds of cooperative interactions that typically characterise social feeding (Alcock 1998), but to aggregate they must be able to tolerate having members of the same species in close proximity. Thus, plasticity in this type of affinity for members of the same species may be a prerequisite for more extensive social interaction.

Social Regulation of Gene Expression and Behaviour

Life in animal societies is often highly structured, with nearly all activities influenced by interactions with other society members. Social regulation influences when, how often, how intensely, and with whom these activities are performed. As the following examples illustrate, social regulation is now understood to involve changes in gene expression in the brain in response to specific social stimuli, which in turn affect behaviour.

Dominance-Related Interactions in *Haplochromis burtoni* and GnRH

Social status has profound influence on the physiology of society members. In vertebrates, this is mediated primarily by circulating stress hormones, such as cortisol, and their effects on immune and brain systems (Cacioppo *et al.* 2003), including neurogenesis (Kozorovitskiy & Gould 2004). In the African teleost (*Astatotilapia*) *Haplochromis burtoni,* the gene encoding the neuropeptide gonadotropin-releasing-hormone (GnRH) is involved in orchestrating changes in behaviour that enable an individual to respond adaptively to its current social status.

H. burtoni has two forms of males. Dominant males are aggressively territorial, brightly coloured, have high levels of circulating testosterone, and enjoy high levels of reproductive success. Subordinate males lack all these attributes and their derived reproductive advantages. Dominant males have larger hypothalamic neurons containing GnRH than do subordinate males (Hofmann *et al.* 1999; White *et al.* 2002). This neurohormone has a crucial function in the hypothalamic pituitary axis, which controls physiological and behavioural aspects of reproductive maturation in vertebrates. The larger size of these neurosecretory cells indicates the capacity for increased neurohormone release (Robison 2000). Larger cells also reflect increased expression of the GnRH gene.

GnRH expression in *H. burtoni* is sensitive to changes in social context (White *et al.* 2002). Dominance hierarchies are fluid, with a great deal of turnover of the territories used by males to attract females. Nonterritorial males that move up in social rank and acquire a territory rapidly show an increase in GnRH gene expression and acquire the suite of characteristics associated with dominance.

Parental Care in Rats and the Glucocortocoid Receptor Gene

Rat mothers (*Rattus norvegicus*) differ strikingly in how they care for their offspring. Those that lick, groom, and nurse their pups extensively endow them with two important attributes: better tolerance of stress and good mothering skills when they themselves get old enough to reproduce (Meaney 2001). This is because frequent contacts of these types increase the expression of the gene encoding a glucocortocoid receptor in the hippocampus, and greater hippocampal density of these receptors enables the animals to better regulate their response to stress hormones. Pups that receive less care grow up with fewer glucocortocoid receptors in the hippocampus, larger fluxes of stress hormones, and increased fearfulness, and they bestow less care upon their offspring.

The effects of high levels of maternal care involve histone acetylation and DNA demethylation in the promoter region of the glucocortocoid receptor gene, specifically of a response element for nerve growth factor-inducible protein A (NGFI-A) (Weaver *et al.* 2004). These epigenetic changes increase the ability of NGFI-A to up-regulate the expression of the glucocortocoid receptor gene. Individuals from litters that experienced poor maternal care and were treated with an inhibitor of histone deacetylation showed the high levels of stress tolerance and glucortocoid receptor gene expression typically seen after a more attentive upbringing.

Epigenetic inheritance of behaviour might have an adaptive significance by enabling rat mothers to produce offspring with temperaments appropriate for prevailing environmental conditions (Suomi 2004). For example, if rats in nature responded to harsh conditions by reducing maternal care, the resulting fearful and cautious offspring might themselves fare better under such conditions. Maternal effects similar to those observed in the rat have been detected in rhesus macaques (*Macaca mulatta*): stressful rearing conditions cause changes in adult behaviour, but epigenetic mechanisms have not yet been reported (Suomi 2004). The strength of the maternal effects in the rhesus macaque varies with genotype at the locus encoding a serotonin transporter (5HTT), providing an excellent example of how the interaction of genotype at an identified locus and the social environment can influence behaviour.

Pheromone Regulation of Brain Gene Expression Profiles and Behaviour in Honey Bees

Division of labour in honeybee colonies is stereotyped as described earlier, but not rigid. Bees are sensitive to changes in their environment, especially their social environment (Robinson 2002b). A flexible system of division of labour presumably is very important to colony fitness because a bee colony must develop and produce reproductive individuals despite constant changes in external and colony conditions. One response of worker bees to changing conditions is an alteration in their typical pattern of behavioural maturation. The transition from working in the hive to foraging can be accelerated, delayed, or even reversed. Plasticity in behavioural development in honey bees is socially regulated, mediated in part by pheromones produced by the queen, brood, and older adult bees (Leoncini et al. 2004).

Effects of queen mandibular pheromone (QMP) have been particularly well studied. QMP is a well-characterised blend that is part of a recently identified 9-component pheromone that attracts workers to attend the queen (Keeling et al. 2003). QMP consists of five chemicals: (E)-9-keto-2-decenoic acid (9-ODA); (R,E)-(–)- and (S,E)-(+)-9-hydroxy-2-decenoic acid (9HDA); methyl p-hydroxybenzoate (HOB); and 4-hydroxy-3-methyoxyphenylethanol (HVA). QMP plays many roles in social regulation of physiology and behaviour in bee colonies including the prevention of worker reproduction, development of the olfactory system, and age-related division of labour (Morgan et al. 1998; Hoover et al. 2002). QMP delays honey bee behavioural maturation (Pankiw et al. 1998).

Microarray analysis revealed that QMP exposure causes changes in gene expression profiles in the brain (Grozinger et al. 2003). QMP exposure resulted in changes in expression of ~2,500 genes in the bee brain, about half of them up-regulated and half down-regulated. This is about 40% of the ~5,500 genes on the microarray (estimated to represent ~40% of the genes in the bee genome). Many of these QMP-induced changes in brain gene expression correlate with the downstream behavioural effects of the pheromone. Comparing these results with those from another microarray study (Whitfield et al. 2003), Grozinger and colleagues (2003) reported that QMP tends to up-regulate genes associated with brood care and down-regulates genes associated with foraging. This is consistent with previous results showing that QMP delays honey bee behavioural maturation (Pankiw et al. 1998). It appears that transcription factors are important targets of pheromone activation because the proportion of transcription factors regulated by QMP was relatively high compared with other functional groups of genes. Because transcription factors regulate the expression of other genes, they may initiate socially regulated "transcriptional programmes" that control the behavioural effects of pheromones.

Conclusions and Future Prospects

This chapter highlights two emerging themes relating to the connection between genes and social behaviour. First, genes involved in solitary behaviour are also used for social behaviour. The possible existence of such evolutionarily labile pathways suggests that studies on the evolution of social behaviour can parallel the successful gene-based approach to the study of the evolution of development (Carroll *et al.* 2005). At a more practical level, molecular insights from simple behaviour can be used to generate candidate genes for more highly derived patterns of social behaviour.

The second emerging theme is that the genome is highly sensitive to social influence. Social regulation of gene expression has a powerful influence on behaviour. Two-way communication between the nervous system and the genome may contribute fundamentally to the control of social behaviour. Information acquired by the nervous system on social conditions likely induces changes in genomic function that, in turn, adaptively modify the structure and functioning of the nervous system. As gene regulation becomes better understood (Harbison *et al.* 2004), it will be important to determine the extent that sociality involves unique forms of transcriptional regulatory codes, as well as novel genes (Robinson & Ben-Shahar 2002).

Several components are essential for a truly rigorous molecular analysis of social behaviour. There must be strong efforts to further enhance the value of "model social species" by developing genomic resources such as expressed sequence tags (EST) collections, microarrays, and a wide variety of freely available cDNA and genomic libraries. For the most compelling species, strong efforts should also be made to obtain full genome sequences, which at present is the ultimate resource for analysing genes and genomes.

It is also necessary to establish causal relationships between the effects of genes on social behaviour, and vice versa. This means increasing or decreasing the expression of specific genes in specific tissues or brain regions at specific points in an animal's life. Gene targeting is done routinely in the model genetic organisms, notably in studies of learning and memory and chronobiology (Sokolowski 2002; Rankin 2002; Bucan and Abel 2002). New approaches likely will be developed because of intense interest by the pharmaceutical industry in developing new therapeutics that act on the genome, using techniques such as RNAi, viral vectors, and nanovectors (Kreuter 2001). RNAi already is being used to test hypotheses of gene function in the honey bee, an example of a species that is favourable for studies of social behaviour but lacks efficient breeding-based transgenic resources (Beye *et al.* 2003; Farooqui *et al.* 2004).

Behaviour is orchestrated by interplay between inherited and environmental influences acting on the same substrate: the genome (Robinson 2004). A complete understanding of genes and behaviour will come only by studying many different types of naturally occurring behaviours in a diverse array of behavioural model organisms. It is now possible to exploit advances in molecular biology and genomics to do this. This enterprise, if grounded in the deep insights into behavioural ecology achieved over the past several decades, promises to illuminate our understanding of both the mechanisms and evolution of behaviour.

Acknowledgments

Portions of this chapter appeared in Robinson *et al.* (2005); I thank my coauthors for permission to use some material from that article here. I am grateful for grants from the National Institutes of Health, National Science Foundation, U.S. Department of Agriculture, University of Illinois Critical Research Initiatives, and the Burroughs-Wellcome Fund that funded research in my laboratory, and I especially thank the members of my laboratory, past and present, who contributed to it.

References

Alcock, J. 1998. *Animal Behavior; An Evolutionary Approach*, 8th edn., Sunderland, Massachusetts: Sinauer.

Ben-Shahar, Y., Robichon, A., Sokolowski, M. B. & Robinson, G. E. 2002. Behavior influenced by gene action across different time scales. *Science*, **296**, 742–744.

Ben-Shahar, Y., Leung, H. T., Pak, W. L., Sokolowski, M. B. & Robinson, G. E. 2003. cGMP-dependent changes in phototaxis: a possible role for the foraging gene in honey bee division of labour. *Journal of Experimental Biology*, **206**, 2507–2515.

Ben-Shahar, Y., Dudek, N. L. & Robinson, G. E. 2004. Phenotypic deconstruction reveals involvement of manganese transporter malvolio in honey bee division of labour. *Journal of Experimental Biology*, **207**, 3281–3288.

Beye, M., Hasselmann, M., Fondrk, M. K., Page, R. E. & Omholt, S. W. 2003. The gene csd is the primary signal for sexual development in the honeybee and encodes an SR-type protein. *Cell*, **114**, 419–429.

Boake, C. R. B., Arnold, S. J., Breder F., Meffert, L. M., Ritchie, M. J., Taylor, B., Wolf, J. B. & Moore, A. J. 2002. Genetic tools for studying adaptation and the evolution of behavior. *American Naturalist*, **160**, S143–S159.

Bucan, M. & Abel, T. 2002. The mouse: genetics meets behaviour. *Nature Reviews Genetics*, **3**, 114–123.

Cacioppo, J. T., Berntson, G. G., Taylor, S. E., & Schacter, D. L. ed. 2002. *Foundations in Social Neuroscience*. Cambridge, Massachusetts: Bradford Books, MIT Press.

Carroll, S. B., Grenier, J. K. & Weatherbee, S. D. 2005. *From DNA to Diversity: Molecular Genetics and the Evolution of Animal Design*, 2nd edn. Oxford: Blackwell Science.

de Bono, M. & Bargmann, C. I. 1998. Natural variation in a neuropeptide Y receptor homolog modifies social behavior and food response in *C. elegans*. *Cell*, **94**, 679–689.

de Bono, M., Tobin, D. M., Davis, M. W., Avery, L. & Bargmann, C. I. 2002. Social feeding in *Caenorhabditis elegans* is induced by neurons that detect aversive stimuli. *Nature*, **419**, 899–903.

7. Genes and Social Behaviour **111**

Farooqui, T., Vaessin, H. & Smith, B. H. 2004. Octopamine receptors in the honeybee (*Apis mellifera*) brain and their disruption by RNA-mediated interference. *Journal of Insect Physiology,* **50,** 701–713.

Fitzpatrick, M. J., Ben-Shahar, Y., Smid, H. M., Vet, L. E. M., Robinson, G. E. & Sokolowski, M. B. 2005. Candidate genes for behavioural ecology. *Trends in Ecology & Evolution,* **20,** 96–104.

Fitzpatrick, M. J. & Sokolowski, M. B. 2004. In search of food: exploring the evolutionary link between cGMP-dependent protein kinase (PKG) and behaviour. *Integrated Comparative Biology,* **44,** 28–36.

Fujiwara, M., Sengupta, P. & McIntire, S. L. 2002. Regulation of body size and behavioral state of *C. elegans* by sensory perception and the EGL-4 cGMP-dependent protein kinase. *Neuron,* **36,** 1091–1102.

Gray, J. M., Karow, D. S., Lu, H., Chang, A. J., Chang, J. S., Ellis, R. E., Marletta, M. A., Bargmann, C. I. 2004. Oxygen sensation and social feeding mediated by a *C. elegans* guanylate cyclase homologue. *Nature,* **430,** 317–322.

Grozinger, C. M., Sharabash, N. M., Whitfield, C. W. & Robinson, G. E. 2003. Pheromone-mediated gene expression in the honey bee brain. *Proceedings of the National Academy of Sciences of the USA,* **100,** Suppl 2, 14519–14525 (2003).

Harbison, C. T., Gordon, D. B., Lee, T. I., Rinaldi, N. J., Macisaac, K. D., Danford, T.W., Hannett, N. M., Tagne, J. B., Reynolds, D. B., Yoo, J., Jennings, E. G., Zeitlinger, J., Pokholok, D. K., Kellis, M., Rolfe, P. A., Takusagawa, K. T., Lander, E. S., Gifford, D. K., Fraenkel, E., Young, R. A. 2004. Transcriptional regulatory code of a eukaryotic genome. *Nature,* **431,** 99–104.

Hofmann, H. A., Benson, M. E. & Fernald, R. D. 1999. Social status regulates growth rate: consequences for life-history strategies. *Proceedings of the National Academy of Sciences of the USA,* **96,** 14171–14176.

Hoover, S. E. R., Keeling, C. I., Winston, M. L. & Slessor, K. N. 2002. The effect of queen pheromones on worker honey bee ovary development. *Naturwissenschaften,* **90,** 477–480.

Ingram, K. K., Oefner, P. & Gordon, D. M. 2005. Task-specific expression of the *foraging* gene in harvester ants. *Molecular Ecology,* **14,** 813–818.

Insel, T. R. & Young, L. J. 2001. The neurobiology of attachment. *Nature Reviews. Neuroscience,* **2,** 129–136.

Keeling, C. I., Slessor, K. N., Higo, H. A. & Winston, M. L. 2003. New components of the honey bee (*Apis mellifera L.*) queen retinue pheromone. *Proceedings of the National Academy of Sciences of the USA,* **100,** 4486–4491.

Kozorovitskiy, Y. & Gould, E. 2004. Dominance hierarchy influences adult neurogenesis in the dentate gyrus. *Journal of Neuroscience,* **24,** 6755–6759.

Kreuter, J. 2001. Nanoparticulate systems for brain delivery of drugs. *Advanced Drug Delivery Reviews,* **47,** 65–81.

Leoncini, I., Le Conte, Y., Costagliola, G., Plettner, E., Toth, A. L., Wang, M., Huang, Z., Becard, J. M., Crauser, D. Slessor, K. N., Robinson, G. E. 2004. Regulation of behavioral maturation in honey bees by a new primer pheromone. *Proceedings of the National Academy of Sciences of the USA,* **101,** 17559–17564.

Lim, M. M., Wang, Z., Olazabal, D. E., Ren, X., Terwilliger, E. F., Young, L. J. 2004. Enhanced partner preference in a promiscuous species by manipulating the expression of a single gene. *Nature,* **429,** 754–757.

Maynard Smith, J. & Szathmáry, E. 1995. *The Major Transitions in Evolution.* New York: Oxford University Press.

Meaney, M. J. 2001. Maternal care, gene expression, and the transmission of individual differences in stress reactivity across generations. *Annual Review of Neurosciences,* **4,** 1161–1192.

Morgan, S. M., Butz Huryn, V. M., Downes, S. R. & Mercer, A. R. 1998. The effects of queenlessness on the maturation of the honey bee olfactory system. *Behavioural Brain Research,* **91,** 115–126.

Orgad, S., Nelson, H., Segal, D. & Nelson, N. 1998. Metal ions suppress the abnormal taste behavior of the *Drosophila* mutant *malvolio*. *Journal of Experimental Biology,* **201,** 115–120.

Osborne, K. A., Robichon, A., Burgess, E., Butland, S., Shaw, R. A., Coulthard, A., Pereira, H. S., Greenspan, R. J., Sokolowski, M. B. 1997. Natural behaviour polymorphism due to a cGMP-dependent protein kinase of *Drosophila. Science,* **277,** 834–836.

Pankiw, T., Huang, Z-Y., Winston, M. L. & Robinson, G. E. 1998. Queen mandibular gland pheromone influences worker honey bee (*Apis mellifera L.*) juvenile hormone titers and foraging ontogeny. *Journal of Insect Physiology,* **44,** 685–692.

Pfaff, D. W. 1999. *Drive: Neurobiological and Molecular Mechanisms of Sexual Motivation.* Cambridge, Massachusetts: Bradford Books, MIT Press.

Rankin, C. H. 2002. From gene to identified neuron to behaviour in *Caenorhabditis elegans. Nature Reviews Genetics,* **3,** 622–630.

Robinson, G. E. 1997. Integrative animal behaviour and sociogenomics. *Trends in Ecology & Evolution,* **14,** 202–205.

Robinson, G. E. 1999. Integrative animal behaviour and sociogenomics. *Trends in Ecology & Evolution,* **14,** 202–205.

Robinson, G. E. 2002a. Sociogenomics takes flight. *Science,* **297,** 204–205.

Robinson, G. E. 2002b. Genomics and integrative analyses of division of labor in honeybee colonies. *American Naturalist,* **160,** S160–S172.

Robinson, G. E. 2004. Beyond nature and nurture. *Science,* **304,** 397–399.

Robinson, G. E. & Ben-Shahar Y. 2002. Social behavior and comparative genomics: new genes or new gene regulation? *Genes, Brain & Behavior,* **4,** 197–203.

Robinson G. E., Fahrbach, S. E. & Winston, M. L. 1997. Insect societies and the molecular biology of social behavior. *Bioessays,* **19,** 1099–1108.

Robinson, G. E., Grozinger, C. M. & Whitfield, C. W. 2005. Sociogenomics: social life in molecular terms. *Nature Reviews Genetics,* **6,** 257–270.

Robison, R. R. 2000. Social regulation of reproduction. Doctoral dissertation, Stanford University.

Ruppell, O., Pankiw, T. & Page, R. E. Jr. 2004. Pleiotropy, epistasis and new QTL: The genetic architecture of honey bee foraging behavior. *Journal of Heredity,* **95,** 481–491.

Schneider, J. E. & Watts, G. A. 2002. Energy balance, ingestive behavior and reproductive success. In: *Hormones, Brain, and Behavior* (Ed. by D. W. Pfaff A. P. Arnold, A. M. Etgen, S. E. Fahrbach & R. Rubin), pp. 435–525. New York: Academic Press.

Sokolowski, M. B. 2001. Drosophila: genetics meets behaviour. *Nature Reviews Genetics,* **2,** 879–890.

Sokowloski, M. B. 2002. Social eating for stress. *Nature,* **419,** 893–894.

Stearns, S. C. & Magwene, P. 2003. The naturalist in a world of genomics. *American Naturalist,* **161,** 171–180.

Suomi, S. J. 2005. Genetic and environmental factors influencing the expression of impulsive aggression and serotonergic functioning in rhesus monkeys. In: *Developmental Origins of Aggression* (Ed. by R. M. Tremblay, W. W. Hartup & J. Archer), pp. 63–82. New York: Guilford Press.

Tully, T. 1996. Discovery of genes involved with learning and memory: An experimental synthesis of Hirschian and Benzerian perspectives. *Proceedings of the National Academy of Sciences of the USA,* **93,** 13460–13467.

von Frisch, K. 1967. *Dance Language and Orientation of the Honey Bee.* Cambridge, Massachusetts: Harvard University Press.

Weaver, I. C. Cervoni, N., Champagne, F. A., D'Alessio, A. C., Sharma, S., Seckl, J. R., Dymov, S., Szyf, M. & Meaney, M. J. 2004. Epigenetic programming by maternal behavior. *Nature Reviews Neuroscience,* **7,** 847–854.

White, S. A., Nguyen, T. & Fernald, R. D. 2002. Social regulation of gonadotropin-releasing hormone. *Journal of Experimental Biology,* **205,** 2567–2581.

Whitfield, C. W., Cziko, A. M. & Robinson, G. E. 2003. Gene expression profiles in the brain predict behavior in individual honey bees. *Science,* **302,** 296–299.

Wilson, E. O. 1975. *Sociobiology: The New Synthesis,* Cambridge, Massachusetts: Harvard University Press.

Wu, Q., Wen, T., Lee, G., Park, J. H., Cai, H. N. & Shen, P. 2003. Developmental control of foraging and social behavior by the *Drosophila* neuropeptide Y-like system. *Neuron,* **39,** 147–161.

8

Control of Behavioural Strategies for Capricious Environments

John C. Wingfield
Department of Zoology
University of Washington

Abstract

In addition to seasonal changes in morphology, physiology and behaviour that occur in predictable annual cycles, there are facultative responses to unpredictable events known as labile (i.e. short-lived) perturbation factors. These rapid behavioural and physiological changes have been termed the 'emergency life-history stage' and serve to enhance lifetime fitness. There are four major components: (1) proactive/reactive coping styles for responding to psychosocial stress, predation, and so forth; (2) fight-or-flight responses to rapid emergencies such as an attack by a predator or sudden severe storm; (3) 'take-it-or-leave-it' behavioural and physiological responses to longer-term perturbations of the physical environment; and (4) sickness behaviour and fever designed to respond to infection. Glucocorticosteroids interact with cytokines and with other hormones in the hypothalamo-pituitary-adrenal cascade and in the autonomic nervous system to initiate and orchestrate the emergency life-history stage within minutes to hours. Some traits of the emergency life-history stage include: redirection of behaviour from a normal life-history stage to increased foraging, irruptive-type migration during the day, enhanced restfulness at night, elevated gluconeogenesis, and recovery once the perturbation passes. These physiological and behavioural changes allow an individual to avoid potential deleterious effects of stress that may result from chronically elevated levels of circulating glucocorticosteroids over days and weeks. Thus, acute rises in gluco-corticosteroids following perturbations of the environment may serve primarily as 'antistress' hormones, potentially allowing individuals to avoid chronic stress. Several field studies in diverse habitats indicate that individuals in free-living populations show elevated circulating levels of corticosteroids when they are in an emergency life-history stage. Some simple models based on food availability, body condition, social status and life-history stage, may allow predictions of sensitivity of the hypothalamo-pituitary-adrenal axis to labile perturbation factors. Although there is now extensive evidence for behavioural components of the emergency life-history stage in birds, there remains much to be learned about how other vertebrate groups, especially fish, cope with perturbations of the environment. Because of the unpredictable nature of these perturbations, systematic study of behavioural responses to them is not possible and investigators need to be 'opportunistic'. There is also a growing need to expand our knowledge of these phenomena because human disturbance, global climate change and pollution are all major perturbations of the environment. How vertebrates respond to the unpredictable in general will thus have important conservation value for the future.

One of the most critical actions any animal will take is to deal with a perturbation of its environment. Sometime during the like cycle, an individual will have to cope with a sudden event such as an attack by a predator or dominant conspecific. It must also be ready to respond to slower environmental challenges such as inclement weather, change in food supply, and so forth. Not surprisingly, vertebrates have evolved highly effective behavioural and physiological strategies to cope with a capricious environment. Because virtually no habitat on earth is static except, perhaps, thermal vents in the deep ocean, organisms must anticipate environmental change and respond appropriately (Jacobs 1996). If the changes in environmental conditions are highly predictable, no matter how severe, organisms are able to modify their morphology, physiology and behaviour in anticipation of the change and reduce the potential for stress. However, unpredictable events in the environment have the potential to disrupt the predictable life cycle with potentially disastrous consequences. Indeed, in some cases, mass mortality in a population may occur, but in the majority of instances, individuals within a population are able to cope with a remarkably broad spectrum of perturbations. These can be physical, such as an attack or violent weather, internal as in the case of wounding and infection, or of longer duration as in response to prolonged inclement weather or a change in population density of predators. Is there any pattern to the physiological and behavioural responses to these diverse perturbations? Furthermore, are there any underlying hormone control mechanisms? Information on the behavioural and physiological responses to perturbations is fragmentary but patterns do possibly exist. Hormonal control mechanisms are better known, but most have been conducted under highly artificial conditions in the laboratory. Here, I review some examples of environmental perturbations and then outline hypotheses put forward to explain how vertebrate organisms respond to them. Finally, I discuss the hormonal mechanisms underlying these behavioural and physiological responses.

Many organisms adjust their phenotype to maximize fitness in any given habitat (Stearns 1989; West-Eberhard 1989). This is especially true if predictable changes occur between generations as in many invertebrates. However, in long-lived organisms such as vertebrates, predictable changes in environmental conditions occur within generations. In these cases, a single phenotype must be able to change its physiology, morphology and behaviour as environmental conditions fluctuate (i.e. analogous to a genotype expressing different phenotypes at the population level; Jacobs & Wingfield 2000). In other words, a single phenotype in a predictably oscillating environment must express several phenotypic or life-history stages (i.e. breeding, nonbreeding, migration, moult, etc.) that maximize fitness throughout the organism's lifetime. Each stage has its own characteristic set of substages that can be expressed in varying ways (Jacobs 1996; Jacobs & Wingfield 2000; Fig. 8-1), and the combination of substages expressed at any point in an individual's lifetime represents its state (Wingfield & Jacobs 1999).

A crucial factor that is often overlooked is that day-to-day conditions also have a highly unpredictable component that has great potential to be stressful. Thus, in addition to the predictable series of life-history stages within an organism's life cycle, there is an 'emergency life-history stage' (Fig. 8-1) triggered by unpredictable events in the environment, termed modifying factors or labile perturbation factors (Jacobs 1996; Wingfield *et al.* 1998; Wingfield & Kitaysky 2002). These unpredictable perturbations trigger facultative behavioural and physiological responses that make up the emergency life-history stage. They also include 'fight-or-flight' responses, proactive/reactive coping styles and sickness behaviour (Fig. 8-2). In general, the components of this stage allow an organism to tailor the most appropriate response to any combination of environmental perturbations.

Examples of Labile Perturbation Factors

Floods can have dramatic effects on survival and growth of fish such as in *Oncorhynchus* salmon (Heard 1991; Sandercock 1991). An unpredictable

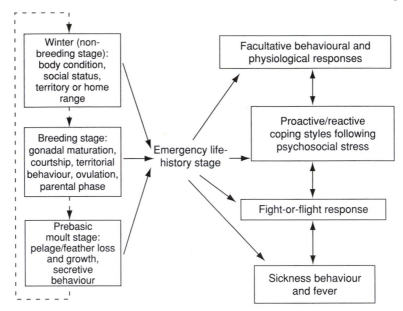

Figure 8-1 Scheme showing examples of life-history stages and components of the emergency life-history stage for a nonmigratory bird. Each has a unique set of substages. The progression of life-history stages is one way, with each cycle taking 1 year. The temporal progression of normal life-history stages (breeding, non-breeding, moult) is regulated by the predictable annual cycle. Superimposed upon this predictable life cycle are unpredictable events, such as severe storms, predator pressure and human disturbance. These labile perturbation factors have the potential to trigger the emergency life-history stage, which redirects the individual away from the normal life-history stage into survival mode. Once the perturbation passes, the individual can then return to a life-history stage appropriate for that time of year. The emergency life-history stage has four characteristic components. Proactive/reactive coping styles define how an individual responds to a given perturbation. The 'fight-or-flight response' is typical of very rapid responses to, for example, sudden attack by a predator. If the perturbation is an infection, or a wounding following an attack by a predator, then sickness behaviour and fever may result. Responses to other less acute labile perturbation factors such as a severe storm trigger facultative behavioural and physiological responses (see Koolhaas *et al.* 1999; Jacobs & Wingfield 2000; Wingfield & Romero 2001).

flood can scour the stream bed, destroying redds (nests) and even disrupting spawning behaviour. High water velocity, increased turbidity and moving gravel and detritus increase energy required to stay on territory, decrease feeding efficiency and may elevate risk of injury due to moving objects. A population of cutthroat trout, *O. clarkii,* in the Cascade Mountains of Oregon, U.S.A., was decimated by flood-induced debris flow that scoured the creek. However, recovery was rapid, and within a year, young cutthroat trout had repopulated the area (Lamberti *et al.* 1991). In coho salmon, *O. kisutch,* yearlings can be swept downstream during spates. They will take up new territories if good habitat is found, or may be harassed further by local

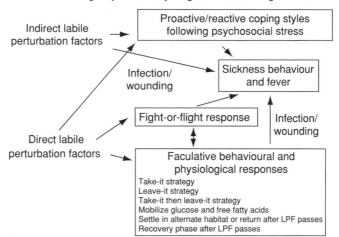

Emergency life-history stage and its substages

Figure 8-2 The emergency life-history stage can be divided into several substages within four major components: proactive/reactive coping styles, fight-or-flight responses, facultative behavioural and physiological responses (such as seeking a refuge, leaving the area, mobilization of energy, etc.; see text) and sickness behaviour and fever. All of these components and their substages are interconnected and can be expressed sequentially or simultaneously depending upon the circumstances. Indirect labile perturbation factors are usually very rapid and do not necessarily interrupt the normal sequence of life-history stages. Thus, they only trigger fight-or-flight responses. However, if wounding or infection results from this type of perturbation, then sickness behaviour and fever may follow (upper part of figure). Direct labile perturbation factors have the potential to disrupt the sequence of life-history stages and may also trigger a fight-or-flight response in some circumstances. Once again, wounding or infection would then trigger sickness behaviour and fever. These components and their substages allow the individual to tailor the expression of an emergency life-history stage precisely to the circumstances and the type of labile perturbation factor (LPF) experienced.

resident fish (Healey 1991). During winter when floods are more frequent, or when freezing is possible in shallow water, coho salmon move into deeper, slow-flowing side channels or into ponds (e.g. created by beavers, *Castor canadensis,* etc.) that provide shelter from spates and severe winter weather. Although these deeper-water habitats may decrease feeding opportunities, increase risk of predation, and force formation of large aggregations, aggression is decreased (Healey 1991). In general, such spates may have potentially catastrophic effects on stream- and river-dwelling fish, but recovery can be rapid. Unpredictable spates appear to be the most devastating, especially in river systems highly modified by humans (Junk *et al.* 1989).

For terrestrial vertebrates, storms can be equally disruptive. Severe weather such as prolonged heavy rain and low temperatures reduce insect food available for breeding songbirds to feed young. As a result, adults lose weight and eventually may abandon the nest and temporarily leave the territory to find food to sustain themselves (Wingfield *et al*. 1983). Rains may also flood nests, resulting in reproductive failure (Wingfield 1984, 1985a, b). After the storm passes, most of the population may begin breeding again, often on the same territory and with the same mate (Wingfield 1988).

In complete contrast, the 10-year cycle of abundance in snowshoe hares, *Lepus americanus,* is an example of a longer-term perturbation. Expansion of hare populations is accompanied by a similar increase in numbers of predators such as the lynx, *Lynx canadensis*. Soon thereafter, a population decline of hares occurs, followed by a decline in predators. The approximately 10-year cycle appears to be driven by predation risk on hares, and is not a function of increasing population outstripping food supplies. Nor does it appear to be caused by increased social interactions as the population peaks (Krebs *et al*. 2001). Evidence to date suggests that as the numbers of predators increase following the rise in hare numbers, risk of predation (by far the major cause of mortality) forces hares into habitat that provides sanctuary but is poor in food. Hares are thus forced to move into open areas where predation increases dramatically, indicating that the population cycle appears to be driven by an interaction of food and predation (Krebs *et al*. 2001). Although the 10-year cycle could be interpreted as predictable, the actual demise of the hares is probably a result of chronic stress resulting from the increasing risk of predation, a true perturbation.

It appears that all vertebrates may have behavioural and physiological strategies for dealing with unpredictable events in the environment. Much more work is needed to investigate what these strategies may be in less well-known vertebrate groups, and whether the emergency life-history stage is ubiquitous among vertebrates in general. Given that effective strategies to cope with perturbations have the potential to greatly enhance lifetime fitness, it seems likely that they may be widespread.

Next, I describe the different types of labile perturbations and how these can affect normal life-history stages and trigger emergency strategies.

Types of Labile Perturbations or Modifying Factors

A wide variety of environmental events have been shown to disrupt an organism's life cycle. Some of these include human disturbance, global climate change, and so forth, providing application of these kinds of studies to conservation biology. Such disruptive environmental factors are usually transient (i.e. 'labile'). On the other hand, human development and disturbance may represent permanent changes that force organisms to leave the area. Nevertheless, labile perturbation factors can be divided into two major groups.

Indirect

Indirect labile perturbations are rapid events that do not affect the organism directly in the sense of reducing food or access to it. An example in birds is when an individual loses a nest or offspring to a predator. Renesting may follow immediately (Wingfield 1988). Another example is a sudden severe storm (e.g. hail storm) that temporarily interrupts migration or destroys a nest. Once again, the normal life-history stage will resume quickly, once the storm passes.

Direct

Direct labile perturbations are usually longer-term environmental events that force an individual, for example, to abandon a nest or offspring, or interrupt migration because of reduced resources such as food. Examples are weather, an influx of predators, a drop in social status, human disturbance, pollution/endocrine disrupters and disease. Note that in these cases, the nest of a breeding bird may not be affected (as in indirect perturbations) and thus the stimulus to continue feeding young or incubating remains. However, after exposure to a direct labile perturbation factor, birds will eventually abandon the nest despite the normal stimuli to keep on breeding. That is, they are redirected into a survival mode and away from the normal life-history stage (Wingfield et al. 1998; Fig. 8-1). Once the perturbation passes, the individuals return to the same life-history stage, or the next one in the cycle if the perturbation is prolonged (Wingfield & Kitaysky 2002). Once again, there is a great need to investigate the types of perturbations that affect other vertebrates, and whether the behavioural and physiological strategies for dealing with them are common to vertebrates in general.

The Emergency Life-history Stage

Although the effects of indirect perturbations are very transient (minutes or so), recovery from them may be prolonged (e.g. renesting) and is not well studied. However, the longer-lasting effects of direct perturbation factors are better known, especially for birds and mammals, and the control mechanisms involved are complex. To my knowledge, the strategies for responding to direct labile perturbation factors in general have not been summarized before. The scheme below reflects the current view and will hopefully have heuristic value to stimulate further research in this area.

Strategies for Coping with a Capricious Environment

There are four major types of coping strategies within the emergency life-history stage (physiology and behaviour, Fig. 8-2).

(1) Proactive/reactive coping styles in response to psychosocial stress (Koolhaas *et al.* 1999). In general, these coping styles are mediated by the hypothalamopituitary-adrenal axis and the hypothalamo-pituitary gonad axis (e.g. testosterone).

(2) The fight-or-flight responses such as antipredator aggression. These behavioural strategies are mediated by the sympathetic branch of the autonomic nervous system, particularly epinephrine.

(3) The 'take-it-or-leave-it' physiological and behavioural strategy mediated by the hypothalamo-pituitary-adrenal cortex (steroids and associated peptides). Free-living animals exposed to direct labile perturbation factors often have elevated circulating levels of glucocorticosteroids (e.g. Kitaysky *et al.* 1999a, b, 2001a; Wingfield & Romero 2001).

(4) Sickness behaviour and associated responses of the immune system including fever. These are mediated by cytokines such as interleukin and also by prostaglandins (e.g. Hart 1988; Kent *et al.* 1992; Brebner *et al.* 2000).

These four types of emergency life-history stage are not mutually exclusive and, during very severe perturbations, may be expressed simultaneously, or in various combinations. Furthermore, there is growing evidence that specific coping 'styles' gained from prior experience through maternal effects and/or during development (Kitaysky *et al.* 2001b, 2003) or determined genetically (e.g. Koolhaas *et al.* 1999; Veenema *et al.* 2003) may overlap extensively with other components of the emergency life-history stage. Much more work is needed to explore these exciting new areas in vertebrates in general.

Proactive/Reactive Coping Styles for Psychosocial Stress

There is an extensive literature on individual differences in how vertebrates deal with psychosocial stress among conspecifics. Although the concept of 'coping styles' has been debated for many years, it is clear that two major types occur. These two coping styles are identifiable despite domestication in agricultural animals and genetic selection in laboratory mammals, but they have been classified in various ways. Koolhaas *et al.* (1999) suggested a grouping that would be applicable to vertebrates in general: (1) a proactive coping style is an active response to a social challenge involving aggression and (2) a reactive coping style is characterized by behavioural immobility and low aggression. Koolhaas *et al.* (1999) then evaluated whether these coping styles and aggression, at the individual level, are related to how individuals respond to perturbations in general. For example, proactive males may show an aggressive behavioural response to challenges, whereas reactive males respond to the same cues with mild aggression, and then, only when absolutely necessary. Not surprisingly, the two coping styles also show characteristic hormonal responses (Table 8-1). The hypothalamo-pituitary-adrenal axis (e.g. glucocorticosteroid) activity at baseline (before exposure to a challenge) and responsiveness (to a challenge) are low in the proactive style and normal or high in the reactive style (Koolhaas *et al.* 1999). Sympathetic and parasympathetic branches of the autonomic nervous system respond differently as well, and testosterone responses to challenges may be higher in proactive than in reactive coping styles (Koolhaas *et al.* 1999; Table 8-1). This hypothesis is eminently testable and future investigations on all the vertebrate taxa would provide valuable information in relation to individual differences in coping styles.

The Fight-or-Flight Response

The proactive/reactive styles of coping can also be extended to interactions of other kinds, including those with other species such as predators. One of the immediate responses (i.e. within seconds or less) to perturbations such as an attack by a predator, dominant individual or severe storm (e.g. hail, tornado) is the fight-or-flight response that triggers immediate avoidance behaviour and self-defence. This well-known physiological and behavioural response, which is regulated by the sympathetic branch of the autonomic nervous system (e.g. via the vagus nerve), includes release of epinephrine by the adrenal medulla and its equivalent (chromaffin tissue) in nonmammalian vertebrates (Axelrod & Reisine 1984; Norris 1996; Young & Landsberg 2001). Responses in mammals include increased heart rate, dilation of capillaries in muscles, dilation of pupils of the eyes, constriction of blood flow to the gut, rapid mobilization of glucose from glycogen, piloerection and increased respiration rate. Together these effects increase metabolism and direct energy to the brain and muscles rather than less immediately critical organs such as the gut. They also increase awareness and performance in the face

Table 8-1 Physiological and neuroendocrine responses to proactive and reactive coping styles of vertebrates to psychosocial stress

Endocrine system	Proactive	Reactive
Hypothalamo-pituitary-adrenal axis activity	Low	Normal
Hypothalamo-pituitary-adrenal axis response	Low	High
Sympathetic response	High	Low
Parasympathetic response	Low	High
Testosterone activity	High	Low

Summarized from Koolhaas *et al.* (1999).

of possible attack. Simultaneous release of endorphins in the brain may also act as an analgesic to defer pain and distraction from the immediate fight-or-flight response (see Sapolsky 1992).

Take-It-or-Leave-It Strategy

There are several components to this complex behavioural and physiological strategy (Wingfield & Ramenofsky 1999; Wingfield & Kitaysky 2002). First, the current life-history stage must be deactivated (e.g. reduced territorial behaviour, abandonment of current reproductive effort, etc.). Second, there are two, and possibly three, substrategies that may be adopted.

(1) Movements away from the source of the perturbation factor ('leave-it' strategy).
(2) If the individual remains, it will seek a refuge ('take-it' strategy).
(3) Seek a refuge first, then move away if conditions do not improve (first 'take-it', then 'leave-it' strategy).

The third component involves mobilization of stored energy sources such as fat and perhaps protein to fuel movement away from the source of the perturbation, or to provide energy while sheltering in a refuge. Fourth, if the animal leaves its habitat, then suitable alternate habitat must be sought, or movement will continue until the perturbation passes. Fifth, the organism must settle in alternate habitat once an appropriate site is identified or return to the original site and resume the normal sequence of life-history stages (Wingfield & Ramenofsky 1999; Wingfield & Kitaysky 2002).

There is now strong evidence that increased secretion of glucocorticosteroids from adrenocortical tissue and other peptides involved in the hypothalamo-pituitary-adrenal axis regulate all aspects of the take-it or leave-it strategies. These mechanisms may be largely conserved throughout the vertebrate classes (Wingfield et al. 1998; Wingfield & Ramenofsky 1999; Wingfield & Romero 2001; Wingfield & Kitaytsky 2002). This suite of physiological and behavioural responses is temporary (hours to days) and maximizes the likelihood of survival in the face of direct labile perturbation factors. If future research indicates that all vertebrates respond in a similar manner, then there may have been strong selection for the mechanisms that trigger an emergency life-history stage for a long period of evolutionary history.

Effects of Glucocorticosteroids in an Emergency Life-history Stage

Growing evidence suggests that within minutes to hours of a response to a labile perturbation, elevated levels of glucocorticosteroids have multiple effects. These effects include suppression of reproductive behaviour (without regression of the reproductive system), regulation of the immune system, increased gluconeogenesis, increased foraging behaviour, promotion of escape (irruptive) behaviour during the day, enhanced night restfulness, and more rapid recovery on return to the normal life-history stage (reviewed in Wingfield & Ramenofsky 1999; Sapolsky *et al.* 2000; Wingfield & Romero 2001). Contrast these effects with those of prolonged high levels of glucocorticosteroids resulting from chronic stress (days to weeks): inhibition of the reproductive system, suppression of the immune system, promotion of severe protein loss (muscle wasting), disruption of second cell messengers, neuronal cell death and suppression of growth (Sapolsky 1992; Sapolsky *et al.* 2000; Wingfield & Romero 2001).

The short-term effects of glucocorticosteroids during a response to direct labile perturbation factors may be advantageous because they suppress unnecessary physiological and behavioural functions, activate alternate behavioural patterns that promote survival (i.e. temporary emergency behaviour) and increase gluconeogenesis to avoid the long-term effects of high levels of glucocorticosteroids induced by stress. Effects on the immune system may be particularly complex in response to perturbations. Although stress alters immunocompetence, it is not necessarily immunosuppressive per se and may even enhance some aspects of immune function (Apanius 1998). Both the proactive/reactive coping styles and the 'take-it' or 'leave-it' strategies may prepare immune systems of organisms for wounding, infection, and so forth. In laboratory rats, acute stress (2 h) results in increased movement of immune cells to the skin and this may be mediated by corticosteroids. Immuno-enhancing effects may also involve gamma interferon (Dhabar 2002). Clearly, our understanding of how stress hormones and the immune system interact is changing, and more investigation in ecological settings for other vertebrates will advance our knowledge of coping behaviour considerably.

What mediates the different effects of glucocorticosteroids, especially as levels increase? This is a rapidly developing area. Glucocorticosteroids probably act through rapid membrane-type receptors, as well as the slower, well-known intracellular receptors acting on gene expression (Wingfield *et al.* 1998). Under a variety of different labile perturbation factors (e.g. osmotic stress, heat, cold), other hormones, such as prolactin, insulin, atrial natriuretic factor, may also be involved that give further specificity to the emergency response.

Facultative metamorphosis. Some variants of the 'take-it' or 'leave-it' strategies include facultative developmental changes. In western spadefoot toads, *Scaphiopus hammondi,* premature drying of ponds results in facultative metamorphosis. This metamorphosis can be accelerated experimentally by artificially lowering the water level in captive conditions (Denver 1998), and is accompanied by precocial increases of the thyroid hormones triodothyronine, thyroxine and corticosterone in whole-body contents of tadpoles.

Injections of corticotrophin-releasing factor activate both thyroid hormone and corticosterone secretion that, in turn, precipitate facultative metamorphosis (Denver 1997). Crowding, limited resources and predation as well as habitat desiccation also may trigger facultative metamorphosis (reviewed in Denver 1997; Hayes 1997). Similarly, crowding and other stress factors may increase corticosterone levels and precipitate premature metamorphosis in the toad *Bufo boreas* (Hayes 1997).

Concept of allostatsis. Living organisms have regular patterns and routines that involve obtaining food in life-history stages such as breeding, migrating, moulting and hibernating. Here the concept of allostasis, maintaining stability through change, has been introduced as a process through which organisms actively adjust to both predictable and unpredictable events on a continuum (McEwen 2000; McEwen & Wingfield 2003). A particularly attractive component of this concept is that the word 'stress' can now be specifically identified with the environmental perturbations and not the process of responding (allostasis). Frequently one reads about the 'stress' of reproduction or migration even though these life-history stages are part of the predictable life cycle and not, in the true sense of the word, stressful at all. They are energetically demanding and may make an individual more susceptible to stress, but they are not stressful per se (McEwen & Wingfield 2003). The allostasis concept has some useful terms that are relevant to coping biology in general. Allostatic load refers to the cumulative cost to the body of allostasis, with allostatic overload (accompanied by elevated plasma levels of glucocorticosteroids) being a state in which serious pathophysiology can occur. In other words, daily routines of feeding and sheltering have 'costs', with breeding, migrating, and so forth, adding further to those costs. If a perturbation strikes, allostatic load may increase to a point where daily food intake and/or body reserves cannot fuel the cumulative cost. At this point, glucocorticosteroid levels surge and an emergency life-history stage may be triggered (McEwen & Wingfield 2003).

Using the balance between energy input and expenditure as the basis for applying the concept of allostasis, two types of allostatic overload have been proposed. Type 1 allostatic overload occurs when energy demand exceeds supply, resulting in activation of the emergency life-history stage. Activation of the emergency life-history stage decreases allostatic load so that the individual regains positive energy balance (McEwen & Wingfield 2003). The normal life cycle (appropriate life-history stage) can be resumed when the perturbation passes. Type 2 allostatic overload begins when there is sufficient or even excess energy consumption accompanied by social conflict and other types of social dysfunction. This is the case in human society, and in certain situations affecting animals in captivity. In all cases, secretion of glucocorticosteroids and activity of other mediators of allostasis, such as the autonomic nervous system, neuro-transmitters and inflammatory cytokines, wax and wane with allostatic load. If allostatic load is chronically high, then pathologies develop. Type 2 allostatic overload does not trigger an escape response, and can only be counteracted through learning and changes in social structure (McEwen 2000; McEwen & Wingfield 2003).

Chronic perturbations. Long-term or permanent changes in the environment have major consequences for population dynamics. For example, during a decline in numbers of snowshoe hares in the Yukon, Canada, in the 1990s, hares appeared to be chronically stressed, as indicated by higher levels of free cortisol and lower corticosteroid-binding protein capacity. Circulating corticosteroid-binding protein is thought to play a role in maintaining high plasma levels of glucocorticosteroids and also influences the entry of these steroids into target tissues. Although baseline plasma testosterone levels in hares did not differ before and during the decline, hares showed reduced responsiveness to dexamethasone (a potent agonist of glucocorticosteroids, especially for negative feedback) and to adrenocorticotrophin treatment (stimulates glucocorticosteroid release by the adrenal cortex) in the decline years (Boonstra *et al.* 1998). During the population collapse, hares also showed reduced leucocyte counts in blood, increased glucose mobilization and higher overwinter loss of body weight compared with hares already at a population low. High predation risk, not population density or poor nutrition, accounted for chronic stress and impaired reproductive function. The stress response did not abate, and reproductive function did not improve until predation risk declined (Boonstra *et al.* 1998). This example of chronic stress in a free-living animal may be a form of type 2 allostatic overload.

Although most perturbations are short-lived (labile), increasing evidence suggests that environmental perturbations of anthropogenic origin may be an increasing problem for free-living vertebrates (possibly as type 2 allostatic overload). Field evidence also points to serious problems arising from chronically elevated glucocorticosteroid levels if an emergency life-history stage is not triggered or fails to reduce allostatic load. Baseline corticosterone levels in American redstarts, *Setophaga ruticilla,* wintering in Jamaica differ according to the habitat occupied. Individuals in 'female-biased' habitat, which tends to be of poorer quality, have higher plasma levels of corticosterone and reduced responses to a standardized acute stressor (capture and handling). This effect is most apparent later in the wintering period and may result in fitness deficits, such as reduced body condition, late departure on spring migration and arrival schedules in the breeding area (Marra & Holberton 1998). During an El Niño southern oscillation event in the Galapagos Islands, marine iguanas, *Amblyrhynchus cristatus,* show both higher levels of baseline corticosterone and higher levels of circulating corticosterone induced by handling stress when food resources on many islands are reduced to virtually zero. During a La Niña event, when many islands have an abundance of food, plasma corticosterone levels in iguanas are much lower. Furthermore, higher levels of corticosterone appear to predict later mortality (Romero & Wikelski 2002). Stressful events during development may also be detrimental when those individuals become adults (reviewed in Dufty *et al.* 2002).

Sickness Behaviour

One major consequence of labile perturbation factors is the potential for infection following injury. Moreover, contraction of a disease may be a labile perturbation factor in itself. A suite of reactions typically involves fever as well as specific behavioural traits associated with sickness. Fever is an elevated thermoregulatory 'set point' that occurs in all vertebrates from fish to mammals and is usually triggered in response to infection with certain pathogens. The wide spectrum of species that can express fever suggests that it has an adaptive or beneficial role coupled with the host's immune response. Several studies have shown that elevated body temperature in ectotherms, as well as endotherms, may increase survival rate of the infected individual. Experimental injection of a pathogen causes ectotherms to seek out environments that are warmer than those that they would normally inhabit (i.e. behaviourally induced fever). The same experiments in endotherms result in endogenously increased temperature, producing a fever (Kluger 1979). Physiological effects of fever include shivering thermogenesis, nonshivering thermogenesis and 'behavioural fever' in ectotherms.

In mammals, including humans, responses to infectious diseases (Hart 1988) include lethargy (as well as soporific behaviour), depression, anorexia, increased threshold for thirst, reduction in grooming and altered physical appearance. These responses to infection may not be maladaptive nor simply an effect of debilitation, but instead may reflect a behavioural strategy that, in conjunction with fever, combats viral and bacterial infections (Hart 1988). For example, individuals infected with bacteria show a reduction in serum iron concentrations, an element that is essential for bacterial growth (i.e. bacteria chelate free iron in the host's serum). Anorexia may also be a way of reducing serum iron concentrations (especially in carnivores), although there may be other costs (Hart 1988). There are also energetic costs to maintaining fever in endotherms, but these may be reduced by piloerection in mammals and its equivalent (feather erection) in birds.

Reduced activity saves energy, and altered postures (e.g. curled up or puffed out) reduce surface-to-volume ratio. In contrast, less grooming results in a scruffy appearance, and possibly, reduced efficiency of heat retention and increased ectoparasite load (Hart 1988). Seeking shelter and soporific behaviour may also reduce predation. Other effects of sickness include decreased libido, low levels of territorial and social aggression, and loss of interest in normal activities associated with various life-history stages. Impaired memory and learning may also occur (Dantzer 2000; Dunn &

Swiergiel 2000). Together, these observations indicate that sickness behaviour is an organized defence response to antigenic challenge. This response is mediated by neural effects of cytokines such as interleukin 1 (IL 1), interleukin 6 (IL-6), tumour necrosis factor alpha (TNF-α, also known as cachectin) and interferon-α (Kent *et al.* 1992; Fig. 8-3). IL-1, TNF and interferon-α can act directly on temperature-sensitive neurons in the preoptic area of the hypothalamus to induce fever. These cytokines also increase slow wave sleep.

Some effects of cytokines are mediated by prostaglandins (such as PGE2). Additionally, IL-1 can increase release of corticotrophin-releasing factor, thus stimulating the hypothalamo-pituitary-adrenal axis. There is evidence that IL-1 and TNF suppress activity of glucose-sensitive neurons in the ventromedial hypothalamus, possibility indicating an effect on food intake (Kent *et al.* 1992).

Injection of lipopolysaccharide into chickens reduces food intake, increases soporific behaviour, decreases plasma iron and zinc, and elevates plasma corticosterone levels. Complex interaction of cytokines may also regulate amine turnover as well as corticosterone (Brebner *et al.* 2000; Dantzer 2000). The effect on fever is much greater and longer lasting if lipopolysaccharide is injected centrally (Johnson *et al.* 1993a). Prostaglandin inhibitors such as indomethacin reverse the effects of lipopoly-saccharide

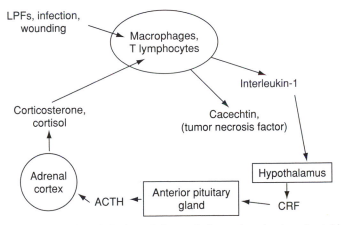

Figure 8-3 Inter-relationships of the hypothalamo-pituitary-adrenal axis and cytokines of the immune system. Increases in corticosteroid secretion following a labile perturbation factor may initially help to activate the immune system (Dhabhar 2002). Release of cytokines then, in turn, further enhances the hypothalamo-pituitary-adrenal axis. However, as corticosteroid levels in blood rise, they begin to inhibit immune cell function and act as a negative feedback system to hold the immune system in check to avoid autoimmune responses. If the labile perturbation factor is prolonged (i.e. chronic stress), the immune system may be suppressed, resulting in increased susceptibility to disease (Sapolsky 1992). LPFs: Labile perturbation factors; CRF: corticotrophin-releasing factor; ACTH: adrenocorticotrophin.

injection (Johnson *et al.* 1993b) consistent with a regulatory pathway via prostaglandin action. IL-6 may be the endogenous pyrogen that results in fever, stimulated by lipopolysaccharide through IL-1 (Bluthé *et al.* 2000). Note that IL-1 reduces activity in the western fence lizard, *Sceloporus occidentalis* (Dunlap & Church 1996) and that corticosterone implants reduce extended metabolic rate and promote night restfulness in passerines (Buttemer *et al.* 1991). Thus, the interaction of cytokines and glucocorticosteroids in regulation of sickness behaviour may be widespread in vertebrates, but more information is needed from comparative studies.

The Emergency Life-history Stage

In this brief review, I have outlined some emerging ideas from both the laboratory and the field that contribute to the ways in which organisms deal with unpredictable events in the environment. A great deal of field work needs to be done to determine the types of strategies that different organisms use to deal with diverse perturbations. This in itself is very difficult because environmental perturbations are so unpredictable! However, field workers who are willing to be opportunists and investigate how animals respond to perturbations when they occur will provide valuable new data. Laboratory studies in response to artificial perturbations are always possible, and essential to work out the mechanisms. However, these studies will always be dependent upon parallel observation in natural settings.

The scheme outlined here describes the emergency life-history stage and four major components. (1) Proactive/reactive coping styles for responding to psychosocial stress, predation, and so forth. (2) 'Fight-or-flight' responses tailored for responding to rapid emergencies such as an attack by a predator or sudden severe storm. (3) 'Take-it' or 'leave-it' strategies designed to cope with longer-term perturbations such as major weather changes and increased predator populations. These responses redirect the individual away from its normal life-history stages into survival mode until the perturbation passes. (4) Sickness behaviour and fever represent a highly organized suite of responses that allow individuals to cope with infection. Note that these four major components of the emergency life-history stage are not mutually exclusive. In some severe perturbations, a few individuals may express all four components simultaneously. Varying degrees of overlap are also possible. This scheme may change profoundly as more taxa are studied in response to unpredictable events in the environment.

The hormonal mechanisms underlying each component of the emergency life-history stage have been studied extensively in mammals and in birds, but much less so in other vertebrate groups. Much remains to be done.

The endocrine aspects of these concepts also allow investigators to manipulate individuals in the field to test how they might respond to real perturbations and whether there are consequences for fitness. Other ideas that are emerging, such as the concept of allostasis and the ability of many organisms to modulate the mechanisms by which they respond to labile perturbation factors, will require much comparative research in the field and in the laboratory in the future.

Acknowledgments

I am grateful for several grants from the Division of Integrated Biology and Neuroscience and the Office of Polar Programs, National Science Foundation. I also acknowledge a John Simon Guggenheim Fellowship, a Benjamin Meaker Fellowship (University of Bristol, U.K.) and a Russell F. Stark University Professorship (University of Washington).

References

Apanius, V. 1998. Stress and immune defense. *Advances in the Study of Behaviour*, **27**, 133–153.

Axelrod, J. & Reisine, T. D. 1984. Stress hormones: their interaction and regulation. *Science*, **224**, 452–459.

Bluthé, R., Michaud, B., Poli, V. & Dantzer, R. 2000. Role of IL-6 in cytokine-induced sickness behaviour: a study with IL-6 deficient mice. *Physiology & Behavior*, **70**, 367–373.

Boonstra, R., Hik, D., Singleton, G. R. & Tinnikov, A. 1998. The impact of predator-induced stress on the snowshoe hare cycle. *Ecological Monographs*, **79**, 371–394.

Brebner, K., Hayley, S., Zacharko, R., Merali, Z. & Anisman, H. 2000. Synergistic effects of interleukin-1 beta, interleukin-6, and tumor necrosis factor-alpha: central monoamine, corticosterone and behavioural variations. *Neuropsychopharmacology*, **22**, 566–580.

Buttemer, W. A., Astheimer, L. A. & Wingfield, J. C. 1991. The effect of corticosterone on standard metabolic rates of small passerines. *Journal of Comparative Physiology B*, **161**, 427–431.

Dantzer, R. 2000. Cytokine-induced sickness behaviour: where do we stand? *Brain Behavior and Immunology*, **10**, 1–18.

Denver, R. J. 1997. Proximate mechanisms of phenotypic plasticity in amphibian metamorphosis. *American Zoologist*, **37**, 172–184.

Denver, R. J. 1998. Hormonal correlates of environmentally induced metamorphosis in the western spadefoot toad, *Scaphiopus hammondii*. *General and Comparative Endocrinology*, **110**, 326–336.

Dhabhar, F. S. 2002. A hassle a day may keep the doctor away: stress and the augmentation of immune function. *Integrative and Comparative Biology*, **42**, 556–564.

Dufty, A. M., Jr, Clobert, J. & Møller, A. P. 2002. Hormones, developmental plasticity and adaptation. *Trends in Ecology and Evolution*, **17**, 190–196.

Dunlap, K. D. & Church, D. R. 1996. Interleukin-1 reduces activity level in fence lizards. *Brain, Behavior and Immunity*, **10**, 68–73.

Dunn, A. J. & Swiergiel, A. H. 2000. The role of cytokines in infection-related behavior. *Annals of the New York Academy of Sciences*, **840**, 577–585.

Hart, B. L. 1988. Biological basis of the behavior of sick animals. *Neuroscience and Biobehavioral Reviews,* **12,** 123–137.

Hayes, T. B. 1997. Steroids as potential modulators of thyroid hormone activity in anuran metamorphosis. *American Zoologist,* **37,** 185–194.

Healey, M. C. 1991. Life history of chinook salmon (*Oncorhynchus tshawytscha*). In: *Pacific Salmon Life Histories* (Ed. by C. Groot & L. Margolis), pp. 311–394. Vancouver: University of British Columbia Press.

Heard, W. R. 1991. Life history of pink salmon (*Oncorhynchus gorbuscha*). In: *Pacific Salmon Life Histories* (Ed. by C. Groot & L. Margolis), pp. 119–230. Vancouver: University of British Columbia Press.

Jacobs, J. D. 1996. Regulation of life history strategies within individuals in predictable and unpredictable environments. Ph.D. thesis, University of Washington, Seattle.

Jacobs, J. D. & Wingfield, J. C. 2000. Endocrine control of life-cycle stages: a constraint on response to the environment? *Condor,* **102,** 35–51.

Johnson, R. W., Curtis, S. E., Dantzer, R., Bahr, J. M. & Kelley, K. W. 1993a. Sickness behavior in birds caused by peripheral or central injection of endotoxin. *Physiology & Behavior,* **53,** 343–348.

Johnson, R. W., Curtis, S. E., Dantzer, R. & Kelley, K. W. 1993b. Central and peripheral prostaglandins are involved in sickness behavior in birds. *Physiology & Behavior,* **53,** 127–131.

Junk, W. J., Bayley, P. B. & Sparks, R. E. 1989. The flood pulse concept in river-floodplain systems. *Special Publication of the Canadian Journal of Fisheries and Aquatic Sciences,* **106,** 110–127.

Kent, S., Bluthé, R.-M., Kelley, K. W. & Dantzer, R. 1992. Sickness behavior as a new target for drug development. *Trends in Pharmacology,* **13,** 24–28.

Kitaysky, A. S., Piatt, J. F., Wingfield, J. C. & Romano, M. 1999a. The adrenocortical stress response of black-legged kittiwake chicks in relation to dietary restrictions. *Journal of Comparative Physiology B,* **169,** 303–310.

Kitaysky, A. S., Wingfield, J. C. & Piatt, J. F. 1999b. Dynamics of food availability, body condition and physiological stress response in breeding black-legged kittiwakes. *Functional Ecology,* **13,** 577–584.

Kitaysky, A. S., Wingfield, J. C. & Piatt, J. F. 2001a. Corticosterone facilitates begging and affects resource allocation in the black-legged kittiwake. *Behavioral Ecology,* **12,** 619–625.

Kitaysky, A. S., Kitaiskaia, E. V., Wingfield, J. C. & Piatt, J. F. 2001b. Dietary restriction causes chronic elevation of corticosterone and enhances stress response in red-legged kittiwake chicks. *Journal of Comparative Physiology B,* **171,** 701–709.

Kitaysky, A. S., Kitaiskaia, E. V., Piatt, J. F. & Wingfield, J. C. 2003. Benefits and costs of increased levels of corticosterone in seabird chicks. *Hormones and Behavior,* **43,** 140–149.

Kluger, M. J. 1979. Fever in ectotherms: evolutionary implications. *American Zoologist,* **19,** 295–304.

Koolhaas, J. M., Korte, S. M., Boer, S. F., Van Der Vegt, B. J., Van Renen, C. G., Hopster, H., De Jong, I. C., Ruis, M. A. W. & Blokhuis, H. J. 1999. Coping styles in animals: current status in behavior and stress-physiology. *Neuroscience and Biobehavioral Reviews,* **23,** 925–935.

Krebs, C. J., Boonstra, R., Boutin, S. & Sinclair, A. R. E. 2001. What drives the 10-year cycle of snowshoe hares? *BioScience,* **51,** 25–35.

Lamberti, G. A., Gregory, S. V., Ashkenas, L. R., Wildman, R. C. & Moore, K. M. S. 1991. Stream ecosystem recovery following a catastrophic debris flow. *Canadian Journal of Fisheries and Aquatic Sciences,* **48,** 196–208.

Marra, P. P. & Holberton, R. L. 1998. Corticosterone levels as indicators of habitat quality: effects of habitat segregation in a migratory bird during the non-breeding season. *Oecologia,* **116,** 284–292.

McEwen, B. 2000. Allostasis and allostatic load: implications for neuropsychopharmacology. *Neuropsychopharmacology,* **22,** 108–124.

McEwen, B. S. & Wingfield, J. C. 2003. The concept of allostasis in biology and medicine. *Hormones and Behavior*, **43**, 2–15.

Norris, D. O. 1996. *Vertebrate Endocrinology*. 3rd edn. New York: Academic Press.

Romero, L. M. & Wikelski, M. 2002. Corticosterone levels predict survival probabilities of Galapagos marine iguanas during EI Niño events. *Proceedings of the National Academy of Sciences, U.S.A.*, **98**, 7366–7370.

Sandercock, F. K. 1991. Life history of coho salmon (*Oncorhynchus kisutch*). In: *Pacific Salmon Life Histories* (Ed. by C. Groot & L. Margolis), pp. 395–446. Vancouver: University of British Columbia Press.

Sapolsky, R. M. 1992. Neuroendocrinology of the stress-response. In: *Behavioural Endocrinology* (Ed. by J. B. Becker, S. M. Breedlove & D. Crews), pp. 287–324. Cambridge, Massachusetts: MIT Press.

Sapolsky, R. M., Romero, L. M. & Munck, A. U. 2000. How do glucocorticosteroids influence stress responses? Integrating permissive, suppressive, stimulatory and preparative actions. *Endocrine Review*, **21**, 55–89.

Stearns, S. C. 1989. The evolutionary significance of phenotypic plasticity. *BioScience*, **39**, 436–445.

Veenema, A. H., Meijer, O. C., De Kloet, E. R. & Koolhaas, J. M. 2003. Genetic selection for coping style predicts stressor susceptibility. *Journal of Neuroendocrinology*, **15**, 256–267.

West-Eberhard, M. L. 1989. Phenotypic plasticity and the origin of diversity. *Annual Review of Ecology and Systematics*, **20**, 249–278.

Wingfield, J. C. 1984. Influences of weather on reproduction. *Journal of Experimental Zoology*, **232**, 589–594.

Wingfield, J. C. 1985a. Influences of weather on reproductive function in male song sparrows, *Melospiza melodia*. *Journal of Zoology*, **205**, 525–544.

Wingfield, J. C. 1985b. Influences of weather on reproductive function in female song sparrows, *Melospiza melodia*. *Journal of Zoology*, **205**, 545–558.

Wingfield, J. C. 1988. Changes in reproductive function of free-living birds in direct response to environmental perturbations. In: *Processing of Environmental Information in Vertebrates* (Ed. by M. H. Stetson), pp. 121–148. Berlin: Springer-Verlag.

Wingfield, J. C., Breuner, C., Jacobs, J., Lynn, S., Maney, D., Ramenofsky, M. & Richardson, R. 1998. Ecological bases of hormone-behavior interactions: the 'emergency life history stage'. *American Zoologist*, **38**, 191–206.

Wingfield, J. C. & Jacobs, J. D. 1999. The interplay of innate and experiential factors regulating the life history cycle of birds. In: *Proceedings of the 22nd International Ornithologi-cal Congress* (Ed. by N. Adams & R. Slotow), pp. 2417–2443. Johannesburg: BirdLife South Africa.

Wingfield, J. C. & Kitaysky, A. S. 2002. Endocrine responses to unpredictable environmental events: stress or anti-stress hormones? *Integrative and Comparative Biology*, **42**, 600–610.

Wingfield, J. C., Moore, M. C. & Farner, D. S. 1983. Endocrine responses to inclement weather in naturally breeding populations of white-crowned sparrows. *Auk*, **100**, 56–62.

Wingfield, J. C. & Ramenofsky, M. 1999. Hormones and the behavioral ecology of stress. In: *Stress Physiology in Animals* (Ed. by P. H. M. Balm), pp. 1–51. Sheffield: Academic Press.

Wingfield, J. C. & Romero, L. M. 2001. Adrenocortical responses to stress and their modulation in free-living vertebrates. In: *Handbook of Physiology. Section 7: The Endocrine System. Vol. 4: Coping with the Environment: Neural and Endocrine Mechanisms* (Ed. by B. S. McEwen), pp. 211–236. Oxford: Oxford University Press.

Young, J. B. & Landsberg, L. 2001. Synthesis, storage, and secretion of adrenal medullary hormones: physiology and pathophysiology. In: *Handbook of Physiology. Section 7: The Endocrine System. Vol. 4: Coping with the Environment: Neural and Endocrine Mechanisms* (Ed. by B. S. McEwen), pp. 3–19. Oxford: Oxford University Press.

9

Costing Reproduction

Andrew I. Barnes
Linda Partridge
Department of Biology
University College London

Abstract

The placing of animal behaviour in an evolutionary context is one of the great achievements of biologists in the last century. Life history theory has been a powerful tool in explaining both adapation and constraint in phenotypic evolution, but rarely addresses the mechanistic bases of the traits it discusses. Recent advances in molecular biology have begun to uncover these mechanisms, and provide a challenge to the traditional view that life history trade-offs are the result of the differential allocation of limiting resources. In particular, costs of reproduction in *Caenorhabditis elegans* appear to arise from molecular signals, which have been claimed to be arbitrary with respect to fitness. We review the evidence that costs of reproduction in *C. elegans* are not resource based, and find that this is not necessarily the case. However, we welcome the challenge to traditional thinking, and suggest that integrating an understanding of mechanisms into life history theory will be one of the most exciting tasks facing evolutionary biologists in the 21st century.

Animal Behaviour and Life History Trade-offs

Interactions between animals and their environments have been at the forefront of zoology ever since Darwin's (1859) realization that the latter played an important role in shaping the former. It has been recognized that all existing organisms are the result of a long evolutionary history in which natural selection is believed to have played a prominent part. The 20th century saw this powerful paradigm extended from being used to explain changes in morphology over evolutionary time, to being applied to all manifestations of the organismal phenotype, including animal behaviour.

Animal behaviours are, of course, manifold. To understand behaviours outside of the context of any one species, it is necessary to translate them into a currency that measures evolutionary success. This currency is fitness (Fisher 1930; Haldane 1932; Pianka 1970), and it is the idea that animals behave in such a way that fitness is maximized that allows behaviours to be unified under the umbrella of 'life history theory'. Life history theory (the age-specific schedule of fecundity and mortality) relates an individual's phenotype to its fitness, and is essential for understanding the role of natural selection in adaptive evolution (Crow & Kimura 1970; Gustaffson 1986). Life history theory also forms the basis of so-called 'why' questions in animal behaviour (i.e. questions that address the ultimate causation of behavioural traits; Alcock 1989). Students of animal behaviour have long been encouraged to keep these distinct from the 'how' questions (those addressing proximate or mechanistic causations), with the latter being discussed largely without reference to natural selection. The task of integrating proximate mechanisms and life history theory has begun, however, as advances in molecular biology allow the mechanistic bases of traits previously viewed as 'black boxes' to be understood. The immediate challenge for evolutionary and developmental biologists is to synthesize approaches that have been, at times, conceptually very different.

The evolution of life histories has long been at the forefront of the study of natural selection (Fisher 1930; Hamilton 1966; Charlesworth 1973, 1980). Law's (1979) Darwinian demon started reproduction immediately after birth and continued to reproduce frequently and with high fecundity throughout a long life. That no such organism has taken over the world leads inexorably to the conclusion that life histories must involve compromises between what selection can achieve (adaptation) and what selection is prevented from achieving (constraint; Gould & Lewontin 1979; Charlesworth 1990; Parker & Maynard Smith 1990; Partridge & Sibly 1991; Stearns 1992; Barton & Partridge 2000). Evidently only some combinations of life history traits can be achieved in practice. It is this distinction between the actual and the possible that provides evolutionary biology with some of its most challenging problems, not least of which is to identify the specific nature of these constraints.

The history of the analysis of constraints on life history evolution has been dominated by the idea that resources required for the expression of life history traits are environmentally limited. Life histories have been compartmentalized into categories such as 'growth', 'maintenance' and 'reproduction', each of which is conceptualized as competing with the others for resources. Fitness can then be maximized by adjusting resource allocation between these (Levins 1968; Calow 1979). Several models of life history evolution based on resource allocation to competing life history traits have been developed. This framework has allowed evolutionary biologists to explore both adaptation of life histories to different regimes of external hazard (Cole 1954; Charlesworth 1973; Schaffer 1974; Pianka & Parker 1975) and the nature of constraints limiting this adaptation (Gould & Lewontin 1979; Schmidt-Nielsen 1984; Lewontin 1986; Arnold 1992; de Jong & van Noordwijk 1992; de Jong 1993).

Resource allocation models of life history evolution were developed in the light of the results of experimental studies demonstrating that different life history traits are traded off against each other. A classic instance of such a trade-off is the cost of reproduction, where elevated reproductive rate leads to lowered subsequent fecundity or survival (Fisher 1930; Williams 1966; Calow 1979; Bell & Koufopanou 1985; Partridge & Harvey 1985; Reznick 1985). The near universality of this finding suggests that current reproduction is involved in an obligate trade-off with other life history traits. The cost of reproduction has traditionally been interpreted as a consequence of conflicting demands for resources by reproduction, growth and somatic maintenance. This fundamental assumption is, for instance, the basis of the 'disposable soma' theory of ageing (Kirkwood 1977). Empirical work in model systems, such as *Drosophila,* has provided evidence that one cost of reproduction is acceleration of the rate of ageing (Rose 1984; Simmons & Bradley 1997; Partridge *et al.* 1999; Sgró & Partridge 1999). Extrinsic hazards such as disease and predation set a limit to potential life span no matter how slow the intrinsic rate of ageing. The disposable soma theory hypothesizes that, because maintenance of somatic tissue uses resources that could otherwise be used for reproduction, somatic maintenance is not maximized, but is instead set at a level that maximizes lifetime reproduction. In less hazardous environments, this compromise is adjusted further towards somatic maintenance at the expense of current reproduction, and so a slower rate of ageing evolves.

Although resource-allocation-based trade-offs have been successfully used as a conceptual tool for modelling the evolution of life histories, their precise mechanistic bases have rarely been analysed. Evolutionary biologists have tended to accept that trade-offs between life history traits occur, and have been more interested in quantifying them than in understanding how they are implemented at the physiological level. This separation between work on evolution and mechanism is sometimes justified; it is not necessary to understand exactly how a female dunnock counts the males in her home range in order to measure the fitness consequences of her reproductive responses. However, some recent challenges to the idea of resource allocation as the basis of life history trade-offs have come from work on mechanisms. These findings have been thought to show that obligate trade-offs between reproduction and other life history traits need not occur. We therefore examine the conclusions of these mechanistic studies in some detail, to determine whether they are indeed at variance with the results from evolutionary analysis of life histories.

Challenges to Resource Allocation and Trade-offs

The nematode worm *Caenorhabditis elegans* has become a Nobel-Prize-winning model laboratory organism, used especially for studying the genetic control of development and ageing. The worm shows a cost of reproduction. Longevity of hermaphrodites (*C. elegans* consists of hermaphrodites and males) declines when mating rates are increased (Gems & Riddle 1996). In addition, mutations in the genes encoding components of the insulin/IGF-like signalling (IIS) pathway extend life span (Braeckman *et al.* 2001; Gems & Partridge 2001). This signalling pathway was discovered in the worm because it regulates the entry of developing worms into an alternative ('dauer') larval stage when food is short or the worms are crowded. These are nonmobile, nongrowing, nonfeeding, lipid-storing and stress-resistant larvae. Strong mutations in genes in the IIS pathway (e.g. in the gene encoding the insulin/IGF-like receptor *daf-2*) cause the worms to enter the dauer stage regardless of conditions. Weaker mutations in the same genes extend adult life span, up to doubling it in some instances (Kenyon *et al.* 1993). In general, these mutations also cause a decline in fecundity, the extent of which is correlated with the degree of extension of life span (Gems *et al.* 1998). The mutations also result in increased lipid storage (Sze *et al.* 2000). The phenotype that they produce is therefore suggestive of a reallocation of nutrients from reproduction to somatic maintenance and nutrient storage. Furthermore, reduction of nutrient supply, which reduces reproductive rate in the worm, also increases life span (Klass 1977). These findings are all consistent with the idea of a trade-off between reproduction and survival based upon allocation of available nutrients. However, more recent work on the worm has suggested that the rate of reproduction and survival can be uncoupled. Furthermore, it seems that the negative association between reproduction and survival, when it occurs, is a consequence of independent control of the two processes by a signalling mechanism, rather than of a direct competition for nutrients. These conclusions, if correct, would pose a challenge to the idea of a cost of reproduction brought about by nutrient allocation.

To assess the validity of these conclusions it is necessary to consider the mechanics of reproduction in the worm. The adult gonads are derived from four precursor cells (designated Z1, Z2, Z3, Z4). Z1 and Z4 give rise to the somatic gonad, Z2 and Z3 to the germ line cells. Ablating all four gonad precursor cells in the preadult stage, which results in complete absence of the gonad, has no effect on adult life span. However, ablation solely of the germ line precursors gives rise to adult worms that have a somatic gonad but no germ line, and these adults live up to 60% longer than untreated worms (Hsin & Kenyon 1999). This extension of life span by removal of the germ line relies on normal functioning of genes in the IIS pathway encoding components downstream of *daf-2*. Specifically, both *daf-16* (a forkhead transcription factor) and *daf-12* (a steroid hormone receptor) must be functioning normally for germ line ablation to extend life span. Normal function of these genes is also required for extension of life span by mutations in *daf-2*. These findings imply that germ cell ablation and the insulin receptor extend life span by overlapping mechanisms that require an intact IIS pathway.

An intriguing and potentially important explanation has been proposed for these results. A signal that downregulates longevity could be passed from the germ line to the soma. In the absence of the germ line, this signal does not exist and longevity is extended. The somatic gonad produces an equal counter-signal that upregulates life span. Life span is unaffected in the absence of the entire gonad (germ line and somatic) because removal of both signals results in no net effect. These (as yet unidentified) signals feed into the insulin/IGF signalling pathway through the action of *daf-12* and *daf-16*. Further work suggests that the germ line signal is generated during germ cell proliferation and may be a steroid hormone (Arantes-Oliveria *et al.* 2002). The insulin/IGF-like pathway is responsive to nutrients, plays a major role in metabolic control and also regulates fecundity and life span. Potentially, therefore, it is a mechanism that regulates the allocation of nutrients between reproduction and somatic maintenance. This could represent the first mechanistic description of a resource-based life history trade-off in an animal.

The results from the worm can be viewed as entirely consistent with the idea of a life history trade-off based on resource allocation. However, it has been suggested that, far from controlling resource-allocation-based trade-offs, molecular signals may be an alternative mechanism for producing negative relations between life history traits (Kenyon 1996; Leroi 2001). In worms, as in other organisms, direct evidence that the effect of germ line ablation on longevity is brought about by reallocation of nutrients to somatic maintenance is largely lacking. Indeed, reproduction can be eliminated entirely without a concomitant rise in longevity by eliminating all four gonadal precursor cells, which might also be expected to result in reallocation of resources. If resources that are no longer required for reproduction are automatically diverted to somatic maintenance, then the effect of the absence of the gonad (whether it be the entire gonad or the germ line only) should be constant. An additional argument against resource-based trade-off is that, in *C. elegans,* reduction in fecundity does not appear to be necessary for extension of life span. Although there is a negative relation between fecundity and life span induced by the *daf-2* mutations, at least one allele of *daf-2* (*e1365*) appears to increase longevity without any significant reduction in fecundity (Gems *et al.* 1998). It thus appears that the use of resources by one aspect of the putative trade-off, reproduction, is not obligately related to withdrawal of resources from the other, somatic maintenance. Furthermore, if mutations such as *daf-2* extend life span by shifting resources away from reproduction, then in those *daf-2* mutant worms that have already reduced fecundity, germ cell ablation might be expected to have a lesser effect on life span (Leroi 2001). Contrary to this prediction, germ cell ablation extends life span more, not less, in the *daf-2* mutants than in wild-type worms (Hsin &

Kenyon 1999). This finding suggests that resource reallocation to somatic maintenance in *daf-2* mutant worms, and in worms with the germ line ablated, may not account for their greater longevity. This idea is reinforced by the finding that germ cell ablation extends life span to differing extents in different strains of *C. elegans*, implying that the germ line signals can evolve to mediate a variety of relations between reproduction and somatic maintenance (Patel *et al.* 2002).

It seems that molecular signals can be manipulated and can evolve in the worm in such a way that fecundity becomes uncoupled from somatic maintenance, something that should not be possible if the two aspects of life history are obligately linked by a resource-based trade-off. If molecular signals do mediate life history trade-offs independently of environmentally derived limiting factors, then such signals can be thought of as wiring connecting different life history components in an arbitrary manner. If signals controlling life history decision are arbitrary with respect to resources then so, by implication, are the trade-offs that they mediate. This conclusion is clearly problematic for evolutionary biologists. If it is possible to increase fitness by simultaneously increasing two fitness-related life history traits such as fecundity and longevity, then it makes no sense for selection to have produced a negative relation between them. The implication is that natural selection on life histories, rather than being constrained by ineluctable choices between competing processes, may instead be able to act upon arbitrary biochemical signals. These act independently of limitations imposed either by the environment or by the physiology of the organism, so as to maximize all life history traits simultaneously. Where, then, is Darwin's demon? The idea that adaptation to the environment is less than perfect is one that has become orthodox, but the suggestion that it is less than important is not.

The conflict between the findings from *C. elegans* and the evolutionary life history trade-offs may be more apparent than real. However, the findings do force a reappraisal of exactly what the evolutionary theories predict and of the degree of current empirical support for the idea that resource allocation is the critical determinant of life history trade-offs. The evidence that life history trade-offs do not occur and signals are arbitrary in *C. elegans* is questionable. On the other hand, direct evidence that resource allocation is involved in any or all reproductive trade-offs in *C. elegans* or any other organism is largely lacking, and there are other possibilities.

Reappraisal of Resource-based Life History Trade-offs

The evidence that trade-offs between reproduction and somatic maintenance do not occur in the worm is three-fold: ablation of the gonad does not extend life span, not all long-lived mutant worms have reduced fecundity and germ cell ablation does not cause a greater extension of lifespan in wild-type than in *daf-2* mutant worms (Leroi 2001). However, none of these findings excludes resource-based trade-offs as an explanation.

Ablation of the gonad may not abolish the cost of reproduction because cessation of one aspect of reproduction may not ablate the mechanism that generates the cost. In the context of resource allocation, this point has been illustrated with a 'tap' analogy (Lessells & Colegrave 2001). If a bucket is being filled from a tap, then removing the bucket will not stop the tap. Processes that contribute to reproduction are not confined to the gonad. The metabolic processes that enable reproduction to occur may cause damage directly or may be energy consuming. Depending upon the exact form of the physiological control of different aspects of the whole reproductive process, generation of damage or consumption of nutrients outside the gonad itself may continue unabated in the absence of the gonad. Only detailed understanding of the mechanisms at work will allow the precise effects of this intervention to be specified. The anomaly is the finding that ablation of the germ line extends life span while ablation of the gonad does not. This finding has been interpreted as a result of exactly cancelling negative and positive signals to life span from the germ line and the somatic gonad (Hsin & Kenyon 1999). Although this is a logically possible explanation, no function has been suggested for the form of this signalling system. Figure 9-1 illustrates an alternative wiring diagram. In this version of events, in the intact worm (Fig. 9-1a) the germ line sends a negative signal to the somatic gonad that suppresses a second signal from the somatic gonad that in turn suppresses those somatic activities that enable reproduction but also generate damage. Because this last signal is suppressed, the worm is short lived. When the germ line is ablated (Fig. 9-1b) the second signal from the somatic gonad suppresses somatic processes that generate damage, and life span is long. If the whole gonad is removed, neither signal is sent and the worm is short lived. The function of such a wiring diagram could be to ensure that costly somatic damage is generated to enable reproduction only in the presence of proliferating germ line cells. The presence of proliferating germ cells might in turn depend upon the availability of nutrients. The parameterization of theoretical models of the cost of reproduction could be changed by basing them on this idea of an enabling system for reproduction that generates damage, rather than on altered resource allocation.

The scenario illustrated in Figure 9-1 would produce a trade-off between reproduction and life span. The proximate mechanism producing this trade-off would be molecular signals, but these signals would not be arbitrary. The ultimate function of both the form of the signalling system and the trade-off would be incompatibility between low generation of somatic damage, on the one hand, and reproduction on the other. It would not be based upon investment of resources into somatic maintenance. The net result would be the

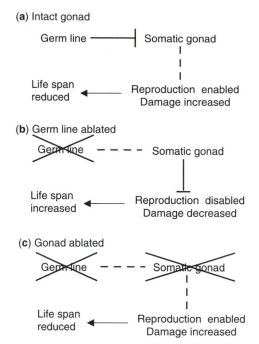

Figure 9-1 A model for reproductive signalling in which putative signals from the germ line and somatic gonad coordinate reproduction and life span adaptively. (a) In an organism capable of reproducing, signals from the germ line block a somatic signal, enabling reproduction at the expense of somatic maintenance. (b) Organisms unable to produce a germ line signal, such as those in which the germ line has been artificially removed, produce this somatic signal, disabling reproduction and reallocating resources to somatic maintenance and, consequently, increasing life span. (c) In organisms in which the gonad has been entirely removed, the signalling between gonad and somatic tissue is identical to (a), and hence so is the effect on life span. (a) and (b) represent adaptive responses to an organism's reproductive state, whereas (c) represents an experimental manipulation that is informative with respect to signalling pathways, but tells us little about adaptation, owing to the absence of any reproductive tissues.

same if 'Damage' in Figure 9-1 was relabelled as 'Somatic maintenance', which would go down in (a), up in (b) and down in (c). We would then have a model of a trade-off where the ultimate function of the signalling system was allocation of resources between somatic maintenance and reproduction. The conclusion is that the effects of removal of germ cells and gonad in the worm are easily compatible with a trade-off between reproduction and life span. One source of confusion in the literature has been the usual one between proximate mechanisms and ultimate function (Lessells & Colegrave 2001), which in this instance has led to the incorrect conclusion that molecular signals must be arbitrary. A trade-off that has the ultimate function of resource allocation need not be implemented mechanistically by the competing processes withdrawing nutrients from a communal bucket. On the other hand, the data are also entirely compatible with a trade-off that is not based on resource allocation. Time will tell.

The second argument against life history trade-offs was the finding that life span in *C. elegans* can be extended without concomitant reduction in fecundity (Apfeld & Kenyon 1998, 1999; Gems *et al.* 1998). This finding does not establish either that trade-offs have been unimportant in the evolution of the *C. elegans* life history or that they do not occur in extant *C. elegans*. Life histories and the proximate signals that control them have evolved in a specific range of nutritional environments. A substantial body of work has established that life history trade-offs are in general less evident in the presence of more abundant nutrients (de Jong & van Noordwijk 1992; Reznick *et al.* 2000; Zera & Harshman 2001). This finding has been one of the major planks in the argument that resource allocation underlies life history trade-offs. However, this finding is also compatible with a model under which enabling processes for reproduction inflict damage, if the level of somatic damage inflicted changes more rapidly with nutrition at lower levels of nutrition.

Little is known about *C. elegans* outside of its laboratory conditions, but the worms are almost certainly cultured in conditions that are much more resource rich than those in the wild. Recent work on another mutation known to extend life span in the worm has shown the importance of the environment for the detection of trade-offs. The *age-1* (a kinase in the IIS pathway) worms have an adult life span approximately 80% longer than wild types. In conditions of food abundance, there is no selection against an allele of *age-1* relative to the wild-type allele, indicating that the increase in life span does not trade off against fecundity. This is another example of the apparent uncoupling of life history traits. However, when the worms are put into a more biologically realistic environment (cycles of abundance and starvation) the frequency of *age-1* mutant alleles drops from 0.5 in the starting populations to less than 0.2 within six generations (Walker *et al.* 2000). Under the latter conditions there is clearly a large fitness cost associated with the extension in life span.

The third argument against a cost of reproduction in *C. elegans* was that germ cell ablation does not extend life span more in wild-type worms than in *daf-2* mutant worms (Hsin & Kenyon 1999). However, interpretation of the interactions between two interventions that individually extend life span should be handled with caution. It is not possible to use this approach to deduce that each intervention acts in different pathways. The reason is that neither one may maximize life span through the underlying mechanism. Under these circumstances, the two together will increase life span more than will either alone even if they do act through the same pathway (Clancy *et al.* 2001, 2002; Bartke *et al.* 2002). To show that pathways are truly separate, it is necessary to maximize the phenotypic effect of a single intervention and then determine whether the second intervention can have any further effect (Clancy *et al.* 2002). This has not been done in gonadectomized *daf-2* worms, so the conclusion that *daf-2* functions independently of reproductive processes may be erroneous.

The work with *C. elegans* has provided a welcome challenge to the current consensus in evolutionary analysis of life histories. The idea of a cost of reproduction has survived the challenge, and in that sense evolutionary life history theory has been left unchanged. However, the work has revealed that evolutionary biologists have been making an unwarranted assumption that the cost of reproduction must be attributable to resource allocation. This idea may be true for other life history trade-offs such as that between growth on the one hand and age at first reproduction and fecundity on the other. It may also be true for the cost of reproduction itself. However, in neither case is the point yet proven. The relative roles of somatic maintenance and generation of damage in the determination of life span have yet to be established. Until they are, evolutionary biologists should not assume that that the cost of reproduction must be a consequence of resource allocation.

References

Alcock, J. 1989. *Animal Behavior.* 4th edn. Sunderland, Massachusetts: Sinauer.

Apfeld, J. & Kenyon, C. 1998. Cell nonautonomy of *C. elegans daf-2* function in the regulation of diapause and life span. *Cell,* **95,** 199–210.

Apfeld, J. & Kenyon, C. 1999. Regulation of lifespan by sensory perception in *Caenorhabditis elegans. Nature,* **402,** 804–809.

Arantes-Oliveira, N., Apfeld, J., Dillin, A. & Kenyon, C. 2002. Regulation of life-span by germ-line cells in *Caenorhabditis elegans. Science,* **295,** 502–505.

Arnold, S. J. 1992. Constraints on phenotypic evolution. *American Naturalist,* **140,** S85–S107.

Bartke, A., Wright, J. C., Mattison, J. A., Ingram, D. K., Miller, R. A. & Roth, G. S. 2002. Dietary restriction and life-span. *Science,* **296,** 2141.

Barton, N. & Partridge, L. 2000. Limits to natural selection. *Bioessays,* **22,** 1075–1084.

Bell, P. D. & Koufopanou, V. 1985. The cost of reproduction. In: *Oxford Surveys of Evolutionary Biology* (Ed. by R. Dawkins), pp. 83–131. Oxford: Oxford University Press.

Braeckman, B. P., Houthoofd, K. & Vanfleteren, J. R. 2001. Insulin-like signaling, metabolism, stress resistance and aging in *Caenorhabditis elegans. Mechanisms of Ageing and Development,* **122,** 673–693.

Calow, P. 1979. The cost of reproduction: a physiological approach. *Biological Reviews,* **54,** 23–40.

Charlesworth, B. 1973. Selection in populations with overlapping generations. V. Natural selection and life histories. *American Naturalist,* **107,** 303–311.

Charlesworth, B. 1980. *Evolution in Age-structured Populations.* Cambridge: Cambridge University Press.

Charlesworth, B. 1990. Optimization models, quantitative genetics and mutation. *Evolution,* **44,** 520–538.

Clancy, D. J., Gems, D., Harshman, L. G., Oldham, S., Stocker, H., Hafen, E., Leevers, S. J. & Partridge, L. 2001. Extension of life-span by loss of CHICO, a *Drosophila* insulin receptor substrate protein. *Science,* **292,** 104–106.

Clancy, D. J., Gems, D., Hafen, E., Leevers, S. & Partridge, L. 2002. Dietary restriction and life-span: response to Bartke *et al. Science,* **296,** 2141–2142.

Cole, L. C. 1954. The population consequences of life history phenomena. *Quarterly Review of Biology,* **29,** 103–137.

Crow, J. F. & Kimura, M. 1970. *An Introduction to Population Genetics Theory.* New York: Harper & Row.

Darwin, C. R. 1859. *The Origin of Species.* 1st edn. London: J. Murray.

Fisher, R. A. 1930. *The Genetical Theory of Natural Selection.* Oxford: Clarendon Press.

Gems, D. & Partridge, L. 2001. Insulin/IGF signaling and ageing: seeing the bigger picture. *Current Opinion in Genetics and Development,* **11,** 287–292.

Gems, D. & Riddle, D. L. 1996. Longevity in *Caenorhabditis elegans* is reduced by mating but not gamete production. *Nature,* **376,** 723–725.

Gems, D., Sutton, A. J., Sundermeyer, M., Albert, P. S., King, K. V., Edgley, M., Larsen, P. L. & Riddle, D. L. L. 1998. Two pleiotropic classes of daf-2 mutation affect larval arrest, adult behavior, reproduction and longevity in *Caenorhabditis elegans. Genetics,* **150,** 129–155.

Gould, S. J. & Lewontin, R. C. 1979. The spandrels of San Marco and the panglossian paradigm: a critique of the adaptationist programme. *Proceedings of the Royal Society of London, Series B,* **205,** 581–598.

Gustaffson, L. 1986. Lifetime reproductive success and heritability: empirical support for Fisher's fundamental theorem. *American Naturalist,* **128,** 761–764.

Haldane, J. B. S. 1932. *The Causes of Evolution.* London: Longmans.

Hamilton, W. D. 1966. The moulding of senescence by natural selection. *Journal of Theoretical Biology,* **12,** 12–45.

Hsin, H. & Kenyon, C. 1999. Signals from the reproductive system regulate the lifespan of *C. elegans. Nature,* **399,** 362–366.

de Jong, G. 1993. Covariance between traits deriving from successive allocations of a resource. *Functional Ecology,* **7,** 75–83.

de Jong, G. & van Noordwijk, A. J. 1992. Acquisition and allocation of resources: genetic (co)variances, selection and life histories. *American Naturalist,* **139,** 749–770.

Kenyon, C. 1996. Ponce d'elegans: genetic quest for the fountain of youth. *Cell,* **84,** 501–504.

Kenyon, C., Chang, J., Gensch, E., Rudner, A. & Tabtiang, R. A. 1993. A *C. elegans* mutant that lives twice as long as wild type. *Nature,* **366,** 461–464.

Kirkwood, T. B. L. 1977. Evolution of ageing. *Nature,* **270,** 301–304.

Klass, M. R. 1977. Aging in the nematode *Caenorhabditis elegans*: major biological and environ-mental factors influencing life span. *Mechanisms of Ageing and Development,* **6,** 413–429.

Law, R. 1979. Optimal life histories under age-specific predation. *American Naturalist,* **113,** 3–16.

Leroi, A. M. 2001. Molecular signals versus the *Loi de Balancement. Trends in Ecology and Evolution,* **16,** 24–29.

Lessells, C. M. & Colegrave, N. 2001. Molecular signals or the *Loi de Balancement? Trends in Ecology and Evolution,* **16,** 284–285.

Levins, R. 1968. *Evolution in Changing Environments.* Princeton, New Jersey: Princeton University Press.

Lewontin, R. C. 1986. How important is genetics for an understanding of evolution? *American Zoologist,* **26,** 811–820.

Parker, G. A. & Maynard Smith, J. 1990. Optimality theory in evolutionary biology. *Nature,* **348,** 27–33.

Partridge, L. & Harvey, P. H. 1985. Evolutionary biology: costs of reproduction. *Nature,* **316,** 20–21.

Partridge, L. & Sibly, R. 1991. Constraints in the evolution of life histories. *Philosophical Transactions of the Royal Society of London,* **332,** 3–13.

Partridge, L., Prowse, N. & Pignatelli, P. 1999. Another set of responses and correlated responses to selection on age at reproduction in *Drosophila melanogaster. Proceedings of the Royal Society of London, Series B,* **266,** 255–261.

Patel, M. N., Knight, C. G., Karageorgi, C. & Leroi, A. M. 2002. Evolution of germ-line signals that regulate growth and aging in nematodes. *Proceedings of the National Academy of Sciences of the U.S.A.*, **99**, 769–774.

Pianka, E. R. 1970. On *r*- and *K*-selection. *American Naturalist*, **104**, 592–597.

Pianka, E. R. & Parker, W. S. 1975. Age-specific reproductive tactics. *American Naturalist*, **109**, 453–464.

Reznick, D. N. 1985. Costs of reproduction: an evaluation of the empirical evidence. *Oikos*, **44**, 257–267.

Reznick, D. N., Nunney, L. & Tessier, A. 2000. Big houses, big cars, superfleas and the costs of reproduction. *Trends in Ecology and Evolution*, **15**, 421–425.

Rose, M. R. 1984. Laboratory evolution of postponed senescence in *Drosophila melanogaster*. *Evolution*, **38**, 1004–1010.

Schaffer, W. M. 1974. Selection for optimal life histories: the effects of age structure. *Ecology*, **55**, 291–303.

Schmidt-Nielsen, K. 1984. *Scaling: Why is Animal Size so Important?* Cambridge: Cambridge University Press.

Sgró, C. M. & Partridge, L. 1999. A delayed wave of death from reproduction in *Drosophila*. *Science*, **286**, 2521–2524.

Simmons, F. H. & Bradley, T. J. 1997. An analysis of resource allocation in response to dietary yeast in *Drosophila melanogaster*. *Journal of Insect Physiology*, **43**, 779–788.

Stearns, S. C. 1992. *The Evolution of Life Histories*. Oxford: Oxford University Press.

Sze, J. Y., Victor, M., Loer, C., Shi, Y. & Ruvkun, G. 2000. Food and metabolic signaling defects in a *Caenorhabditis elegans* serotonin-synthesis mutant. *Nature*, **403**, 804–809.

Walker, D. W., McColl, G., Jenkins, N. L., Harris, J. & Lithgow, G. J. 2000. Evolution of lifespan in *C. elegans*. *Nature*, **405**, 296–297.

Williams, G. C. 1966. Natural selection, the costs of reproduction, and a refinement of Lack's principle. *American Naturalist*, **100**, 687–690.

Zera, A. J. & Brink, T. 2000. Nutrient absorption and utilization by wing and flight muscle morphs of the cricket *Gryllus firmus*: implications for the trade-off between flight capability and early reproduction. *Journal of Insect Physiology*, **46**, 1207–1218.

Zera, A. J. & Harshman, L. G. 2001. The physiology of life-history trade-offs in animals. *Annual Review of Ecology and Systematics*, **32**, 95–126.

10

The Promise of Behavioural Biology

Patrick Bateson
Sub-Department of Animal Behaviour
University of Cambridge

Abstract

The studies of behaviour that are strongly rooted in biology have a long tradition of bringing together the "how" and the "why" questions. This integrative approach will serve the subject well in the postgenomic era as the long trend towards analysis at lower and lower levels starts to reverse. The new studies make use of the resources uncovered by molecular biology and the neurosciences, but use the behaviour of the whole animal to measure outcomes and the context in which behaviour occurs to frame analytical questions. Two examples are given of how movement between levels of analysis is being used with increasing power and promise. The first is the study of filial imprinting in birds, where many of the molecular and neural mechanisms involved have been uncovered and are now being integrated to explain the behaviour of the whole animal. The second is the triggering by environmental events during sensitive periods in early life of one of several alternative modes of development leading to different phenotypes.

Introduction

In their time, the founding fathers of ethology were successful partly because they brought to behavioural biology a coherent theory of how behaviour is organised, and partly because they were interested in what behaviour is for. Their functional approach marked them out as being quite different from the comparative psychologists. Niko Tinbergen was as clear as anybody about the distinctions that should be drawn between "how" and "why" questions, but he saw the value of keeping the two approaches in play at the same time (Dawkins 1989).

By the early 1970s, ethology itself was ripe for takeover. Its "Grand Theory" was in ruins and the much-hoped-for understanding of the links between behaviour and underlying mechanisms was still fragmentary. Meanwhile, field studies relating behaviour patterns to the social and ecological conditions in which they normally occur led to the enormous popularity and success of behavioural ecology, in which an understanding of mechanisms played little part. The change was apparent in the great success of the Krebs and Davies' (1981) textbook and its subsequent editions.

Sociobiology moved into the available space, bringing to the study of behaviour important concepts and methods from population biology, together with some grandiose claims of its own (Wilson 1975). Imaginations were captured by the way the ideas from evolutionary biology were used, and the majority of aspiring graduate students wanted to work on a problem in this new area. The appeal of evolutionary theory and population biology, in which sociobiology was embedded, was that it seemed to make a complicated subject manageable (Barlow 1989). The drawback was that large chunks of behavioural biology, which had been central concerns of ethology, were deemed to be irrelevant or uninteresting. Few students interested in whole animals wanted to work on how behaviour develops or on how it is controlled. Therefore, for many years, issues to do with mechanism were largely ignored. In the last decade, however, the atrophied links between the "why" and the "how" questions have been rebuilt (Bateson & Gomendio 1992; Krebs & Davies 1997; Stamps 1991).

Understanding Process

The ebb and flow of fashions in behavioural biology seems relatively trivial by comparison with the overall trend in biology as a whole. The sheer excitement of uncovering the molecular biology of the gene has provided a powerful incentive for young biologists entering the field. Moreover, as the possibilities for biotechnology opened up, this new generation could look forward to certain employment. Anybody working in a biology department of a university for many years must have been aware of the way in which whole areas of comparative physiology and behaviour have been depleted of active research workers over the decades.

Two changes in thought are bringing this long trend to a halt. First, it has become obvious that there are limits to the usefulness of reductionism. Eventually, the mass of detail from lower levels of analysis provides no more explanatory power. An appropriate base for understanding the whole organism will be the gene at the lowest level and, in the case of an animal's behaviour, it will usually be at the level of its nervous system. The point is well illustrated in many essays in the book edited by Bock and Goode (1998). Second, the drive to understand the molecular mechanisms of inheritance has reached its apogee, though much detailed work doubtless remains to be done.

The ability to sequence genomes was a great scientific achievement. The much-heralded publication of the human genome does not and cannot provide the hoped-for "Book of Life" that would enable us to understand all aspects of human nature. Numerous postgenomic projects are based on the assumption that if clever enough mathematics and sufficient informatics were applied to the problem, somehow the code for the characteristics of whole human beings would be laid bare. The problem for biology in the postgenomic era is not, however, one of cryptography. Genes code for proteins, not people. If we want to understand what happens in the lifelong process from conception to death, we must study the process by which an embryo becomes a child and a child becomes an adult. Moreover, the nexus of interactions between gene expression and behaviour of the individual must be related to the current utility of behaviour and its evolutionary origins.

As developmental biology has come of age, the links with evolutionary theory have grown in the so-called "evo-devo" movement (Akam *et al.* 1994; Raff 1996). In the thinking about the origin of species, increasing emphasis has been placed on the importance of gene–gene interaction (epistasis). Postzygotic isolation is thought to result from an interaction between two or more genes (Orr & Presgraves 2000). Suppose the initial genotype is *aabb*, the population splits and in one population an *A* mutation appears and goes to fixation, and in the other population a *B* mutation appears and also goes to fixation. If *A* and *B* do not function well together, then hybrids between the two populations will be less viable or infertile. As Orr and Presgraves (2000) point out, this model highlights the importance of epistasis in evolution. Though credit is usually given to Dobzhansky (1937) and Muller (1940), Orr and Presgraves (2000) noted that the problem was first solved by William Bateson (1909). Once epistasis was recognised as important in the developmental process, the factors influencing phenotypic characters were less profitably thought about in terms of the genes as units, but in terms of the factors that are generated downstream. "Interaction" is really referred to in the statistical sense. Even in the simplest case, the physical interplay is not strictly between genes, but between the products of genes.

At one time, a commonly expressed view in the behaviour genetics literature was that genes usually interact in additive fashion (Broadhurst 1979). In part, this may have arisen because the biometrical advice was to rescale data until a way has been found to minimise the nonadditive interactions (Mather & Jinks 1971). This procedure made for simple genetic models but did not in itself provide evidence for the absence of interplay between the different factors affecting development. Equally important, epistasis could easily be missed if only first-generation hybrids between two pure-bred lines were examined. F1 hybrids carry an almost complete set of alleles from each relatively homozygous parent. Consequently, when relevant genes are not suppressed, the hybrid phenotype is influenced by and benefits from either or both sets of genes from the parents. In such circumstances, the possibility of statistical interactions between genes at different loci only becomes apparent after resegregation in the F2 hybrids (Bateson & D'Udine 1986). These general issues raise the question of what precisely happens in an individual's development.

I was supervised as a graduate student by Robert Hinde in the early 1960s. His opposition to the nature–nurture dichotomies (Hinde 1969) commonly deployed at that time had a strong influence on me (Bateson 1991, 2001a). Many contemporaries have been writing about developmental process in a similar vein as myself (e.g., Oyama 1985; Gottlieb 1992; Johnston 1988), and I have greatly benefited from many interactions with them. An important synthesis, sometimes described as Developmental Systems Theory, has been assembled by Oyama et al. (2001), and their edited book provides an invaluable modern source. In general, Lehrman (1970) argued that the interaction out of which the organism develops is between organism and environment, as opposed to heredity and environment. His wise point has been accepted in the literature on behavioural development for a long time. The importance becomes obvious when examining specific examples, and I shall give two here.

Behavioural Imprinting

Imprinting in birds is an example of tightly constrained learning occurring at a particular stage in the life cycle. The predispositions to respond to particular features and give particular responses to the stimulus are central to understanding the process. Perhaps the most important conclusion from the behavioural work is the need to think of a given phenomenon in terms of a series of subprocesses. These subprocesses were referred to as "modules" by Bateson and Horn (1994), who developed a neural net model. The work on imprinting has focused on analysis of the features of stimuli that begin the formation of the social attachment, establish a representation of that combination of features, and link such a representation to the system controlling social behaviour (Bateson 1990; Hollis et al. 1991). Different subprocesses have different underlying rules for plastic change. Contiguity of the various elements is likely to be important in forming a category, whereas contingency is crucial in learning that depends on external reward (Bateson 2000).

Inferences about the subprocesses involved in an overall transaction with an individual's environment are being examined at the neural level. An array of different neurobiological techniques have implicated the intermediate and medial part of the hyperstriatum ventrale (IMHV) on both sides of the brain as being sites of a neural representation of the imprinting object (Horn 1985, 2000). In locating the neural seat of imprinting, it was not good enough simply to show that a particular part of the brain was active when the bird was learning about the imprinting object. This is because lots of other things happen during the imprinting process: the young bird is visually stimulated and aroused by the imprinting object, and it also tries to approach and follow the object. All these processes produce their own changes in brain activity. When experimental evidence is open to a variety of different interpretations, greater confidence in one particular explanation can be attained by tackling the problem from a number of different angles.

In the case of imprinting, the first approach took advantage of the fact that in birds all the sensory input to the brain from one eye can be restricted to one hemisphere of the brain by cutting a bundle of nerve fibres running between the two hemispheres. After this had been done, one of the chick's eyes was covered with a patch, so that it could only see the imprinting object (a flashing rotating light) through one eye. This procedure meant that only one side of the chick's brain was exposed to sensory information about the imprinting object. When this was done, a difference in brain activity between the exposed and unexposed sides of the chick's brain was found only in the forebrain roof. No differences between the two sides were observed in other regions of the brain. This "split brain" technique eliminated the possibility that both sides of the brain were affected equally by training (Horn *et al.* 1973). However, it did not exclude the possibility that the enhanced brain activity resulted from greater visual stimulation of the trained side. Other procedures were, therefore, needed.

Another set of experiments exploited individual variation in the chicks. Various aspects of the chicks' behaviour were measured while the chicks were being trained, and their preferences for the familiar object were then tested. This procedure opened up to examination the relationships between behavioural measures of imprinting and neural activity in different parts of the brain. Only one behavioural measure was positively correlated with biochemical activity in the roof of the anterior forebrain, namely, how much the chicks preferred the familiar object to a novel object when given a choice. This index of learning was not correlated with biochemical activity in any other region of the brain and, equally important, was only weakly linked with other behavioural measures such as the birds' overall activity and responsiveness (Bateson *et al.* 1975). The analysis, therefore, revealed a specific link between a behavioural measure of imprinting and biochemical activity in a part of the brain that had already been implicated as the seat of imprinting in other experiments.

The final component in narrowing down the range of explanations was to exploit the asymptotic character of learning: a phase of rapid change is followed by one of much slower change. Therefore, animals that are in the rapid phase will be likely to show greater activity in brain sites that are specifically involved in learning than those that have moved on to the slower phase, even though many other aspects of the animals' experience and activity are matched. Animals may be prepared in advance by under-training them or over-training them on the task in question. This technique was successfully exploited when identifying the role of IMHV as a site for the neural representation of the imprinting object in imprinting (Bateson *et al.* 1973; Horn *et al.* 1979).

Each piece of evidence obtained by the different approaches was ambiguous, but the ambiguities were different in each case. When the whole body of evidence was considered, therefore, much greater confidence could be placed on a particular meaning. An analogy is trying to locate the position of a visible mountain top on a map. One compass bearing is rarely enough. Two bearings from different angles provide a much better fix, and three bearings give the most reliable position for the top. The strong inference from the triangulation studies of the neural basis of imprinting was that the IMHV did, indeed, represent the site where a representation of the imprinting object was formed.

Chicks that have had both left and right IMHV removed surgically are unable to imprint, and if bilateral lesions are placed immediately after imprinting, the birds show no recognition of the imprinting object (Horn 1985). Nevertheless, these lesioned chicks will show a preference for a stimulus that has a head and neck feature over one that does not, thereby dissociating the analysis component of the imprinting process from the recognition component. The lesioning experiments also dissociated recognition learning from learning involving external reward. Chicks will learn a visual discrimination rewarded with heat after bilateral removal of IMHV (Cipolla-Neto *et al.* 1982; Honey *et al.* 1995). They will also learn to press a pedal that rewards them with a view of an imprinting stimulus, even though they do not go on to learn the characteristics of that stimulus (Johnson & Horn 1986).

Many of the detailed cellular and molecular events occurring in IMHV are beginning to be worked out (Solomonia *et al.* 2000), and the physiology of the system is described (Horn 1998, 2000, 2004). However, the links between imprinting and other learning processes occurring in parallel with it are still poorly understood. The behavioural theories undoubtedly make assumptions about the nervous system and these assumptions may prove to be false. As the neural understanding grows, the inquiry has to return to the behavioural level so that the parts may be reassembled and, if necessary, new behavioural experiments may have to be done. This is a very different picture from that of a classical reductionist approach in which the behavioural people hand a problem to the neural people who, having made their contribution, hand it on to the molecular people. The return flow of ideas from lower to higher levels of analysis now seems a much more attractive and plausible picture of collaboration between disciplines (Johnston & Edwards 2002).

Environmental Triggers

Behavioural imprinting provides one of the classic examples of sensitive periods in development, where a given input from the environment is much more effective at one stage in the life cycle, usually an early one, than at others. Gradually, it has been appreciated how widespread sensitive periods are and, when the development of a range of phenotypes can be triggered during these periods, how important they can be to the life history of the organism. Many species of both plants and animals have the capacity to develop in a variety of different ways (Caro & Bateson 1986; Lott 1991; Schlichting & Pigliucci 1998; West-Eberhard 2003). These alternative modes of development are often referred to as "reaction norms" (Schmalhausen 1949) or "polyphenisms" (Mayr 1963). The castes of the social insects and solitary–migratory phases of locusts have been known for many years. Another striking insect example is provided by the alternative phenotypes of grasshoppers. After a fire on the high grassland plains of eastern Africa, the recently hatched grasshoppers of the eggs that survived are black instead of being the normal grey or yellowish green. Something has switched the course of their development onto a different track. The grasshopper's colour makes a big difference to the risk that it will be spotted and eaten by a bird, and the scorched grassland may remain black for many months after a fire. Therefore, matching its body colour to the blackened background is important for its survival. The developmental mechanism for making this switch in body colour is automatic and depends on the amount of light reflected from the ground. If the young grasshoppers are placed on black paper, they are black when they moult to the next stage (Rowell 1971). However, if they are placed on pale paper, the moulting grasshoppers are the normal grey or green colour. The grasshoppers actively select habitats with colours that match their own. If the colour of the background changes, they can also change their colour at the next moult to match the background, but they are committed to a colour once they reach adulthood.

Turtles, alligators, and some other reptiles commit themselves early in life to developing along one of two different developmental tracks and, like grasshoppers, they do so in response to a feature of their environment. Each individual starts life with the capacity to become either a male or a female (Bull 1980). The outcome depends on environmental temperature during the middle third of embryonic development (Yntema & Mrosovsky 1982). If the eggs from which they hatch are buried in sand lower than 30°C, the young turtles become males. If, however, the eggs are incubated at higher than 30°C they become females. Temperatures lower than 30°C activate genes responsible for the production of male sex hormones and male sex hormone receptors. If the incubation temperature is higher than 30°C, a different set of genes is activated, producing female hormones and receptors instead. It so happens that in alligators, the sex determination works the other way around, such that eggs incubated at higher temperatures produce males.

Each grasshopper and turtle starts life with the capacity to take one of two distinctly different developmental routes—becoming green or black, male or female. A particular feature of the environment determines the path taken by the individual for the rest of its life. And once committed, the individual cannot switch to the other route. Once black as an adult, the grasshopper cannot subsequently change its colour to green, just as a male turtle cannot transform itself into a female.

The implication of many of the phenomena described in this chapter is that environmental induction involves a prediction about the conditions of the world that the individual will subsequently inhabit. In mammals, the best route for such a forecast is often via the mother. Vole pups born in the autumn have much thicker coats than those born in spring: the cue to produce a thicker coat is provided by the mother before birth (Lee & Zucker 1988). The value of preparing in this way for colder weather is obvious.

Weaning represents a period of major transition for young mammals, marking a change from complete dependence on parental care to partial or complete independence. This transition, which is shown most obviously by the change in food source, involves a whole range of behavioural and physiological changes on the part of both mother and offspring (Martin 1984). If, as is likely for a variety of reasons, the time of weaning varies according to factors such as maternal food supply, then the developing offspring must be able to adapt by altering its behaviour accordingly (Bateson 1981). Domestic cats do so (Bateson et al. 1981; Bateson & Young 1981; Bateson et al. 1990; Martin & Bateson 1985; Tan & Counsilman 1985), exhibiting a higher rate of play after early weaning. This may mark a conditional response by the kitten to enforced early independence, boosting the benefits of play before complete independence. Similar contingent development is found in the rat (Gomendio et al. 1995; Smith 1991).

Human development may also involve environmental cues that prepare the individual for the sort of environment in which it is likely to live. Men who had the lowest body weights at birth and at 1 year of age were most likely to die from cardiovascular disease later in life (Barker 1998). Those born as the heaviest babies and brought up in affluent environments enjoyed a much-reduced risk of dying from cardiovascular disease or developing many other diseases such as noninsulin-dependent diabetes. These ill-effects of low birth weight are usually treated as yet another pathological consequence of poverty. However, a functional and evolutionary approach suggests that possibly the pregnant woman in poor nutritional condition unwittingly signals to her unborn baby that the environment that her child is about to enter is likely to be harsh. If so, this weather forecast from the mother's body may result in her baby being born with adaptations, such as a small body and a modified metabolism, helping the child to cope with a shortage of food. This hypothetical set of adaptations has been called the "thrifty phenotype" (Hales & Barker 1992;

Hales *et al.* 1997). Perhaps these individuals with a thrifty phenotype, having small bodies and specialised metabolisms adapted to cope with meagre diets, run into problems if, instead, they find themselves growing up in an affluent industrialised society to which they are poorly adapted.

If the functional explanation is correct, why don't individuals adapt continuously to changes in their local conditions during their own lifetimes? The image of the adaptive landscape used by Wright (1963) in evolutionary biology may be helpful here. His thought was that in the same environment, individuals with different gene combinations might be equally well adapted (on equally high mountains, using his image), but that going from one mountain to another entailed a loss of fitness. Engineers and economists dealing with optimisation problems often find local optima, knowing full well that better solutions can be found. In the context of the evolutionary adaptive landscape, an organism may reach the top of one mountain. Although it might be beneficial to cross over to a higher mountain, getting from a low mountaintop to a higher one involves going downhill before climbing once again. The same image may be used in development. Once a phenotype is fully formed, it may be difficult to switch to another phenotype that has become more beneficial because of a change in local conditions. A body, once built, is difficult to alter. Making fundamental changes to mature behaviour patterns or personality traits will similarly take time, resources and, quite possibly, support from others. Adults have important tasks to carry out, such as feeding and caring for their family, and cannot readily dissolve themselves and reconstruct their behaviour without others to care for them during the transition phase (Bateson 2001b).

The general point is that humans, along with many other animals and plants, are capable of developing in different ways and, in stable conditions, their characteristics are well adapted to the environmental conditions in which they find themselves (Bateson *et al.* 2004; McNamara & Houston 1996; Moran 1992). Generally, such systems of developmental plasticity work well, but in a changing environment they generate poorly adapted phenotypes because the environmental forecast proved to be incorrect. The cues for the way in which the individual develops are provided during sensitive periods early in development. When things go wrong, the effects of adaptive developmental plasticity have to be disentangled from disruption of normal development or the adverse long-term consequences when an individual has had to cope with difficult conditions during early life. Gluckman *et al.* (2005) discuss ways in which this may be done.

The mechanisms involved in the triggering process are largely to be discovered (Chapman *et al.* 2000; Waterland & Garza 1999), but a good rat model has been developed. When pregnant mother rats are given restricted diets, their offspring are smaller, and when given plenty food they become much more obese than the offspring of mothers given an unrestricted diet

(Jones & Friedman 1982; Vickers *et al.* 2000). Hyperphagia, obesity, and hypertension induced during the mother's pregnancy can be reduced in their offspring by one of the most powerful regulators of growth: insulin-like growth factor 1 (IGF-I) (Vickers *et al.* 2001). A powerful hint was provided by a study of the honeybee: the reproductive queen expressed different genes from the sterile workers (Evans & Wheeler 2000, 2001). Use of such genomic techniques holds much promise for uncovering the mechanisms involved in developmental plasticity and these are now being applied to the induction of particular phenotypes in the rat (Gluckman & Hanson 2004).

Conclusions

I was asked to provide a personal view of some important trends in behavioural biology and provide some guesses about the future of the subject. I have done so largely from the area I know best, namely, the attempts to understand the processes of behavioural development, but I have tried to show some ways in which asking the "why" questions relate to answering the "how" questions. Asking *what* something is for is never going to reveal directly the *way* in which it works. But the functional approach does help to distinguish between independent mechanisms underlying behaviour and can lead fruitfully to the important controlling variables of each system. This is important in the design of experiments in which, inevitably, only a small number of independent variables are manipulated while the others are held constant or randomised. The experiment is a waste of time if important conditions that are going to be held constant are badly arranged. A functional approach can provide the knowledge that prevents expensive and time-consuming mistakes. In behavioural development, functionally inspired approaches have played a useful role in making sense of what otherwise seems a confused area. Asking what might be the current use of behaviour helps distinguish juvenile specialisations from emerging adult behaviour and helps to understand the developmental scaffolding used in the assembly process. Functional assembly rules are important, for instance, in determining when an animal gathers crucial information from its environment. With attention focused on the problem, attempts can be made to analyse the mechanisms. As in other areas, the optimal design approach frames and stimulates research on the processes of development (Bateson & Martin 2000).

The streams of ideas between "how" and "why" approaches flow both ways. The need for knowledge of the mechanisms to address functional and evolutionary questions is also being recognised. This has happened notably in the studies of perceptual factors and learning processes influencing mate choice and their implication for associated evolutionary theories of sexual selection (Wilczynski *et al.* 2001). It is also happening in areas of work generally lumped under the heading of "life-history strategies," which raise important issues about conditional responses to environmental conditions (McNamara & Houston 1996; Moran 1992; West-Eberhard 2003). In general, these changes in thought are occurring because what animals do is being seen as important in stimulating (as well as constraining) ideas about function and evolution. Finally, the mechanisms involved in the development and control of behaviour may often generate ratchets in evolutionary processes, as seems likely to be the case in the active control of the social environment (Bateson 1988, 2004).

In this much-changed intellectual environment, the time seems right to rebuild an integrated approach to behavioural biology. With a whole array of promising new research areas and techniques emerging, behavioural biologists have a lot to be excited about. This matters in a highly competitive world in which determined and well-placed people can, in a remarkably short time, change what is and what is not funded, close research institutes, and radically alter the departmental structure of universities. It is important, therefore, to offer to the new generation of young scientists who are coming into the field a sense of what is becoming once again one of the most exciting areas in biology.

Acknowledgments

I am grateful to Leigh Simmons for inviting me to contribute this chapter and for his helpful suggestions.

References

Akam, M., Holland, P., Ingham, P. & Wray, G. 1994. *The Evolution of Developmental Mechanisms*. Cambridge: Company of Biologists.

Barker, D. J. P. 1998. *Mothers, Babies and Health in Later Life*. Edinburgh: Churchill Livingstone.

Barlow, G. W. 1989. Has sociobiology killed ethology or revitalized it? In: *Perspectives in Ethology, Vol. 8, Whither Ethology?* (Ed. by P. P. G. Bateson & P. H. Klopfer), pp. 1–45. New York: Plenum.

Bateson, P. 1981. Discontinuities in development and changes in the organization of play in cats. In: *Behavioral Development* (Ed. by K. Immelmann, G. W. Barlow, L. Petrinovich & M. Main), pp. 281–295. Cambridge: Cambridge University Press.

Bateson, P. 1988. The active role of behaviour in evolution. In: *Process and Metaphors in Evolution* (Ed. by M-W. Ho & S. Fox), pp. 191–207. Chichester: Wiley.

Bateson, P. 1990. Is imprinting such a special case? *Philosophical Transactions of the Royal Society of London, Series B*, **329**, 125–131.

Bateson, P. 1991. Are there principles of behavioural development? In: *The Development and Integration of Behaviour* (Ed. by P. Bateson), pp. 19–39. Cambridge: Cambridge University Press.

Bateson, P. 2000. What must be known in order to understand imprinting? In: *The Evolution of Cognition* (Ed. by C. Heyes & L. Huber), pp. 85–102. Cambridge, Massachusetts: MIT Press.

Bateson, P. 2001a. Where does our behaviour come from? *Journal of Biosciences,* **26,** 561–570.

Bateson, P. 2001b. Fetal experience and good adult design. *International Journal of Epidemiology,* **26,** 561–570.

Bateson, P. 2004. The active role of behaviour in evolution. *Biology and Philosophy,* **19,** 283–298.

Bateson, P., Barker, D., Clutton-Brock, T., Deb, D., D'Udine, B., Foley, R. A., Gluckman, P., Godfrey, K., Kirkwood, T., Lahr, M. M., McNamara, J., Metcalfe, N. B., Monaghan, P., Spencer, H. G. & Sultan, S. E. 2004. Developmental plasticity and human health. *Nature,* **430,** 419–421.

Bateson, P. & D'Udine, B. 1986. Exploration in two inbred strains of mice and their hybrids: additive and interactive models of gene expression. *Animal Behaviour,* **34,** 1026–1032.

Bateson, P. & Gomendio, M. 1992. *Behavioural Mechanisms in Evolutionary Perspective.* Madrid: Instituto Juan March.

Bateson, P. & Horn, G. 1994. Imprinting and recognition memory—a neural-net model. *Animal Behaviour,* **48,** 695–715.

Bateson, P. & Martin, P. 2000. *Design for a Life: How Behaviour Develops.* London: Vintage Paperbacks.

Bateson, P., Martin, P. & Young, M. 1981. Effects of interrupting cat mothers' lactation with bromocriptine on the subsequent play of their kittens. *Physiology and Behavior,* **27,** 841–845.

Bateson, P., Mendl, M. & Feaver, J. 1990. Play in the domestic cat is enhanced by rationing the mother during lactation. *Animal Behaviour,* **40,** 514–525.

Bateson, P. & Young, M. 1981. Separation from mother and the development of play in cats. *Animal Behaviour,* **29,** 173–180.

Bateson, P. P. G., Horn, G. & Rose, S. P. R. 1975. Imprinting: correlations between behaviour and incorporation of (l4C) Uracil into chick brain. *Brain Research,* **84,** 207–220.

Bateson, P. P. G., Rose, S. P. R. & Horn, G. 1973. Imprinting: lasting effects on uracil incorporation into chick brain. *Science,* **181,** 576–578.

Bateson, W. 1909. Heredity and variation in modern lights. In: *Darwin and Modern Science* (Ed. by A. C. Seward), pp. 85–101. Cambridge: Cambridge University Press.

Bock, G. R. & Goode, J. A. E. 1998. *The Limits of Reductionism in Biology. Novartis Foundation Symposium 213.* Chichester: Wiley.

Broadhurst, P. L. 1979. The experimental approach to behavioural evolution. In: *Theoretical Advances in Behavioural Genetics* (Ed. by J. R. Royce & L. P. Mos). Alphen aan den Rijn, Netherlands: Sijthoff & Noordhoff.

Bull, J. J. 1980. Sex determination in reptiles. *Quarterly Review of Biology,* **55,** 3–21.

Caro, T. M. & Bateson, P. 1986. Organisation and ontogeny of alternative tactics. *Animal Behaviour,* **34,** 1483–1499.

Chapman, C., Morgan, L. M. & Murphy, M. C. 2000. Maternal and early dietary fatty acid intake: changes in lipid metabolism and liver enzymes in adult rats. *Journal of Nutrition,* **130,** 146–151.

Cipolla-Neto, J., Horn, G. & McCabe, B. J. 1982. Hemispheric asymmetry and imprinting: the effect of sequential lesions to the hyperstriatum ventrale. *Experimental Brain Research,* **48,** 22–27.

Dawkins, M. S. 1989. The future of ethology: how many legs are we standing on? In: *Perspectives in Ethology. Vol. 8. Whither Ethology?* (Ed. by P. P. G. Bateson & P. H. Klopfer), pp. 47–54. New York: Plenum.

Dobzhansky, T. 1937. *Genetics and Origin of Species.* New York: Columbia University Press.

Evans, J. D. & Wheeler, D. E. 2000. Expression profiles during honeybee caste determination. *Genome Biology,* **2,** 1–6.

Evans, J. D. & Wheeler, D. E. 2001. Gene expression and the evolution of insect polyphenisms. *Bioessays,* **54,** 62–68.

Gluckman, P. D. & Hanson, M. A. 2004. *The Fetal Matrix.* Cambridge: Cambridge University Press.

Gluckman, P. D., Hanson, M. A., Spencer, H. G. & Bateson, P. 2005. Environmental influences during development and their later consequences for health and disease: implications for the interpretation of empirical studies. *Proceedings of the Royal Society, Series B,* **272,** 671–677.

Gomendio, M., Cassinello, J., Smith, M. W. & Bateson, P. 1995. Maternal state affects intestinal changes of rat pups at weaning. *Behavioral Ecology & Sociobiology,* **37,** 71–80.

Gottlieb, G. 1992. *Individual Development and Evolution.* New York: Oxford University Press.

Hales, C. N. & Barker, D. J. P. 1992. Type 2 (non-insulin-dependent) diabetes mellitus: the thrifty phenotype hypothesis. *Diabetologia,* **35,** 595–601.

Hales, C. N., Desai, M. & Ozanne, S. E. 1997. The thrifty phenotype hypothesis: how does it look after 5 years? *Diabetic Medicine,* **14,** 189–195.

Hinde, R. A. 1969. Dichotomies in the study of development. In: *Genetic and Environmental Influences on Behaviour* (Ed. by J. M. Thoday & A. S. Parkes), pp. 3–14. Edinburgh: Oliver & Boyd.

Hollis, K. L., ten Cate, C. & Bateson, P. 1991. Stimulus representation: a subprocess of imprinting and conditioning. *Journal of Comparative Psychology,* **105,** 307–317.

Honey, R. C., Horn, G., Bateson, P. & Walpole, M. 1995. Functionally distinct memories for imprinting stimuli: behavioral and neural dissociations. *Behavioral Neuroscience,* **109,** 689–698.

Horn, G. 1985. *Memory, Imprinting, and the Brain.* Oxford: Oxford University Press.

Horn, G. 1998. Visual imprinting and the neural mechanisms of recognition memory. *Trends in Neurosciences,* **21,** 300–305.

Horn, G. 2000. In memory. In: *Brain, Perception, Memory: Advances in Cognitive Neuroscience* (Ed. by J. J. Bolhuis), pp. 329–363. Oxford: Oxford University Press.

Horn, G. 2004. Pathways to the past: the imprint of memory. *Nature Neuroscience,* 5, 108–121.

Horn, G., McCabe, B. J. & Bateson, P. P. G. 1979. An autoradiographic study of the chick brain after imprinting. *Brain Research,* **168,** 361–373.

Horn, G., Rose, S. P. R. & Bateson, P. P. G. 1973. Monocular imprinting and regional incorporation of tritiated uracil into the brains of intact and "split-brain" chicks. *Brain Research,* **56,** 227–237.

Johnson, M. H. & Horn, G. 1986. Dissociation between recognition memory and associative learning by a restricted lesion to the chick forebrain. *Neuropsychologia,* **24,** 329–340.

Johnston, T. D. 1988. Developmental explanation and the ontogeny of birdsong: Nature/nurture redux. *Behavioral and Brain Sciences,* **11,** 617–663.

Johnston, T. D. & Edwards, L. 2002. Genes, interactions, and the development of behavior. *Psychological Reviews,* **109,** 26–34.

Jones, A. P. & Friedman, M. I. 1982. Obesity and adipocyte abnormalities in offspring of rats undernourished during pregnancy. *Science,* **215,** 1518–1519.

Krebs, J. R. & Davies, N. B. 1981. *Introduction to Behavioural Ecology.* Oxford: Oxford University Press.

Krebs, J. R. & Davies, N. B. 1997. *Behavioural Ecology: an Evolutionary Approach.* 4th edn. Oxford: Blackwell.

Lee, T. M. & Zucker, I. 1988. Vole infant development is influenced perinatally by maternal photoperiodic history. *American Journal of Physiology,* **255,** R831–R838.

Lehrman, D. S. 1970. Semantic and conceptual issues in the nature-nurture problem. In: *Development and Evolution of Behavior* (Ed. by L. R. Aronson, E. Tobach, D. S. Lehrman & J. S. Rosenblatt), pp. 17–52. San Francisco: Freeman.

Lott, D. F. 1991. *Intraspecific Variation in the Social Systems of Wild Vertebrates.* Cambridge: Cambridge University Press.

Martin, P. 1984. The meaning of weaning. *Animal Behaviour,* **32,** 1024–1026.

Martin, P. & Bateson, P. 1985. The influence of experimentally manipulating a component of weaning on the development of play in domestic cats. *Animal Behaviour,* **33,** 511–518.

Mather, K. & Jinks, J. L. 1971. *Biometrical Genetics.* London: Chapman & Hall.

Mayr, E. 1963. *Animal Species and Evolution.* Cambridge, Massachusetts: Harvard University Press.

McNamara, J. M. & Houston, A. I. 1996. State-dependent life-histories. *Nature,* **380,** 215–221.

Moran, N. A. 1992. The evolutionary maintenance of alternative phenotypes. *American Naturalist,* **139,** 249–278.

Muller, H. J. 1940. Bearing of the Drosophila work on systematics. In: *The New Systematics* (Ed. by J. S. Huxley), pp. 125–268. Oxford: Oxford University Press.

Orr, H. A. & Presgraves, D. C. 2000. Speciation by postzygotic isolation: forces, genes and molecules. *Bioessays,* **22,** 1085–1094.

Oyama, S. 1985. *The Ontogeny of Information.* Cambridge: Cambridge University Press.

Oyama, S., Griffiths, P. E. & Gray, R. D. 2001. *Cycles of Contingency: Developmental Systems and Evolution.* Cambridge, Massachusetts: MIT Press.

Raff, R. A. 1996. *The Shape of Life: Genes, Development and Evolution of Animal Form.* Chicago: University of Chicago Press.

Rowell, C. H. F. 1971. The variable coloration of the Acridoid grasshoppers. *Advances in Insect Physiology,* **8,** 145–198.

Schlichting, C. D. & Pigliucci, M. 1998. *Phenotypic Evolution: a Reaction Norm Perspective.* Sunderland, Massachusetts: Sinauer.

Schmalhausen, I. I. 1949. *Factors of Evolution.* Philadelphia: Blakiston.

Smith, E. F. S. 1991. Early social development in hooded rats (*Rattus norvegicus*): a link between weaning and play. *Animal Behaviour,* **41,** 513–524.

Solomonia, R. O., Kiguradzw, T., McCabe, B. J. & Hprn, G. 2000. Neural cell adhesion molecules, CAM kinase II and long-term memory in the chick. *Neuroreport,* **11,** 3139–3143.

Stamps, J. A. 1991. Why evolutionary issues are reviving interest in proximate mechanisms. *American Zoologist,* **31,** 338–348.

Tan, P. L. & Counsilman, J. J. 1985. The influence of weaning on prey-catching behaviour in kittens. *Zeitschrift für Tierpsychologie,* **70,** 148–164.

Vickers, M. H., Breier, B. H., Cutfield, W. S., Hofman, P. L. & Gluckman, P. D. 2000. Fetal origins of hyperphagia, obesity, and hypertension and postnatal amplification by hypercaloric nutrition. *American Journal of Physiology. Endocrinology and Metabolism,* **279,** E83–E87.

Vickers, M. H., Ikenasio, B. A. & Breier, B. H. 2001. IGF-I Treatment reduces hyperphagia, obesity, and hypertension in metabolic disorders induced by fetal programming. *Endocrinology,* **142,** 3964–3973.

Waterland, R. A. & Garza, C. 1999. Potential mechanisms of metabolic imprinting that lead to chronic disease. *American Journal of Clinical Nutrition,* **69,** 179–197.

West-Eberhard, M. J. 2003. *Developmental Plasticity and Evolution.* Oxford: Oxford University Press.

Wilczynski, W., Rand, A. S. & Ryan, M. 2001. Evolution of calls and auditory tuning in the *Physalaemus pastulosus* species. *Brain, Behavior and Evolution,* **58,** 137–151.

Wilson, E. O. 1975. *Sociobiology: The New Synthesis.* Cambridge, Massachusetts: Harvard University Press.

Wright, S. 1963. Genic interaction. In: *Methodology in Mammalian Genetics* (Ed. by W. J. Burdette), pp. 159–192. San Francisco: Holden Day.

Yntema, C. L. & Mrosovsky, N. 1982. Critical periods and pivotal temperatures for sexual differentiation in loggerhead sea turtles. *Canadian Journal of Zoology,* **60,** 1012–1016.

11

Theoretical and Empirical Approaches to Understanding When Animals Use Socially Acquired Information and from Whom They Acquire It

Bennett G. Galef, Jr.
Department of Psychology
McMaster University

Abstract

I review empirical studies of the integration of individually and socially acquired information by animals faced with a choice between alternative courses of action. Focus on results of empirical studies is intended as a compliment to recent reviews of similar material that have focused on predictions from formal models. In introduction and conclusion, I consider both the relatioship between empirical and theoretical approaches to the study of social learning and implications of the material reviewed for future work in the area.

Introduction

Many of the biologically important decisions that animals make can be biased by interaction with conspecifics making similar decisions. However, even when information acquired socially affects behaviour, socially acquired information does not act in a vacuum. Before an individual chooses to act, it integrates information extracted from the social environment with: (1) information acquired during previous experience with the asocial environment, (2) affective responses to alternative potential goal objects, and (3) information as to its own internal state.

Great progress has been made in both identifying behavioural domains where social learning is important and understanding behavioural processes that underlie social influences on behaviour. However, we still know relatively little about how socially acquired and other sources of information are integrated before action is initiated.

There are two quite different approaches to understanding how animals achieve such integration. The first is a theoretical approach admirably presented in Laland's (2004) review of formal models of social learning. Laland's paper discusses predictions, derived from both game theory and evolutionary models, as to when animals might be expected to use social cues to guide their behaviour ("when strategies"), and whose behaviour social learners might be expected to copy ("who strategies"), as well as tests of some of those predictions.

The alternative approach to the theoretical one is empirical. It involves direct investigation of variables that might determine whether animals use available social information when making decisions. Often, variables are selected for examination because they are known to be important in determining whether animals acquire and perform behaviours when no social learning is involved. Such extrapolation from asocial to social learning is reasonable because although exposition is made simpler by categorising learning as either "social" or "asocial," the dichotomy is not so real as the terminology implies.

As Heyes (1993) pointed out some years ago, with the exception of learning by imitation (that appears to be relatively rare in animals), animal social learning does not involve learning directly about the *behaviour* of others. Rather, socially acquired information directs an individual's behaviour towards objects in the environment with which the "social learner" then interacts directly. Consequently, most social learning in animals is, in fact, socially biased individual learning (Galef 1995), and variables that affect individual learning might be expected to influence social learning as well.

To synthesise and organise information, general theories of social learning have had to ignore much of the detail of learning processes and social interactions. Such detail, although of relatively little obvious theoretical significance, can place boundary conditions on theories and determine whether predictions from theory are confirmed in particular instances.

Empirical approaches exploring variables that affect the probability of social learning will invariably be more intuitive and less integrative than theoretical approaches. Still, empirical approaches result in discovery of phenomena that theory does not predict and reveal the impact of variables that general models have yet to consider. For example, as Laland (2004) indicates in his review, functional considerations lead to the conclusion that animals should copy the behaviour of others when: (1) their ongoing behaviour is relatively unproductive, (2) asocial learning is costly, and (3) asocial learning is uncertain. However, as indicated later, lack of productivity, uncertainty, and costliness can each have many causes, and not all need have similar effects on the probability that social learning will occur.

Here, I review empirical studies that contribute to our understanding of how socially acquired information interacts with other sources of information to determine the decisions animals reach and suggest ways in which the interplay between theory and data might guide future research. The chapter is organised first in terms of the type of information that is being integrated with socially acquired information and, second, with respect to whether effects of socially acquired information are on the acquisition of behaviour or its subsequent performance.

Integration of Social Information with Other Sources of Information When Making Decisions

Internal State

It has been predicted on functional grounds that an animal doing poorly will be more likely to adopt the behaviour of others than an individual that has independently acquired behaviour leading to success (Laland 2004). However, it is not clear from general theory just how an animal might determine whether it is succeeding or failing. A possibility considered here is that an individual might gauge its success by monitoring its internal state. For example, an animal experiencing hunger or deficiency in some necessary nutrient (e.g., protein, sodium) might be more likely than a well-fed animal to consider itself unsuccessful, to abandon its individually acquired foraging patterns or food choices and adopt those of others.

Theory suggests further that if a relatively unsuccessful animal could identify successful conspecifics, it should be more likely to affiliate with, attend to, and adopt the behaviour of successful rather than of unsuccessful individuals. However, and obviously, for relatively unsuccessful individuals to be able to copy the behaviour of the relatively successful, relatively unsuccessful individuals must both assess their own relative success and identify the more successful.

Ward and Zahavi's (1973) information-centre hypothesis implicitly assumed that unsuccessful avian foragers can both recognise their own failure and detect successful individuals so that the unsuccessful can follow the successful when the latter leave a roost to forage. Thirty years of observation and experiment in natural circumstances have provided little data consistent with the information-centre hypothesis regarding the function of avian roosts (Mock *et al.* 1988). Even if, in some species, unsuccessful foragers do follow successful foragers from aggregation to foraging sites (e.g., Sonerud *et al.* 2001; Wilkinson 1992), considerable empirical work will be required to understand why the phenomenon is not observed in other central-place foraging avian species, as theory suggests it should be. Are central-place foragers whose aggregation sites do not function as information centres insensitive to their own relative success? Are they unable to detect or unable to follow successful individuals, or is there some other reason why they fail to exploit useful social information that appears to be available to them?

Laboratory studies undertaken to look for effects of deprivation states on social learning of food preferences in Norway rats have provided a partial picture of the influence of lack of success on reliance on social learning, as well as information on the ability of rats to discriminate successful from unsuccessful conspecifics. Galef and colleagues (1991) presented individual protein-deprived and protein-replete Norway rats with a cafeteria of four distinctively flavoured, protein-deficient foods and found no differences in their food choices. However, when both protein-deprived and protein-replete rats were presented with the same cafeteria of four foods in the presence of a "demonstrator" rat trained to eat only the least palatable of the foods in the cafeteria, protein-deprived observers ate far more of that food than did protein-replete observers. The findings are consistent with theory in that a state of protein deprivation, a sign of lack of success, increased reliance on socially acquired information (Beck & Galef 1989).

However, further evidence suggested: (1) that not all deprivation states affected reliance on social information in the same way, and (2) that a particular deprivation state may have different effects in different species. For example, and as theory predicts, food-deprived juvenile Norway rats prefer a food bowl where a conspecific adult is feeding to a food bowl where no adult is present. However, water-deprived juvenile rats do not prefer to drink from a water bowl where an adult rat is drinking (Galef 1978).

Unlike food-deprived rats, which are more strongly influenced by social stimuli than their replete fellows, food-deprived banded killifish (*Fundulus diaphanous*) spend more time alone and less time shoaling than do well-fed killifish (Hensor *et al.* 2003). Perhaps competition for food is more severe in killifish than in rats. Perhaps there is some other cause for their differing responses to food deprivation.

A focal individual's deprivation state can also affect its choice between replete and deprived conspecifics as companions (Galef & Whiskin 2001). Food- or sodium-deprived Norway rats choosing to affiliate with either food-deprived or food-replete rats preferred to remain near well-fed individuals. However, both sodium-deprived and food-deprived rats were indifferent as to whether potential partners were sodium-deprived.

In sum, as formal models predict, internal states indicative of a lack of success sometimes increase an animal's probability of using social information. However, theory does not yet predict which internal states indicative of lack of success affect use of social information, and gives no indication of which species might be expected to increase affiliation or social learning when unsuccessful. Indeed, "successful" and "unsuccessful" are probably not sufficient descriptors of either potential social learners or their potential models. What is needed, but not available, is programmatic examination of the effects of various sorts of lack of success on susceptibility to various types of social learning. When are deficient animals more likely to affiliate with conspecifics than healthy animals? What types of social learning are affected by lack of success: are deficient animals more susceptible to local enhancement, more likely to follow conspecifics to food, or to copy conspecifics' food choices? Do different deprivation states affect differently which potential models deprived animals choose to copy? Theory does not yet provide much guidance in asking or answering such mechanistic questions.

Affective Responses

Whether an animal chooses to adopt another's behaviour can depend not only on its internal state, but also on its affective response to the outcomes of alternative behaviours in which others are engaged. Such "direct bias" (Boyd & Richerson 1985) can have important effects on the probability of socially acquired information affecting behaviour. For example, Dugatkin (1996) set in opposition the tendency of female guppies to affiliate with physically attractive males (those with large orange-coloured areas on their bodies; Houde 1988) and with males that they had been previously seen courting other females (Dugatkin 1992; Dugatkin & Godin 1992). He found that a female guppy that had watched the less-orange-coloured of two males court subsequently preferred to affiliate with him, but only if his areas of orange colouration were slightly smaller (4% to 24%) than those of his competitor (Dugatkin 1996). If two males differed 40% or more in orange colouration, then females preferred the male with larger orange patches even after seeing the male with smaller orange patches court another female.

In analogous fashion, observer rats that interacted with demonstrator rats that were fed a diet flavoured with unpalatable cayenne pepper before choosing between a standard diet and a diet flavoured with varying concentrations of cayenne pepper showed less social influence on their diet choice the greater the concentration of cayenne pepper in the flavoured diet offered to them (Galef & Whiskin 1998). When the relative palatability of two diets offered to observer rats was manipulated by increasing rather than by decreasing the palatability of the food that demonstrators ate, once again, as the difference in palatability of the diets offered to demonstrators increased, the effects of demonstrators on their observers' food choices decreased (Galef & Whiskin 1998).

In general, as theory predicts, the greater the difference in affective response of naïve individuals to two stimuli, the less the impact of demonstrators on their observers' subsequent choices between those stimuli.

Preparedness

In a classic series of studies of social learning of predator avoidance, Cook and Mineka (1989, 1990) demonstrated that laboratory-reared, juvenile rhesus monkeys learn to respond fearfully to snakes or snake-like objects by watching adults of their species exhibit fearful responses to such stimuli. However, such social learning of avoidance was limited to specific stimuli. After watching video sequences of conspecifics appearing to behave fearfully towards either a toy rabbit or flowers, rhesus monkeys failed to acquire fear responses to them. However, similar video presentations were sufficient to induce fear of snake-like stimuli (Cook & Mineka 1989, 1990).

Similar preferential social learning to certain stimuli has also been found in birds, although it is of lesser degree (Griffin 2004). Curio and colleagues (1978) found that socially learned antipredator responses to a stuffed bird were stronger than similar responses learned to a plastic bottle. Initial responses of naïve birds were greater to presentation of a stuffed bird than a plastic bottle, and may have been responsible for the different strengths of subsequent social learning. Thus, empirical investigations suggest the need for theoretical developments to extend the notion of "preparedness" (Seligman 1970), "cue to consequence specificity" (Garcia & Koelling 1966), or "adaptive specialisation of learning" (Rozin & Kalat 1971) from individual learning to social learning.

Characteristics of Demonstrators

Boyd and Richerson (1985) have discussed the effects on social learning not only of affective responses to outcomes of alternative actions (direct bias), but also of the characteristics of models on the probability that their behaviour will be adopted (indirect bias). Effects of a number of different attributes of potential models on the probability that the naïve will adopt their behaviour have been explored.

Success

Both common sense and theory suggest that observers should be more likely to adopt the behaviour of successful than of unsuccessful demonstrators (Laland 2004). Surprisingly, observers do not always make the predicted discrimination. For example, although Norway rats can readily distinguish poisoned from unpoisoned conspecifics, they are no more likely to adopt the food choices of the healthy than of the ill (Galef *et al.* 1990; Galef *et al.* 1983). Perhaps similarly, domestic hens are no more likely to learn socially from previously highly successful than from the less successful foragers (Nicol & Pope 1994, 1999). Norway rats and domestic fowl appear to lack the behavioural machinery needed to learn differentially from successful and unsuccessful potential demonstrators, though functional considerations lead to the prediction that they should.

Reliability

Norway rats are also unable to distinguish reliable from unreliable demonstrators. Galef and colleagues (1999) poisoned observer rats on several occasions after the rats ate whatever foods one demonstrator had eaten and never poisoned the rats after they ate the foods that a second demonstrator had eaten. The observers were subsequently equally likely to copy the food choices of the two demonstrators.

Proficiency

Both theory and common sense also suggest that individuals should be more likely to adopt the behaviour of proficient than of ineffective conspecifics (Laland 2004), but this is often not the case. Swaney and colleagues (2001) found that guppies were more likely to use socially acquired information to learn a path to concealed food when conspecific demonstrators were poorly trained than when they were well trained. Well-trained demonstrators appeared to move too quickly for naïve individuals to join them en route to food (van Bergen *et al.* 2004).

Similar superiority of nonproficient to proficient demonstrators as tutors has been reported in two sets of experiments in which birds watched proficient and less proficient tutors perform arbitrary operant responses (Beauchamp & Kacelnik 1991; Biederman & Vanayan 1988). Beauchamp and Kacelnik (1991) interpreted the superiority of nonproficient to proficient demonstrators, both in their own experiment and that of Biederman and Vanayan (1988), to proficient demonstrators providing a reliable cue for the opportunity to forage that interfered with learning about any other cues that predicted food availability. Studies of asocial learning have shown repeatedly that learning to respond to a reliable cue of the occurrence of a rewarding event interferes with subsequent learning to respond to a second cue that predicts occurrence of the same event.

Although theory led to the posing of interesting questions about the relationship of demonstrator proficiency to demonstrator effectiveness, the observed relationship between proficiency and effectiveness depended on details of mechanisms of little current interest from an evolutionary perspective. The importance of such mechanistic detail in determining behavioural outcomes suggests the need for further integration of mechanistic and functional perspectives in theory building.

Frequency

Some theory has been developed to reflect social learners' sensitivity to the frequency with which other individuals engage in each of two or more alternative behaviours (Boyd & Richerson 1985; Chou & Richerson 1992). Both, Chou and Richerson (1992) and Galef and Whiskin (1995b) found that observer rats offered a choice between two diets after interacting with groups of demonstrator rats, some of whose members had eaten each of the two diets, showed diet choices reflecting the proportion of group members that had eaten each diet. For example, observer rats offered a choice of cinnamon- and cocoa-flavoured diets after interacting with a group of four demonstrators, three of which had eaten cocoa-flavoured diet and one cinnamon-flavoured diet, ate more cocoa-flavoured diet than observer rats that had interacted with a group of four demonstrators, three of which had eaten cinnamon-flavoured diet and one cocoa-flavoured diet.

Social and Individual Learning

Individual experiences of various kinds can affect the probability that an observer will subsequently copy the behaviour of others. Conversely, social learning can affect both the probability that subsequent individual learning will occur and the stimuli towards which individual learning will be directed.

Individual Experience and Subsequent Social Acquisition of Behaviour

Several types of individual experience (e.g., simple exposure, Pavlovian conditioning, operant conditioning) can affect the probability that an individual's subsequent acquisition of behaviour will be influenced by interaction with others.

Familiarity

Familiarity of Demonstrators

Coussi-Korbel and Fragaszy (1995: 1444) have distinguished between instances of social learning where the relationship between a demonstrator and its observer affects the strength of social learning ("directed social learning") and those where the relationship between demonstrator and observer is irrelevant ("nonspecific social learning"). The distinction is similar to an earlier one proposed by Boyd and Richerson (1985) between indirectly biased and unbiased social learning.

Several laboratories have looked for and found effects of a prior relationship between an observer and its demonstrator on subsequent social learning. The general finding, as Coussi-Korbel and Fragaszy (1995) observed, is that naïve individuals are more likely to learn from interaction with familiar rather than with unfamiliar conspecifics, though there are both exceptions to that rule and no obvious functional reason why familiar individuals should be preferred to nonpreferred individuals as sources of information.

In a very early study of local enhancement, Chesler (1969) found that kittens that had watched their mothers press a lever for a food reward subsequently learned the same behaviour faster than did kittens that had watched an unfamiliar cat engage in the same behaviour. More recently, Lupfer and colleagues (2003) reported that young golden hamsters exhibit enhanced preference for novel foods eaten by their dam, but not for those eaten by an unfamiliar adult. Moreover, Benskin and colleagues (2002) showed that the probability that young zebra finches will copy the food choice of a male model increases when he is familiar with his observers. Swaney and colleagues (2001) provide data indicating, similarly, that naïve guppies learned a path to a concealed food source more rapidly when a demonstrator shoal consisted of familiar rather than of unfamiliar individuals.

Cadieu and Cadieu (2002, 2004) compared effects of parents and unfamiliar conspecific adult demonstrators on ingestion of a novel food by young canaries and found that parents were more effective in inducing feeding on novel food. Juveniles' manipulation of unfamiliar seed was more frequent in the presence of fathers than of unfamiliar males, and juveniles ingested more seed in the presence of a parent of either sex than in the presence of an unfamiliar adult. Cadieu and Cadieu (2004) suggested that the greater efficacy of fathers than of unfamiliar male canaries as demonstrators resulted from fathers exhibiting the relevant behaviour more often in the presence of their own offspring than in the presence of others' young.

Kaveliers and colleagues (2005) report that naïve, laboratory-bred deer-mice (*Peromyscus maniculatus*) show greater social learning of defensive responses to biting flies after observing siblings or familiar non-kin than after observing unfamiliar individuals respond defensively to biting flies. Further, within familiar pairs, social status affected acquisition, with subordinate observers displaying better social learning than dominants.

In a possible exception to the rule that increasing familiarity of demonstrators increases their effectiveness as demonstrators, Hatch and Lefebvre (1997) reported that juvenile ring doves tend to learn a novel foraging technique better from unrelated but familiar adults than from their fathers, possibly because parental tolerance permits scrounging of food that inhibits social learning.

Valsecchi and colleagues (1996) reported striking differences in social enhancement of food preferences in Mongolian gerbils exposed to either familiar or unfamiliar demonstrators, a somewhat unexpected finding given that Galef and colleagues (1984) had previously reported no effect of familiarity between demonstrator and observer Norway rats on social learning of food preferences. Subsequent analysis (Galef *et al.* 1998) suggested that whether familiarity of demonstrator and observer affected social learning of food preferences depended not on species differences, but on the strength of the cues that demonstrators provided for their observers. When demonstrators were fed immediately before interacting with observers, and were therefore presumably emitting relatively strong diet-identifying cues for their observers to learn about, both familiar and unfamiliar demonstrator rats and gerbils had equivalent effects on conspecific observers' subsequent food choices. When demonstrators ate some hours before they interacted with observers, and presumably therefore provided weaker diet-identifying cues than demonstrators fed immediately before they interacted with their observers, familiarity of demonstrators had a significant effect on observers' food preferences.

In general, there is a need for further experimental work to determine the conditions under which familiarity influences the strength of social learning and, for further theoretical work exploring possible functional implications of the apparent greater effectiveness of familiar than of unfamiliar demonstrators. Coussi-Korbel and Fragaszy (1995) suggested that individual differences in the efficacy of demonstrators result from differences in the salience of their behaviour to their observers, though, obviously, differences in salience are only one of many possible causes of differences in the effectiveness of familiar and unfamiliar demonstrators in altering the behaviour of their observers.

Familiarity of Stimuli

Galef (1993) and Galef and Whiskin (1994) found that rats maintained on a single type of food for several days did not show an enhanced preference for that food after interacting with a demonstrator rat that had eaten it; however, rats that were unfamiliar with the food that a demonstrator ate exhibited a marked enhancement of their preference for that food. Because the effect of personal experience of a food on subsequent social learning of a preference for it is to restrict socially learned food preferences to foods not eaten in the recent past, Galef (1993) interpreted this familiarity-induced inhibition of social learning as indicating that social learning about foods evolved to facilitate individuals increasing or maintaining dietary breadth. However, subsequent findings suggest that it is probably incorrect to infer that effects of diet familiarity on social learning are adaptations related to social learning about foods.

Recent work indicates that maintenance on a single food causes a surprisingly powerful, though relatively short-lived (24 to 48 hours), reduction in Norway rats' (and golden hamsters') subsequent preference for that food (DiBattista 2002; Galef & Whiskin 2003, 2005). Consequently, an observer rat that has eaten a food for 3 days before encountering a conspecific demonstrator that has eaten the same food experiences social induction of preference for a food to which it has already developed an aversion (Galef & Whiskin 2003). As discussed earlier, animals' affective responses towards stimuli to which socially acquired information directs them can affect the probability that social learning will occur.

Aversion to a maintenance diet may also underlie Forkman's (1991) finding that Mongolian gerbils resume eating novel but not familiar foods when a hungry, feeding conspecific is placed with them. Whether Mongolian gerbils, like Norway rats and golden hamsters, develop an aversion to a food after eating it for several days in succession is not known. However, if they do, then the difference that Forkman found in social facilitation of gerbils eating familiar and unfamiliar foods might reflect a difference in social facilitation of ingestion of relatively palatable and unpalatable foods.

Social Learning and Subsequent Independent Acquisition and Performance of Behaviour

Students of individual learning have discovered that variables can have rather different effects on the acquisition of behaviour and on the performance of previously acquired behaviours (Staddon & Simmelhag 1971). The same distinction can be applied to social learning (Galef 1995). In the following sections, I discuss issues relevant to the acquisition and performance of behaviour separately, though the distinction is seldom made in the literature on social learning.

Acquisition

Whether social influences on acquisition of behaviour lead to optimal or sub-optimal performance is situation-dependent. In particular, social learning in relatively stable environments tends to promote adaptive interactions between social and individual learning, whereas social learning in more variable environments can result in delayed acquisition of novel adaptive responses (Boyd & Richerson 1985).

Studies of social influence on the acquisition of aversions by Norway rats provide examples of possibly adaptive effects of prior social learning on individual learning. For example, an observer rat that: (1) interacts with a conspecific demonstrator eating an unfamiliar food, (2) then eats the food that its demonstrator ate and becomes ill, is relatively unlikely to learn an aversion to the food that it ate before experiencing illness (Galef 1989). Similarly, if an observer rat: (1) interacts with a conspecific demonstrator that has eaten a food; (2) then eats two foods for the first time, one of which is the food its demonstrator ate; and (3) is poisoned, the observer learns an aversion to whichever food it ate that its demonstrator had not eaten (Galef 1989). Such social influence on acquisition might increase the probability that ill rats would avoid the lost opportunity costs of learning an aversion to a food when illness experienced in the hours following ingestion of a novel food results from some cause other than food poisoning.

Laland and Williams (1998) provide evidence of circumstances in which social learning appears to reduce the probability of later adaptive individual learning. Guppies tested while members of shoals that were taking the longer of two routes to food learned an alternative, more efficient route to food more slowly than did naïve guppies tested individually. Testing of the trained guppies in shoals and of the naïve animals individually, though appropriate from a functional perspective, makes it difficult to determine the relative contribution of social learning and a tendency to remain in a shoal to slowed acquisition of a novel, adaptive response.

Pongracz and colleagues (2003) also discuss a situation where social learning interferes with subsequent individual acquisition of more efficient behaviours. They found that dogs that had learned socially to make a detour around a fence were subsequently less likely than naïve dogs to use an open door in the fence to access reward. The greater the number of demonstrations of detouring around the fence a dog had received, the slower it was to learn the direct route. Whether social learning itself or experience of rewards after social leaning occurred was responsible for retardation of individual acquisition of the more efficient route to food remains to be determined.

Performance

Interaction with conspecifics can influence not only acquisition of behaviour, but also how long a previously independently learned behaviour is expressed.

For example, after a focal animal, a rat (Galef 1986) or a hyena (Yoerg 1991), learns independently to avoid a food because ingestion of that food preceded experience of illness, the focal animal will abandon its learned aversion after interacting with one or more conspecifics that have recently eaten the food that the focal animal had learned independently to avoid. In a conceptually similar study, Pongracz and colleagues (2003) trained dogs to go through an open door to reach food or a favourite toy. When the door was closed, the dogs' perseverance was substantially reduced if a human demonstrated a detour around the fence.

Effects of Individual Learning on Subsequent Acquisition and Performance of Socially Learned Behaviours

Following, I now consider the inverse relationship to that discussed in the preceding section, reviewing evidence of effects of individual learning on subsequent acquisition and performance of socially learned behaviours.

Acquisition

Theory suggests that individuals should "copy when uncertain," and prior individual experience in an environment should affect judgement as to its predictability. For example, as theory suggests, maintaining rats in constantly changing conditions, a circumstance that should increase uncertainty, increased their dependence on information acquired from others. For 12 days, Galef and Whiskin (2004) fed rats a different food, at a different hour, for different lengths of time, and found a small, but statistically reliable increase in subjects' subsequent use of social information in food choice relative to rats fed on predictable schedules.

On the other hand, feeding observer rats two foods for a week (which should have reduced their uncertainty concerning those foods) and then allowing them to interact with demonstrators that had eaten one of the two foods did not reduce demonstrators' influence on their observers' preferences for those foods (Galef & Whiskin 2001). As discussed earlier, although maintenance on a single food temporarily blocks subsequent social induction of preference for that food, such inhibition results from exposure-induced aversion and probably does not involve reduced uncertainty (Galef 1993; Galef & Whiskin 2005).

Individual learning can determine the attractiveness of the stimuli encountered as a result of copying the behaviour of another, and as discussed in a preceding section, affective responses to behavioural outcomes can alter the probability that an individual will adopt the behaviour of another individual. For example, Galef (1985) varied the strength of toxin used to induce an aversion to a palatable food in observer rats and then examined the effect of interaction with a demonstrator rat eating that food on observer rats' subsequent choice of it. The greater the pharmacological insult used to induce an aversion to the palatable food, and consequently the greater the strength of the aversion learned, the smaller the effect of interaction with a demonstrator rat fed the palatable diet on its observers' intake of the food that they had previously learned to avoid.

Galef and colleagues (1987) found, similarly, that the probability that a hungry Norway rat would follow a trained leader rat through a maze to food was affected by potential followers' information regarding the safety of the food that a potential leader had eaten. Galef and colleagues (1987) either poisoned or did not poison rats immediately after they ate a palatable food. When a trained leader rat was fed the same palatable food that its potential followers had learned to avoid, the poisoned rats failed to follow the leader, although the poisoned rats readily followed leader rats that had eaten other foods.

Performance

A number of experiments have been undertaken to examine factors that affect the longevity of a socially learned behaviour when a superior alternative becomes available. The general method of such studies has been similar. An observer learns socially to perform some behaviour that is less rewarding than an alternative subsequently made available to it, and the number of trials or time taken under various conditions for the observer to adopt the superior behaviour is measured. As might be expected, strength of initial social learning (determined by the number of demonstrators, the number of demonstrations, or the temporal distribution of demonstrations) affects the longevity of performance of a socially learned behaviour (Galef & Whiskin 1998), as does the opportunity to evaluate consequences of engaging in alternative courses of action (Galef 1999; Galef & Allen 1995; Galef & Whiskin 1997, 2001). For example, longevity of rats' socially enhanced food preferences, when choosing between a food that demonstrators had eaten and an alternative, decreased with an increase in either the time available to sample foods or the palatability of an alternative food (Galef & Allen 1995; Galef & Whiskin 1997, 2001).

Results of such experiments suggest that socially learned behaviours, similar to behaviours learned individually, are not maintained when they lead to insufficient reward. For example, McQuoid and Galef (1992) found that observer Burmese jungle fowl that watched conspecific demonstrators fed from a visually distinctive bowl on television were equally likely to initiate pecking at a similar bowl when it was presented in a choice situation, whether food was present in the bowl or it was empty. When food was present in the bowl that looked like the one from which demonstrators had fed, observers continued to peck at that bowl for many minutes. However, when that bowl was empty, pecking by observers ceased in seconds. Effects of individual experience were clearly on performance of a socially learned behaviour, not on its acquisition.

The little evidence available suggests that socially learned behaviours are abandoned as rapidly as individually learned behaviours by those discovering alternative behaviours that produce either greater reward or equal reward at less cost (Mason *et al.* 1984; Galef & Whiskin 1995a). Mason and colleagues (1984) trained red-winged blackbirds to avoid distinctively coloured food cups either directly, by poisoning them after they ate from those cups, or socially, by watching conspecifics who became ill after eating from those cups. They then offered the birds a choice between two food cups containing the same food. One cup was the colour associated with illness, and the other a different colour. Mason and colleagues (1984) found that birds that had learned directly and birds that had learned socially continued to avoid the food cup associated with illness for the same length of time. If, as seems to be the case, socially learned behaviours extinguish rapidly without differential reward, the probability of a suboptimal behaviour becoming fixed in a population diminishes and perseverance of "maladaptive" traditions (Laland 1996) becomes less likely (Galef 1995, 1996).

Acquisition and Performance

Giraldeau and Lefebvre (1987) examined effects of the opportunity to "scrounge" seeds produced by another's foraging on the frequency with which pigeons acquired a behaviour that resulted in access to seeds by observing others engage in that behaviour. Scrounging food produced by a demonstrator that removed a stopper from an inverted test tube and released seed that both producer and observer could eat reduced the probability that observers would both learn and perform the behaviour that they had observed. Naïve observers that scrounged some of the food that their demonstrators produced while demonstrating were less likely to open tubes when subsequently tested alone than were observers assigned to a control group that watched demonstrators open tubes, but had no access to the food that their demonstrators produced.

When observers that had learned socially to open tubes foraged together with a bird trained to produce, the observers stopped opening tubes and scrounged seeds released by producers. When producers were removed, observers produced. Thus, scrounging interfered with performance of a socially learned behaviour as well as with its acquisition. No subsequent study has provided such clear evidence of social effects on both learning and performance, and results of some studies have failed to provide evidence that scrounging interferes with social learning (McQuoid & Galef 1994; Giraldeau & Templeton 1991: experiment 2; Mason & Reidinger 1981).

Conclusion

Theoretically and empirically based approaches to the study of variables affecting the probability of social learning are clearly complementary. Formal models reveal unexpected order in previously unconnected observations and serve as heuristics to identify areas in need of empirical exploration. Empirical studies, undertaken to explore mechanisms of social learning, often reveal effects that formal models have not, and perhaps, given the current state of our knowledge, cannot predict. For example, and as discussed earlier, theory predicts that animals should be more likely to adopt the behaviour of successful than unsuccessful potential models. Yet, naïve Norway rats show as great an enhancement of their preferences for those foods eaten by healthy demonstrators as for those eaten by unconscious demonstrators or retching demonstrators with uncontrollable diarrhoea.

The reasons for the failure of observation to confirm theory are unclear. For example, although the potential benefits of copying food choices of healthy individuals seem obvious, there may be hidden costs of responding differently to successful and unsuccessful demonstrators that have resulted in the failure of rats to evolve that ability. Perhaps, in natural circumstances, ill or unconscious rats are only rarely incapacitated by ingesting toxic substances. If so, lost opportunity costs of ignoring information about foods that unhealthy potential demonstrators have eaten may be greater than the benefits of ignoring such information. Alternatively, costs of maintaining neural structures needed to inhibit acquiring a preference for foods eaten by unhealthy demonstrators may be greater than benefits resulting from ignoring information extracted from the unwell. Whatever the ultimate cause of the inability of rats to inhibit acquisition of preferences for foods eaten by ill demonstrators, empirical investigations suggest boundary conditions on theoretical predictions that point the way for the next generation of theories.

It might be argued that variables that influence the acquisition and performance of socially learned behaviours are simply specific examples of factors identified in formal models as determinants of when animals should rely on socially acquired information in decision making. For instance, theorists tell us that animals should copy when their established behaviour is unproductive. Suffering protein deficiency or hunger might indicate to an animal that its current behaviour is unproductive. If so, experiencing either protein or caloric deprivation should increase the probability that animals will adopt the behaviour of others. Of course, at a mechanistic level, there is no guarantee that experiencing caloric deficiency and protein deficiency will have similar effects on the probability of social learning, and the evidence to date suggests that they may not.

In closing his review of formal models of social learning, Laland (2004) calls for empirical research that explicitly evaluates predictions derived from such models. As this chapter makes clear, there is also a need for theoretical models to take into account the rich empirical literature demonstrating boundary conditions that appear to restrict the generality of current theoretical formulations. Dewar (2004) developed a formal model of the effects of previous experience on social learning using as a starting point previously reported differences among species in both willingness to ingest unfamiliar foods and responsiveness to social influences on food choice. Such integration of theoretical and empirical approaches in modelling is clearly necessary.

Perhaps both the most interesting and, at the same time the most challenging, feature of social learning as a field of inquiry is the requirement to integrate work undertaken from divergent perspectives. In isolation, neither theoretical nor empirical approaches are sufficient to provide a full understanding of the role of social learning in the development of behavioural repertoires of animals. The future of the field lies in integration of two quite different approaches.

Acknowledgments

Preparation of the manuscript was facilitated by a Discovery Grant from the Natural Sciences and Engineering Research Council of Canada. Thanks to Kevin Laland for pointing out, in a most helpful way, the many inadequacies of an earlier draft and to Jeff Lucas for making the text of the present manuscript easier to read.

References

Beauchamp, G. & Kacelnik, A. 1991. Effects of the knowledge of partners on learning rates in zebra finches, *Taeniopygia guttata*. *Animal Behaviour*, **41**, 247–253.

Beck, M. & Galef, B. G. Jr. 1989. Social influences on the selection of a protein-sufficient diet by Norway rats. *Journal of Comparative Psychology*, **103**, 132–139.

Benskin, C. Mc., Mann, W. H., Lachlin, R. F., & Slater, P. J. B. 2002. Social learning directs feeding preferences in the zebra finch, *Taeniopygia guttata*. *Animal Behaviour*, **64**, 823–828.

Biederman, G. B. & Vanayan, M. 1988. Observational learning in pigeons: the function of the quality of observed performance in simultaneous discrimination. *Learning and Motivation*, **19**, 31–43.

Boyd, R. & Richerson, P. J. 1985. *Culture and the Evolutionary Process*. Chicago: University of Chicago Press.

Cadieu, N. & Cadieu, J.-C. 2002. Is use of a novel food source by young canaries (*Serinus canaries*) influenced by the sex and familiarity of the adult demonstrator? *Behaviour,* **139,** 825–846.

Cadieu, N. & Cadieu, J.-C. 2004. The influence of free interactions and partner familiarity on social transmission in young canary. *Animal Behaviour,* **67,** 1051–1057.

Chesler, P. 1969. Maternal influence in learning by observation in kittens. *Science,* **166,** 901–903.

Chou, L.-S. & Richerson, P. L. 1992. Multiple models of social transmission of food selection by Norway rats, *Rattus norvegicus. Animal Behaviour,* **44,** 337–343.

Cook, M. & Mineka, S. 1989. Observational conditioning of fear to fear-relevant and fear-irrelevant stimuli in rhesus monkeys. *Journal of Abnormal Psychology,* **98,** 448–459.

Cook, M. & Mineka, S. 1990. Selective associations in the observational conditioning of fear in rhesus monkeys. *Journal of Experimental Psychology: Animal Behavior Processes,* **16,** 372–389.

Coussi-Korbel, S. & Fragaszy, D. M. 1995. On the relation between social dynamics and social learning. *Animal Behaviour,* **50,** 1441–1453.

Curio, E., Ernst, U. & Vieth, W. 1978. Adaptive significance of avian mobbing: II. Cultural transmission of enemy recognition in blackbirds: effectiveness and some constraints. *Zeitschrift fur Tierpsychologie,* **48,** 184–202.

Dewar, G. 2004. Social and asocial cues about new food: cue reliability influences intake in rats. *Learning & Behavior,* **32,** 82–89.

DiBattista, D. 2002. Preference for novel flavors in golden hamsters (*Mesocricetus auratus*). *Journal of Comparative Psychology,* **116,** 63–72.

Dugatkin, L. A. 1992. Sexual selection and imitation: females copy the mate choices of others. *American Naturalist,* **139,** 1384–1389.

Dugatkin, L. A. 1996. Interface between culturally based preferences and genetic preferences: female mate choice in *Poecilia reticulata. Proceedings of the National Academy of Sciences,* **93,** 2770–2773.

Dugatkin, L. A. & Godin, J.-G. J. 1992. Reversal of female choice by copying in the guppy (*Poecilia reticulata*). *Proceedings of the Royal Society of London, Series B,* **249,** 179–184.

Forkman, B. 1991. Social facilitation is shown by gerbils when presented with novel but not with familiar food. *Animal Behaviour,* **42,** 860–861.

Galef, B. G. Jr. 1977. The social transmission of food preferences: an adaptation for weaning in rats. *Journal of Comparative and Physiological Psychology,* **91,** 1136–1140.

Galef, B. G. Jr. 1978. Differences in the affiliative behavior of weanling rats selecting eating and drinking sites. *Journal of Comparative and Physiological Psychology,* **92,** 431–438.

Galef, B. G. Jr. 1985. Direct and indirect behavioral processes for the social transmission of food avoidance. *Proceedings of the New York Academy of Sciences,* **443,** 203–215.

Galef, B. G. Jr. 1986. Social identification of toxic diets by Norway rats (*R. norvegicus*). *Journal of Comparative Psychology,* **100,** 331–334.

Galef, B. G. Jr. 1986. Social interaction modifies learned aversions, sodium appetite, and both palatability and handling-time induced dietary preference in rats (*R. norvegicus*), *Journal of Comparative Psychology,* **100,** 432–439.

Galef, B. G. Jr. 1989. Socially-mediated attenuation of taste-aversion learning in Norway rats: preventing development of "food phobias." *Animal Learning & Behavior,* **17,** 468–474.

Galef, B. G. Jr. 1993. Functions of social learning about foods by Norway rats: a causal analysis of effects of diet novelty on preference transmission. *Animal Behaviour,* **46,** 257–265.

Galef, B. G. Jr. 1995. Why behaviour patterns that animals learn socially are locally adaptive. *Animal Behaviour,* **49,** 1325–1334.

Galef, B. G. Jr. 1996. The adaptive value of social learning: a reply to Laland. *Animal Behaviour,* **52,** 641–644.

Galef, B. G. Jr. 1999. Effects of time for resource sampling on use of public information while foraging. *Animal Cognition,* **2,** 103–107.

Galef, B. G. Jr. 2004. Approaches to the study of traditional behaviors of free-living animals. *Learning & Behavior*, **32**, 53–61.

Galef, B. G. Jr. 2004. Social learning: promoter or inhibitor of innovation. In: *Animal Innovation* (Ed. by S. Reader & K. N. Laland), pp. 137–155. Cambridge: Cambridge University Press.

Galef, B. G. Jr. & Allen, C. 1995. A new model system for studying animal tradition. *Animal Behaviour*, **50**, 705–717.

Galef, B. G. Jr., Beck, M. & Whiskin, E. E. 1991. Protein deficiency magnifies social influences on the food choices of Norway rats (*Rattus norvegicus*). *Journal of Comparative Psychology*, **105**, 55–59.

Galef, B. G. Jr., Kennett, D. J. & Wigmore, S. W. 1984. Transfer of information concerning distant foods in rats: a robust phenomenon. *Animal Learning & Behavior*, **12**, 292–296.

Galef, B. G. Jr., Lee, W. Y. & Whiskin, E. E. 2005. Lack of interference effects in long-term memory for socially learned food preferences. *Journal of Comparative Psychology*, **119**, 131–135.

Galef, B. G. Jr., Mischinger, A. & Malenfant, S. A. 1987. Hungry rats following of conspecifics to food depends on the diets eaten by potential leaders. *Animal Behaviour*, **35**, 1234–1239.

Galef, B. G. Jr., McQuoid, L. M., & Whiskin, E. E. 1990. Further evidence that Norway rats do not socially transmit learned aversions to toxic baits. *Animal Learning & Behavior*, **18**, 199–205.

Galef, B. G. Jr., Rudolf, B., Whiskin, E. E., Choleris, E., Mainardi, M. & Valsecchi, P. 1998. Familiarity and relatedness: effects on social learning about foods by Norway rats and Mongolian gerbils. *Animal Learning & Behavior*, **26**, 448–454.

Galef, B. G. Jr. & Whiskin, E. E. 1994. Passage of time reduces effects of familiarity on social learning: functional implications. *Animal Behaviour*, **48**, 1057–1062.

Galef, B. G. Jr. & Whiskin, E. E. 1995a. Are socially learned behaviours irreversible? *Behavioural Processes*, **34**, 279–284.

Galef, B. G., Jr. & Whiskin, E. E. 1995b. Learning socially to eat more of one food than of another. *Journal of Comparative Psychology*, **109**, 99–101.

Galef, B. G. Jr. & Whiskin, E. E. 1997. Effects of social and asocial learning on longevity of food-preference traditions. *Animal Behaviour*, **53**, 1313–1322.

Galef, B. G. Jr. & Whiskin, E. E. 1998. Determinants of the longevity of socially learned food preferences of Norway rats. *Animal Behaviour*, **55**, 967–975.

Galef, B. G. Jr. & Whiskin, E. E. 1998. Limits on social influences on food choices of Norway rats. *Animal Behaviour*, **56**, 1015–1020.

Galef, B. G. Jr. & Whiskin, E. E. 2001. Effects of caloric, protein, and sodium deprivation on affiliative behavior of Norway rats. *Journal of Comparative Psychology*, **115**, 192–195.

Galef, B. G. Jr. & Whiskin, E. E. 2001. Interaction of social and asocial learning in food preferences of Norway rats. *Animal Behaviour*, **62**, 41–46.

Galef, B. G. Jr. & Whiskin, E. E. 2003. Preference for novel flavors in adult Norway rats (*Rattus norvegicus*). *Journal of Comparative Psychology*, **117**, 96–100.

Galef, B. G. Jr. & Whiskin, E. E. 2004. Effects of environmental stability and demonstrator age on social learning of food preferences by young Norway rats. *Animal Behaviour*, **68**, 897–902.

Galef, B. G. Jr. & Whiskin, E. E. 2005. Differences between golden hamsters and Norway rats in preference for the sole diet that they are eating. *Journal of Comparative Psychology*, **119**, 8–13.

Galef, B. G. Jr., Whiskin, E. E. & Horn, C. S. 1999. What observer rats don't learn about food from demonstrator rats. *Animal Learning & Behavior*, **27**, 316–322.

Galef, B. G. Jr. & Wigmore, S. W. 1983. Transfer of information concerning distant foods: A laboratory investigation of the "information-centre" hypothesis. *Animal Behaviour*, **31**, 748–758.

Galef, B. G. Jr., Wigmore, S. W. & Kennett, D. J. 1983. A failure to find socially mediated taste-aversion learning in Norway rats (*R. norvegicus*). *Journal of Comparative Psychology*, **97**, 358–363.

Garcia, J. & Koelling, R. A. 1966. The relationship of cue to consequence in avoidance learning. *Psychonomic Science*, **4**, 123–124.

Giraldeau, L-A. & LeFebvre, L. 1987. Scrounging prevents cultural transmission of food-finding behaviour in pigeons. *Animal Behaviour*, **35**, 387–394.

Giraldeau, L-A. & Templeton, J. J. 1991. Food scrounging and diffusion of foraging skills in pigeons, *Columbia livia*, the importance of tutor and observer rewards. *Ethology*, **89**, 63–72.

Griffin, A. S. 2004. Social learning about predators: a review and prospectus. *Learning & Behavior*, **32**, 131–140.

Hatch, K. K. & Lefebvre, L. 1997. Does father know best? Social learning from kin and non-kin in juvenile ring doves. *Behavioral Processes*, **41**, 1–10.

Hensor, E. M. A., Godin J., G. J., Hoare, D. J. & Krause, J. 2003. Effects of nutritional status on the shoaling tendency of banded killifish, *Fundulus diaphanous*, in the field. *Animal Behaviour*, **65**, 663–669.

Heyes, C. M. 1993. Imitation, culture and cognition. *Animal Behaviour*, **46**, 999–1010.

Houde, A. E. 1988. Genetic difference in female choice between two guppy populations. *Animal Behaviour*, **36**, 510–516.

Kaveliers, M., Colwell, D. D. & Choleris, E. 2005. Kinship, familiarity and social status modulate social learning about "micropredators" (biting flies) in deer mice. *Behavioural Ecology & Socioliology*, **58**, 60–71.

Laland, K. N. 1996. Is social learning always locally adaptive? *Animal Behaviour*, **52**, 637–640.

Laland, K. N. 2004. Social leaning strategies. *Learning & Behavior*, **32**, 4–14.

Laland, K. N. & Williams, K. 1998. Social transmission of maladaptive information in the guppy. *Behavioral Ecology*, **9**, 493–499.

Lupfer, G., Frieman, J. & Coonfield, D. 2003. Social transmission of flavor preferences in two species of hamsters (*Mesocricetus auratus* and *Phodopus campbelli*). *Journal of Comparative Psychology*, **117**, 449–455.

Mason, J. R., Artz, A. H. & Reidinger, R. F. 1984. Comparative assessment of food preferences and aversions acquired by blackbirds via observational learning, *The Auk*, **101**, 796–803.

Mason, J. R. & Reidinger, R. F. 1981. Effects of social facilitation and observational learning on feeding behavior of the red-winged blackbird (*Agelaius phoeniceus*). *The Auk*, **98**, 778–784.

McQuoid, L. M. & Galef, B. G. Jr. 1992. Social influences on feeding site selection by Burmese fowl (*Gallus gallus*). *Journal of Comparative Psychology*, **106**, 137–141.

McQuoid, L. M. & Galef, B. G. Jr. 1994. Effects of access to food during training on social learning by Burmese jungle fowl. *Animal Behaviour*, **48**, 737–739.

Mock, D. W., Lamey, T. C. & Thompson, D. B. A. 1988. Falsifiability and the information centre hypothesis. *Ornis Scandinavica*, **19**, 231–248.

Nicol, C. J. & Pope, S. J. 1994. Social learning in small flocks of laying hens. *Animal Behaviour*, **47**, 1289–1296.

Nicol, C. J. & Pope, S. J. 1999. The effects of demonstrator social status and prior foraging success on social learning in domestic hens. *Animal Behaviour*, **57**, 163–171.

Pongracz, P., Miklosi, A. Kubinyi, E. Topal, J. & Csanyi, V. 2003. Interaction between individual experience and social learning in dogs. *Animal Behaviour*, **65**, 595–603.

Popper, K. 1959. *The Logic of Scientific Discovery*. London: Hutchinson.

Rozin, P. & Kalat, J. W. 1971. Specific hungers and poison avoidance as adaptive specializations of learning. *Psychological Review*, **78**, 459–486.

Seligman, M. E. P. 1970. On the generality of the laws of learning. *Psychological Review*, **77**, 406–418.

Sonerud, G. A., Smedshaug, C. A. & Brathen, O. 2001. Ignorant hooded crows follow knowledgeable roost-mates to food: support for the information centre hypothesis. *Proceedings of the Royal Society of London, Series B*, **268**, 827–831.

Staddon, J. E. R. & Simmelhag, V. L. 1971. The 'superstition' experiment: a reexamination of its implications for the principle of adaptive behavior. *Psychological Review*, **78**, 3–43.

Swaney, W., Kendal, J. R., Capon, H. Brown, C. & Laland, K. N. 2001. Familiarity facilitates social learning of foraging behaviour in the guppy. *Animal Behaviour*, **62**, 591–598.

Valsecchi, P., Choleris, E., Moles, A., Guo, C. & Mainardi, M. 1996. Kinship and familiarity as factors affecting social transfer of food preferences in adult Mongolian gerbils. *Journal of Comparative Psychology,* **110,** 243–251.

van Bergen, Y. Laland, K. N. & Hoppitt, W. 2004. Intelligence in fish. In: *Comparative Vertebrate Cognition* (Ed. by L. J. Rogers and G. Kaplan), pp. 141–168. Dordrecht, The Netherlands: Kluwer Academic/Plenum.

Ward, P. & Zahavi, A. 1973. The importance of certain assemblages of birds as "information centres" for food finding. *Ibis,* **115,** 517–534.

Wilkinson, G. 1992. Information transfer at evening bat colonies. *Animal Behaviour,* **44,** 501–518.

Yoerg, S. I. 1991. Social feeding reverses flavor aversions in spotted hyena *(Crocuta crocuta). Journal of Comparative Psychology,* **105,** 185–189.

12

Behavioural Processes Affecting Development: Tinbergen's Fourth Question Comes of Age

Judy Stamps
Evolution and Ecology
University of California at Davis

Abstract

Interest in relationships between behaviour and development has been spurred by research on related topics, including phenotypic plasticity, parental effects, extragenetic inheritance, individual differences and trait syndromes. Here, I consider several emerging areas of research in the interface between behaviour and development, with a focus on behavioural processes that are likely to affect the development and maintenance of interindividual variation in a wide array of morphological, physiological and behavioural traits. Using a norm of reaction approach, I introduce and illustrate the complexities of phenotypic development. Next, I consider the implications of environmental selection and niche construction for phenotypic development, and consider why these behavioural processes are likely to encourage the development and maintenance of repeatable, stable individual differences and trait syndromes. Parental effects involving behaviour also affect the development of a wide array of phenotypic traits; differential allocation is a currently underappreciated type of parental effect, by which males can affect the development of their offspring via nongenetic means, even if those males have no contact with their young. Behavioural parental effects also contribute to extragenetic inheritance, and recent studies suggest that this phenomenon may be more widespread than previously suspected. The effects of behavioural processes on phenotypic development have interesting implications for problems in related disciplines (e.g. ecology, evolution and conservation biology), providing additional impetus for future research on the effects of behavioural mechanisms on the development of behavioural and other traits.

In the middle of the last century, Tinbergen (1963) was sufficiently interested in development to add this topic to his list of the 'four questions' of animal behaviour, having borrowed his other three questions (on immediate causation, survival value and evolution, respectively) from J. S. Huxley. Subsequently, research on developmental topics was temporarily eclipsed by the growth of sociobiology (Wilson 1975), behavioural ecology (Krebs & Davies 1997) and evolutionary psychology (Buss 1999), but the last few years have seen a resurgence of interest in relationships between behaviour and development (Bateson 2001a; Oyama et al. 2001; Johnston & Edwards 2002). In this essay, I suggest that we are poised for a surge in research on topics involving behaviour and development, impelled in part by the salience of these topics for related disciplines, including behavioural ecology, ecology and evolutionary biology. In particular, I suggest that behavioural processes may play a larger role than previously suspected in the development and maintenance of interindividual variation in a wide array of phenotypic traits, including morphological and physiological as well as behavioural traits.

Interest in behavioural processes affecting development has been encouraged by a renewed focus on developmental issues by ecologists and evolutionary biologists. One example is the literature on phenotypic plasticity and reaction norms, which considers the effects of experiential factors on the development of morphological and physiological traits (reviews in West-Eberhard 1989; Schlichting & Pigliucci 1998). For instance, fish that eat hard prey items (e.g. snails) as juveniles develop much larger jaw muscles than otherwise equivalent juveniles provided with softer prey items (Mittelbach et al. 1999); similarly striking effects of early diet on the development of trophic structures have been reported for primates (Corruccini & Beecher 1984), insects (Bernays 1986) and birds (Piersma et al. 1999). These and other recent studies of phenotypic plasticity have helped lay to rest the assumption that behavioural traits are necessarily more plastic than morphological traits, and have encouraged research on the ways that experiential factors influence the development of a wide range of morphological, physiological and behavioural traits (reviews in Gilbert 2001; Oyama et al. 2001).

Interest in relationships between behaviour and development has also been encouraged by the recent spate of studies on parental effects (also known as maternal effects), which consider situations in which phenotypic traits in parents affect patterns of development in their offspring (Mousseau & Fox 1998; McAdam et al. 2002; Sheldon 2002). Of course, many parental effects explicitly involve behavioural processes. In addition, parental effects can contribute to 'extragenetic inheritance': the transmission of phenotypic traits across generations via mechanisms that do not involve the transmission of genetic material (Jablonka 2001; Fleming et al. 2002).

Finally, interest in developmental processes that generate individual variation has been encouraged by a growing appreciation among behavioural and evolutionary biologists that selection often favours phenotypic diversity, rather than favouring a single phenotype that is optimal for every individual in a given population. It is easy to see that selection might favour the development of phenotypic polymorphisms when members of the same species live in different types of habitats, where they are subjected to different types of selective pressures (Hedrick 1986; Gillespie & Turelli 1989). For example, spiders that vigorously attack prey and conspecifics grow more rapidly than timid spiders in arid habitats with low prey availability, but timid spiders have the advantage in nearby riparian habitats, where bolder individuals suffer higher predation rates (Riechert & Hall 2000). However, selection can also favour phenotypic diversity even if every individual in the population lives in the same environment. For instance, animal behaviourists are familiar with the notion that alternative phenotypes can evolve as a result of negative frequency-dependent selection, which occurs when rare phenotypes are favoured by selection (Ayala & Campbell 1974; Maynard Smith 1982; Dugatkin & Reeve 1998). Thus, Sinervo & Lively (1996) suggested that three alternative reproductive morphs of lizards might be maintained by frequency-dependent selection, because individuals of each type perform best when the other morphs are more common. In addition, selection can favour the development and maintenance of phenotypic diversity when there are strong trade-offs among traits related to fitness, such that individuals with high values of particular fitness traits necessarily have lower values on other fitness traits (Whitlock 1996; Orzack & Tuljapurkar 2001). For instance, trade-offs between growth and mortality rates can produce situations in which individuals growing at a wide range of different rates end up with virtually the same fitness (Mangel & Stamps 2001).

This literature suggests that, from an evolutionary perspective, one should not necessarily expect natural or sexual selection to favour a single developmental trajectory, which generates a single 'typical', 'normal', or 'optimal' phenotype that is best for every individual in the population. Instead, this literature suggests that we should be actively looking for behavioural processes that encourage the development and maintenance of interindividual differences in behavioural, physiological and morphological traits. As we will see below, certain types of behavioural processes are prime candidates for the development of predictable patterns of phenotypic diversity among the individuals in a given population.

Although the current essay focuses on the role of behavioural processes in the development of variation in phenotypic traits, a modest amount of 'background' material is required before we reach this point. I begin with definitions of some of the key terms in the paper, with an emphasis on topics (e.g. behavioural trait syndromes) that may be unfamiliar to some readers. Then, I use a norm of reaction approach to introduce and illustrate some of the complexities of interactions between genes and experiential factors on the development of behavioural and other traits. At that point, we can consider three behavioural processes with major potential effects on development: (1) environmental selection and modification, (2) parental effects (including differential allocation) and (3) extragenetic inheritance via behavioural processes. Finally, the last section considers some of the implications of these behavioural processes for problems in related disciplines, including ecology and evolution.

Definitions

To consider processes that affect development, we first need to consider the products of development (i.e. the morphological, physiological or behavioural traits that are generated via developmental processes). Here, 'trait' refers to any variable that can be measured for a given individual at a given point in time. Traits can be morphological (e.g. wing length), physiological (concentration of testosterone in the bloodstream) or behavioural (rate of production of an aggressive display). In this essay, I focus on behavioural traits that vary between individuals but are consistent (repeatable) within individuals over an appreciable period of their lifetimes; hereafter, I use the term 'individual differences' to refer to this situation (e.g. Wilson 1998).

When behavioural biologists measure different traits in the same individuals, they often observe correlations among different traits across individuals (Koolhaas et al. 1997; Wilson 1998; Gosling 2001; Sih et al. 2004, A. Bell, J. C. Johnson & R. E. Ziemba, unpublished data). In this essay, the term 'trait syndrome' refers to correlations among different traits across individuals in the same population; and recent studies indicate that behavioural trait syndromes are common in animals (Sih et al. 2004). One example is 'sociability' in primates, a trait syndrome that reflects positive correlations across individuals between different behavioural measures related to social interactions with conspecifics (e.g. see Capitanio 1999; Gosling 2001). In spiders, individuals that are quick to attack intruders (competitive behaviour) also have a shorter latency to emerge after a simulated predator attack (antipredator behaviour) and are more likely to engage in wasteful killing of prey (foraging behaviour) (Riechert & Hedrick 1993; Maupin & Riechert 2001). In great tits, *Parus major* (Verbeek et al. 1996), individuals that quickly (but superficially) explore novel environments attack conspecifics more quickly, are more likely to win aggressive interactions with opponents, are less likely to respond to changes in familiar environments and are more likely to follow a previously learned 'routine' when faced with environmental change than individuals that slowly and thoroughly explore novel environments. These differences in exploratory style and the traits correlated with them are consistent (repeatable) across time, and juvenile great tits have exploratory scores similar to those of their parents (Dingemanse et al. 2003). As we will see, the existence of trait syndromes raises important questions

about the processes that are responsible for generating and maintaining correlations among different traits across individuals.

With respect to behavioural development, we rely on Tinbergen's original
definition of ontogeny: a change in behaviour machinery during development. This definition emphasizes the physiological and morphological
systems that are responsible for producing behavioural traits at any given
point of time. Note that this definition is silent with respect to the duration
or reversibility of changes in behaviour or behavioural machinery, reflecting an
early appreciation among behaviourists that distinctions between long-versus
short-term changes, or more versus less reversible changes in behaviour are
arbitrary (see also Hinde 1970, page 5). Also, note that this definition is more
general than 'maturation', or the achieving of 'adult' function. Changes in the
machinery affecting behaviour do not cease when an animal matures, as evidenced by studies indicating that neural plasticity is characteristic of adults as
well as juveniles (Stiles 2000). Nor do phenotypic traits expressed in juveniles
simply reflect preparation or practice for adult function. Instead, they are
shaped by selective forces that affect juveniles during the periods when those
traits are expressed. For instance, Galef (1981) discusses the many specialized
traits that young mammals use to extract resources from their mothers, and
suggests that mammalian offspring might be more properly viewed as highly
adapted parasites than as incompletely formed adults. Conversely, if a trait has
the same form in juveniles and adults, there is no a priori reason to assume that
the trait must have been shaped by selection acting on adults. Thus, water
snakes, *Neroidia sipedon,* show colour polymorphisms that are expressed in
neonates and continued into adulthood (King 1993). Field studies indicate that
natural selection is currently operating on the distribution of colour patterns in
neonates and juveniles, but not in adults, results that are consistent with the
hypothesis that differential predation by visual predators on juveniles is
responsible for the distribution of colour patterns in this species (King 1993).

Genes, Experience and the Development of Phenotypic Diversity

To consider how behavioural processes contribute to the development and
maintenance of phenotypic variation, we first need to consider how any experiential factor (not just those related to behaviour) affects the development of
behavioural and other traits. One of the easiest ways to appreciate the complex ways that experiential factors interact with genetic factors to affect
development is via reaction norms. The term 'reaction norm' refers to the set
of phenotypes that can produced by an individual genotype that is exposed
to a range of different environmental conditions (Schlichting & Pigliucci
1998; Falk 2001). In turn, the term 'genotype' refers to all of the genes in a

given individual, not just to a particular gene of interest. This is because the effects of a particular gene on development often vary as a function of other genes in that same individual, such that individuals with the same alleles at a given genetic locus, but with a different genetic background, develop differently under the same environmental conditions (e.g. Greenspan 2001).

Unfortunately, the perfect norm of reaction experiment is achievable only in science fiction: a series of 'parallel universes' in which the same individual experiences different sets of environmental conditions during its development. Given the impracticability of this experimental design, empirical studies of reaction norms typically rely on model systems in which the subjects destined to be raised in different environments are as genetically similar as possible (e.g. clones, partheno-genetically generated individuals, hybrid crosses of inbred strains, or very closely related individuals, such as full siblings). In this way, it is possible to raise different individuals with comparable genotypes in different environments at the same time.

Graphical depictions of reaction norms plot trait values against a range of environmental conditions for a number of different genotypes, each of which is represented by a different line.

A highly idealized set of reaction norms for three genotypes (individuals) from the same population is illustrated in Figure 12-1. Assume that each of three genotypes is maintained from the time of conception to the time of measurement in several different environments, and that a behavioural trait (or an individual's score on a trait syndrome) is measured at the end of this period. Depending on the study, 'environment' might refer to a single experiential factor of interest (e.g. temperature, Imasheva *et al.* 1997), or it might

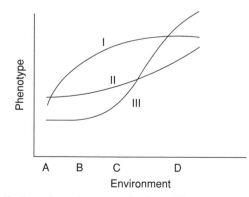

Figure 12-1 An idealized set of reaction norms for three different genotypes (I, II and III), which develop under a range of environmental conditions (A through D). Each individual's phenotype at a specified point in time results from interactions involving all of its genes (genotype) and the environmental conditions it experienced prior to that point in time. Variation among genotypes with respect to the intercept, slope and shape of their reaction norms makes it difficult to assign phenotypic variation to genetic or environmental influences.

refer to localities that differ from one another in a number of respects, only some of which are apparent to the experimenter (e.g. 'common garden' experiments, cf. Clausen *et al.* 1948). Similarly, 'phenotype' can refer to a single behavioural trait, or to a composite variable reflecting a cluster of correlated traits (e.g. an individual's score from a factor analysis).

Several general points can be illustrated using this idealized set of reaction norms. First, reaction norms span the entire range of environmental conditions in which the members of a population might be able to live and reproduce, not just those in which they currently live (Schlichting & Pigliucci 1998). For instance, imagine that most members of a population currently live in one of two environments indicated by points B and C. Not unnaturally, a reaction norm study might focus on development in these two environments. However, in the past, the ancestors of this population lived in other types of environments (e.g. A), and as a result of global warming, members of this population will soon find themselves in a new type of environment, indicated by D. Hence, a reaction norm that considers experimental conditions beyond those currently experienced by the members of a population may uncover phenotypes that used to be common in their ancestors, and provide insights into new phenotypes that might be expressed by members of that population in the future.

Reaction norm diagrams also illustrate why it is so difficult to partition phenotypic variation into genetic and environmental components (Lewontin 1974; Gupta & Lewontin 1982; Bateson 2001b; Falk 2001). Reaction norms typically do not form a neat set of parallel straight lines. Instead, genotypes often vary with respect to the shape, intercept and slope of their reaction norms, so that all of these factors need to be specified when comparing reaction norms for different genotypes (Via *et al.* 1995; Schlichting & Pigliucci 1998). One consequence of interindividual variation in the shape and position of reaction norms is that the proportion of phenotypic variance that can be attributed to genotype and to environment varies as a function of both the genotypes and the environments that are included in a given study. For instance, if genotypes I and III were raised in the environments indicated by points B and C, most of the observed variance in the phenotypic trait would be attributable to variation between genotypes. In contrast, if genotypes I and II were raised in the environments at points A and D, most of the phenotypic variation in the same trait would be attributable to differences between environments A and D.

As a practical matter, variation among genotypes in the shape and position of their reaction norms greatly complicates efforts to identify genes that affect the development of behavioural and other traits. For example, behavioural geneticists using house mice, *Mus domesticus,* as a model system have crossed standard inbred lines to produce different genotypes, each of which has a stable genetic composition, making it possible to raise and test the same genotype under a range of environmental conditions (Wahlsten 2001). However, complicated interactions between genotype and environment are common, such that some genotypes respond more than others to particular features of the environments in which they are raised or tested. Thus, in an attempt to identify quantitative trait loci (QTLs) related to locomotion in mice, Flint *et al.* (1995) used an F2 hybrid cross from two strains (C57BL/6J × BALB/cJ) and tested their subjects in a circular, white, open field measuring 60 cm in diameter; these investigators reported QTLs for locomotor activity on chromosomes 1, 4, 12 and 15. In another study on the same question, Gershenfeld *et al.* (1997) used the F2 hybrid cross of C57BL/6J × A/J, tested them in a square, clear, open field measuring 42 × 42 cm, and reported QTLs for locomotor activity on chromosomes 1, 10 and 19. At this point, it is not clear whether the differences in the genetic loci associated with locomotor behaviour were a result of rearing mice in different laboratory environments, differences in the test apparatus, genetic differences between the crosses, or interactions between these factors (Wahlsten 2001).

Because this degree of variation in results is unacceptable for biologists interested in specifying the effects of genes on behavioural development, investigators typically handle the problem by concentrating on one (or a few) genotypes, which are maintained under rigidly controlled, standardized conditions in the laboratory (e.g. Gilbert & Jorgensen 1998; Schaffner 1998; Wahlsten 2001). In effect, such studies reduce the effects of environment and of genotype–environment interactions on development by focusing on a single genotype in a single environment (e.g. genotype I in condition C, Fig. 12-1). The difficulty, of course, is that even the most complete description of the genes involved in behavioural development for this individual in this environment might not tell us much about the genes related to the development of the same trait in other individuals in that same population, or about other genes that would have influenced the development of this trait, had the same individual been raised under a different set of conditions.

Even as an idealized diagram, Figure 12-1 is still a gross oversimplification because it assumes that genotypes are maintained in the same environments from the time of conception. There are at least two problems with this scenario. First, investigators virtually always initiate experimental treatments well after the point of conception, after a variety of factors in the egg, the uterus, or the postnatal environment have had an opportunity to affect the developmental trajectories of the experimental subjects. Many of these factors are produced by the individual's parents (see parental effects, below), so at the very least, investigators must control for parental effects when studying the reaction norms of different genotypes raised in different environments (e.g. Holtmeier 2001; Laurila *et al.* 2002). Second, from a conceptual point of view, Figure 12-1 glosses over the fact that the effects of experience on development often depend on the state of the individuals when that experience occurs, and, in turn, that an individual's state at any point in development is affected by interactions between its genotype and experiences prior to that point in time (Gottlieb 1992; McNamara & Houston 1996; Schlichting & Pigliucci 1998; Oyama *et al.* 2001). Indeed, even introductory students of animal behaviour are taught that the effects of experience on development depend on the period during development when the organism receives that experience, as reflected in the familiar concept of 'sensitive periods' (e.g. Alcock 1998).

The temporal contingencies that affect behavioural development are difficult to capture in a simple diagram, but Figure 12-2 may provide a useful starting point for thinking about them. Assume that individuals are placed into the environments of interest at a convenient point in early development (e.g. at hatching), and that each individual's state at hatching is determined by its genes, factors its mother placed into its egg, and all of the other environmental factors that impinge on an individual from conception to hatching. For simplicity, assume that there are only two sets of conditions that individuals experience prior to hatching (α or β), and that we are interested in the reaction norms for two genotypes (I and II). After hatching, individuals with different genotypes and early experience are reared in a range of environments, after which their phenotypes are measured, as in Figure 12-1. In this graph, a two-way interaction between early experience and later experience on the development of the phenotypic trait is indicated by the fact that for each genotype, the effect of the second environment (e.g. B versus C) on the development of the phenotype varies as a function of previous experience (α or β). A three-way interaction between genotype, early experience and later experience on development is indicated by the fact that the interaction between

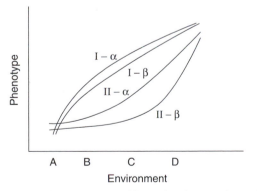

Figure 12-2 An idealized set of reaction norms illustrating the ways that early experience (α or β), later experience (environments A through D) and genotype can interact to influence the development of phenotypic traits. The shape and position of these curves illustrates a three-way interaction between the effects of genotype, early experience and later experience on development: for genotype II, early experience has a strong impact on phenotypic development in environment C, but a weaker effect on development in environment B, whereas for genotype I, early experience has a weak effect on development in both environments B and C.

early experience and later experience varies as a function of genotype: in genotype II, early experience has a much stronger effect on the relationship between later experience and phenotypic development than is the case for genotype 1. Although still highly oversimplified, Figure 12-2 illustrates why it is so important to keep an individual's prior history in mind when designing and interpreting studies of the development of behavioural and other traits.

In summary, diagrams of reaction norms can be quite useful for illustrating some of the complexities of development that have been obvious to animal behaviourists for many years (e.g. see Lehrman 1953), but are sometimes difficult to grasp when presented in a descriptive format. In addition, a norm of reaction approach provides a useful point of departure for a discussion of behavioural processes that are likely to influence the production and maintenance of phenotypic variation within populations, a topic I explore in greater depth below.

Development and Maintenance of Individual Differences and Trait Syndromes

Selection and Modification of the Environment

The classic norm of reaction approach implicitly assumes that experience affects the individual but that the reverse is not the case: the individual does not influence its own experience. However, any animal behaviourist is aware that animals are not merely passive organisms at the mercy of external environmental forces. Instead, animals frequently select their own environments, or modify their environments through their own actions (Waddington 1959; Lewontin 1983; Bateson 1988; Olding-Smee 1988; Laland et al. 2001). Of course, environmental selection and environmental modification are both explicitly behavioural processes. As we will see below, both of these processes can profoundly affect the patterns of phenotypic variation that we observe in natural populations.

Over the years, behavioural ecologists have documented many situations in which individuals select the environments that they will experience in the future. Thus, dispersers in heterogeneous landscapes select the habitats in which they will spend their lives (Stamps 2001), and within those habitats, individuals choose particular microhabitats in which to conduct particular activities, including foraging, mating and raising offspring. An example are cryptic species in which individuals improve their degree of crypsis by selecting microhabitats based on their visual characteristics (Broadman et al. 1974; Gillis 1982; Steen et al. 1992).

In many animals, the social environment is at least as important as the physical environment: the group, mate or neighbourhood with which an individual lives will affect its social behaviour over extended periods. Individuals in nature often have a choice of social situations available to them, as a result of which, the social environment experienced by a particular individual can be at least partially determined by choices made by that individual. In socially monogamous birds, animals select the partner with whom they will interact for subsequent months to years (Gowaty & Mock 1985; Black 1996), and in group-living animals, natal dispersers select a new group in which they are likely to remain for the rest of their lives (Brown & Brown 1996; Kunkele & Von Holst 1996). Even in territorial species, dispersers often have a choice of neighbourhoods that differ with respect to the density or type of residents living within them (Stamps 2001; Doligez et al. 2002).

Selection of an environment is not the only process by which individuals can affect the environment in which they develop: animals can also modify the environment(s) in which they will live. Traditional studies of niche construction have focused on modifications of the physical environment; examples include beaver dams, termite mounds, or spider webs (review in Laland et al. 2001). Less widely appreciated is the extent to which animals control their social environment through their own behaviour, a situation we might term 'social construction'. Social construction occurs when an individual affects its future social environment, by initiating particular types of social interactions with conspecifics with whom it might interact in the future.

For instance, consider a situation in which an individual remains in a particular area, and vigorously attacks conspecifics whenever it encounters them. If the members of this species tend to avoid areas where they have been attacked (i.e. 'punished'), then an individual who attacks conspecifics will eventually construct a social environment that features low spatial overlap and low encounter rates with those conspecifics. In other words, using aggressive behaviour, the individual has constructed a territory (Stamps & Krishnan 1999, 2001; Switzer et al. 2001). Other examples of social construction include the use of aggressive behaviour to affect the rates and types of subsequent agonistic interactions with group members, through the establishment of dominance relationships (Drews 1993; Pagel & Dawkins 1997), or the use of affiliative behaviour to increase the likelihood of engaging in a range of positive interactions with particular individuals in the future (Capitanio 1999).

The ability of animals to select or modify their environments has implications for the development and maintenance of phenotypic diversity in natural populations. Returning to Figure 12-1, imagine that genotype I prefers environment C, while genotype II prefers environment B. In that case, most individuals would express one of two alternative phenotypes: one a result of the combination of genotype I and environment C, and the other a result of the combination of genotype II and environment B. Note that this bimodal distribution of phenotypes requires that individuals be able to select their own environments; it would not develop if those same genotypes were randomly assigned to environments (as is typically the case in norm of reaction experiments).

Indeed, variation among genotypes in environmental selection or construction is not required, behavioural processes alone could encourage the development and maintenance of alternative phenotypes within the same population. The development of stable individual differences and trait syndromes is expected whenever the following conditions are satisfied: (1) a population lives in a heterogeneous environment, (2) each individual selects an environment that it can use for an extended period, (3) experience in a particular type of environment affects development in a way that improves subsequent performance in that type of environment, and (4) individuals prefer to remain in or return to environments in which they perform at relatively high levels. If these four conditions are satisfied, an initial choice of environment (perhaps made on a purely random basis) will encourage the development and maintenance of adaptive trait syndromes involving a suite of behavioural, physiological and morphological traits.

I am unaware of any empirical study that directly bears on this point, but juvenile fish might be suitable candidates for such a study. Many fish live in habitats that are heterogeneous at the spatial scale of a home range or territory. For instance, juvenile brook charr, *Salvelinus fontinalis,* can spend their time in fast- or in slow-moving water, and fish living in these two types of microenvironments within the same stream significantly differ with respect to a number of traits, including site fidelity, aggressive rates, foraging styles, diet, body shape and caudal fin height (Grant & Noakes 1988; McLaughlin & Grant 1994). Current evidence suggests that the differences between the juveniles inhabiting fast- and slow-flowing water could be a result of phenotypic plasticity (e.g. significant differences in caudal fin heights can be generated by raising randomly selected charr in different flow regimes; Imre *et al.* 2002), and in other fish, foraging on a particular type of prey has been shown to improve subsequent performance with that type of prey, for example, because particular diets induce changes in musculature or skeletal components of the feeding apparatus (Wainwright *et al.* 1991; Day & McPhail 1996), or because the ability of individuals to recognize, attack and handle particular types of prey improves as a function of previous experience with that type of prey (Kieffer & Colgan 1991; Skulason *et al.* 1993). Hence, current evidence implies that even if two young brook charr were identical when they first selected a location in which to live, behavioural processes would encourage the development of predictable clusters of correlated traits for individuals that selected fast- versus slow-moving water.

Parental Effects and the Development of Individual Differences and Trait Syndromes

Every animal develops in an environment that is influenced, in one way or the other, by its parents (Rossiter 1996). Social learning is obviously one process by which the behaviour of parents affects the development of traits in their offspring, but there are many others. For instance, a mother lizard's choice of incubation temperature for her eggs can affect the antipredator behaviour of her hatchlings (Downes & Shine 1999), or the amount of food dung beetle parents provide to their offspring can affect the body size of their offspring (Hunt & Simmons 2000).

Even in species with extensive amounts of parental care, important parental effects may occur via behavioural mechanisms that do not involve social learning. A particularly salient example is provided by Meaney (2001) and his colleagues, who studied how variation in 'maternal style' in rats affects the development of a cluster of correlated behavioural and physiological traits in their pups. Some mothers lick and groom offspring at high rates, and adopt a nursing posture that allows pups easy access to the nipples, and other mothers lick and groom at lower rates, and adopt a more restrictive posture while nursing. In turn, maternal behaviour has profound effects on the development of a suite of correlated traits in their young, effects that appear to be mediated by changes in the development of corticotropin-releasing factor (CRF) systems. For instance, cross-fostering studies indicate that pups reared by high-licking mothers are less fearful and less responsive to stress at adulthood, and have reduced resistance to certain pathogens, than pups reared by low-licking mothers. Hence, in this case, differences in maternal behaviour during the first week after birth contribute to the development of central CRF systems that affect a suite of behavioural and physiological traits throughout life.

Differential allocation is another parental effect with the potential to affect the development of an impressive list of phenotypic traits. Differential allocation occurs when the allocation of resources to offspring by one parent varies as a function of phenotypic traits in the mate (Burley 1986). Thus, differential allocation explicitly involves behavioural processes, in that stimuli from one parent influences parental effects mediated by the other parent. Burley (1988) provided the first evidence for this hypothesis, by experimentally manipulating the attractiveness of male and female zebra finches, *Taeniopygia guttata*, using coloured leg-bands, and showing that the mates of individuals with attractive bands invested more time caring for their offspring than did the mates of individuals with unattractive bands. Subsequent studies have shown that female zebra finches sequentially mated to males with attractive and unattractive bands alter the amount of testosterone in their eggs, as a function of male band colour (Gil *et al.* 1999; but see Petrie *et al.* 2001). In turn, exposure to testosterone deposited in avian eggs affects the begging rates, aggression and growth rates of the nestlings that hatch from those eggs (Schwabl 1993, 1996; Eising *et al.* 2001; C. M. Eising & T. G. Groothuis, unpublished data). Taken together, this literature suggests that stimuli from a male bird could influence the development of a suite of behavioural and physiological traits in his offspring, via the effects of those stimuli on hormones placed into the eggs by his mate.

In recent years, differential allocation has been reported in a wide range of taxa, suggesting that this phenomenon may be quite common in animals (review in Sheldon 2000; see also Kolm 2002; Nilsson *et al.* 2002; Saino *et al.* 2002). This indicates that a hitherto unsuspected behavioural process may provide yet another way that traits in parents can influence the development of their offspring. In particular, differential allocation provides a nongenetic route by which phenotypic traits in fathers can influence the development of their offspring, even in species in which fathers have no contact with those offspring.

Extragenetic Inheritance and the Development of Individual Differences and Trait Syndromes

Any discussion of parental effects leads directly to a closely related topic: extragenetic inheritance. Extragenetic inheritance occurs when there is a correlation between phenotypic traits in parents and offspring for reasons other than the transmission of genetic material between parents and their offspring. The fact that extragenetic inheritance is defined in negative terms reflects the prevalent assumption that the inheritance of phenotypic traits is virtually always due to the inheritance of genetic material (Jablonka 2001). This emphasis on genes as the primary, if not the only, mode of inheritance has broadened over the years to encompass other processes affecting development. For instance, parental effects can be subsumed within the genetic-primary paradigm by including genes that affect traits in the parents (Rossiter 1996; Mousseau & Fox 1998; Wolf 2000); genes are still assumed to govern inheritance, but now we consider two sets of genes, those in parents, and those in offspring, and estimate the effects of the former on the latter (Kirkpatrick & Lande 1989; Oklejewicz *et al.* 2001). Reaction norms can also be accommodated under the same paradigm, by assuming that reaction norms, and the plasticity they generate, have a genetic basis (Schlichting & Smith 2002).

Over the years, animal behaviourists have provided several clear counterexamples of extragenetic inheritance in animals. Familiar cases include the cultural transmission of songs in birds (e.g. Grant & Grant 1996; MacDougall-Shackleton & MacDougall-Shackleton 2001), or the transmission of food preferences from mothers to their offspring (Galef & Whiskin 1997). Even so, many biologists still seem to view examples of extragenetic inheritance via behavioural processes as interesting curiosities, exceptions to the general rule that modes of inheritance are almost always genetic.

One possible reason for the widespread dismissal of behavioural extragenetic inheritance is the equally widespread assumption that social learning is the mechanism responsible for most, if not all, extragenetic inheritance in animals (Cavalli-Sforza & Feldman 1981; Boyd & Richerson 1985, 1996; Takahasi 1999; Jablonka 2001). However, only a limited number of species and situations satisfy the conditions required for the transmission of behavioural traits via social learning (Caro & Hauser 1992; Brooks 1998; Galef

2001), and empirical support for cultural inheritance in animals is sparse (Boyd & Richerson 1996; Sterelny 2001).

Recently, however, it has become apparent that social learning is only one of several behavioural processes that can encourage correlations between traits in parents and their offspring. Generally speaking, two components are required for any type of extragenetic inheritance. First, extragenetic inheritance requires parental effects: some physiological, behavioural or morphological trait X in parents that directly affects the development of trait Y in their offspring. Second, mechanisms must exist in the offspring that increase the likelihood that individuals that develop trait Y early in life will express trait X later in life, when they themselves mature and become parents. This second mechanism is required to ensure that the parental trait(s) that shape offspring developmental trajectories reliably reappear in successive generations.

Cultural transmission provides a simplified version of this scenario, because in this situation, X and Y are the same trait. The same is true when parents directly pass substances to their young during the period of parental care (e.g. when the transfer of odours in maternal milk affects the food odours preferred by young after they begin to forage on their own; Galef & Sherry 1973; Provenza & Balf 1987). In these situations, the critical question is why individuals that learned motor patterns or preferences for particular stimuli from their parents early in life would continue to express these same behaviour patterns much later in life, when they have offspring of their own. One possible answer to this question is that the behaviour X learned from its parents will be maintained into adulthood when the rewards that are contingent upon the production of behaviour X as an adult are higher than the rewards that are contingent upon the production of alternative forms of behaviour (Galef 1996; Galef & Whiskin 1997).

Recently, a small but growing group of investigators has begun to investigate examples of extragenetic inheritance that do not rely on social learning. One particularly interesting example follows from the studies discussed earlier of the effects of maternal behaviour (licking, nursing posture) on the development of a trait syndrome involving stress reactivity of young rodents. An important addition to this story is that the behaviour of mothers affects the development of maternal behaviour in their daughters (Meaney 2001; Fleming et al. 2002). Cross-fostering studies show that females raised by high-licking mothers develop into high-licking mothers themselves, and vice versa (i.e. the maternal behaviour of a female is similar to that of her foster mother, not to that of her biological mother). In this case, a trait syndrome is maternally inherited by non-genetic means: high-licking, low-reactivity mothers produce low-reactivity offspring of both sexes, and their low-reactivity daughters lick their own offspring at high rates after they mature, producing grandchildren with low reactivity.

Although thus far, most studies of extragenetic inheritance of maternal behaviour have focused on rodents and primates (Berman 1990; Fairbanks

1996; Maestripieri 1999; Fleming *et al.* 2002), researchers working with other taxa are also beginning to study this phenomenon. For instance, in dung beetles, maternal provisioning behaviour (amount of dung in the brood mass) affects the growth trajectories and final sizes of both male and female offspring, and, in turn, large adult females produce large brood masses for their offspring. As a result, females that provision their young with large brood masses produce daughters that are also likely to provision their offspring with large brood masses (Hunt & Simmons 2002).

Even if behavioural modes of extragenetic inheritance turn out to be common in mammals, birds and other species with extensive parental care, this would leave the genetic-primary paradigm intact for biologists studying taxa in which neither parent cares for the offspring. Unless mechanisms for extragenetic inheritance exist in species lacking parental care, extragenetic inheritance is likely to remain a curiosity, of little relevance to the inheritance of phenotypic traits for most of the animals on earth.

However, virtually all animals engage in one type of parental behaviour that has the potential to profoundly affect the development of phenotypic traits in their offspring: females select a location for their eggs. By selecting a natal habitat for their eggs, females provide their offspring with a broad range of environmental conditions that affect embryos during the period between laying and hatching. In addition, in many species, offspring remain near their natal location for an extended period after hatching; in this situation, maternal choice of oviposition site determines the environment that will be experienced by offspring over an extended period of juvenile development (West & King 1987).

Because the burgeoning literature on parental effects clearly shows that a mother's choice of a natal habitat can greatly impact the development of her offspring, the critical question is whether extragenetic mechanisms exist that encourage a correlation between the habitat preferences of parents and their offspring. This question has a long and illustrious history. In 1864, Walsh proposed that insects become conditioned to the host in which they develop, a process that would encourage adult females to deposit her eggs on the same host that was selected by her mother. In the entomological literature, this idea evolved into the Hopkins' host-selection principle, which, in its broadest sense, predicts that insects will develop a preference for the host species on which they developed (Jaenike 1983). At the same time, biologists working with vertebrates became interested in a similar phenomenon they termed 'habitat imprinting', in which an individual's experience with a particular type of habitat early in life increases that individual's level of preference for the same type of habitat later in life (Hilden 1965; Klopfer & Ganzhorn 1985). Currently, these and related phenomenon are subsumed under the general term of 'preference induction', which refers to situations in which experience (not necessarily restricted to learning) in a natal habitat encourages an individual to select the same type of habitat for reproduction later in life (J. N. Davis, J. A. Stamps & T. P. Coombes-Hahn, unpublished data).

To date, empirical support for preference induction has been obtained for animals from a wide range of taxa, including mammals (Wecker 1963), birds (Teuschl *et al.* 1998), fish (Arvedlund & Nielsen 1996), amphibians (Hepper & Waldman 1992) and insects (Anderson & Hilker 1995; Djieto-Lordon & Dejean 1999; Barron 2001). In addition, interest in this phenomenon is growing, in part because of the obvious relevance of preference induction to problems in population and conservation biology (Stamps 2001; Davis *et al.*, unpublished data). At this point, the available evidence suggests that preference induction is likely to contribute to extragenetic inheritance in many animals, including many species in which neither parent provides any care to their young after the eggs are laid. Given the potential importance of preference induction for the extragenetic inheritance of a wide range of traits, this phenomenon clearly warrants additional attention from animal behavourists.

Implications for Problems in Ecology and Evolutionary Biology

A norm of reaction approach implies that any dramatic change in environmental factors during development is likely to generate equally dramatic changes in behavioural traits and trait syndromes, and that these changes can be expressed within a very short period (as little as a single generation). In turn, if animals are exposed to novel conditions during development, they may display 'behavioural neophenotypes': behavioural traits or trait syndromes never before observed for the members of their species (Kuo 1976; Gottlieb 1992, 2002). Behavioural neophenotypes are expected when individuals find themselves in a new habitat that differs in a number of respects from other habitats used by that species, and that is suitable for at least modest levels of survival and reproduction. Most captive environments satisfy these criteria, and behavioural neophenotypes are routinely generated in the laboratory (e.g. see West *et al.* 1994). In nature, behavioural neophenotypes are expected in any situation in which the members of a population find themselves in a new habitat that differs in a number of respects from their previous habitats. For instance, invasion biology considers situations in which the members of a species establish themselves in new localities, where they experience a different set of selective pressures than those experienced by their ancestors in the habitat of origin (Vermeij 1996; Kolar & Lodge 2001). A norm of reaction approach suggests that novel behavioural phenotypes, or novel clusters of traits involving behaviour could emerge within a generation or two after the invaders arrived at the new habitat. Thus, new behaviour observed in animals colonizing new habitats (e.g. Holway & Suarez 1999) need not necessarily reflect genetic changes as a consequence of founder effects or strong directional selection in those new habitats.

Similarly, many applied biologists, including conservation biologists and integrated pest managers, seek to establish populations in new habitats using individuals raised in captivity or in other types of natural habitats. A norm of reaction approach argues that if animals develop for extended periods in one type of environment and are then transferred to another type of environment, they may have difficulty making the transition, because so much of their morphology, physiology and behaviour has already been shaped by factors experienced in their previous environment. Conservation biologists are already aware of this problem (e.g. as evidenced by attempts to 'train' captive-raised animals to recognize predators before releasing them in their new habitats; Griffin *et al.* 2000). However, a norm of reaction approach suggests that instead of trying to change the behavioural phenotypes of subadults or adults prior to release, it might be more practical to provide them with protection, food and other forms of support in the new habitat (i.e. soft release; Letty *et al.* 2000). Assuming that these individuals are able to survive and reproduce in the new habitat, their offspring would be exposed throughout ontogeny to experiential factors that are likely to encourage the development of phenotypes appropriate to the new habitat. Captive–release programmes for golden lion tamarins, *Leontopithecus rosalia,* illustrate the utility of this approach: efforts to provide 'training' to captive-raised animals prior to release had no appreciable effect on success rates, but the wild offspring born to captive-raised individuals were far more efficient than their parents at surviving and reproducing in their new habitats (Beck *et al.* 2002).

Behavioural processes can also encourage the development and maintenance of stable, predictable patterns of individual differences in behaviour, and stable, predictable clusters of correlated traits. Thus, variation in maternal styles among rodents generates a trait syndrome featuring a variety of correlated behavioural and physiological traits in their offspring, and selection of a foraging habitat may encourage the development of a complex syndrome involving behavioural and morphological traits in brook charr. These and related studies suggest that biologists should not assume that stable, repeatable individual differences in phenotypic traits, or predictable correlations among phenotypic traits, are necessarily the product of underlying genetic variation between those individuals.

Biologists should also be cautious when extrapolating from developmental patterns in the laboratory to developmental patterns in nature, because the subjects of most laboratory studies are severely restricted with respect to their ability to select or modify their physical or social environments. If the development and maintenance of individual differences and trait syndromes requires that individuals be able to select or modify the environments that will shape their own development, then phenotypes in the laboratory will diverge rather dramatically from those in the field. This may help to explain situations in which trait syndromes reliably appear under natural conditions, but disappear when animals are confined. For instance, in pumpkinseed sunfish, *Lepomis gibbosus*, stable individual differences in behavioural traits reflecting 'shyness' and 'boldness' were observed when individuals were living in seminatural enclosures, but these differences gradually disappeared when those individuals were transferred to the laboratory (Wilson *et al.* 1993). Hence, predictable patterns of phenotypic diversity and stable behavioural polymorphisms may be more common in nature than in captivity, because their development requires a degree of free choice and free expression that is typically denied to animals housed in captive environments.

Differential allocation is another behavioural process with important implications for evolutionary biology. Currently, most scientists assume that in species lacking male parental care, correlations between the phenotypes of fathers and the phenotypes of their offspring must be the result of the transfer of genetic material from fathers to offspring. Differential allocation provides an alternate, extragenetic route by which fathers can influence the development of traits in their offspring. As we have seen, differential allocation is a type of indirect parental effect, by which sensory stimuli from fathers influence the development of their offspring via the effects of these stimuli on maternal traits affecting offspring development.

The emerging literature on differential allocation suggests that this phenomenon may be widespread in nature. If this is the case, then research programmes and paradigms that ignore this phenomenon may need to be revised. For instance, standard techniques for estimating heritability using a paternal half-sibling design are based on the assumption that correlations between phenotypic traits in fathers and offspring can be attributed to genes transferred from fathers to offspring (Falconer & Mackay 1996). However, if differential allocation is occurring, this technique will produce inflated estimates of the contributions of genes to inheritance. Similarly, in species that lack male parental care, a positive correlation between attractive traits in fathers and viability traits in their offspring is usually construed as supporting the hypothesis that the attractive male traits are correlated with 'good genes' (Sheldon 2000). However, in any species in which a female receives sensory stimuli from her mate before investing in her young, differential allocation by mothers may also encourage positive correlations between attractive traits in fathers and viability traits in their offspring. The implications of differential allocation for genetics, evolutionary biology and behavioural ecology are just beginning to be appreciated. This is clearly one behavioural process with the potential to affect the ways that scientists in related disciplines conduct their research.

Finally, the recent literature suggests that extragenetic inheritance via behavioural processes may be more common, and may involve a much wider range of phenotypic traits, than previously suspected. As we have seen, social learning is only one of several behavioural mechanisms that may contribute to the extragenetic inheritance of morphological, physiological and behavioural traits. One general way that females can affect the development of many traits in their young is by selecting a site for their eggs, and there is growing evidence in a wide range of taxa for preference induction, the inheritance of habitat preferences by extragenetic means. In retrospect, it seems surprising that animal behaviourists have not devoted more attention to processes that are likely to encourage the extragenetic inheritance of habitat preferences, given the potential importance of such processes for the development and evolution of such a wide array of other phenotypic traits.

In conclusion, studies of behavioural processes that affect development are not only interesting in their own right, but this line of inquiry may shed light on questions and issues of concern to scientists working in related disciplines. At this point, animal behaviourists have just begun to study several behavioural processes with large potential effects on the development of individual differences and trait syndromes. Hence, if the recent past is any indication, Tinbergen's fourth question should attract attention from animal behaviourists for many years to come.

Acknowledgments

I am very grateful to the following colleagues for stimulating discussion and comments on earlier drafts of this manuscript: A. Badyaev, A. Bell, J. Capitanio, J. Davis, H. Drummond, J. Lucas, S. Lema, C. Nunn, D. Owings, P. Wainwright, J. Watters, E. Snell-Rood and the graduate students in the Autumn 2002 Behavioural Ecology course.

References

Alcock, J. 1998. *Animal Behavior: an Evolutionary Approach.* 6th edn. Sunderland, Massachusetts: Sinauer.

Anderson, P. & Hilker, M. 1995. Larval diet influence on oviposition behaviour in *Spodoptera littoralis. Entomologia Experimentalis et Applicata,* **74,** 71–82.

Arvedlund, M. & Nielsen, L. E. 1996. Do the anemonefish *Amphiprion ocellaris* (Pisces: Pomacentridae) imprint themselves on their host anemone *Heteractis magnifica* (Anthozoa: Actinidae)? *Ethology,* **102,** 197–211.

Ayala, F. J. & Campbell, C. A. 1974. Frequency dependent selection. *Annual Review of Ecology and Systematics,* **5,** 115–138.

Barron, A. 2001. The life and death of Hopkins' host-selection principle. *Journal of Insect Behaviour,* **14,** 725–737.

Bateson, P. 1988. The active role of behaviour in evolution. In: *Evolutionary Processes and Metaphors* (Ed. by M. W. Ho & S. Fox), pp. 191–207. Chichester: J. Wiley.

Bateson, P. 2001a. Where does our behaviour come from? *Journal of Biosciences,* **26,** 561–570.

Bateson, P. 2001b. Behavioural development and Darwinian evolution. In: *Cycles of Contingency* (Ed. by S. Oyama, P. Griffiths & R. E. Gray), pp. 149–166. Cambridge, Massachusetts: MIT Press.

Beck, B. B., Castro, M. I., Stoinski, T. S. & Ballou, J. 2002. The effects of pre-release environments on survivorship in golden lion tamarins. In: *The Lion Tamarins: Twenty-Five Years of Research and Conservation* (Ed. by D. G. Kleiman & A. Rylands), pp. 283–301. Washington, D.C.: Smithsonian Institution Press.

Berman, C. M. 1990. Intergenerational transmission of maternal rejection rates among free-ranging rhesus monkeys on Cayo Santiago. *Animal Behaviour,* **44,** 247–258.

Bernays, E. A. 1986. Diet-induced head allometry among foliage-chewing insects and its importance for gramnivores. *Science,* **231,** 495–497.

Black, J. M. 1996. *Partnerships in Birds, the Study of Monogamy.* New York: Oxford University Press.

Boyd, R. & Richerson, P. J. 1985. *Culture and the Evolutionary Process.* Chicago: University of Chicago Press.

Boyd, R. & Richerson, P. J. 1996. Why culture is common, but cultural evolution is rare. *Proceedings of the British Academy,* **88,** 77–93.

Broadman, M., Askew, R. R. & Cook, L. M. 1974. Experiments on resting site selection by nocturnal moths. *Journal of Zoology,* **172,** 343–355.

Brooks, R. 1998. The importance of mate copying and cultural inheritance of mating preferences. *Trends in Evolution and Ecology,* **13,** 45–46.

Brown, C. R. & Brown, M. B. 1996. *Coloniality in the Cliff Swallow.* Chicago: University of Chicago Press.

Burley, N. 1986. Sexual selection for aesthetic traits in species with biparental care. *American Naturalist,* **127,** 415–445.

Burley, N. 1988. The differential allocation hypothesis: an experimental test. *American Naturalist,* **132,** 611–628.

Buss, D. M. 1999. *Evolutionary Psychology: the New Science of the Mind.* Boston: Allyn & Bacon.

Capitanio, J. P. 1999. Personality dimensions in adult male rhesus macaques: prediction of behaviours across time and situation. *American Journal of Primatology,* **47,** 299–320.

Caro, T. M. & Hauser, M. D. 1992. Is there teaching in nonhuman animals? *Quarterly Review of Biology,* **67,** 151–174.

Cavalli-Sforza, L. L. & Feldman, M. W. 1981. *Cultural Transmission and Evolution.* Princeton, New Jersey: Princeton University Press.

Clausen, J. D., Keck, D. & Hiesey, W. M. 1948. *Experimental Studies on the Nature of Plant Species. III. Environmental Responses of Climatic Races of Achillea.* Washington, D.C.: Carnegie Institution, Publication 581.

Corruccini, R. S. & Beecher, R. M. 1984. Occlusofacial morphological integration lowered in baboons raised on soft diet. *Journal of Craniofacial Genetics and Development Biology,* **4,** 135–142.

Day, T. & McPhail, J. D. 1996. The effect of behavioural and morphological plasticity on foraging efficiency in the threespine stickleback (*Gasterosteus* sp.). *Oecologia,* **108,** 380–388.

Dingemanse, N. J., Both, C., Drent, P. J. & van Oers, K. 2003. Repeatability and heritability of exploratory behaviour in great tits. *Animal Behaviour,* **64,** 929–937.

Djieto-Lordon, C. & Dejean, A. 1999. Tropical arboreal ant mosaics: innate attraction and imprinting determine nest site selection in dominant ants. *Behavioral Ecology and Sociobiology,* **45,** 219–225.

Doligez, B., Danchin, E. & Clobert, J. 2002. Public information and breeding habitat selection in a wild bird population. *Science,* **297,** 1168–1170.

Downes, S. J. & Shine, R. 1999. Do incubation-induced changes in a lizard's phenotype influence its vulnerability to predators? *Oecologia,* **120,** 9–18.

Drews, C. 1993. The concept and definition of dominance in animal behaviour. *Behaviour,* **125,** 283–313.

Dugaktin, L. A. & Reeve, H. K. 1998. *Game Theory and Animal Behaviour.* New York: Oxford University Press.

Eising, C. M., Eikenaar, C., Schwabl, H. & Groothuis, T. G. 2001. Maternal androgens in black-headed gull (*Larus ridibundus*) eggs: consequences for chick development. *Proceedings of the Royal Society of London, Series B,* **268,** 839–846.

Fairbanks, L. M. 1996. Individual differences in maternal style. *Advances in the Study of Behaviour,* **25,** 579–611.

Falconer, D. S. & Mackay, T. F. 1996. *Introduction to Quantitative Genetics.* Essex: Longman.

Falk, R. 2001. Can the norm of reaction save the gene concept? In: *Thinking About Evolution, Historical, Philosophical and Political Perspectives* (Ed. by R. S. Singh, C. B. Krimbas, D. B. Paul & J. Beatty), pp. 119–140. Cambridge: Cambridge University Press.

Fleming, A. S., Kraemer, G. W., Gonzalez, A., Lovic, V., Rees, S. & Melo, A. 2002. Mothering begets mothering: the transmission of behaviour and its neurobiology across generations. *Pharmacology, Biochemistry and Behaviour,* **73,** 61–75.

Flint, J., Corley, R., DeFries, J. C., Fulker, D. W., Gray, J. A., Miller, S. & Collins, A. C. 1995. A simple genetic basis for a complex psychological trait in laboratory mice. *Science,* **269,** 1432–1435.

Galef, B. G. 1981. The ecology of weaning: parasitism and the achievement of independence by altricial mammals. In: *Parental Care in Mammals* (Ed. by D. Gubernick & P. H. Klopfter), pp. 211–241. New York: Plenum.

Galef, B. G. 1996. The adaptive value of social learning: a reply. *Animal Behaviour,* **52,** 641–644.

Galef, B. G. 2001. Where's the beef? Evidence of culture, imitation and teaching, in cetaceans? *Behavioural and Brain Sciences,* **24,** 335.

Galef, B. G. & Sherry, D. F. 1973. Mother's milk: a medium for transmission of cues reflecting the flavour of mother's diet. *Journal of Comparative Physiological Psychology,* **83,** 374–378.

Galef, B. G. & Whiskin, E. E. 1997. Effects of social and asocial learning on longevity of food-preference traditions. *Animal Behaviour,* **53,** 1313–1322.

Gershenfeld, H. K., Neumann, P. E., Mathis, C., Crawley, J. N., Li, X. & Paul, S. M. 1997. Mapping quantitative trait loci for open-field behaviour in mice. *Behaviour Genetics,* **27,** 201–210.

Gil, D., Graves, J., Hazon, N. & Wells, A. 1999. Male attractiveness and differential testosterone investment in zebra finch eggs. *Science,* **286,** 126–128.

Gilbert, S. F. 2001. Ecological developmental biology: developmental biology meets the real world. *Developmental Biology,* **233,** 1–12.

Gilbert, S. F. & Jorgensen, E. M. 1998. Wormholes: a commentary on K. F. Schaffner's *Genes, Behaviour and Developmental Emergentism. Philosophy of Science,* **65,** 259–266.

Gillespie, J. H. & Turelli, M. 1989. Genotype-environmental interactions and the maintenance of polygenic variation. *Genetics,* **121,** 129–138.

Gillis, J. E. 1982. Substrate colour-matching cues in the cryptic grasshopper *Circotettix rabula rabula* (Rehn and Hebard). *Animal Behaviour,* **30,** 113–116.

Gosling, S. 2001. From mice to men: what can we learn about personality from animal research. *Psychological Bulletin,* **127,** 45–86.

Gottlieb, G. 1992. *Individual Development and Evolution: the Genesis of Novel Behaviour.* New York: Oxford University Press.

Gottlieb, G. 2002. Developmental-behavioural initiation of evolutionary change. *Psychological Review,* **109,** 211–218.

Gowaty, P. A. & Mock, D. W. 1985. *Avian Monogamy.* Washington, D.C.: American Ornithologists' Union.

Grant, B. R. & Grant, P. R. 1996. Cultural inheritance of song and its role in the evolution of Darwin's finches. *Evolution,* **50,** 2471–2487.

Grant, J. W. A. & Noakes, D. L. G. 1988. Aggressiveness and foraging mode of young-of-the-year brook charr, *Salvelinus fontinalis* (Pisces, Salmonidae). *Behavioral Ecology and Sociobiology,* **22,** 435–445.

Greenspan, R. J. 2001. The flexible genome. *Nature Reviews Genetics,* **2,** 383–387.

Griffin, A., Blumstein, D. & Evans, C. 2000. Training captive-bred or translocated animals to avoid predators. *Conservation Biology,* **14,** 1317–1326.

Gupta, A. P. & Lewontin, R. C. 1982. A study of reaction norms in natural populations of *Drosophila pseudoobscura. Evolution,* **36,** 934–948.

Hedrick, P. W. 1986. Genetic polymorphism in heterogeneous environments: a decade later. *Annual Review of Ecology and Systematics,* **17,** 535–566.

Hepper, P. G. & Waldman, B. 1992. Embryonic olfactory learning in frogs. *Quarterly Journal of Experimental Psychology B, Comparative and Physiological Psychology,* **44,** 179–197.

Hilden, O. 1965. Habitat selection in birds: a review. *Annales Zoologici Fennici,* **2,** 53–75.

Hinde, R. A. 1970. *Animal Behaviour.* New York: McGraw-Hill.

Holtmeier, C. L. 2001. Heterochrony, maternal effects and phenotypic variation among sympatric pupfishes. *Evolution,* **55,** 330–338.

Holway, D. A. & Suarez, A. V. 1999. Animal behaviour: an essential component of invasion biology. *Trends in Ecology and Evolution,* **14,** 328–330.

Hunt, J. & Simmons, L. W. 2000. Maternal and paternal effects on offspring phenotype in the dung beetle *Onthophagus taurus,* **54,** 936–941.

Hunt, J. & Simmons, L. W. 2002. The genetics of maternal care: direct and indirect genetic effects on phenotype in the dung beetle *Onthophagus taurus. Proceedings of the National Academy of Sciences, U.S.A.,* **99,** 6828–6832.

Imasheva, A. G., Loeschcke, L. A., Zhivotovsky, L. A. & Lazenby, O. E. 1997. Effects of extreme temperatures on phenotypic variation and developmental stability in *Drosophila melanogaster* and *Drosophila buzzatii. Biological Journal of the Linnean Society,* **61,** 117–126.

Imre, I., McLaughlin, R. L. & Noakes, D. L. G. 2002. Phenotypic plasticity in brook charr *Salvelinus fontinalis:* changes in caudal fin induced by water flow. *Journal of Fish Biology,* **61,** 1171–1181.

Jablonka, E. 2001. The systems of inheritance. In: *Cycles of Contingency* (Ed. by S. Oyama, P. Griffiths & R. E. Gray), pp. 99–116. Cambridge, Massachusetts: MIT Press.

Jaenike, J. 1983. Induction of host preference in *Drosophila melanogaster. Oecologia,* **58,** 320–325.

Johnston, T. D. & Edwards, L. 2002. Genes, interactions, and the development of behaviour. *Psychological Review,* **109,** 26–34.

Kieffer, J. D. & Colgan, P. W. 1991. Individual variation in learning by foraging pumpkinseed sunfish, *Lepomis gibbosus:* the influence of habitat. *Animal Behaviour,* **41,** 603–611.

King, R. B. 1993. Color-pattern variation in Lake Erie water snakes: prediction and measurement of natural selection. *Evolution,* **47,** 1819–1833.

Kirkpatrick, M. & Lande, R. 1989. The evolution of maternal characters. *Evolution,* **43,** 485–503.

Klopfer, P. H. & Ganzhorn, J. U. 1985. Habitat selection: behavioural aspects. In: *Habitat Selection in Birds* (Ed. by M. L. Cody), pp. 435–453. Orlando, Florida: Academic Press.

Kolar, C. S. & Lodge, D. 2001. Progress in invasion biology: predicting invaders. *Trends in Ecology and Evolution,* **16,** 199–204.

Kolm, N. 2002. Male size determines reproductive output in a paternal mouthbrooding fish. *Animal Behaviour,* **63,** 727–733.

Koolhaas, J. M., de Boer, S. F. & Bohus, B. 1997. Motivational systems or motivational states: behavioural and physiological evidence. *Applied Animal Behaviour Science,* **53,** 131–143.

Krebs, J. R. & Davies, N. B. 1997. *Behavioural Ecology: an Evolutionary Approach.* Cambridge, Massachusetts: Blackwell Scientific.

Kunkele, J. & Von Holst, D. 1996. Natal dispersal in the European wild rabbit. *Animal Behaviour,* **51,** 1047–1059.

Kuo, Z. Y. 1976. *The Dynamics of Behaviour Development: an Epigenetic View.* New York: Plenum.

Laland, K. N., Odling-Smee, F. J. & Feldman, M. W. 2001. Niche construction, ecological inheritance, and cycles of contingency in evolution. In: *Cycles of Contingency* (Ed. by S. Oyama, P. E. Griffiths & R. D. Gray), pp. 117–126. Cambridge, Massachusetts: MIT Press.

Laurila, A., Karttunen, S. & Merila, J. 2002. Adaptive phenotypic plasticity and the genetics of larval life histories in two *Rana temporaria* populations. *Evolution,* **56,** 617–627.

Lehrman, D. S. 1953. A critique of Konrad Lorenz's theory of instinctive behaviour. *Quarterly Review of Biology,* **28,** 337–363.

Letty, J., Marchandeau, S., Clobert, J. & Aubineau, J. 2000. Improving translocation success: an experimental study of antistress treatment and release method for wild rabbits. *Animal Conservation,* **3,** 211–219.

Lewontin, R. C. 1974. The analysis of variance and the analysis of causes. *American Journal of Human Genetics,* **26,** 400–411.

Lewontin, R. C. 1983. Gene, organism and environment. In: *Evolution: from Molecules to Men* (Ed. by D. S. Bendall), pp. 273–285. Cambridge: Cambridge University Press.

MacDougall-Shackleton, E. A. & MacDougall-Shackleton, S. A. 2001. Cultural and genetic evolution in mountain white-crowned sparrows: song dialects are associated with population structure. *Evolution,* **55,** 2568–2575.

McAdam, A. G., Boutin, S., Reale, D. & Berteaux, D. 2002. Maternal effects and the potential for evolution in a natural population. *Evolution,* **56,** 846–851.

McLaughlin, R. L. & Grant, J. W. A. 1994. Morphological and behavioural differences among recently emerged brook charr, *Salvelinus fontinalis,* foraging in slow- and fast-running water. *Environmental Biology of Fishes,* **39,** 289–300.

McNamara, J. M. & Houston, A. I. 1996. State-dependent life histories. *Nature,* **380,** 215–221.

Maestripieri, D. 1999. The biology of human parenting: insights from nonhuman primates. *Neuroscience and Biobehavioural Review,* **23,** 411–422.

Mangel, M. & Stamps, J. 2001. Trade-offs between growth and mortality and the maintenance of individual variation in growth. *Evolutionary Ecology Research,* **3,** 583–593.

Maupin, J. L. & Riechert, S. E. 2001. Superfluous killing in spiders: a consequence of adaptation to food-limited environments? *Behavioral Ecology,* **12,** 569–576.

Maynard Smith, M. 1982. *Evolution and the Theory of Games.* Cambridge: Cambridge University Press.

Meaney, M. J. 2001. Maternal care, gene expression, and the transmission of individual differences in stress reactivity across generations. *Annual Review of Neuroscience,* **240,** 1161–1192.

Mittelbach, G. C., Osenberg, C. W. & Wainwright, P. C. 1999. Variation in feeding morphology between pumpkinfish populations: phenotypic plasticity or evolution? *Evolutionary Ecology Research,* **1,** 111–128.

Mousseau, T. A. & Fox, C. W. 1998. *Maternal Effects as Adaptations.* New York: Oxford University Press.

Nilsson, T., Fricke, C. & Arnqvist, G. 2002. Patterns of divergence in the effects of mating on female reproductive performance in flour beetles. *Evolution,* **56,** 111–120.

Oklejewicz, M., Pen, I., Durieux, G. C. R. & Daan, S. 2001. Maternal and pup genotype contribution to growth in wild-type and tau mutant Syrian hamsters. *Behavior Genetics,* **31,** 383–391.

Olding-Smee, R. J. 1988. Niche-constructing phenotypes. In: *The Role of Behaviour in Evolution* (Ed. by H. C. Plotkin), pp. 73–132. Cambridge, Massachusetts: MIT Press.

Orzack, S. H. & Tuljapurkar, S. 2001. Reproductive effort in variable environments, or environmental variation is for the birds. *Ecology,* **82,** 2659–2665.

Oyama, S., Griffiths, P. & Gray, R. E. 2001. *Cycles of Contingency.* Cambridge, Massachusetts: MIT Press.

Pagel, M. & Dawkins, M. S. 1997. Peck orders and group size in laying hens: 'futures contracts' for non-aggression. *Behavioural Processes,* **40,** 13–25.

Petrie, M., Schwabl, H., Brande-Lavridsen, N. & Burke, T. 2001. Sex differences in avian yolk hormone levels. *Nature,* **412,** 498–499.

Piersma, T., Dietz, M. W., Dekinga, A., Nebel, S., van Gils, J., Battley, P. F. & Spaans, B. 1999. Reversible size-changes in stomachs of shorebirds: when, to what extent, and why? *Acta Ornithologica,* **34,** 175–181.

Provenza, F. D. & Balf, D. F. 1987. Diet learning by domestic ruminants: theory, evidence and practical implications. *Applied Animal Behavioural Science*, **18**, 221–232.

Riechert, S. E. & Hedrick, A. V. 1993. A test of correlations among fitness-related behavioural traits in the spider, *Agelenopsis aperta* (Araneae, Agelinadae). *Animal Behaviour*, **46**, 669–675.

Riechert, S. E. & Hall, R. A. 2000. Local population success in heterogeneous habitats: reciprocal transplant experiments completed on a desert spider. *Journal of Evolutionary Biology*, **13**, 541–550.

Rossiter, M. 1996. Incidence and consequences of inherited environmental effects. *Annual Review of Ecology and Systematics*, **27**, 451–476.

Saino, N., Ferrari, R. P., Martinelli, R., Romano, M., Rubolini, D. & Møller, A. P. 2002. Early maternal effects mediated by immunity depend on sexual ornamentation of the male partner. *Proceedings of the Royal Society of London, Series B*, **269**, 1005–1009.

Schaffner, K. F. 1998. Genes, behaviour, and the developmental emergentism: one process, indivisible? *Philosophy of Science*, **65**, 209–252.

Schlichting, C. & Pigliucci, M. 1998. *Phenotypic Evolution: a Reaction Norm Perspective*. Sunderland, Massachusetts: Sinauer.

Schlichting, C. D. & Smith, H. 2002. Phenotypic plasticity: linking molecular mechanisms with evolutionary outcomes. *Evolutionary Ecology*, **16**, 189–211.

Schwabl, H. 1993. Yolk is a source of maternal testosterone for developing birds. *Proceedings of the National Academy of Sciences, U.S.A.*, **90**, 11446–11450.

Schwabl, H. 1996. Maternal testosterone in the avian egg enhances postnatal growth. *Comparative Biochemistry and Physiology*, **114**, 271–276.

Sheldon, B. C. 2000. Differential allocation: tests, mechanisms and implications. *Trends in Ecology and Evolution*, **15**, 397–402.

Sheldon, B. C. 2002. Adaptive maternal effects and rapid population differentiation. *Trends in Ecology and Evolution*, **17**, 247–249.

Sih, A., Bell, A. M., Johnson, J. C. & Ziemba, R. E. 2004. Behavioural syndromes: an integrative approach. *Quarterly Review of Biology*, **79**, 241–277.

Sinervo, B. & Lively, C. M. 1996. The rock-paper-scissors game and the evolution of alternative male strategies. *Nature*, **380**, 240–243.

Skulason, S., Snorrason, S., Ota, D. & Noakes, D. L. G. 1993. Genetically based differences in foraging behaviour among sympatric morphs of arctic charr (Pisces: Salmonidae). *Animal Behaviour*, **45**, 1175–1192.

Stamps, J. A. 2001. Habitat selection by dispersers: integrating proximate and ultimate approaches. In: *Dispersal* (Ed. by J. Clobert, E. Danchin, A. A. Dhondt & J. D. Nichols), pp. 230–242. Oxford: Oxford University Press.

Stamps, J. A. & Krishnan, V. V. 1999. A learning-based model of territory establishment. *Quarterly Review of Biology*, **74**, 291–318.

Stamps, J. A. & Krishnan, V. V. 2001. How territorial animals compete for divisible space: a learning-based model with unequal competitors. *American Naturalist*, **157**, 154–169.

Steen, J. B., Erikstad, K. E. & Hoidal, K. 1992. Cryptic behaviour in moulting hen willow ptarmigan *Lagopus lagopus* during snow melt. *Ornis Scandinavica*, **23**, 101–104.

Sterelny, K. 2001. Niche construction, developmental systems and the extended replicator. In: *Cycles of Contingency* (Ed. by S. Oyama, P. Griffiths & R. E. Gray), pp. 333–350. Cambridge, Massachusetts: MIT Press.

Stiles, J. 2000. Neural plasticity and cognitive development. *Developmental Neuropsychology*, **18**, 237–272.

Switzer, P. V., Stamps, J. A. & Mangel, M. 2001. When should a territory resident attack? *Animal Behaviour*, **62**, 749–759.

Takahasi, K. 1999. Theoretical aspects of the mode of transmission of cultural inheritance. *Theoretical Population Biology*, **55**, 208–225.

Teuschl, Y., Taborsky, B. & Taborsky, M. 1998. How do cuckoos find their hosts? The role of habitat imprinting. *Animal Behaviour,* **56,** 1425–1433.

Tinbergen, N. 1963. On aims and methods of ethology. *Zietscrift für Tierpsychologie,* **20,** 410–433.

Verbeek, M. E., Boon, A. & Drent, P. J. 1996. Exploration, aggressive behaviour and dominance in pairwise confrontations of juvenile male great tits. *Behaviour,* **133,** 945–963.

Vermeij, G. J. 1996. An agenda for invasion biology. *Biological Conservation,* **78,** 3–9.

Via, S., Gomulkiewicz, R., de Jong, G., Scheiner, S. M., Schlichting, C. D. & van Tienderen, P. H. 1995. Adaptive phenotypic plasticity: consensus and controversy. *Trends in Ecology and Evolution,* **10,** 212–216.

Waddington, C. H. 1959. Evolutionary systems: animal and human. *Nature,* **183,** 1634–1638.

Wahlsten, D. 2001. Standardizing tests of mouse behaviour: reasons, recommendations and reality. *Physiology & Behavior,* **73,** 695–704.

Wainwright, P. C., Osenberg, S. W. & Mittelbach, G. 1991. Trophic polymorphis in the pumpkinseed sunfish (*Lepomis gibbosus* Linnaeus): effects of environment on ontogeny. *Functional Ecology,* **5,** 40–45.

Walsh, B. D. 1864. On phytophagic varieties and phytophagic species. *Proceedings of the Entomological Society of Philadelphia,* **3,** 403–430.

Wecker, S. C. 1963. The role of early experience in habitat selection by the prairie deer mouse, *Peromyscus maniculatus bairdi. Ecological Monographs,* **33,** 307–325.

West, M. J. & King, A. P. 1987. Settling nature and nurture into an ontogenetic niche. *Developmental Psychobiology,* **20,** 549–562.

West, M. J., King, A. P. & Freeberg, T. M. 1994. The nature and nature of neo-phenotypes: a case study. In: *Behavioural Mechanisms in Evolutionary Ecology* (Ed. by L. A. Real), pp. 238–257. Chicago: Chicago University Press.

West-Eberhard, M. J. 1989. Phenotypic plasticity and the origins of diversity. *Annual Review of Ecology and Systematics,* **20,** 249–278.

Whitlock, M. C. 1996. The red queen beats the jack-of-all-trades: the limitations on the evolution of phenotypic plasticity and niche breadth. *American Naturalist,* **148,** S65–S77.

Wilson, D. S. 1998. Adaptive individual differences within single populations. *Philosophical Transactions of the Royal Society of London, Series B,* **353,** 199–205.

Wilson, D. S., Coleman, K., Clark, A. B. & Biederman, L. 1993. Shy-bold continuum in pumpkinseed sunfish (*Lepomis gibbosus*): an ecological study of a psychological trait. *Journal of Comparative Psychology,* **107,** 250–260.

Wilson, E. D. 1975. *Sociobiology: the New Synthesis.* Cambridge, Massachusetts: Belknap Press.

Wolf, J. B. 2000. Gene interactions from maternal effects. *Evolution,* **54,** 1882–1898.

13

The Case for Developmental Ecology

Meredith J. West
Andrew P. King
Department of Psychology
Indiana University

David J. White
Department of Psychology
University of Pennsylvania

Abstract

We call for renewed emphasis on the tasks confronting animals as they develop and learn. We are extending the use of the term 'developmental ecology' employed by plant biologists who have studied how fitness can be influenced by the ecological context present during development (Watson *et al.* 2001, *Evolutionary Ecology,* **15,** 425–442). We seek an expanded venue for the term, arguing that for animal behaviourists to understand some of the traits so familiar in behavioural ecology, they must consider the fundamental phenomena of development. Not doing so runs the risk of misidentifying both the proximal and functional causes of traits. For example, without a developmental view, macro-geographical variation in species-typical behaviour may be viewed as evidence of genotypic differences when, in fact, the variation is being produced by developmental contexts. Detailed below are some general issues about how development can be studied if it is to contribute to our knowledge of the adaptive value of behavioural systems. We argue for a prospective and longitudinal orientation, with an emphasis on relatively continuous observation and measurement. Both behaviours and contexts that may only occur during ontogeny are examined, as well as the reproductive outcome of the traits of interest. We present examples from our work on courtship and communication in brown-headed cowbirds, *Molothrus ater,* to show that a prospective and ecological view of development reveals pronounced variation in patterns of reproductive behaviour that cannot be understood without taking into account developmental ecology.

Behavioural ecology is now a dominant approach to the study of animal behaviour. It combines ethology, ecology, economics and natural selection as it evaluates the adaptive value of behavioural traits (Krebs & Davies 1997). Although ethology is part of the foundation of behavioural ecology, not all of its aims are equally represented in this approach to the study of behaviour. The focus is generally on adaptive function and, more recently, on proximal cause. Here we argue for the inclusion of development, a point of view that has been acknowledged by behavioural ecologists to have been downplayed despite its fundamental role in ethology (Tinbergen 1963; Krebs & Davies 1997). Our belief is that cause and function of behaviour cannot be understood without an analysis of ontogeny.

Developmental studies were a common part of ethology at the height of popularity of the nature-nurture paradigm, where the goal was generally to label a behaviour as innate or learned. In the aftermath of the debates begun by Lorenz (1965) and Lehrman (1971), nature/nurture was generally acknowledged to be a false dichotomy and the paradigm eventually lost heuristic value. The method used to establish innate origins, the use of animals reared in isolation, also lost its theoretical power as it was recognized that such a condition was not a developmental baseline, but an aberrant context (Slater 1985). More and more evidence accumulated about the presence of phenotypic plasticity in a wide variety of taxa, making it clear that ontogeny could produce multiple outcomes (West-Eberhard 1989). Despite these events, few new general theories of behavioural development emerged and the popularity of developmental studies in animal behaviour waned. At this point, the central driving theory in the study of behaviour was evolution, and the popular (neo-Darwinian) evolutionary theory had little to say about development (Raff 1996). Under this particulate model, the genes an individual was born with were the genes the individual would transmit at maturity. Thus, it seemed possible to view the time in between as not critical to an evolutionary analysis.

Currently, however, evolutionary biology has seen a surge of interest in synthesizing development with evolution, with the realization that development does not change genes, but influences which genes are selected. New studies, books, and even journals, have emerged focusing on how developmental processes influence phenotypic form, maintain genetic and phenotypic variation, and respond to selection (Hall 1992; Raff 1996; Schlichting & Pigliucci 1998; Gilbert 2001; Wolf 2002). This new synthesis has led to a new reason for interest in development: studies of development can make direct contributions to understanding the adaptive role of flexible ontogenetic mechanisms in natural and sexual selection.

But what if one's interest is only in behavioural outcomes and the final phenotypes on which selection operates? Is it necessary to delve into developmental underpinnings? We would answer in the affirmative because differences in reproductive success, and thus fitness, are products of differences in development. Without a focus on development, any observed variation in a behaviour either within or across populations may be automatically attributed to genotypic differences, when, in fact, it may be the consequence of common developmental processes. For example, over the last 25 years, our laboratory has studied the development of courtship behaviour in the three subspecies of the North American brown-headed cowbird, *Molothrus ater*. We have found substantial differences in all three subspecies. Specifically, we have found differences in the rate and timing of song development in the male as well as some variation in female song preferences particularly near subspecies' borders (King & West 1990). We have documented differences in patterns of courtship and song use across populations as well as differences in female responsivity to song (West *et al*. 1998). These differences seem biologically significant in that attempts to hybridize distant populations from the different subspecies failed to produce significant numbers of viable offspring (unpublished data). Because these populations were geographically separated and morphologically distinct, we assumed the behavioural differences signalled genetically based macrogeographical variation (King & West 1990). In recent work, however, some of which is detailed below, we manipulated ecological variables and investigated the effects on phenotypic variation within a population. We found that all of the behavioural differences we documented in geographically distant populations can be induced within a single population in a single generation, even including reproductive incompatibilities (West *et al*. 2002; White *et al*. 2002b, c). Thus, without developmental approaches, phenotypic flexibility may go unnoticed or be unappreciated as a target of selection. Said another way, selection acts on traits that vary with developmental context and thus what is selected is the source of behavioural variation, the developmental process itself.

Developmental analyses of behaviour have not always been particularly useful in answering evolutionary questions because of limitations in the methods used, the absence of measures of functional outcome, a lack of focus on process, and little interest in ecological validity (but see Galef 1981; Gottlieb 1992; Hoffman *et al*. 1999). A common developmental practice, for example, is to target a mature behaviour of interest and essentially work backwards, retrospectively tracing its ontogeny guided by notions of a predetermined final form. For example, those looking at the structure of bird song might identify adult stereotyped song and then find its roots in immature sounds (Marler & Peters 1982; King & West 1988). Questions may be asked about when these precursors appear and how they change over time relative to the final outcome. Studies focusing on sensitive periods for learning also tend to be retrospective, because they choose a final behaviour and ask at what point do different variables influence its appearance.

The retrospective approach is a necessary step to find order in the usually more variable activity of the young. But the retrospective method has important limitations. First, behavioural precursors of adult behaviour are generally assumed to be functionless because of their temporary and changing nature.

For example, subsong or plastic song are often not assigned communicative value but categorized only as motor practice. The vocalizations undergo massive change as the animal matures and may never recur. So it may seem unnecessary to think that they are even indirectly related to fitness. These behavioural precursors, however, can provide the variation that can propel individuals down different developmental trajectories. In addition, the retrospective approach assumes what the function of the adult form of the behaviour should be but does not actually test the functional outcome directly. Assuming a single outcome obscures sensitivity to the variation in outcomes, which is critical to understanding what selection may be acting upon. In summary, if different developmental trajectories are not recognized, and their connection to differences in outcomes is missed, then it becomes impossible to determine with certainty what function the final behaviours serve.

Finally, developmental contexts may not be visible using a retrospective view. The specific environments in which behaviours develop are probably one of the most understudied parameters in animal behaviour (Kaufman 1975). Developmental environments contain some of the most important pieces of information about later outcomes. For example, the juvenile social structure contains detailed knowledge about what is available to be learned during development. Identification of juvenile social structure also reveals information about the timing of occurrence or absence of behavioural stimulation such as the quantity and quality of contact between adults and young. As Gould (1977) and others have argued, even small changes in the timing of developmental events can have evolutionary consequences through heterochrony (Moore 2001).

An alternative to a retrospective approach is a prospective one. The prospective approach makes few assumptions about the final form of a behaviour, but tracks organisms and their activities from their origins to their reproductive consequences. The prospective approach also does not assume that behavioural precursors are functionless. Instead, it considers that developing organisms may have capacities similar to adults, but because of a lack of experience, they do not have the same capabilities (Galef 1981). This method assumes multiple outcomes in phenotypic form are possible within and across ecologies and attempts to describe the factors that contribute to variation. This approach also assumes that the contextual variables that structure development are not always obvious, because they are dynamically determined by the animals over time. Such a perspective means giving animals sufficient freedom to reveal the independent variables that matter to them as opposed to measuring how animals respond to a static experimental structure. The burden is on the investigator to know what some of the relevant ecological variables may be, based on the species' natural history (e.g. Payne & Payne 1993; Nordby *et al.* 1999, 2000). Thus, the prospective approach is heavily indebted to field and naturalistic studies to provide information about that history. Fieldwork is often constrained, however, in its ability to isolate developmental mechanisms, because of the difficulty in measuring and manipulating relevant variables.

The prospective approach aims to identify sources of influence that animals use to modify or maintain their behaviour. The goal is to find the ontogenetic structures that shape, sustain or change the emergent behavioural form. One of those structures is the animal's species-typical ecology, its ontogenetic niche (West & King 1987; West *et al.* 1988). The ontogenetic niche encompasses the kinds of information that are potentially available to the developing organism. The animal, by virtue of its particular niche, inherits genes, conspecifics and habitats. Specifically, animals inherit provisions, nest sites, migration routes, territories or social rank, properties directly correlated with their genetic inheritance (West *et al.* 1988; Mousseau & Fox 1998; Wolf *et al.* 1999; Laland *et al.* 2000). It is as likely that songbirds inherit conspecifics that sing as it is that they will have a syrinx with which to sing. There is no shared denominator in the case of exogenetic inheritances; there is no common material comparable to DNA, making it more difficult to categorize exogenetic forms of heredity. But the diversity of form should not deter animal behaviourists from looking for the role of ontogenetic niches in defining developmental contexts. As we will show, knowledge of the ontogenetic niche can generate developmental predictions.

Studying development prospectively means a commitment to behaviour and context as the fundamental unit. Contexts, the immediate or proximate properties of an animal's overall niche, are multifaceted and can be dramatically affected by the specific individuals within them. So, just as there is a reaction norm for genotypes exposed to different environments, there is also a reaction norm for environments created by different individuals. This interaction means that behaviours are codefined by settings and individuals (Lewontin 1983; Moore 2001).

Studying behaviours and contexts requires new integrative concepts. An example of such an integrative structure is what we term a social gateway (White *et al.* 2002a), which is the pattern of recurring social interactions that channels sensory stimulation and subsequent responsiveness throughout a group. In a flock, for example, not all birds may have equal access to one another; a subordinate individual may rarely be physically close to a dominant one. As a result, some animals are differentially exposed to models or competitors and are put in a position to learn more or less from conspecifics. The flock, or comparable social group, thus serves a sensory function, gating stimulation along different social pathways (Payne & Payne 1993; Nordby *et al.* 1999, 2000). Investigating the role of social context requires use of complex and public social ecologies, permitting animals to play multiple roles such as observers, models, competitors, or distracters. Such environments also allow animals to self-select patterns of stimulation while placing the burden on the investigator to see the environment from the animal's point of view.

A study with very young cowbirds demonstrates the early manifestation of niches and gateways (White *et al.* 2002a). Young cowbirds are first seen in groups in late summer (see Hauber *et al.* 2000). How sensitive are the immature birds to peers and to adults and how is such sensitivity displayed right after fledging? The species inhabits a wide range of habitats inheriting different niches: in some populations, adult cowbirds are still present, and in others, the adults have moved away. Thus, we chose to investigate the effects of the presence or absence of adults on newly fledged birds.

In three replications, we housed flocks of fledglings in two adjacent aviaries where they could see and hear each other. Adult conspecifics were alternately moved in and out of the two aviaries. To assess organization, we measured patterns of near-neighbour association and vocalizing among the young birds, many of whom were within a week or two of host independence. We found that young flock members, even at less than 40 days of age, showed clear and rapid responses to the presence of adults, even though the adults appeared to do little and did not generally interact with the fledglings. Young males housed with adults vocalized less than young males without adults. But juveniles with adults showed more social interaction with one another, although not with the adults themselves. The effects were remarkably easy to manipulate: if adults were removed or added from the juvenile flock, changes in vocalizing and social behaviour reversed quickly. Taken as a whole, the data showed that young cowbirds, newly independent, react differently to peers than to adults and react differently to peers as a function of adult presence. The reversibility of the effect shows that the young birds' behaviours are context dependent and highly adaptable.

The experiment demonstrates the operation of a social gateway. The young cowbirds, when housed without adults, could see and hear the adults and could observe the greater rate of social interaction between the adult-housed juveniles. Despite this physical proximity and exposure, we repeatedly obtained robust group differences between the two aviaries as a function of adult presence. These observations tell us that the flock is a perceptual, as well as a social, entity, affecting attentiveness to nearby and potentially accessible stimulation.

From a developmental perspective, these data show that the patterns of organization and vocalization of the young birds are already dependent on social circumstances. These behaviours, social assortment and vocalizing, are ones that cowbirds use throughout ontogeny. The data also showed that different opportunities for social and vocal learning are created as a function of the nature of the young birds' surroundings (O'Loghlen & Rothstein 2002). In populations where adults are present, young birds may learn more about interaction but be delayed in the practice and performance of species-typical vocalizations. In areas without adults, singing may be a more frequent event. Most theories of bird song suggest that rudimentary sounds related to later song produced at this age are by-products of motor programming. But, if so, why the sensitivity to the presence of adults? The data suggest that vocalizing at this early age has significance as a means of communication within the juvenile flock. Birds may, therefore, begin their song ontogeny with a sensitivity to react to vocal and social cues, with a capacity similar to adults, but not with adults' capability, that is, they still have much to learn.

Although we focused on very young birds here, we have replicated the effect of social context affecting attentiveness three times with older birds, including adults. Thus, we have found a mechanism, the social gateway, that helps to organize and regulate plasticity. This finding also marks a change in the way one can view a developmental study, as noted earlier. The aim is not to document plasticity, which has now been done in so many taxa, but to find the ecological variables that create the social structures that define what is available to be learned. These structures can function to channel malleability into stable trajectories. An example of such an ecological variable would be the timing and extent of social contact with adult conspecifics (Nordby *et al*. 1999, 2000).

But what about longer-term effects and functional consequences of these different patterns of behaviour? The fledgling experiment might qualify as a sensitive-period phenomenon with differences disappearing as birds mature. This possibility raises the need to look at ontogeny for sufficient lengths of time to document the functional consequences of different patterns of social organization.

We chose to explore the longer-term development of young birds housed with and without adult males in large indoor–outdoor aviaries (White *et al*. 2002b). We configured two flocks of 20–25 birds each. Both flocks had juvenile males and both had females, but one flock also had adult males present (+ADM) whereas the other flock did not (−ADM). Juvenile males in the two conditions developed along different pathways and showed reliably different courtship and communication skills. As in the fledging experiment, +ADM juveniles affiliated with other juvenile males and females more frequently than did the −ADM juveniles. +ADM juveniles also sang more to males and females. In the breeding season, the +ADM males were aggressive with other males and courted and copulated with females in patterns common for cowbirds in the midwestern U.S.A. In this condition, all females that coupled were monogamous. In contrast, −ADM juvenile males displayed very different social patterns. They rarely associated with females or each other, and sang in long bouts of undirected soliloquies. In the breeding season, they showed no aggression towards other males, courted with minimal pursuit, and even after copulation, they did not guard females, allowing multiple males to copulate with their females. Females were promiscuous and laid fewer eggs than did the +ADM females. The +ADM and −ADM juveniles also developed structurally different songs at different rates. The −ADM juveniles advanced sooner to stereotyped song and developed songs that were more effective at eliciting females' copulatory responses than were the songs of the +ADM males. We followed the −ADM males for another year and found the −ADM phenotypes persisted even when we introduced new females. We have recently found that the now adult −ADM males could transmit their behaviour patterns to a new set of juveniles (unpublished data). Thus, this work shows that in the cowbird system, variation in developmental trajectories exists, trajectories are (culturally) heritable, and can have substantial effects on fitness.

The patterns of behaviour seen before the breeding season revealed the facultative nature of cowbird social development. Developmental trajectories were organized as a result of recurring social interactions. In addition to revealing mechanisms of social development, the different outcomes in mating strategies (social monogamy versus promiscuity) also had functional consequences. The conditions differed in the variance in mating success, copulation patterns and egg production. Thus, cowbirds in different developmental ecologies may experience differential variation in reproductive success and intensity of sexual selection (White *et al.* 2002b).

We have gone on to carry out many other aviary manipulations that are not described here (West *et al.* 2002; White *et al.* 2002c; King *et al.* 2003). Some were done to replicate previous effects and some explored the effects of new social variables (see also Freeberg 1998; Freeberg *et al.* 1999). Traits yielding the highest degree of reproductive success differed depending on the context created by social organization during development. For example, in some contexts, males with the best-quality song (as measured by playback) were most successful, in other contexts, males with the best-quality songs were least successful (correlations between song quality and copulations varied from -0.89 to $+0.81$). These data suggest that the function of song in this species cannot be understood without understanding the ecology in which song is produced.

Our work over the past two decades had been premised on the role of song as a stimulus for female mate choice. But we had taken a unitary view of song function: the better the song, the greater the chances of reproductive success. We must now qualify that statement to say that song bears the imprint of a male's social and vocal history: its efficacy and use during the breeding season depends on the kind of social organization experienced during that history. A playback test of vocal effectiveness can thus be misleading as to the honesty of song as a signal of a high-quality male, because it evaluates the signal in the absence of its context. The playback test, however, does differentiate songs by structural properties and thus can be used as a clue that social development has measurable effects on the properties of vocal signals. We also know that song quality, as measured by playback, can change from year to year depending on a male's experience between breeding seasons, reinforcing the idea that song is a sensitive marker of changes in the nature of the local social ecology (West & King 1980; West *et al.* 1996; Nowicki *et al.* 2002).

Thus, the young cowbird develops critical reproductive skills opportunistically through recurring social interactions with others in its niche. That cowbirds will respond to a diversity of local differences is supported by findings showing strong cultural transmission of different phenotypes across generations in captive populations (Freeberg *et al.* 1999). The range of phenotypes transmitted underscores the facultative nature of the developmental system. The relation of such phenotypes to the social context during development cannot be seen using a retrospective view and thus may obscure the fact that selection is acting on the system of development itself (i.e. on the ability to deal with environmental contingencies that can alter developmental trajectories; see Schlichting & Pigliucci 1998).

An example of an environmental contingency is apparent in the differences during the year in the behaviour of song recipients in the ±ADM aviaries. When −ADM males sang to one another, the recipient generally left without returning a song. In the +ADM aviary, males, especially adult males, stayed until the song overture, which led to sustained singing and aggressive interactions. +ADM juveniles learned to sing with other males and as a result developed competitive and aggressive mating behaviour. −ADM juveniles never learned to maintain male–male singing interactions but did engage in more undirected singing. This led these males to be less aggressive, but to develop more effective courtship song than the +ADM males. The differences in the breeding behaviour of the two groups of juveniles emerged from their singing experience with other males during development.

Here we have focused on flock composition and social organization as developmental parameters, but migratory status and hatching time, which also affect contact with adults, have also proved to be heuristic in other avian species (Kroodsma & Pickert 1980; Nelson et al. 1995). These variables are of special interest because they affect the timing of developmental events. A way to think about evolution is that it necessarily incorporates changes in an animal's developmental system, changes that in part reflect selection on the timing of the developmental progression. We saw differences in the timing of song development, both its structure and use, come about as a function of social context from as early as it could be measured (White et al. 2002a). We also know from past work that female stimulation can modulate the rate of vocal development (Smith et al. 2000). Thus, another way to think about the timing differences is from the perspective of the context. An animal may be developmentally ready to learn new song material or improvise on material already acquired but not have close physical access to adult models or tutors or other singers. The pattern of social organization, the gateway, can thus create differences in timing.

In summary, we hope to have shown that developmental approaches, when grounded in ecological perspectives, can contribute organizing variables to the study of behaviour. A specific kind of contribution such studies can make is to uncover how animals learn the pragmatics of employing species-typical behaviours such as vocalizing. In all of the studies we have done, male cowbirds vocalize, and although this capacity need not be learned, almost every other aspect of their song development is sensitive to the social context in which it occurs. The study of pragmatics, the use of communicative signals, has lagged behind the study of syntax or semantics with respect to the analysis of communication in many species, and the reason may be the lack of developmental analyses where behaviour and context are considered together.

Thus, we end by arguing the case for a developmental ecology to unite and inform the study of function, cause and phylogeny of behaviour. Developmental ecology is the study of the ontogenetic interactions between organisms, contexts and behaviours. But instead of merely stating or inferring that interactions occur, developmental ecology seeks to identify the specific nature and effects of the interactions. How? By manipulating ecologically based features of the proximate environment and observing how the effects change behavioural trajectories while they are still ongoing and by testing the reproductive significance of these trajectories (Freeberg *et al.* 1999). Observing and manipulating the ongoing processes of development is the hallmark of this approach and the feature that distinguishes it from other approaches to the study of behavioural change. The greater our sensitivity to behavioural reactions to developmental ecology, the more likely it is that the research will yield answers that are useful to understanding how selection acts on behaviour.

Acknowledgments

The authors thank the Animal Behaviour Society for inviting us to contribute this essay to the journal. The authors were supported by a grant from NSF. Todd Freeberg, Jeff Galef, Julie Gros-Louis and Hunter Honeycutt provided valuable comments on an earlier draft of the manuscript.

References

Freeberg, T. M. 1998. The cultural transmission of courtship patterns in cowbirds, *Molothrus ater. Animal Behaviour,* **56,** 1063–1073.

Freeberg, T. M., Duncan, S. D., Kast, T. L. & Enstrom, D. A. 1999. Cultural influences on female mate choice: an experimental test in cowbirds, *Molothrus ater. Animal Behaviour,* **57,** 421–426.

Galef, B. G., Jr. 1981. The ecology of weaning: parasitism and the achievement of independence by altricial mammals. In: *Parental Care* (Ed. by D. J. Gubernick & P. H. Klopfer), pp. 211–241. New York: Plenum.

Gilbert, S. F. 2001. Ecological developmental biology: developmental biology meets the real world. *Developmental Biology,* **233,** 1–12.

Gottlieb, G. 1992. *Individual Development and Evolution: the Genesis of Novel Behavior.* New York: Oxford University Press.

Gould, S. J. 1977. *Ontogeny and Phylogeny.* Cambridge, Massachusetts: Belknap Press of Harvard University Press.

Hall, B. K. 1992. *Evolutionary Developmental Biology.* London: Chapman & Hall.

Hauber, M. E., Sherman, P. W. & Paprika, D. 2000. Self-referent phenotype matching in a brood parasite: the armpit effect in brown-headed cowbirds (*Molothrus ater*). *Animal Cognition,* **3,** 113–117.

Hoffman, C. M., Flory, G. S. & Alberts, J. R. 1999. Ontogenetic adaptation and learning: a developmental constraint in learning for a thermal reinforcer. *Developmental Psychobiology*, **34**, 73–86.

Kaufman, I. C. 1975. Learning what comes naturally: the role of life experience in the establishment of species-typical behavior. *Ethos*, **3**, 129–142.

King, A. P. & West, M. J. 1988. Searching for the functional origins of cowbird song in eastern brown-headed cowbirds (*Molothrus ater ater*). *Animal Behaviour*, **36**, 1575–1588.

King, A. P. & West, M. J. 1990. Variation in species-typical behavior: a contemporary theme for comparative psychology. In: *Contemporary Issues in Comparative Psychology* (Ed. by D. A. Dewsbury), pp. 331–339. Sunderland, Massachusetts: Sinauer.

King, A. P., White, D. J. & West, M. J. 2003. Female proximity stimulates development of male competition in juvenile brown-headed cowbirds, Molothrus ater. *Animal Behaviour*, **66**, 817–828.

Krebs, J. R. & Davies, N. B. 1997. *Behavioural Ecology: an Evolutionary Approach*. Oxford: Blackwell Scientific.

Kroodsma, D. E. & Pickert, R. 1980. Environmentally dependent sensitive periods for avian vocal learning. *Nature*, **288**, 477–479.

Laland, K. N., Odling-Smee, J. & Feldman, M. W. 2000. Niche construction, biological evolution and cultural change. *Behavioral and Brain Sciences*, **23**, 131–175.

Lehrman, D. S. 1971. Conceptual and semantic issues in the nature–nurture problem. In: *Development and the Evolution of Behaviour: Essays in the Memory of T. C. Schneirla* (Ed. by L. R. Aronson, E. Tobach, D. S. Lehrman & J. S. Rosenblatt), pp. 17–52. San Francisco: W. H. Freeman.

Lewontin, R. C. 1983. The organism as the subject and object of evolution. *Scientia*, **118**, 65–82.

Lorenz, K. Z. 1965. *Evolution and Modification of Behavior*. Chicago: University of Chicago Press.

Marler, P. & Peters, S. 1982. Developmental overproduction and selective attrition: new processes in the epigenesis of bird song. *Developmental Psychobiology*, **15**, 369–378.

Moore, D. S. 2001. *The Dependent Gene: the Fallacy of Nature vs. Nurture*. New York: Times Books.

Mousseau, T. A. & Fox, C. W. 1998. *Maternal Effects as Adaptations*. New York: Oxford Press.

Nelson, D. A., Marler, P. & Palleroni, A. 1995. A comparative analysis of vocal learning: intraspecific variation in the learning process. *Animal Behaviour*, **50**, 83–97.

Nordby, J. C., Campbell, S. E. & Beecher, M. D. 1999. Ecological correlates of song learning in song sparrows. *Behavioral Ecology*, **10**, 287–297.

Nordby, J. C., Campbell, S. E., Burt, J. M. & Beecher, M. D. 2000. Social influences during song development in the song sparrow: a laboratory experiment simulating field conditions. *Animal Behaviour*, **59**, 1187–1197.

Nowicki, S., Searcy, W. A. & Peters, S. 2002. Quality of song learning affects female response to male bird song. *Proceedings of the National Academy of Sciences, U.S.A.*, **269**, 1949–1954.

O'Loghlen, A. L. & Rothstein, S. I. 2002. Ecological effects on song learning: delayed development is widespread in wild populations of brown-headed cowbirds. *Animal Behaviour*, **63**, 475–486.

Payne, R. B. & Payne, L. L. 1993. Song copying and cultural transmission in indigo buntings. *Animal Behaviour*, **46**, 1045–1065.

Raff, R. A. 1996. *The Shape of Life: Genes, Development and the Evolution of Animal Form*. Chicago: University of Chicago.

Schlichting, C. D. & Pigliucci, M. 1998. *Phenotypic Evolution: a Reaction Norm Perspective*. Sunderland, Massachusetts: Sinauer.

Slater, P. J. B. 1985. *An Introduction to Ethology*. Cambridge: Cambridge University Press.

Smith, V. A., King, A. P. & West, M. J. 2000. A role of her own: female cowbird influences on vocal development. *Animal Behaviour*, **60**, 599–609.

Tinbergen, N. 1963. On aims and methods of ethology. *Zeitschrift für Tierpsychologie*, **20**, 410–433.

Watson, M. A., Scott, K., Griffith, J., Dieter, S., Jones, C. S. & Nanda, S. 2001. The developmental ecology of mycorrhizal associations in mayapple, *Podophyllum peltatum*, Berberidaceae. *Evolutionary Ecology*, **15**, 425–442.

West, M. J. & King, A. P. 1980. Enriching cowbird song by social deprivation. *Journal of Comparative and Physiological Psychology,* **94,** 263–270.

West, M. J. & King, A. P. 1987. Settling nature and nurture into an ontogenetic niche. *Developmental Psychobiology,* **20,** 549–562.

West, M. J., King, A. P. & Arberg, A. A. 1988. An inheritance of niches: the role of ecological legacies in ontogeny. In: *Developmental Psychobiology and Behavioral Ecology* (Ed. by E. M. Blass), pp. 41–62. New York: Plenum.

West, M. J., King, A. P. & Freeberg, T. M. 1996. Social malleability in cowbirds: new measures reveal new evidence of plasticity in the eastern subspecies (*Molothrus ater ater*). *Journal of Comparative Psychology,* **110,** 15–26.

West, M. J., King, A. P. & Freeberg, T. M. 1998. Dual signaling during mating in brown-headed cowbirds (*Molothrus ater*; Family Emberizidae/Icterinae). *Ethology,* **104,** 250–267.

West, M. J., White, D. J. & King, A. P. 2002. Female brown-headed cowbirds' (*Molothrus ater*) organization and behaviour reflects male social dynamics. *Animal Behaviour,* **64,** 377–385.

West-Eberhard, M. J. 1989. Phenotypic plasticity and the origins of diversity. *Annual Review of Ecology and Systematics,* **20,** 249–278.

White, D. J., King, A. P., Cole, A. & West, M. J. 2002a. Opening the social gateway: early vocal and social sensitivities in brown-headed cowbirds (*Molothrus ater*). *Ethology,* **108,** 23–37.

White, D. J., King, A. P. & West, M. J. 2002b. Facultative development of courtship and communication skills in juvenile male cowbirds, *Molothrus ater. Behavioral Ecology,* **23,** 487–496.

White, D. J., King, A. P. & West, M. J. 2002c. Plasticity in adult development: experience with young males enhances mating competence in adult male cowbirds, *Molothrus ater. Behaviour,* **139,** 713–728.

Wolf, J. B. 2002. The geometry of phenotypic evolution in developmental hyperspace. *Proceedings of the National Academy of Sciences, U.S.A.,* **99,** 15849–15851.

Wolf, J. B., Brodie, E. D., III & Moore, A. J. 1999. Interacting phenotypes and the evolutionary process. II. Selection resulting from social interactions. *American Naturalist,* **153,** 254–266.

14

Beyond Extra-Pair Paternity: Constraints, Fitness Components, and Social Mating Systems

Patricia Adair Gowaty
Institute of Ecology
University of Georgia

Abstract

During the 50 years commemorated by this volume, three thematic questions marked discussions of the social systems of birds and mammals. These were: (1) What is the value of male parental care to females and their offspring? (2) What are the origins of sexual conflict? Which sex is in "control?" (3) Is the behaviour of mating systems fixed, that is, variable only in evolutionary time, or flexible, that is, induced by ecological, social, and demographic circumstances that individuals experience? Despite the persistence of these questions, the discovery of extra-pair paternity (EPP), in which a socially paired female reproduces with an extra-pair male, reoriented investigation away from the factors favouring emergent patterns of social organisation and mating systems and towards the extent and sources of variation in EPP. EPP is about concurrent multiple mating by females in a species with persistent male–female social bonds, not unlike those that predominate in humans— which might explain why the last 20 years have witnessed an almost exclusive focus on EPP, at least in the field of avian mating systems.

Indeed, EPP is the current key issue in mating systems research in birds and mammals. This was not always so. What is noteworthy in the long view suggested by this chapter is that the questions we asked about mating systems abruptly changed in the mid 1980s. Before that time, the rarer cases of socially polygynous mating systems in birds and socially monogamous mating systems in mammals dominated discussions about the ecological and evolutionary causes of variation in mating systems—of vertebrates, at least. In the 1970s, it was important news to report multiple mating in insects, because the common assumption was that mating once would provide sperm-storing females with a lifetime supply of sperm. Similarly, from 1984 until about 1994, it remained important news in studies of birds and mammals. After that, the important news was pair fidelity, the absence of multiple mating in insects and EPP in socially monogamous birds and mammals. Our perspectives and assumptions changed radically in a very short time. Access to new technologies for genetic parentage testing fuelled the transitions, and once EPP was discovered, the quest to understand how fitness varied with extra-pair copulations (EPC), extra-pair fertilisations (EPF), EPP, and caring for extra-pair offspring (EPO) fuelled further study. Social associations alone were no longer adequate indicators of Darwinian fitness (genetic parentage). Early debates centred on whether males were primarily responsible for EPP and resisted by females, or perhaps sought by females. The possibility that females seek EPP was hotly debated during the transition period. Now, questions about EPP focus mostly on the benefits of polyandry for females, with most investigators assuming that EPC, EPF, and EPP are sought and, in birds at least, mostly controlled by females. ("What *do* females want?") Along with this is an interest in the proximate cues mediating multiple mating by females. ("Why does she like *him*?")

This essay is about the questions that we left behind, some previously thematic, some now almost forgotten, and the questions we might profitably confront in future studies of animal mating systems. The pivotal message here is that variation among females in the ecological and social constraints they experience, the effects of constraints on their reproductive decisions, and the fitness of their offspring are the missing ensemble components to a fuller understanding of the selective factors favouring emergent social systems.

Introduction

I begin this chapter with a history of the questions about animal (mostly birds and mammal) mating systems as I experienced them in the 1970s, when my then vertebrate-centric view focused my questions about the *ecology* of social organisation and mating systems. I next discuss the tension around the initial "discovery" of EPP in socially monogamous birds as I experienced it in the early 1980s, and describe the current consensus about the ecological and social forces (correlates) of EPP in birds. I discuss constraints theory and compensation theory, which emphasise ecological and social constraints acting on female (and now male) reproductive decisions and their consequences, and how individuals respond to constraints. These theories apply equally well to vertebrates and invertebrates, and data about them have moved past vertebrate-centrism. Finally, I circle back to speculate on the ecological, social, and demographic questions that remain largely unanswered and suggest some of the questions about social organisation and mating systems of organisms, including invertebrates, that I anticipate in our collective future.

1960–1984: Ecology and Variation in Mating Systems

Three themes from this period remain topical today: (1) What is the value of male parental care to females and their offspring? (2) What are the origins of sexual conflict? Which sex is in "control"? (3) Is the behaviour of mating systems fixed, that is, variable only in evolutionary time, or flexible, that is, induced by ecological, social, and demographic circumstances that individuals experience?

During the 1960s and 1970s, the discussion that exercised investigators concerned the origins of social polygyny, the most common mating system in mammals and a distinctive, if rare, variant in birds. The Orians–Verner–Wilson polygyny threshold model (Orians 1969) addressed the origins of social polygyny, and arguably remains the most important mating systems model ever published. It said that in birds and mammals, whether polygyny evolved was largely a matter of how much help from males females required in raising offspring. Because mammal mothers gestate and lactate, usually in the complete absence of help from males, the model implied that mammal males, performing no parental care, were free to attempt to mate with more than one female. In contrast, birds, in which males could perform almost all of the parental duties of a female, were constrained to monogamy because females required male help. The Orians–Verner–Wilson model formalised these assumptions and described female fitness as a function of territory quality and the value of male parental care to female fitness. In this simple graphical model, whether social polygyny occurred was a female decision, determined by whether a female chose to settle with an unmated or already-mated male. The graphical model (Fig. 14-1) has two fitness lines: one for females that mated with an unmated male so that social monogamy resulted; the other fitness line was for females that mated with an already-mated male. For all values of territory quality, the fitness of females in social monogamy was greater than the fitness of female in social polygyny. Thus, a fundamental assumption of this model was that male parental care always had a positive effect on female fit-

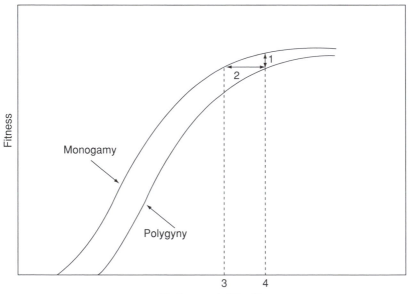

Figure 14-1 The polygyny threshold model from Orians (1969) explains the conditions for the evolution of social polygyny. The model assumed that females choose their mates, males always accept females on their territories, and male parental care always enhances female fitness. It also assumed that social polygyny occurred because of the fitness advantages to the least advantaged member of the polygynous unit, usually the female that joined an already-mated male. The fitness difference, 1, represents the difference between monogamously-mated versus polygynously mated females on the same territory; the polygyny threshold is 2, the difference in environmental quality that favours females that join already-mated males rather than monogamous males.

ness, implying that females fitness depended on male help (theme 1). It was the first explicit model about "female control" (theme 2). Orians emphasised that the females who joined an already-mated male made the critical decision resulting in social polygyny, which introduced the idea that mating systems were emergent properties of the adaptive flexibility of individuals (theme 3).

Trivers's (1972) paper argued that parental investment asymmetries selected for sex-differentiated behaviour. Because it is usually females, rather than males, that invest the most in parental care, selection should favour choosy females and indiscriminate males. A seminal idea in this paper was that selection would favour males who invested in the offspring of one female (theme 1), while simultaneously seeking EPP flexibly (theme 3) and opportunistically with other females. Mixed tactics of males would sometimes conflict with the interests of females so that conflict (theme 2) between male and female interests would result in dynamic interactions over control of breeding decisions by flexibly "cooperating" partners (theme 3).

Kleiman (1977) emphasised two of the period's key themes. Her review showed that among mammals social monogamy was of two kinds: a flexible alternative (theme 3) associated with small populations so that individuals' only options were monogamy. The other form was obligate, occurring when a solitary female is unable to rear a litter without aid from conspecifics (theme 1), or in which carrying capacity is too low to allow more than one female to breed at a time. Among the subtleties exposed by Kleiman's review was that few socially monogamous mammals live in bird-type social monogamy. Instead, socially monogamous mammals live in cooperative systems with a single dominant male and female who sometimes suppress the breeding activities of subordinates. These systems are more like avian helpers-at-the-nest systems, where sharing of offspring care, which might or might not be associated with monogamous breeding, appears to be the key adaptation.

Emlen and Oring's (1977) paper is another classic bearing on the period's three themes. They argued that ecology and demography shaped mating systems and that "ecological constraints imposed limits on the degree to which sexual selection can operate" (p. 215). They centred their arguments around the "environmental potential for polygamy," which theoretically was determined by the distribution of the limiting sex usually females, in space and time and the factor that affected the abilities of the limited sex (usually males) to monopolise individuals of the opposite sex. In practice "emancipation" usually was "emancipation from *male* parental care." The distribution of limiting resources—food, roost sites, and the like—controlled the distribution of females in space. Similarly, the degree of breeding synchrony controlled the distribution of females in time. Emlen and Oring were the first to suggest that the operational sex ratio (defined as the average ratio of fertilisable females to sexually active males) provided an empirical measure of the intensity of sexual selection. Here again, the dependence of females on male parental care was a key variable. Although they did not make claims about female control in typical mating systems, their emphasis on the distribution of females in space and time could be easily associated with female control, whenever one assumed that females' availability—their location in space and their receptivity to mating—were under their own control. Emlen and Oring's focus was on interspecific variation in mating systems; however, readers with an intraspecific perspective easily adapted their ideas to within-species flexible individuals, who adjusted their behaviour to ecological and social conditions.

An influential review by Wittenberger and Tilson (1980) on the evolution of monogamy listed five hypotheses for monogamy. As a set, these hypotheses focused on constraints to monogamy. If females could not achieve social polyandry and males could not achieve social polygyny, then monogamy was a default (Gowaty & Mock 1985; Mock & Fujioka 1990) mating system. These five hypotheses are as follows.

(1) Monogamy should evolve when male parental care is both nonsharable and indispensible to female reproductive success.
(2) Monogamy should evolve in territorial species if pairing with an unavailable unmated male is always better than pairing with an already mated male.
(3) Monogamy should evolve in nonterritorial species when the majority of males can reproduce most successfully by defending exclusive access to a single female.
(4) Monogamy should evolve even though the polygyny threshold is exceeded if aggression by mated females prevents males from acquiring additional mates.
(5) Monogamy should evolve when males are less successful with two mates than with one. (Wittenberger & Tilson 1980: 198)

Again, two of the period's themes were obvious: the indispensability of male parental care (theme 1) and the issue of male versus female control (theme 2) (e.g., as in the ability of a male to defend exclusive access to a single female, or the likelihood that female aggression was key to keeping other females out of a male's territory). Given that aggression is induced behaviour, readers easily took home the lesson of implied adaptive flexibility (theme 3) of individual behaviour.

Thus, the value of male parental care to female fitness appears *almost universally* in theories of mating systems. Each of these seminal papers noted that a key disposing factor was "male emancipation from parental care," to use Emlen and Oring's phrase, or alternatively, the indispensability to females of male parental care. The early comparisons of mammal and bird mating systems had theoretical relevance, despite the almost complete lack of male parental care in the vast majority of mammals and invertebrates that others were studying at the same time. In mammals, mothers most often enjoyed (or suffered) few further interactions with the sires of their offspring after copulation. However, in birds, there are few ecological constraints or morphological limitations to male participation in nest building, incubation, and nestling provisioning. Furthermore, in birds, male parental care is common; thus, many assumed, as Lack (1968) had, that it was compulsory, leading to obligate monogamy. The first tests of this assumption yielded surprising and controversial results (Gowaty 1983). In this field experiment using free-living eastern bluebirds *Sialia sialis,* removal of males revealed that females with or without the help of males were as likely to fledge young, as likely to have adult offspring recruit to the local breeding population, and to survive to the next breeding season. Notably, females helped by males suffered a higher, not a lower, rate of nest predation. The conclusion was that male help was not essential to female fitness. The results begged additional testing, and many tests followed (e.g., Wolf *et al.* 1988; Wolf *et al.* 1990; Wolf *et al.* 1991). Bart and Tornes's (1989) review of the studies following Gowaty (1983) focused on interspecific differences in the degree of male help. They concluded that male help was more likely to be essential when males not only fed nestlings, but incubated eggs as well. This was a reasonable conclusion based on larger effect sizes for fitness of lone and paired females in species with male incubation. Their balanced analysis also underscored that within-population variation among females was impressive. I believe many investigators still hold fast to the idea that male parental care is an evolved adaptation that is essential to females, making social monogamy obligate in most cases. If true, the question of the evolution of social monogamy is put to rest. Yet, accumulating data continue to challenge this typological idea and hold open the door to a fuller examination of classical (Kleiman 1977; Wittenberger & Tilson 1980) and new explanations for social monogamy (Gowaty 1996a; Gowaty & Buschhaus 1998), besides the indispensability of male parental care.

Our field might have developed differently if we discussed male parental care in terms of whether females *allowed* the care of offspring by males or other conspecifics, a reasonable inference in mammals. Is parental care a type of control (Gowaty 1996b)? Are winners the ones who got the prize, the opportunity to care? This perspective is admittedly different from those of theorists worried over desertion. What would theories of male parental care look like if we thought of it in terms of a benefit to male fitness independent of its effects on females? Could we imagine fitness enhancements beyond a season's number of offspring (Freeman-Gallant 1997b)? Is enhanced survival a critical component of fitness for males that care? Do caring males experience survival costs from caring? Do caring males have enhanced opportunities for EPP (Gowaty 1996c)? My point with this list of questions is to emphasise that data at hand show that we are still a long way from answers to some basic questions about the evolutionary forces shaping monogamy.

1984–1990: Social Monogamy is Genetic Polyandry

Analysis of genetic parentage in socially monogamous birds revolutionised our understanding of and questions about mating systems. Despite the prevalence of social monogamy in birds, EPP often occurs, and often at relatively high frequencies. Before the mid-1980s, when EPP in socially monogamous birds was first reported (Gowaty & Karlin 1984), monogamy implied an exclusive mating relationship between one male and one female. Among the results of the discovery of EPP in socially monogamous animals was that previous definitions of monogamy that required "exclusivity" became inadequate descriptors of the social system. Then the focus changed from exclusivity to more operational descriptors: "genetic monogamy," "social monogamy,"or both. Genetic patterns of shared gametes could reflect many kinds of mating patterns, although individuals continued to interact in social monogamy (Gowaty & Mock 1985). This conceptual advance also reinforced the idea that flexible phenotypes contributed to the variation in social behaviour that emerged as critical to mating systems.

A concern that many investigators had was just how divergent conclusions about fitness are when based on behaviour alone in comparison to genetic evidence. The question is not yet generally solved, yet there is consensus that much behaviour and physiology intimately associated with fitness is cryptic (Oring *et al.* 1992; Eberhard 1996; Carling *et al.* 2003).

After the report of EPP in eastern bluebirds (Gowaty & Karlin 1984), the number of socially monogamous species with EPP rapidly increased (Gavin & Bollinger 1985; Evarts & Williams 1987; Westneat 1987; Sherman & Morton 1988; Birkhead *et al.* 1990; Morton *et al.* 1990; Westneat 1990; Bollinger & Gavin 1991; Gowaty & Bridges 1991a, 1991b). In part, the increase resulted from interest and the availability of the new tools of multilocus DNA fingerprinting. There are numerous reviews from just after this period of the occurrence and frequency of EPP in socially monogamous birds (Birkhead & Moller 1992). What was really remarkable was that after about 1991 or 1992, a report of very low or absent EPP in socially monogamous birds was the important news (Lifjeld *et al.* 1991). In fewer than 10 years, our perception of what monogamy meant changed. Before that time, most investigators I talked to thought extra-pair mating would be limited to a very few species, or would occur only through forced copulation (Morton *et al.* 1990). One senior scientist told me he just did not believe my data on eastern bluebirds. Another investigator, perhaps tongue-in-cheek, told me, "Not in my birds!" Thus, it is pleasing to know that recently some have argued that "the discovery of EPP is the most important empirical discovery in avian mating systems over the last 30 years" (Griffith *et al.* 2002: 2195). What is really remarkable, however, is that we used to emphasise, as Lack (1968) did, that 90% of bird species were monogamous and infidelity unknown; now we know that 90% of socially monogamous species are genetically polyandrous (Griffith *et al.* 2002), a sea change. Furthermore, among temperate breeding birds, EPP is twice as frequent among socially monogamous than socially polygynous species (Hasselquist & Sherman 2001).

This time period was crucial too, because it was when other questions (e.g., those of Sutherland [1985a, 1985b, 1987] and Hubbell and Johnson [1987]) that asked about stochastic forces acting on fitness variances fell away and were simply lost to collective attention. Yet, these questions are still compelling (Gowaty & Hubbell 2005). Sutherland's papers emphasised that fixed (nonheritable) life history differences between males and females could result in typically observed differences between the sexes in mating success variances. His papers were the first to challenge the idea that mating success variances were due solely to sexual selection. Hubbell and Johnson added other time-sensitive parameters to their models of mating success variance. They recommended a components of variance approach to the description of the opportunity for sexual selection. They explicitly asked investigators to subtract those effects on mating success variances resulting from fixed sex differences in life history and chance to estimate the true "opportunity for sexual selection."

Other more prosaic questions were also lost. For example, almost no one investigates the significance of female–female aggression to social mating systems anymore, or even to EPP frequencies (see later). It was as if the existence of EPP blinded investigators, reducing, rather than expanding, studies of mating systems.

1991 to the Present: Ecological and Social Correlates of EPP

Recent reports of EPP are still descriptive of its within-population extent (Gelter & Tegelstrom 1992; Gelter *et al.* 1992; Graves *et al.* 1992). But, beginning around 1991, more complex reports of the behavioural, demographic, and ecological correlates of EPP (Gowaty & Bridges 1991a) along with experimental tests (Gowaty & Bridges 1991b) began to appear. These focused on how EPP correlated with breeder ages, male mate guarding intensity, female breeding synchrony, the duration of consortships, and the intensity of male parental care. Experimental studies examined the effects of breeder density and availability of essential resources on the rates of EPP. Some generalisations and surprises emerged from these studies, but the older seminal theories of mating systems (e.g., Orians 1969; Emlen & Oring 1977; Trivers 1972) continued to inform the study of EPP. In this section I briefly review evidence about correlates of EPP to explicitly connect this field to the three themes that have dominated previous discussions—the significance of paternal care, debates about male versus female control, and the preeminence of adaptively flexible behaviour.

Males *and Females* Seek EPP

Because male reproductive success is limited by access to females, the possibility that males actively seek EPP was easy to understand. The first published evidence that females might actively seek EPP was inferred from the significantly positive association between the time fertile eastern bluebird females were off of their territories and the frequency of extra-pair offspring she produced (Gowaty & Bridges 1991b). The idea that females would actively seek EPP was controversial at first. But more detailed studies in hooded warbles *Wilsonia citrina* followed (Stutchbury *et al.* 1994; Stutchbury & Morton 1995; Neudorf *et al.* 1997; Ogden & Stutchbury 1997; Stutchbury *et al.* 1997) and demonstrated that females in this species, at least, control EPP rates. It is controversial whether males or females control EPP rates in red-winged blackbirds (Gray 1996, 1997).

Do Females or Males Control EPP Rates?

EPP may result from active female and/or male solicitations, from male manipulation of females' reproductive decisions through aggressive or "helpful coercion," or from forced EPC. Thus, it is obvious that a global hypothesis of female control is unlikely to be true. Debate continues about forced copulations in birds: are they successful in transferring sperm or achieving fertilisation success? Are forced "copulations" actually just male aggression against females (Gowaty & Buschhaus 1998), a tactic males use to condition female behaviour for male advantage?

The first paper to examine such questions in experimental context was Burley and colleagues (1996). In this study, the investigators recorded copulations in captive colonies of zebra finches *Taeniopygia guttata castanotis,* scoring them as forced or solicited by females as a function of the band colour worn by males. The forced EPCs of green-banded males (unattractive) failed to influence EPP rates. Burley and coworkers concluded that females control EPP rates. In the common gull *Larus canus,* forced copulation is common, but EPP rates are less then 10% (Bukacinska *et al.* 1998), also suggesting female control of fertilisations. In passerines, forced EPCs are surprising given that successful insemination depends as much on active female participation, as male participation in copulation. In both sexes, the second compartment of the cloaca, the urodeum, must be everted through the coprodeum and the vent during the "cloacal kiss," when sperm transfer takes place. Thus, the mechanics of copulation in passerines makes it unlikely that forced copulation is always successful in sperm transfer. In contrast, investigators commonly report forced copulations in ducks (Gowaty & Buschhaus 1998). Male waterfowl have an intromittant organ so that males can forcibly place sperm into the urodeum of females. Whether forced copulation commonly enhances immediate fertilisation success of males remains debatable because females may be able to resist by denaturing sperm using secretions from urodeal glands similar to those in the digestive tract.

Mate Guarding Intensity May Commonly Vary Inversely with EPP

Before Gowaty and Bridges (1991a), investigators expected mate guarding to be something that males did to keep other males from approaching "their" females. We reported that mate guarding intensity significantly correlated positively, not negatively as expected, with the frequency of EPO in the nests of males. This observation suggested that mate guarding was a conditional tactic of males, induced by males' observation of female cues of infidelity. Debates that followed our first report of these data at a scientific meeting in 1988 focused on their meaning for male or female control of extra-pair behaviour. If guarding is something males do to keep other males away from "their" females, one would expect random variation in between-male guarding intensity. But if guarding is something males do to keep "their" females from approaching other males, one would expect males to follow or closely attend fertile mates only when female behaviour suggested infidelity. In yellowhammers *Emberiza citrinella,* males' presence on territories where they can repel intruding rivals, not their behaviour of closely following females, appears to reduce the potential for EPP (Sundberg 1994). In black-throated blue warblers *Dendroica caeruleseens,* males that guarded their mates most closely were less likely to have EPO in their nests, although males that sought more EPP of their own also had more EPO in their nests, suggesting a trade-off between mate guarding and a male's realised EPP (Chuang-Dobbs *et al.* 2001a). Currently, there is no consensus about the effect of mate-guarding on EPP rates. More experimental studies would likely prove interesting.

EPP Varies Positively with Conspecific Densities and Encounter Rates

The first demonstration that birds engage in EPP as a function of opportunity or individual encounter rates with potential mates was an experimental manipulation of eastern bluebird nest site densities (Gowaty & Bridges 1991b). EPP was highest when nest sites were close together and breeder densities and encounter rates with conspecifics high; EPP was lowest when nest sites were scarce and breeder densities and encounter rates low. Because this study manipulated artificial nesting sites, critics argued that increasing encounter rates were a likely artefact of using nesting boxes. This explanation seemed unlikely to us because bluebirds nesting in natural cavities are often much closer together than those nesting in artificial cavities. Another criticism was that the three treatment areas were not replicated. This was unlikely to have led to incorrect conclusions, because our unit of analysis was the EPP rates of individual birds, and except for the manipulated densities of conspecifics, the areas were managed in similar ways and were otherwise ecologically equivalent. Nevertheless, given additional resources, it might be useful to redo these large-scale treatments with multiple replicates of each density treatment. A study (Barber *et al.* 1996) comparing EPP rates of individual tree swallows *Tachycineta bicolor* nesting in natural versus artificial nesting boxes tested the idea that EPP rates were artefacts of nesting boxes. In their study, EPP rates were significantly higher in natural cavities than in nest boxes, possibly because naturally occurring cavities were in tree snags in relatively small flooded areas so that individual tree swallows easily encountered other potential mates and opportunistically mated.

Female Breeding Synchrony Sometimes Increases and Sometimes Decreases EPP

Nowhere has the discussion of male versus female control of mating been more interesting than in the debates about how synchrony affects EPP rates. If female breeding synchrony is important to variation in EPP in the same way that Emlen and Oring (1977) suggested for social mating systems, when females breed synchronously, males' opportunities for EPP should be relatively low, but correspondingly higher as females breed asynchronously. Remember that Emlen and Oring argued that males' abilities to defend multiple females from other males and to inseminate them is greater the more asynchronous females are.

The first test of this idea using genetic parentage data (Gowaty & Bridges 1991a) pointed out the male-biased perspective of the prediction. The analysis indicated that EPP was "no more likely and perhaps less likely as female breeding synchrony decreased" (p. 672), and it offered no support for the idea that males alone controlled EPP rates. If EPP is something sought by females as well as by males or by females alone, one would make other predictions. The male perspective focuses on a trade-off (Westneat & Sherman 1993) between male mate guarding, paternal care, and males seeking EPP so that one expects males to lose opportunities to mate with extra-pair females as his work load with a primary female and her offspring increases. But if females seek EPPs, the trade-offs for males would likely be negligible to absent (Gowaty 1996c), partly because avian copulations usually take so little time. If all a male need do is stay put, perhaps singing to alert females seeking EPP of his location, the trade-offs for him may be much smaller than usually imagined.

Stutchbury and Morton (1995) explicitly argued that in passerines, females control copulations. They then argued that breeding synchrony provided enhanced opportunities for females to assess among-male variation in quality, and therefore they expected that when synchrony was tight, EPP would be higher than when synchrony was loose. They argued that strong synchrony allows females to make better-informed choices among high-quality mates so that female synchrony sets up conditions favourable for female-driven EPP. Using this idea, they pioneered a comparative study of EPP in tropical and temperate birds that exhibit notable differences in breeding synchrony. They argued that the tight synchrony of temperate breeders is probably a response to seasonal cues that induce the onset of breeding activity, in comparison to tropical species with much longer, more spread out breeding seasons. The main prediction is that temperate breeding species have higher rates of EPP than tropical breeding congeners.

EPP is often higher when females breed synchronously (Stutchbury & Morton 1995). EPP rates nevertheless are nontrivial when females breed asynchronously (Yezerinac & Weatherhead 1997; Weatherhead 1997; Weatherhead & Yezerinac 1998), challenging the generality of the Stutchbury and Morton model. Stutchbury rebutted these criticisms (1998). Kempenaers's (1997) study of blue tits *Parus caeruleus* found that breeding synchrony and EPP rates positively correlated when analysed over years, but not when analysed within seasons. His study suggested that the scale of analysis might affect conclusions. Supporting data come from a study (Zilberman *et al.* 1999) of orange-tufted sunbirds *Nectarinia osea osea* in which there is a positive correlation between synchrony and EPP. An interspecific comparison between blue-headed *Vireo solitarius* and red-eyed vireos *V. olivaceus* also supports the female breeding synchrony hypothesis (Morton *et al.* 1998).

Obviously, it is still an open question how well-correlated female breeding synchrony is with EPP opportunity in most socially monogamous but genetically polyandrous species of birds. What is certain is that this debate has been productive and led to new questions. For example, why might some species—breeding at very high latitudes and exhibiting uncommonly high levels of female breeding synchrony—show no evidence of EPP? The general expectation is that female breeding synchrony may arise as a by-product of the timing of environmental cues, such as increasing day-length, that initiate physiological cascades necessary for reproduction. Other explanations are also possible; that is, females may breed synchronously in facultative attempts to manipulate social behaviour of others or to encourage or inhibit their own or others' opportunities for EPP, or for some other reason altogether. Addressing the possible selective pressures favouring or disfavouring female breeding synchrony would seem to be an important next step in efforts to understand its relationship to EPP. Is breeding synchrony simply a by-product of increasing day-length or other environmental cues? Or, is female breeding synchrony more finely tuned, as might be expected if synchrony is flexible and induced by social environments? As far as I am aware, no one has yet addressed questions like these in socially monogamous birds.

EPP, Breeder Age, Male Traits, and Pair-Bond Duration and Pair-Identity

Correlative studies predominate here. For example, in eastern bluebirds, older males were less likely to care for offspring not theirs (i.e., to be cuckolded) than younger males (Gowaty & Bridges 1991a). This was so also in brown thornbills *Acanthiza pusilla* (Green *et al*. 2002), purple martins *Progne subis* (Wagner *et al*. 1996), rock sparrows *Petronia petronia* (Pilastro *et al*. 2002), Bullock's orioles *Icterus galbula bullockii* (Richardson & Burke 1999), American redstarts *Setophaga ruticilla* (Perreault *et al*. 1997), and white-crowned sparrows (Sherman & Morton 1988). In bobolinks, younger males paired with older females are more likely to have EPO (Bollinger & Gavin 1991) in their nests. Less evidence is available on female age and EPP. In eastern bluebirds, second-year and after-second-year females are equally likely to have EPO (Gowaty & Bridges 1991a). In contrast, younger hooded warbler *Wilsonia citrina* females have higher EPP rates than older females (Stutchbury *et al*. 1997). In eastern bluebirds, the longer pairs were together the lower the likelihood of EPP (Gowaty & Bridges 1991b). Similar results are reported for coal tits *Parus ater* (Dietrich *et al*. 2004). Male willow warblers *Phylloscopus trochilus* from a Norwegian, subalpine population with EPO in their nests had significantly lower body mass than males with no EPO in their nests (Bjornstad & Lifjeld 1997). In contrast, in sedge warblers *Acrocephalus schoenobaenus* (Buchanan & Catchpole 2000), there were no significant differences between males' behaviour, physical traits, or territories from nests with and without EPO. Further studies are reviewed in Griffith *et al*. (2002). Their conclusion that the key issue is whether within-pair and extra-pair mates differ in both phenotype and in contribution to offspring fitness is essential. So far, data comparing maternal half-sibs are still quite rare. It seems we are still a long way from generalities about individual traits and variation in paternity gained and lost through EPP.

EPP and Male Parental Care

The expected rush of studies showing that paternal care varies with paternal certainty as predicted by Trivers (1972) has not materialised (Sheldon 2002).

Despite extensive study, a consensus has, so far, not been reached. The most convincing study was the earliest to examine how parental care varied with realised paternity (Dixon *et al.* 1994). In most species studied so far, there was no correlation, or only relatively weak evidence, for a negative relationship between male parental care and EPO in the nests of caring males. A list of examples would include yellow warblers *Dendroica petechia* (Yezerinac *et al.* 1996) and red-winged blackbirds *Agelaius phoeniceus* (Westneat 1995; Westneat *et al.* 1995). However, in black-throated blue warblers *Dendroica caerulescens,* older males, but not younger males, adjust their provisioning rates: as realised paternity declines, food provisioning to nestlings also declines (Chuang-Dobbs *et al.* 2001b). In eastern bluebirds, an analysis (Gowaty, Richardson & Burke unpublished data) including only nests with EPO, showed a middling, but statistically significant negative correlation of pair-male feeding rates with the percentage of EPO in nests. Overall, the evidence for adjustment of paternal provisioning as a function of genetic paternity remains weak, and the significance of EPP to the evolution of variation in male parental care remains controversial.

EPP and Female Fitness

Hypotheses to explain why females seek EPP turn on whether EPP enhances mothers' fitness or the fitness of their offspring. Usually, investigators focus on direct fitness benefits for mothers through enhanced access to resources that mothers need, or on indirect benefits, usually increased numbers of offspring that result from enhanced offspring health or quality. Perhaps the best support from wild-living birds for the hypothesis that females seek EPP to enhance offspring health or quality was from two of the earliest reports (Kempenaers *et al.* 1992; Lifjeld & Robertson 1992). A recent report of long-term fitness consequences of EPP for coal tits *Parus alter,* based on a very large-scale cross-fostering field experiment showed that there were no differences in within-pair offspring (WPO) and EPO, providing no support for the hypothesis that females seek EPP for heritable "good genes" in their mates (Schmoll *et al.* 2003). We are nowhere near a solution to this problem, as many studies emphasise (Gray 1997).

EPP on Island versus Mainland Populations

Some data support the idea that islands have bird populations with lower levels of genetic variability than mainland populations (Griffith 2000), and consequently lower levels of EPP rates (Petrie *et al.* 1998). For example, island house sparrows *Passer domesticus* have lower rates of EPP than mainland populations (Griffith *et al.* 1999). However, there were no differences in genetic structure or in EPP paternity rates of island and mainland populations of blue tits *Parus caeruleus* (Krokene & Lifjeld 2000) or Mediterranean blue tits (Charmantier & Blondel 2003). And, in contrast to expectations based on low genetic variation, in some island populations EPP rates seem very high, such as those reported for Seychelles warbler *Acrocephalus sechellensis* (Richardson *et al.* 2001) and savannah sparrows *Passerculus sandwichensis* (Freeman-Gallant 1997a). In populations of island canaries *Serinus canaria,* in which genetic variability is similar to mainland populations of other species, EPP was nonexistent (Voigt *et al.* 2003). In most of these studies EPP rates seemed to vary most consistently with resource variation rather than genetic variation in the studied populations.

EPP is Usually Genetic Polyandry

What we know now is that multiple mating by females is usually genetic polyandry. There are cases, however, in which a female's social mate loses all paternity to an extra-pair mate. In such cases, females are socially monogamous with one male but genetically monogamous with another. Limitations on our methods still do not allow the general conclusion that female multiple mating results in genetic polygyny, although anecdotal evidence of genetic polygyny exists for common quail *Coturnix coturnix* (Rodriguez-Teijeiro *et al.* 2003) and possibly other overlooked species. Thus, a question still generally unanswered is about the distribution of reproductive success among males. Could it be that in birds, male reproductive success is less skewed than many previously thought?

Univariate Theories of EPP Variation

One of the curiosities of recent literature has been the tendency for some authors to promote one or the other *correlate* of EPP as the fundamental *cause* of EPP variation within and between species. Griffiths and colleagues (2002) evaluated several of these univariate hypotheses, yet found them inadequate to explain phylogenetically controlled comparative interspecific patterns of EPP. Their conclusion is unsurprising if one expects that behaviour associated with EPP is adaptively flexible and induced by the environments individuals are in, which the earlier brief review shows is the case. It is, furthermore, unsurprising if different correlates are simultaneously contributors to the same causative factor(s). Given that individual fitness of breeders (both males and females) most likely results from nonlinear interactions between ecological, behavioural, and genetic factors, it is unlikely that any single correlate of EPP will be shown to be causative. Rather, synthetic theories that take account of how ecology and behaviour affect sometimes conflicting demands of fitness accrual for males and females would seem more likely to be productive.

1996 to the Present: Constraints on Females, Components of Fitness, and Mating Systems

Two theories familiar to me use variation in females to anchor predictive theories about variation in EPP rates. One is the female synchrony hypothesis (Stutchbury & Morton 1995) discussed earlier. The other is the constrained female hypothesis (Gowaty 1996a, 1996b, 1997, 2003, 2004; Gowaty & Buschhaus 1998) that explains between-individual, within-population variation in EPP behaviour of females *and males,* and may be used to explore between-population and between-species variation as well. The constrained female hypothesis assumes that sexual conflict exists, that males benefit from attempts to control the reproductive decisions of females, that female fitness is greater when females control their own reproductive decisions, and that female reproductive decisions are based on the fitness payouts to them, particularly through the health of their offspring. This hypothesis explicitly connects the three themes; it predicts that EPP behaviour in both females and males is flexible; induced in both sexes; and dependent on demographic, life-history, social, and ecological variation in the circumstances experienced by individuals. It also predicts that induced, flexible EPP behaviour is adaptive for both sexes.

The Constrained Female Hypothesis

The constrained female hypothesis (Gowaty 1996a, 1996b, 1997, 2003; Gowaty & Buschhaus 1998) says that the balance between female versus male control of female reproductive decisions is a fundamental cause of variation in mating systems and that this balance is influenced primarily by variation among females in their vulnerability to male control. In this model of sexual conflict (Fig. 14-2), highly constrained and unconstrained females may mate multiply, but the conditions and benefits of EPP vary for individuals as their vulnerability to male control varies. The hypothesis predicts that EPP rates will be higher for unconstrained than for constrained females—all else being equal. More important, it predicts that when more constrained females engage in extra-pair mating, they will share genetic paternity between their social and extra-pair partners so that the mating system is socially monogamous, but genetically polyandrous. In contrast, less constrained females will sometimes mate solely with an extra-pair male so that they are genetically

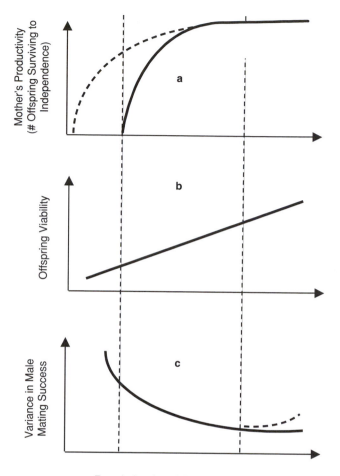

Female Invulnerability to Male Attempts
to Control Female Reproductive Decisions

Figure 14-2 The constrained female hypothesis, generalised from Gowaty (1996), Gowaty and Buschhaus (1998), and Gowaty (2003), makes predictions about within-population components of fitness for females (a), their offspring (b), and their mates (c), and within populations of socially monogamous animals also about the distribution of EPP (see text). Here the x-axis is generalised to represent females' abilities to resist or avoid mechanisms of males that attempt to control or manipulate females' reproductive decisions. In some systems, this could result from males' helpful coercion, when females vary in their abilities to provide food and resources for themselves and their offspring. It could also be females' abilities to avoid aggressive coercion or forced copulation. In (a), the curves represent females helped or protected by conspecifics (the dotted line), and females breeding without help or protection (the solid line). Females highly vulnerable to control of their reproductive decisions by males are those unable to produce any offspring without the help or protection of others. The two fitness curves converge because the model assumes that female fitness is intrinsically limited so that above some threshold no amount of extra help or protection could increase female fitness. Under the

Continued

monogamous with one male but socially monogamous with another. Even more important, the constrained female hypothesis predicts that the fitness payouts of EPP are different for constrained and unconstrained females. For constrained females, it predicts that EPP enhances female survival and her production of offspring (relative to other constrained females), but has no effect on the relative quality of her EPO compared with her WPO. For unconstrained females, it predicts that EPP enhances her fitness, primarily through increases in the viability of her offspring. It predicts for unconstrained females that the quality of EPO offspring is greater than her WPO.

The hypothesis also makes predictions about males. Males mated to lucky and/or skilled females will have more time to seek extra-pair partners; thus, it predicts that these males will have higher rates of achieved EPP than males socially paired to unskilled or unlucky females. It predicts that variance in reproductive success among males mated to skilled and/or lucky females will be higher than among males mated to unlucky and/or unskilled females.

The constrained female hypothesis assumes that variation among females may result from intrinsic differences (e.g., in foraging ability, weaponry, or size), or environmental differences (e.g., local food availability, presence of collaborators, or places to hide) that affect individuals' vulnerabilities to manipulation of their reproductive decisions by others (e.g., their ability to avoid aggressive or helpful coercion by males). The hypothesis assumes that females' reproductive options depend on a composite of these sources of variation. Some of the variation may result from life-history differences (if one takes a more typological between-species approach), some from local ecological and social differences, and some from demographic differences. The curves show variation in female fitness as a function of their vulnerability to manipulation of their reproductive capacities by males—how relatively constrained they are. Female fitness asymptotes in both cases at the same level, emphasising that variation female fitness has similar upper bounds relative to the limits on variation in females. Those females—unlucky, less skilled, or in poorer environments—are more vulnerable to male manipulations so that the hypothesis predicts that some females are relatively free of social constraints while others are far more constrained. Thus, it predicts that lucky (in benign or abundant environments) and/or highly skilled females will be most likely to seek extra-pair mates or

---

assumption that mate preferences assess likely offspring health and survival, the hypothesis predicts that offspring viability, in (b), varies also in terms of mothers' vulnerability to control by males, being higher whenever mothers are less vulnerable than more so. Variance in male mating success, in (c), is predicted to be highest when females' requirements for male help and protection from other males are highest. As females' vulnerabilities decrease, male mating success variance also decreases to a low whenever populations are viscous and outbred. A second dotted line indicates that male mating success variance will increase whenever populations are less viscous and more inbred.

accept EPCs than females who are not so lucky or skilled (Gowaty 1996a). It predicts that among females that have extra-pair young, lucky and/or skilled females will be more likely to be genetically monogamous (have all her offspring sired by her within-pair male) than unskilled females or those in challenging environments. In contrast, it predicts that unskilled females will be more likely to be genetically polyandrous, sharing genetic paternity with pair males and extra-pair males. It predicts that for highly skilled females or those in benign environments, females will mate to enhance the viability of their offspring (Gowaty et al. 2003; Gowaty 2004). It predicts that for less skilled or unlucky females in less benign environments, females will trade copulations and perhaps genetic parentage for food or protection. Thus, one would not expect that for more constrained females that their EPO are healthier or more viable than their WPO.

The most interesting result of these simple models is that mothers' rates of multiple mating, fathers' rates of extra-pair behaviour, variance in male reproductive success, and frequencies of genetic polyandry and genetic monogamy depend on and are predicted by within-population, between-female variation in their vulnerability to manipulation by males (obviously a multivariate parameter). If males can exploit variation in females' abilities to feed themselves and their young, a variable as simple to measure as female foraging skill may functionally account for much of the within-population variation in EPP.

Male Aggression Attempts to Manipulate and Control Females

The key to the first version (Gowaty 1996a) of the constrained female hypothesis was the linkage of within-population, between-female variation in their abilities to provide all care for themselves and their offspring to efforts by males to control or manipulate their reproductive decisions. Another way of describing the importance of variation in females is that the "polygyny threshold may not be the same for all individuals" (Forstmeier et al. 2001a). It was not a stretch after that to extend the constrained female hypothesis to species in which females provide all the parental care, such as ducks and other waterfowl species (Gowaty & Buschhaus 1998). In ducks, because there is no paternal care, one might imagine that no females are vulnerable to trades of shares of female fitness for male parental care. Some females in these species, however, do seem vulnerable to fitness trades for protection against male aggression (Gowaty & Buschhaus 1998). In species in which males cannot or do not build nests, incubate eggs, or feed and defend offspring, the crucial sources of *variation in female vulnerability to male attempts to control them* is not paternal care. Rather, it is likely to be variation in females' responses to the dramatic male aggression against females and forced copulation that is so famous in many ducks, including mallards *Anas platyrhynchos*. If the constrained female hypothesis is right, selection will often act on males to exploit female vulnerabilities to manipulate female reproductive decisions. It is worth emphasising that any time that male control is deleterious to female fitness, selection will act on any available variation *among* females to favour female resistance to male control (Gowaty 1997; Amrhein 1999; Marlowe 2000). Thus, one of the essentials of the constrained female hypothesis is that it is a theory about *dynamic interactions of the sexes*—in response to environmental, demographic, and social variation—that result in induced, flexible individual behaviour.

Tests of the Constrained Female Hypothesis

Evidence in support of the constrained female hypothesis is accumulating. Female breeding success seems fundamentally related to intrinsic differences between females in spotless starlings *Sturnus unicolor* (Moreno *et al.* 2002). EPP of serin *Serinus serinus* is higher in territories with high food (Forstmeier *et al.* 2001b) availability than on territories with low food availability. In addition, socially monogamous females on high-food territories were genetically monogamous with their extra-pair mates (Hoi-Leitner *et al.* 1999). It would be extremely interesting in these cases to know if the quality of EPO is greater than WPO, as also predicted by the constrained female hypothesis. Variation among females of polygynous dusky warblers *Phylloscopus fuscatus* demonstrates that intrinsic differences exist among females in their ability to raise nestlings without assistance (Forstmeier *et al.* 2001b), and that (Forstmeier 2003) females unlikely to have help from males in brood care have higher rates of EPP. In aquatic warblers *Acrocephalus paludicola,* a species with high levels of EPP, food resources are abundant and are not defendable by males and this may free females to seek EPP without jeopardy. Variation in female quality has been associated with females' abilities to manipulate energetically expensive behaviour of males (Hoi 1997).

At the other end of the female constraint spectrum, investigators have documented copulation for food in great skuas *Catharacta skua* (Catry & Furness 1997), common terns *Sterna hirundo* (Gonzalez-Solis *et al.* 2001), osprey *Pandion haliaetus* (Mougeot *et al.* 2002), and in yellow-legged gulls *Larus cachinnans*. It would be interesting to know if there are no differences in the quality of WPO and EPO for females that trade copulations for food, as predicted by the constrained female hypothesis.

Mediterranean blue tits *Parus caeruleus* on Corsica, where food seems limited, seek EPP more often than blue tits in mainland populations, where food is less limited (Charmantier & Blondel 2003), an observation that may be at odds with the constrained female hypothesis. Additional data on the quality of WPO versus EPO in these two populations is needed to know whether the constrained female hypothesis applies. What would be even more interesting is examination of how EPP rates vary with females' abilities to feed themselves and their offspring *within* each population.

Consistent with the constrained female hypothesis, low levels of EPP result sometimes because females that seek EPP jeopardize future aid from their mates (Korpimaki *et al.* 1996; Lawless *et al.* 1997; Stanback *et al.* 2002). A study of house sparrows *Passer domesticus* (Vaclav *et al.* 2003) showed that EPP rates were significantly lower on territories with experimental increases in food availability, suggesting that under nonmanipulated conditions, females that mate multiply trade food for copulations.

None of the studies known to me have yet tested the essential predictions related to offspring viability–quality and fitness as a function of whether females mate in trades for food, protection, or access to essential resources versus when they are free of these sorts of constraints. Nor have investigators examined in systematic ways how variance in male reproductive success changes with the vulnerability status of females. As far as I have been able to tell, no one has tested how variation in female vulnerability to male aggression against them correlates with EPP or with the fitness differences of WPO and EPO.

Fitness Variation under Constraints and the Evolution of Compensation

Constraints theory applies to both sexes because constraints are likely to affect fitness outcomes for both sexes, if under constraints best reproductive decisions are not freely expressed. Partridge's (1980) study was the first to explicitly link offspring viability with mate preferences. My insight was to link variation in offspring viability with social constraints (Gowaty 1996, 1997, 2003; Gowaty & Buschhaus 1998; Drickamer *et al.* 2000) that cause some individuals to not be able to freely express their reproductive decisions. Thus, constraints theory argues that socially imposed constraints (as well as demographic, life-history, and ecological constraints) guarantee that some individuals breed with individuals with whom they are likely to have highly viable offspring and others do not. This predicted that offspring viability would vary with female and *male* mate preferences. Earlier, Hamilton and Zuk (1982) linked heritable fitness benefits from female preferences for fancy traits in males to offspring fitness. But there are few empirical demonstrations of the essential link between fancy male traits and offspring health and survival (Petrie 1994). As a result, I worried that my assumption about offspring viability was not generally true. I also wondered if fancy male traits might not exploit females' sensory biases in ways deleterious to female fitness, an idea that no one has tested directly as far as I can tell, but that has some support in studies showing that females prefer the fancy traits of other species to similar traits in males of their own species. Familiar tests of how mate preferences affect trait variation in males might inadvertently manipulate females against their own best fitness interests, and similar logic applies to how female traits might manipulate males against their own best fitness interests.

Thus, it occurred to me that another way to perform mate preference tests was to ask subjects to discriminate among potential mates drawn at random with respect to phenotypic variation, thus controlling for investigator biases about what cues mediate preferences. Then, if investigators got a reliable and repeatable behavioural response to one discriminatee versus the other(s), one could test for *fitness effects of mating under variation in constraints* (by experimentally manipulating individuals so that they were constrained to breed with a nonpreferred partner, or less constrained and allowed to breed with a preferred partner)—independent of the cues mediating the preferences—and identical tests could be simultaneously done in both sexes.

A consortium of investigators organised in 1995 to 1996 tested predictions about the effects of constraints on offspring viability using a variety of only distantly related organisms. The experiments demonstrated that constraints matter to offspring viability in mice *Mus musculus,* when either females (Drickamer *et al.* 2000), males (Gowaty *et al.* 2003), or both sexes simultaneously (Drickamer *et al.* 2003) are constrained to reproduction with individuals they do not prefer. Constraints matter also in pipefish (Sandvik *et al.* 2000), in female mallards (Bluhm & Gowaty 2004b), in female and male *Drosophila pseudoobscura* (W. W. Anderson, P. A. Gowaty & Y-K. Kim MS), and in female medaka (J. F. Downhower & M. Matsui MS). The only consortium study that failed to show the offspring viability effect of constrained matings was in Tanzanian cockroaches *Nauphoeta cinerea* (Moore *et al.* 2001; Moore *et al.* 2003). However, despite 50 years of captive breeding, *N. cinerea* did evidence costs of constrained breeding for females. Females constrained to breed with males they did not prefer died sooner than females breeding with males they did prefer. The composite results show that constraints matter to offspring viability, and these results increased my confidence that constraints theory might have general significance, whenever ecology, life-history, demography, or social behaviour inhibit the expression of freely made individual reproductive decisions.

When breeders are constrained to reproduction with individuals they do not prefer, and when offspring viability varies with constraints, selection will favour those breeders that compensate or attempt to compensate for offspring viability deficits (Gowaty 2003, 2004). Because selection is expected to act on any available variation, compensation theory predicts that individuals constrained to breed with partners they do not prefer may increase haplotypes available for fertilisation (increased sperm loads), extra-pair mating (by either females or males), fecundity, parental care, and/or other parental effects. In many instances, these predictions are alternative to classic sexual selection hypotheses, making them particularly interesting. For example, older female mallards experimentally constrained to breed with partners they do not prefer compensate by laying larger eggs, giving their offspring a quality advantage that lasts at least until ducklings fledge at 50 days old (Bluhm & Gowaty 2004a).

Among the emerging questions is: how common is compensation? In a study of three species of shore birds in which social pairing with close relatives is common, there was a positive relationship between genetic similarity of social mates and EPP (Blomqvist *et al.* 2002), suggesting that compensation via EPP for expected offspring viability deficits from close inbreeding is common. What remains unknown in the shore bird study is whether a reduction in offspring viability actually exists for WPO and EPO. More studies like Blomqvist and colleagues will surely follow.

The Constrained Female Hypothesis and the Compensation Hypothesis are Based on Variation in Females

I began thinking about these ideas in the late 1980s, as they grew out of my interest in the constraints under which females live (Gowaty 1996a, 1996b, 1997), in the details of what limits females' reproductive success, and females' responses to social, ecological, and demographic constraints. It was perhaps an inevitable outgrowth of more than a decade (then) of field work on bluebirds and my initial studies (Gowaty 1983) of how male parental care did and did not limit the fitness of females and on patterns and consequences of conspecific aggression (Gowaty 1981; Gowaty & Wagner 1987). When I later reviewed the same studies as Bart and Tornes (1989) and additional later studies unavailable to them (Gowaty 1996a, 1996b), what caught my attention was that the value of male parental care obviously varied *between individuals, within populations,* and *within species.* In most populations, some (sometimes all) experimental lone females did as well as control paired females. Even in the populations where there were no statistical differences between experimental and control females, some lone females did quite poorly compared with paired females. A reasonable, unexplored explanation for this was that within populations *females varied* in their abilities to feed themselves and their offspring alone. The variation is in fact striking and suggested that a potential key to understanding dynamically flexible social behaviour and emergent mating systems is the within-population variation among females in their abilities to provide all necessary parental care. This is no longer a minority view (Amrhein 1999; Forstmeier

2003; Hoi-Leitner *et al.* 1999), but when I first began talking about this possibility, other investigators greeted the ideas with scepticism. After all, since the birth of sociobiology, we had been assuring ourselves that among females, relative to males at least, that there was little scope for selection acting on females, because the variances in reproductive success of females is so low. Thus, some suspected that attention to female variation would not be as illuminating as I expected it to be. Similarly today, the idea that females can resist male aggression against them and their children (Fig. 14-3) and that females vary in their vulnerabilities to male aggression and in

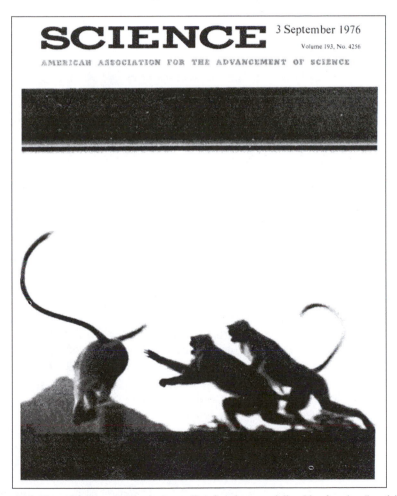

Figure 14-3 Hanuman langurs (*Presbytis entellus*) females, especially older females, "participate in . . . protecting troop infants from assaults by infanticidal males" (Reprinted with permission from *Science* vol. 193 no. 4256, 3 September 1976. Copyright 1976 AAAS. Image: Sarah Blaffer Hrdy, Harvard University, Cambridge MA.)

their abilities to retaliate, remain contentious despite almost 30 years of evidence of female resistance (Hrdy & Hrdy 1976).

Emerging Questions

One of the by-products of tests in flies, cockroaches, pipefish, medaka, mallards, and mice was that we discovered that constraints matter for offspring viability and breeder productivity, not just for female breeders, but male breeders too. Male mate preferences in flies and mice assess offspring viability as reliably and consistently as females' preferences do. Given the theoretical foundations of sex differences research (Williams 1966; Trivers 1972), the existence of fitness enhancing male mate preferences in species with female-biased parental investment begs additional tests and perhaps new theory. Why are males less indiscriminate, in fact far choosier, than we have previously thought?

The distributions of females in space could simply result from the distributions of resources females need, or they might result from interactions among females or between males and females. How female distributions arise is an important question for the future that has so far been addressed by only a few ornithologists. It is a question much more commonly addressed in the mammal literature.

Likewise, breeding synchrony of females might be a passive, inevitable, fixed response to changes in daylight cues, or an adaptive, perhaps flexible response of females induced when their individual circumstances change. It is possible that females regulate their synchrony with neighbours to enhance their own fitness or the fitness of their offspring. Perhaps females adjust their synchrony to manipulate male behaviour or to avoid male manipulation. As far as I know, few studies of nonhumans have yet examined the possibility that female breeding synchrony is an adaptively flexible trait serving female fitness interests. I know of no studies of males manipulating the temporal availability of females, a question also related to female breeding synchrony.

The extent of conspecific brood parasitism relates to female breeding synchrony in some obvious ways. New techniques (Andersson & Ahlund 2001) for studying conspecific brood parasitism are allowing greater resolution to questions about identities of laying females. One of the questions that interests me is how conspecific brood parasitism, EPP, and male aggression against females are related. I believe others will soon be asking similar questions.

Almost totally ignored, ever since Wittenberger and Tilson's (1980) classic review of monogamy, has been the significance of female–female aggression (Gowaty & Wagner 1987) to the evolution of mating systems. Interest in female–female aggression is picking up (Williams 2004; Ptak & Lachmann 2003; Whittingham & Dunn 2000; Cezilly et al. 2000; Elekonich & Wingfield

2000; Slagsvold *et al.* 1999; Snowdon 1998; Sandell & Smith 1997; Kempenaers *et al.* 1995; Kempenaers 1994; Slagsvold & Lifjeld 1994). I anticipate that as more empirical research is accomplished that female–female aggression will be seen as a pivotal aspect of emergent social systems.

With the development of ever more robust methods of genetic parentage assignments, questions about the components of mating success and reproductive success variance differences will emerge as important. Literature suggesting that chance, not female choice or male–male competition alone, can result in mating success variances similar to those predicted by sexual selection are old now (Sutherland 1985a, 1985b, 1987; Hubbell & Johnson 1987). These overlooked models will have greater salience for empiricists once we know more about the identity of males that sire EPO. Thus, I expect that more and more investigators will take a components of fitness approach to their questions (Gowaty 2003). I anticipate studies in which fitness components are examined for fixed (i.e., nonheritable) life-history effects, chance, and sexual selection. Finally, I believe that the question of the origins of sex differences will reemerge (Hrdy 2000; Gowaty 2004). And, that we will begin again to ask in ecological context why the sexes are as they are.

These questions suggest that the themes that informed discussions since the 1970s endure. The theme about the value of male parental care to females has expanded considerably; its derivative questions are richer, explicitly connected to themes of sexual conflict (Forstmeier & Leisler 2004), and adaptively flexible behaviour. It is these richer, more nuanced questions (West-Eberhard 2003) that are likely to dominate mating systems' research in the foreseeable future.

Acknowledgments

I thank the editors for inviting this contribution. I thank Jeff Lucas for collegial and helpful suggestions; Steve Hubbell for discussion and encouragement; and my students Jill Goldstein, Jason Lang, Beth Tyler LeBow, Rebekah Rogers, Leslie Ruyle, and Brian Sydner for challenges. I thank my extraordinary collaborators in the "free mate choice consortium" for their generosity: Wyatt Anderson, Cindy Bluhm, Lee Drickamer, Allen Moore, and the post-docs, especially Yong-Kyu Kim and students, without whom the work would have never been completed. I thank Sarah Hrdy and Jerry Downhower for their enduring interest in my work, for our discussions, and for their always insightful comments. I apologise ahead of time to those authors whose work I overlooked. The Office of the Vice President for Research, University of Georgia, the National Science Foundation, and the National Institute of Mental Health provided partial support for my work discussed here.

References

References

Amrhein, V. 1999. Sexual selection and the evolution of extra-pair copulation: rules of the game from the females' point of view. *Journal fur Ornithologie,* **140,** 431–441.

Andersson, M. & Ahlund, M. 2001. Protein fingerprinting: a new technique reveals extensive conspecific brood parasitism. *Ecology,* **82,** 1433–1442.

Barber, C. A., Robertson, R. J. & Boag, P. T. 1996. The high frequency of extra-pair paternity in tree swallows is not an artifact of nestboxes. *Behavioral Ecology and Sociobiology,* **38,** 425–430.

Bart, J. & Tornes, A. 1989. Importance of monogamous male birds in determining reproductive success: evidence for house wrens and a review of male-removal experiments. *Behavioral Ecology and Sociobiology,* **24,** 109–116.

Birkhead, T. & Moller, A. 1992. *Sperm Competiton in Birds: Evolutionary Causes and Consequences.* San Diego: Academic Press.

Birkhead, T. R., Burke, T., Zann, R., Hunter, F. M. & Krupa, A. P. 1990. Extra-Pair paternity and intraspecific brood parasitism in wild zebra finches *Taeniopygia guttata,* revealed by DNA fingerprinting. *Behavioral Ecology and Sociobiology,* **27,** 315–324.

Bjornstad, G. & Lifjeld, J. T. 1997. High frequency of extra-pair paternity in a dense and synchronous population of Willow Warblers *Phylloscopus trochilus. Journal of Avian Biology,* **28,** 319–324.

Blomqvist, D., Andersson, M., Kupper, C., Cuthill, I. C., Kis, J., Lanctot, R. B., Sandercock, B. K., Szekely, T., Wallander, J. & Kempenaers, B. 2002. Genetic similarity between mates and extrapair parentage in three species of shorebirds. *Nature,* **419,** 613–615.

Bluhm, C. K. & Gowaty, P. A. 2004a. Reproductive compensation for offspring viability deficits by female mallards, *Anas platyrhynchos. Animal Behaviour,* **68,** 985–992.

Bluhm, C. K. & Gowaty, P. A. 2004b. Social constraints on female mate preferences in mallards, *Anas platyrhynchos,* decrease offspring viability and mother productivity. *Animal Behaviour,* **68,** 977–983.

Bollinger, E. K. & Gavin, T. A. 1991. Patterns of extra-pair fertilizations in bobolinks. *Behavioral Ecology and Sociobiology,* **29,** 1–7.

Buchanan, K. L. & Catchpole, C. K. 2000. Extra-pair paternity in the socially monogamous sedge warbler *Acrocephalus schoenobaenus* as revealed by multilocus DNA fingerprinting. *Ibis,* **142,** 12–20.

Bukacinska, M., Bukacinski, D., Epplen, J. T., Sauer, K. P. & Lubjuhn, T. 1998. Low frequency of extra-pair paternity in common gulls (*Larus canus*) as revealed by DNA fingerprinting. *Journal fur Ornithologie,* **139,** 413–420.

Burley, N. T., Parker, P. G. & Lundy, K. 1996. Sexual selection and extra-pair fertilization in a socially monogamous passerine, the zebra finch (*Taeniopygia guttata*). *Behavioral Ecology,* **7,** 218–226.

Carling, M. D., Wiseman, P. A. & Byers, J. A. 2003. Microsatellite analysis reveals multiple paternity in a population of wild pronghorn antelopes (*Antilocapra americana*). *Journal of Mammalogy,* **84,** 1237–1243.

Catry, P. & Furness, R. W. 1997. Territorial intrusions and copulation behaviour in the great skua, *Catharacta skua. Animal Behaviour,* **54,** 1265–1272.

Cezilly, F., Preault, M., Dubois, F., Faivre, B. & Patris, B. 2000. Pair-bonding in birds and the active role of females: a critical review of the empirical evidence. *Behavioural Processes,* **51,** 83–92.

Charmantier, A. & Blondel, J. 2003. A contrast in extra-pair paternity levels on mainland and island populations of Mediterranean blue tits. *Ethology,* **109,** 351–363.

Chuang-Dobbs, H. C., Webster, M. S. & Holmes, R. T. 2001a. The effectiveness of mate guarding by male black-throated blue warblers. *Behavioral Ecology,* **12,** 541–546.

Chuang-Dobbs, H. C., Webster, M. S. & Holmes, R. T. 2001b. Paternity and parental care in the black-throated blue warbler, *Dendroica caerulescens*. *Animal Behaviour*, **62**, 83–92.

Dietrich, V., Schmoll, T., Winkel, W., Epplen, J. T. & Lubjuhn, T. 2004. Pair identity: an important factor concerning variation in extra-pair paternity in the coal tit (*Parus ater*). *Behaviour*, **141**, 817–835.

Dixon, A., Ross, D., O'Malley, C. & Burke, T. 1994. Parental investment inversely related to degree of extra-pair paternity in the reed bunting. *Nature*, **371**, 698–700.

Drickamer, L. C., Gowaty, P. A. & Holmes, C. M. 2000. Free female mate choice in house mice affects reproductive success and offspring viability and performance. *Animal Behaviour*, **59**, 371–378.

Drickamer, L. C., Gowaty, P. A. & Wagner, D. M. 2003. Free mutual mate preferences in house mice affect reproductive success and offspring performance. *Animal Behaviour*, **65**, 105–114.

Eberhard, W. G. 1996. *Female Control: Sexual Selection by Cryptic Female Choice*. Princeton, New Jersey: Princeton University Press.

Elekonich, M. M. & Wingfield, J. C. 2000. Seasonality and hormonal control of territorial aggression in female song sparrows (*Passeriformes: Emberizidae: Melospiza melodia*). *Ethology*, **106**, 493–510.

Emlen, S. T. & Oring, L. W. 1977. Ecology, sexual selection, and evolution of mating systems. *Science*, **197**, 215–223.

Evarts, S. & Williams, C. J. 1987. Multiple paternity in a wild population of mallards. *The Auk*, **104**, 597–602.

Forstmeier, W. 2003. Extra-pair paternity in the dusky warbler, *Phylloscopus fuscatus*: A test of the "constrained female hypothesis". *Behaviour*, **140**, 1117–1134.

Forstmeier, W., Kuijper, D. P. J. & Leisler, B. 2001a. Polygyny in the dusky warbler, *Phylloscopus fuscatus:* The importance of female qualities. *Animal Behaviour*, **62**, 1097–1108.

Forstmeier, W. & Leisler, B. 2004. Repertoire size, sexual selection, and offspring viability in the great reed warbler: changing patterns in space and time. *Behavioral Ecology*, **15**, 555–563.

Forstmeier, W., Leisler, B. & Kempenaers, B. 2001b. Bill morphology reflects female independence from male parental help. *Proceedings of the Royal Society of London, Series B*, **268**, 1583–1588.

Freeman-Gallant, C. R. 1997a. Extra-pair paternity in monogamous and polygynous savannah sparrows, *Passerculus sandwichensis*. *Animal Behaviour*, **53**, 397–404.

Freeman-Gallant, C. R. 1997b. Parentage and paternal care: Consequences of intersexual selection in Savannah sparrows? *Behavioral Ecology and Sociobiology*, **40**, 395–400.

Gavin, T. A. & Bollinger, E. K. 1985. Multiple paternity in a territorial passerine—the bobolink. *The Auk*, **102**, 550–555.

Gelter, H. P. & Tegelstrom, H. 1992. High frequency of extra-pair paternity in Swedish pied flycatchers revealed by allozyme electrophoresis and DNA fingerprinting. *Behavioral Ecology and Sociobiology*, **31**, 1–7.

Gelter, H. P., Tegelstrom, H. & Gustafsson, L. 1992. Evidence from hatching success and DNA fingerprinting for the fertility of hybrid pied X-collared flycatchers *Ficedula-Hypoleuca X Albicollis*. *Ibis*, **134**, 62–68.

Gonzalez-Solis, J., Sokolov, E. & Becker, P. H. 2001. Courtship feedings, copulations and paternity in common terns, *Sterna hirundo*. *Animal Behaviour*, **61**, 1125–1132.

Gowaty, P. A. 1981. The aggression of breeding eastern bluebirds *Sialia sialis* toward each other and intra- and inter-specific intruders. *Animal Behaviour*, **29**, 1013–1027.

Gowaty, P. A. 1983. Male parental care and apparent monogamy among eastern bluebirds (*Sialia sialis*). *American Naturalist*, **121**, 149–157.

Gowaty, P. A. 1996a. Battles of the sexes and origins of monogamy. In: *Partnerships in Birds* (Ed. by J. L. Black), pp. 21–52. Oxford: Oxford University Press.

Gowaty, P. A. 1996b. Field studies of parental care in birds: new data focus questions on variation in females In: *Advances in the Study of Behaviour* (Ed. by C. T. Snowdon & J. S. Rosenblatt), pp. 476–531. New York: Academic Press.

Gowaty, P. A. 1996c. Multiple mating by females selects for males that stay: another hypothesis for social monogamy in passerine birds. *Animal Behaviour,* **51,** 482–484.

Gowaty, P. A. 1997. Sexual dialectics, sexual selection, and variation in mating behavior. In: *Feminism and Evolutionary Biology: Boundaries, Intersections, and Frontiers* (Ed. by P. A. Gowaty), pp. 351–384. New York: Chapman Hall.

Gowaty, P. A. 2003. Power asymmetries between the sexes, mate preferences, and components of fitness. In: *Women, Evolution, and Rape* (Ed. by C. Travis), pp. 61–86. Cambridge, Massachusetts: MIT Press.

Gowaty, P. A. 2004. Sex roles, contests for the control of reproduction, and sexual selection. In: *Sexual Selection in Primates: New and Comparative Perspectives* (Ed. by P. M. Kappeler & C. P. van Schaik), pp. 163–221. Cambridge: Cambridge University Press.

Gowaty, P. A. & Bridges, W. C. 1991a. Behavioral, demographic, and environmental correlates of extrapair fertilizations in eastern bluebirds, *Sialia sialis. Behavioral Ecology,* **2,** 339–350.

Gowaty, P. A. & Bridges, W. C. 1991b. Nestbox availability affects extra-pair fertilizations and conspecific nest parasitism in eastern bluebirds, *Sialia sialis. Animal Behaviour,* **41,** 661–675.

Gowaty, P. A. & Buschhaus, N. 1998. Ultimate causation of aggressive and forced copulation in birds: female resistance, the CODE hypothesis, and social monogamy. *American Zoologist,* **38,** 207–225.

Gowaty, P. A., Drickamer, L. C. & Schmid-Holmes, S. 2003. Male house mice produce fewer offspring with lower viability and poorer performance when mated with females they do not prefer. *Animal Behaviour,* **65,** 95–103.

Gowaty, P. A. & Hubbell, S. P. In press. Chance, time allocation, and adaptively flexible sex roles. *Journal of Integrative and Comparative Biology.*

Gowaty, P. A. & Karlin, A. A. 1984. Multiple maternity and paternity in single broods of apparently monogamous eastern bluebirds (*Sialia sialis*). *Behavioral Ecology and Sociobiology,* **15,** 91–95.

Gowaty, P. A. & Mock, D. W. 1985. *Avian Monogamy.* Lawrence, Kansas: Allen Press.

Gowaty, P. A. & Wagner, S. J. 1987. Breeding season aggression of female and male eastern bluebirds (*Sialia sialis*) to models of potential conspecific and interspecific eggdumpers. *Ethology,* **78,** 238–250.

Graves, J., Hay, R. T., Scallan, M. & Rowe, S. 1992. Extra-pair paternity in the shag, *Phalacrocorax aristotelis* as determined by DNA fingerprinting. *Journal of Zoology,* **226,** 399–408.

Gray, E. M. 1996. Female control of offspring paternity in a western population of red-winged blackbirds (*Agelaius phoeniceus*). *Behavioral Ecology and Sociobiology,* **38,** 267–278.

Gray, E. M. 1997. Do female red-winged blackbirds benefit genetically from seeking extra-pair copulations? *Animal Behaviour,* **53,** 605–623.

Green, D. J., Peters, A. & Cockburn, A. 2002. Extra-pair paternity and mate-guarding behaviour in the brown thornbill. *Australian Journal of Zoology,* **50,** 565–580.

Griffith, S. C. 2000. High fidelity on islands: a comparative study of extra-pair paternity in passerine birds. *Behavioral Ecology,* **11,** 265–273.

Griffith, S. C., Owens, I. P. F. & Thuman, K. A. 2002. Extra-pair paternity in birds: a review of interspecific variation and adaptive function. *Molecular Ecology,* **11,** 2195–2212.

Griffith, S. C., Stewart, I. R. K., Dawson, D. A., Owens, I. P. F. & Burke, T. 1999. Contrasting levels of extra-pair paternity in mainland and island populations of the house sparrow (*Passer domesticus*): is there an "island effect"? *Biological Journal of the Linnaean Society,* **68,** 303–316.

Hamilton, W. D. & Zuk, M. 1982. Heritable true fitness and bright birds: a role for parasites? *Science,* **18,** 384–387.

Hasselquist, D. & Sherman, P. W. 2001. Social mating systems and extra-pair fertilizations in passerine birds. *Behavioral Ecology,* **12,** 457–466.

Hoi, H. 1997. Assessment of the quality of copulation partners in the monogamous bearded tit. *Animal Behaviour,* **53,** 277–286.

Hoi-Leitner, M., Hoi, H., Romero-Pujante, M. & Valera, F. 1999. Female extra-pair behaviour and environmental quality in the serin (*Serinus serinus*): a test of the "constrained female hypothesis". *Proceedings of the Royal Society of London, Series B–Biological Sciences,* **266,** 1021–1026.

Hrdy, S. B. 2000. The optimal number of fathers: evolution, demography, and history in the shaping of female mate preferences. In: *Evolutionary Perspectives on Human Reproductive Behavior* (Ed. by D. LeCroy & P. Moller), pp. 75–96. New York: New York Academy of Sciences.

Hrdy, S. B. & Hrdy, D. B. 1976. Hierarchical relations among female Hanuman langurs (*Primates-Colobinae, Presbytis-Entellus*). *Science,* **193,** 913–915.

Hubbell, S. P. & Johnson, L. K. 1987. Environmental variance in lifetime mating success, mate choice, and sexual selection. *American Naturalist,* **130,** 91–112.

Kempenaers, B. 1994. Polygyny in the blue tit: unbalanced sex ratio and female aggression restrict mate choice. *Animal Behaviour,* **47,** 943–957.

Kempenaers, B. 1997. Does reproductive synchrony limit male opportunities or enhance female choice for extra-pair paternity? *Behaviour,* **134,** 551–562.

Kempenaers, B., Pinxten, R. & Eens, M. 1995. Intraspecific brood parasitism in two tit parus species: occurrence and responses to experimental parasitism. *Journal of Avian Biology,* **26,** 114–120.

Kempenaers, B., Verheyen, G. R., Vandenbroeck, M., Burke, T., Vanbroeckhoven, C. & Dhondt, A. A. 1992. Extra-pair paternity results from female preference for high-quality males in the blue tit. *Nature,* **357,** 494–496.

Kleiman, D. G. 1977. Monogamy in mammals. *Quarterly Review of Biology,* **52,** 39–69.

Korpimaki, E., Lahti, K., May, C. A., Parkin, D. T., Powell, G. B., Tolonen, P. & Wetton, J. H. 1996. Copulatory behaviour and paternity determined by DNA fingerprinting in kestrels: effects of cyclic food abundance. *Animal Behaviour,* **51,** 945–955.

Krokene, C. & Lifjeld, J. T. 2000. Variation in the frequency of extra-pair paternity in birds: a comparison of an island and a mainland population of blue tits. *Behaviour,* **137,** 1317–1330.

Lack, D. 1968. *Ecological Adaptations for Breeding in Birds.* London: Methuen.

Lawless, S. G., Ritchison, G., Klatt, P. H. & Westneat, D. F. 1997. The mating strategies of eastern screech owls: a genetic analysis. *Condor,* **99,** 213–217.

Lifjeld, J. T. & Robertson, R. J. 1992. Female control of extra-pair fertilization in tree swallows. *Behavioral Ecology and Sociobiology,* **31,** 89–96.

Lifjeld, J. T., Slagsvold, T. & Lampe, H. M. 1991. Low frequency of extra-pair paternity in pied flycatchers revealed by DNA fingerprinting. *Behavioral Ecology and Sociobiology,* **29,** 95–101.

Marlowe, F. 2000. Paternal investment and the human mating system. *Behavioural Processes,* **51,** 45–61.

Mock, D. W. & Fujioka, M. 1990. Monogamy and long-term pair bonding in vertebrates. *Trends in Ecology & Evolution,* **5,** 39–43.

Moore, A. J., Gowaty, P. A. & Moore, P. J. 2003. Females avoid manipulative males and live longer. *Journal of Evolutionary Biology,* **16,** 523–530.

Moore, A. J., Gowaty, P. A., Wallin, W. G. & Moore, P. J. 2001. Sexual conflict and the evolution of female mate choice and male social dominance. *Proceedings of the Royal Society of London, Series B–Biological Sciences,* **268,** 517–523.

Moreno, J., Veiga, J. P., Romasanta, M. & Sanchez, S. 2002. Effects of maternal quality and mating status on female reproductive success in the polygynous spotless starling. *Animal Behaviour,* **64,** 197–206.

Morton, E. S., Forman, L. & Braun, M. 1990. Extra-pair fertilizations and the evolution of colonial breeding in purple martins. *The Auk,* **107,** 275–283.

Morton, E. S., Stutchbury, B. J. M., Howlett, J. S. & Piper, W. H. 1998. Genetic monogamy in blue-headed vireos and a comparison with a sympatric vireo with extra-pair paternity. *Behavioral Ecology,* **9,** 515–524.

Mougeot, F., Thibaul, J. C. & Bretagnolle, V. 2002. Effects of territorial intrusions, courtship feedings and mate fidelity on the copulation behaviour of the osprey. *Animal Behaviour,* **64,** 759–769.

Neudorf, D. L., Stutchbury, B. J. M. & Piper, W. H. 1997. Covert extraterritorial behavior of female hooded warblers. *Behavioral Ecology,* **8,** 595–600.

Ogden, L. J. E. & Stutchbury, B. J. M. 1997. Fledgling care and male parental effort in the hooded warbler (*Wilsonia citrina*). *Canadian Journal of Zoology–Revue Canadienne de Zoologie,* **75,** 576–581.

Orians, G. H. 1969. On the evolution of mating systems in birds and mammals. *American Naturalist,* **103,** 589–603.

Oring, L. W., Fleischer, R. C., Reed, J. M. & Marsden, K. E. 1992. Cuckoldry through stored sperm in the sequentially polyandrous spotted sandpiper. *Nature,* **359,** 631–633.

Partridge, L. 1980. Mate choice increases a component of offspring fitness in fruit flies. *Nature,* **283,** 290–291.

Perreault, S., Lemon, R. E. & Kuhnlein, U. 1997. Patterns and correlates of extra-pair paternity in American redstarts (*Setophaga ruticilla*). *Behavioral Ecology,* **8,** 612–621.

Petrie, M. 1994. Improved growth and survival of offspring of peacocks with more elaborate trains. *Nature,* **371,** 598–599.

Petrie, M., Doums, C. & Moller, A. P. 1998. The degree of extra-pair paternity increases with genetic variability. *Proceedings of the National Academy of Sciences of the United States of America,* **95,** 9390–9395.

Pilastro, A., Griggio, M., Biddau, L. & Mingozzi, T. 2002. Extra-pair paternity as a cost of polygyny in the rock sparrow: behavioural and genetic evidence of the "trade-off" hypothesis. *Animal Behaviour,* **63,** 967–974.

Ptak, S. E. & Lachmann, M. 2003. On the evolution of polygyny: a theoretical examination of the polygyny threshold model. *Behavioral Ecology,* **14,** 201–211.

Richardson, D. S. & Burke, T. 1999. Extra-pair paternity in relation to male age in Bullock's orioles. *Molecular Ecology,* **8,** 2115–2126.

Richardson, D. S., Jury, F. L., Blaakmeer, K., Komdeur, J. & Burke, T. 2001. Parentage assignment and extra-group paternity in a cooperative breeder: the Seychelles warbler (*Acrocephalus sechellensis*). *Molecular Ecology,* **10,** 2263–2273.

Rodriguez-Teijeiro, J. D., Puigcerver, M., Gallego, S., Cordero, P. J. & Parkin, D. T. 2003. Pair bonding and multiple paternity in the polygamous common quail *Coturnix coturnix. Ethology,* **109,** 291–302.

Sandell, M. I. & Smith, H. G. 1997. Female aggression in the European starling during the breeding season. *Animal Behaviour,* **53,** 13–23.

Sandvik, M., Rosenqvist, G. & Berglund, A. 2000. Male and female mate choice affects offspring quality in a sex-role-reversed pipefish. *Proceedings of the Royal Society of London, Series B–Biological Sciences,* **267,** 2151–2155.

Schmoll, T., Dietrich, V., Winkel, W., Epplen, J. T. & Lubjuhn, T. 2003. Long-term fitness consequences of female extra-pair matings in a socially monogamous passerine. *Proceedings of the Royal Society of London, Series B,* **270,** 259–264.

Sheldon, B. C. 2002. Relating paternity to paternal care. *Philosophical Transactions of the Royal Society of London, Series B–Biological Sciences,* **357,** 341–350.

Sherman, P. W. & Morton, M. L. 1988. Extra-pair fertilizations in mountain white crowned sparrows. *Behavioral Ecology and Sociobiology,* **22,** 413–420.

Slagsvold, T., Dale, S. & Lampe, H. M. 1999. Does female aggression prevent polygyny? An experiment with pied flycatchers (*Ficedula hypoleuca*). *Behavioral Ecology and Sociobiology,* **45,** 403–410.

Slagsvold, T. & Lifjeld, J. T. 1994. Polygyny in birds: the role of competition between females for male parental care. *American Naturalist,* **143,** 59–94.

Snowdon, C. T. 1998. The nurture of nature: social, developmental, and environmental controls of aggression. *Behavioral and Brain Sciences,* **21,** 384–385.

Stanback, M., Richardson, D. S., Boix-Hinzen, C. & Mendelsohn, J. 2002. Genetic monogamy in Monteiro's hornbill, *Tockus monteiri. Animal Behaviour,* **63,** 787–793.

Stutchbury, B. J. & Morton, E. S. 1995. The effect of breeding synchrony on extra-pair mating systems in songbirds. *Behaviour,* **132,** 675–690.

Stutchbury, B. J., Rhymer, J. M. & Morton, E. S. 1994. Extra-pair paternity in hooded warblers. *Behavioral Ecology,* **5,** 384–392.

Stutchbury, B. J. M. 1998. Female mate choice of extra-pair males: breeding synchrony is important. *Behavioral Ecology and Sociobiology,* **43,** 213–215.

Stutchbury, B. J. M. & Neudorf, D. L. 1998. Female control, breeding synchrony, and the evolution of extra-pair mating systems. In: *Avian Reproductive Tactics: Female and Male Perspectives* (Ed. by P. G. Parker & N. T. Burley), pp. 103–122. Washington, D. C.: American Ornithologists' Union.

Stutchbury, B. J. M., Piper, W. H., Neudorf, D. L., Tarof, S. A., Rhymer, J. M., Fuller, G. & Fleischer, R. C. 1997. Correlates of extra-pair fertilization success in hooded warblers. *Behavioral Ecology and Sociobiology,* **40,** 119–126.

Sundberg, J. 1994. Paternity guarding in the yellowhammer *Emberiza citrinella*: a detention experiment. *Journal of Avian Biology,* **25,** 135–141.

Sutherland, W. J. 1985a. Chance can produce a sex difference in variance in mating success and account for Bateman's data? *Animal Behaviour,* **33,** 1349–1352.

Sutherland, W. J. 1985b. Measures of sexual selection. In: *Oxford's Surveys in Evolutionary Biology* (Ed. by R. Dawkins & M. Ridley), pp. 90–101. Oxford: Oxford University Press.

Sutherland, W. J. 1987. Random and deterministic components of variance in mating success. In: *Sexual Selection: Testing the Alternatives* (Ed. by J. W. Bradbury & M. B. Andersson), pp. 209–219. New York: John Wiley & Sons.

Trivers, R. L. 1972. Parental investment and sexual selection. In: *Sexual Selection and the Descent of Man* (Ed. by B. Campbell), pp. 136–179. Chicago: Aldine.

Vaclav, R., Hoi, H. & Blomqvist, D. 2003. Food supplementation affects extra-pair paternity in house sparrows (*Passer domesticus*). *Behavioral Ecology,* **14,** 730–735.

Voigt, C., Leitner, S. & Gahr, M. 2003. Mate fidelity in a population of island canaries (*Serinus canaria*) in the Madeiran Archipelago. *Journal fur Ornithologie,* **144,** 86–92.

Wagner, R. H., Schug, M. D. & Morton, E. S. 1996. Condition-dependent control of paternity by female purple martins: implications for coloniality. *Behavioral Ecology and Sociobiology,* **38,** 379–389.

Weatherhead, P. J. 1997. Breeding synchrony and extra-pair mating in red-winged blackbirds. *Behavioral Ecology and Sociobiology,* **40,** 151–158.

Weatherhead, P. J. & Yezerinac, S. M. 1998. Breeding synchrony and extra-pair mating in birds. *Behavioral Ecology and Sociobiology,* **43,** 217–219.

West-Eberhard, M. J. 2003. *Developmental Plasticity and Evolution.* New York: Oxford University Press.

Westneat, D. F. 1987. Extra-pair fertilizations in a predominantly monogamous bird: genetic evidence. *Animal Behaviour,* **35,** 877–886.

Westneat, D. F. 1990. Genetic parentage in the indigo bunting: a study using DNA fingerprinting. *Behavioral Ecology and Sociobiology,* **27,** 67–76.

Westneat, D. F. 1995. Paternity and paternal behavior in the red-winged blackbird, *Agelaius phoeniceus. Animal Behaviour,* **49,** 21–35.

Westneat, D. F., Clark, A. B. & Rambo, K. C. 1995. Within-brood patterns of paternity and paternal behavior in red-winged blackbirds. *Behavioral Ecology and Sociobiology,* **37,** 349–356.

Westneat, D. F. & Sherman, P. W. 1993. Parentage and the evolution of parental behavior. *Behavioral Ecology,* **4,** 66–77.

Whittingham, L. A. & Dunn, P. O. 2000. Offspring sex ratios in tree swallows: females in better condition produce more sons. *Molecular Ecology,* **9,** 1123–1129.

Williams, D. A. 2004. Female control of reproductive skew in cooperatively breeding brown jays (*Cyanocorax morio*). *Behavioral Ecology and Sociobiology,* **55,** 370–380.

Williams, G. C. 1966. *Adaptation and Natural Selection.* Princeton, New Jersey: Princeton University Press.

Wittenberger, J. F. & Tilson, R. L. 1980. The evolution of monogamy: hypotheses and evidence. *Annual Review of Ecology Evolution and Systematics,* **11,** 197–232.

Wolf, L., Ketterson, E. D. & Nolan, V. 1988. Paternal influence on growth and survival of dark-eyed junco young: do parental males benefit? *Animal Behaviour,* **36,** 1601–1618.

Wolf, L., Ketterson, E. D. & Nolan, V. 1990. Behavioral response of female dark-eyed juncos to the experimental removal of their bates: implications for the evolution of male parental care. *Animal Behaviour,* **39,** 125–134.

Wolf, L., Ketterson, E. D. & Nolan, V. 1991. Female condition and delayed benefits to males that provide parental care: a removal study. *The Auk,* **108,** 371–380.

Yezerinac, S. M. & Weatherhead, P. J. 1997. Extra-pair mating, male plumage coloration and sexual selection in yellow warblers (*Dendroica petechia*). *Proceedings of the Royal Society of London, Series B–Biological Sciences,* **264,** 527–532.

Yezerinac, S. M., Weatherhead, P. J. & Boag, P. T. 1996. Cuckoldry and lack of parentage-dependent paternal care in yellow warblers: a cost-benefit approach. *Animal Behaviour,* **52,** 821–832.

Zilberman, R., Moav, B. & Yom-Tov, Y. 1999. Extra-pair paternity in the socially monogamous orange-tufted sunbird (*Nectarinia Osea Osea*). *Israel Journal of Zoology,* **45,** 407–421.

15

Condition-Dependent Indicators in Sexual Selection: Development of Theory and Tests

Malte Andersson
Department of Zoology
University of Gothenburg

Abstract

Since ideas addressing sexual selection by condition-dependent indicators began to grow four decades ago there has been continuing progress, both in theoretical development and empirical testing. Mathematical models and empirical tests have led to indicator processes now being viewed as plausible, but their relative importance compared with Fisherian mating advantages ("sexy sons") and mate complementarity remains debated. There is much scope for imaginative empirical work to estimate the fitness consequences of mate choice and the relative strength of the different mechanisms. Measurements of mate choice costs may help determine the applicability of the models. Assumptions and predictions from indicator processes have been corroborated in many animals, but additional well-controlled studies of genetic aspects are needed, based, for instance, on maternal half-sib designs and artificial fertilisation, that also measure fitness and offspring production over more than one generation. This field is still full of open problems requiring a variety of empirical and theoretical approaches for their solution.

Introduction

It is now well known that many animals choose mates based on behavioural and other secondary sex traits that reflect condition and may indicate overall genetic quality. This view is rather new: in spite of Darwin's (1871) early insights, until a few decades ago it was even doubted whether animals chose mates.

An indicator mechanism of sexual selection was already suggested 90 years ago by Ronald Fisher (1915), in a couple of brilliant pages on the evolution of sexual preference, to explain the evolution of female choice. Unfortunately, they remained almost unknown for nearly 70 years. Instead, another great thinker in evolutionary biology, George Williams, began the modern cultivation of this research field in his *Adaptation and Natural Selection* (Williams 1966). This inspiring book gave, perhaps for the first time since Darwin, a succinct, critical, yet creative overview of its field. Among many other important ideas, Williams suggested that "a male whose general health and nutrition enables him to indulge in full development of secondary sexual characters is likely to be reasonably fit genetically. . . . In submitting only to a male with such signs of fitness a female would probably be aiding the survival of her own genes," because "unusually fit fathers tend to have unusually fit offspring." In other words, Williams suggested that

(1) Secondary sex traits are costly indicators that can only be developed fully by males in good, partly genetically determined, condition;
(2) Females choosing such high-fitness males will bear offspring that inherit genes providing high condition and fitness from their father.

Like Williams, I refer for convenience to male secondary sex traits and female choice, although male choice of female traits also occurs (e.g., Andersson 1994).

Williams's (1966) influential book was widely read and led to further thinking about indicator mechanisms (e.g., Trivers 1972; Emlen 1973) Some years later, Zahavi (1975) drew attention to these problems by presenting his generalised "handicap" version of the idea, further emphasising that indicator traits, and many other signals, must be costly. Otherwise, cheating may erode their indicator quality.

So far, the ideas were presented entirely in words, but critics pointed out that purely verbal arguments are not sufficient. The problem is, in essence, quantitative. To see clearly whether the mechanism may work we need to calculate net effects of costs and benefits of the genes involved and trace gene frequency changes and development of linkage (gametic) disequilibrium. As probably few of us can do these calculations in our heads based on words only, mathematical genetic models are needed to see if the process can work. For example, assume that a female mating with a highly ornamented male bears offspring obtaining genes from their father that improve condition and survival. Will this advantage exceed the disadvantage of sons also inheriting genes for the costly male ornament that reduces survival? As Maynard Smith (1976) pointed out, whether this is the case can hardly be decided by verbal arguments only.

Genetic modelling was therefore needed (e.g., Davis & O'Donald 1975; Maynard Smith 1976; Bell 1978; Kirkpatrick 1986). The earliest few-locus models found, however, no realistic conditions under which an indicator process could work. There was also strong doubt as to whether the heritability of fitness can remain high enough to permit such an adaptive mate choice mechanism (reviewed by Kirkpatrick & Ryan 1991; Andersson 1994).

Several authors suggested that more sophisticated mechanisms might make the process work. Williams's reasoning involves adjustment of ornament expression to the condition of the male, and this idea was taken up briefly, for example, by Trivers (1972), Emlen (1973), Zahavi (1977), Borgia (1979), and West-Eberhard (1979), and in more detail by Andersson (1982), Hamilton and Zuk (1982), Kodric-Brown and Brown (1984), and Nur and Hasson (1984) (Fig. 15-1). The importance of condition-dependent trait expression in sexual and other social selection has since received increasing

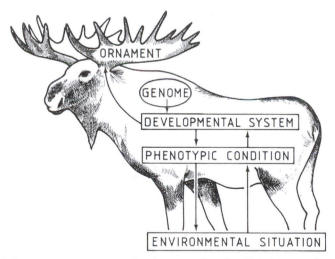

Figure 15-1 Ornaments, weapons, and other sexually selected traits are often condition-dependent indicators, developed in proportion to phenotypic and probably also overall genetic quality. Variation in genome as well as environment will influence their expression via the developmental system. Being part of the reproductive effort, secondary sex traits may be subject to similar allocation constraints and trade-offs as other life-history traits, with expression likely to be influenced more or less by the entire genome (modified from Andersson 1982).

support from empirical as well as theoretical studies. Here, I briefly review some of this continuing interplay between theory and tests.

Indicator Processes and Fisherian Mating Advantages: A Useful Distinction?

In addition to indicators, Fisher (1915, 1930) suggested another major mechanism of sexual selection by female choice, which is now associated with his name. Males with traits preferred by females will have a mating advantage. This advantage is inherited by sons of females with the preference. As genes for preference and trait become associated in offspring, the male trait favoured by female choice will carry the female preference with it. A self-reinforcing positive feedback loop, Fisher's "runaway process," can therefore develop, bringing trait and preference to more extreme values (Lande 1981, reviewed by Mead & Arnold 2004). Although they have sometimes been treated as incompatible alternatives, Fisherian mating advantages ("sexy sons") and viability-based indicator processes are likely to occur together (e.g., Fisher 1915, 1930; Andersson 1982; Iwasa & Pomiankowski 1994; Kirkpatrick & Barton 1997; Kokko et al. 2002; Mead & Arnold 2004). This chapter, however, is focussed mainly on indicator mechanisms.

The usefulness of the distinction between Fisherian (sexy sons) and indicator mechanisms was recently questioned (Kokko 2001; Kokko et al. 2002, 2003). The critics suggested that it is a false dichotomy, and that the two processes are opposite endpoints along a continuum, without any qualitative difference between them. A conceptual distinction is useful if it helps us better understand some interesting aspect of the world that might otherwise go unnoticed, unexplained, or misunderstood. Does the distinction between sexy sons and indicator mechanisms provide such help? I think it does, in several ways. Genetic indicator processes may be driven by advantages derived from overall genetic condition, such as relative freedom from deleterious mutations; that is, by genetic mechanisms that involve other and much larger parts of the genome than do Fisherian mating advantages (see later). The latter can be based on genes that, in essence, influence only mating preferences and preferred traits. Genetic indicator processes on the other hand can work without any sexy sons mating advantage. This has been shown in genetic models by using strict monogamy mating rules (Andersson 1986), and by preventing build-up of gametic disequilibrium between genes for male display and female choice (Houle & Kondrashov 2001), which is a crucial component of the Fisherian runaway process. The two mechanisms are qualitatively different also in that indicator mechanisms can maintain female choice in the face of direct costs of choice, whereas Fisherian mating advantages cannot do so (Kirkpatrick 1985, 1996; Cameron et al. 2003).

These important differences also lead to fundamental differences in evolutionary dynamics and outcomes, which cannot be fully understood without a clear distinction between the two kinds of processes (Cameron *et al.* 2003).

The distinction between sexy sons and indicator mechanisms can also be important for understanding how mate choice translates into various fitness consequences. Many of us seem to be interested in understanding precisely, from a selection point of view, what costs and benefits accrue to offspring from individuals choosing mates with well-developed secondary sex traits. Are the benefits mating advantages (sexy sons), other reproductive advantages, survival advantages, or some combination? The differences between sexy sons and indicator mechanisms concern just these kinds of different consequences, and may therefore be of interest to many. For these reasons it seems to me useful to keep the distinction as clear as possible.

Genetic Models of Condition-Dependent Indicator Traits

Inspired by Maynard Smith (1976, 1978), the first working genetic models of condition-dependent indicator traits used three loci with two alleles each, viability being modelled by one locus, male trait by another, and female mate choice by a third (Andersson 1986; Pomiankowski 1987a, 1987b). Condition-dependence was introduced by letting only high-viability males develop the costly male trait preferred by choosy females. This change turned out to make it much easier for an indicator mechanism to work, also in the absence of any Fisherian mating advantage.

Health and nutritional status of an animal depends on many different processes, such as resistance to pathogens, parasites, and predators, and on foraging and metabolic efficiency. These aspects in turn will probably depend not on a few major genes, but on variation in most of the genome, the quality of which will therefore be reflected in sexual ornaments (Andersson 1982, see Fig. 15-1). Iwasa and colleagues (1991) and Rowe and Houle (1996) showed by genetic modelling how condition-dependence of sexual ornaments combined with high genetic variance in condition will lead to genomewide genetic variance being reflected in the expression of sexually selected traits. These predictions were corroborated in a study of male courtship and female choice in the dung beetle *Onthophagus taurus* by Kotiaho and colleagues (2001; see also Brandt & Greenfield 2004).

Most secondary sex traits show continuous variation and are probably polygenic, as are most traits related to reproductive effort (e.g., Roff 2002). For these and other reasons, a logical next step was to use quantitative genetic modelling and make the three traits continuous. Doing so, Iwasa and colleagues (1991) and Iwasa and Pomiankowski (1994) developed a set of equations to describe how mean female preference $\bar{p}$ and male indicator trait $\bar{s}$ evolve. The following simplified representation (from Pomiankowski & Iwasa 1998) gives some flavour of the important quantities involved.

$$\Delta \bar{p} = B_{pv}\beta_v + B_{ps}\beta_s, \qquad\qquad (1)$$

$$\Delta \bar{s} = B_{sv}\beta_v + G_s\beta_s, \qquad\qquad (2)$$

In these equations describing the change between generations in preference $(\Delta \bar{p})$ and ornament $(\Delta \bar{s})$, β_v represents selection of genetic quality v in males and females, and β_s is selection of male ornament s. G_s is genetic variation in male ornament, and the four B_{ij} are additive genetic covariances between traits i and j. The models showed that costly male traits that reflect differences in male genetic quality can evolve together with a female mate preference because choosy females obtain offspring with higher genetic viability. This requires that the marginal cost of developing a larger trait be lower for males with higher genetic quality. Deleterious mutations that tend to reduce genetic quality are another important assumption.

These models went a long way towards establishing indicator processes as a plausible mechanism of sexual selection by mate choice, and later models have explored additional aspects (e.g., Kirkpatrick 1996; Kirkpatrick & Barton 1997; Houle & Kondrashov 2002; Kokko et al. 2002; Cameron et al. 2003). Nevertheless, conclusions based on different genetic models still diverge over the importance of indicator processes relative to Fisherian mating advantages. The two processes are likely to occur together (see earlier), and Kirkpatrick and Barton (1997) suggested that indicator processes are probably relatively weak compared with Fisherian processes. Houle and Kondrashov (2001; see also Andersson 1986; Kokko et al. 2003; Lorch et al. 2003) on the other hand found that an indicator process can also favour the evolution of costly mate preference and extreme ornaments in the absence of a Fisherian mating advantage. To test between these (and other) models, empirical studies are needed that focus on critical aspects. In particular, costs of female choice and male ornaments may hold a key to clarifying the applicability of different models (e.g., Kirkpatrick & Barton 1997; Houle & Kondrashov 2001; Kotiaho 2001; Cameron et al. 2003; Kokko et al. 2003; Mead & Arnold 2004).

Empirical Testing of Indicator Processes

As genetic models began to support the plausibility of indicator processes, empirical biologists became increasingly motivated to test their predictions. A large number of studies have now done so, many of them by analysing offspring survival to see if females choosing males with larger-than-average ornaments bear offspring with higher-than-average survival. If so, this may be evidence for an indicator process (but see later). This prediction has been corroborated in many studies, 22 of which were examined in a meta-analysis by Møller and Alatalo (1999). They found that the average correlation between preferred male trait and offspring survival was 0.122, suggesting that male traits reflected on average about 1.5% of the variance in offspring fitness measures. Species with high variance in male mating success had stronger correlations than others. The authors concluded that viability-based sexual selection occurs in a variety of taxa, but that its effect is relatively minor, a conclusion that accords with the theoretical view of Kirkpatrick and Barton (1997). Additional evidence for indicator processes has since been presented for several other species (e.g., Iyengar & Eisner 1999; David et al. 2000; Sandvik et al. 2000; Nowicki et al. 2000; Ahtiainen et al. 2001; Ditchkoff et al. 2001; Evans et al. 2004; see also later). Negative evidence was presented by Brooks (2000) and Grether (2000).

In testing indicator mechanisms, it is difficult to control all potentially confounding variables. Because male ornaments are reproductive life-history traits (see Fig. 15-1), trade-offs with other traits might conceal potential viability advantages inherited from highly ornamented males (Kokko 2001; Kokko et al. 2002). Earlier workers in this field, myself included, suggested that benefits of high-quality genes inherited by offspring through an indicator process will be manifested by increased offspring survival, but this is not logically necessary. Even if large ornaments indicate high male condition, high-quality males, under some circumstances, might shunt so much of their resources to mate-attracting traits (see Fig. 15-1) that their male offspring have higher mating success but lower viability than lower-quality males (e.g., Grafen 1990b; Hansen & Price 1995; Höglund & Sheldon 1998; Eshel et al. 2000; Kokko 2001; Kokko et al. 2002). Indicator processes, therefore, cannot be falsified by showing that survival is negatively related to attractiveness, and Kokko (2001) suggested that the low estimates reported by Møller and Alatalo (1999) might in part be caused by such allocation effects.

In a test of this possibility, male field crickets Teleogryllus commodus given high protein food had higher calling rate and reduced survival, whereas females with high-protein food lived longer than others (Hunt et al. 2004a). Whether such an effect can also be brought about by genetic manipulation, comparing offspring inheriting high-quality genes with offspring inheriting lower-quality genes from their fathers, remains to be seen. Such tests need to distinguish effects of genes with narrow influence on calling rate from genes with broader influence on health, nutrition, and other aspects of condition.

As indicator processes and Fisherian mating advantages (sexy sons) are likely to occur together, a challenging problem is to estimate their relative importance (Andersson 1994), but in practice, a clear-cut estimation is no easy task. The extra resources available for individuals of high quality (condition) can be allocated between different functions and traits (see Fig. 15-1). Measures of offspring fitness, therefore, need to distinguish between mating success, other aspects of reproductive success, and viability. Hunt and colleagues (2004b) suggest that total fitness should be measured by counting the number of grandoffspring produced, because some fitness effects do not become apparent until after two generations. This is a desirable goal, but the number of field studies where it can be achieved are few at present. Long-term studies of collared flycatcher *Ficedula albicollis* and red deer *Cervus elaphus* are two potential examples (e.g., Kruuk *et al.* 2002; Sheldon *et al.* 2003a).

Another problem in testing sexual selection models is that processes may vary in space and time. For example, a study of great reed warblers *Acrocephalus arundinaceus* found that viability of extra-pair offspring was strongly correlated with the song repertoire size of the genetic father, suggesting that repertoire size is an indicator of male genetic quality (Hasselquist *et al.* 1996; Nowicki *et al.* 2000). A recent study in another area found no correlation with song repertoire size, instead suggesting high frequency of song syllable switching as a candidate trait (Forstmeier & Leisler 2004).

Testing whether offspring of females mating with highly ornamented males inherit genes that provide higher-than-average fitness can be confounded by effects related to genetic compatibility and complementarity of the mates (reviewed e.g., by Tregenza & Wedell 2000; Zeh & Zeh 2003; Neff & Pitcher 2005), and by maternal effects. The latter can occur, for instance, if the female is of higher-than-average quality herself, or if she invests more resources in offspring after mating with a highly ornamented male (e.g., Kraak & Bakker 1998). Another possibility is that males with high condition have both large ornaments and provide superior resources to female or offspring (e.g., Hill 1991, 2002; Kotiaho *et al.* 2003; Jensen *et al.* 2004).

These potentially confounding factors can be controlled in species with external fertilisation, by using a maternal half-sib experimental design and *in vitro* fertilisation (Fig. 15-2). To test whether call duration in male grey tree frogs *Hyla versicolor* is an indicator of genetic quality, Welch *et al.* (1998; also see Doty & Welch 2001; Welch 2003) split the clutches from each of a number of females in two parts, one artificially fertilised by sperm from a male with a short call duration, the other from a male with a long call duration, and raised the offspring in the laboratory. The offspring of males with long call duration performed significantly better than the others, demonstrating that call duration reflects genetic quality. The female preference for long calls may therefore have evolved at least in part through an indicator process.

Using similar approaches, three more studies provide experimental evidence for genetic benefits from mate choice by an indicator process in three-spined stickleback *Gasterosteus aculeatus* (Barber *et al.* 2001), whitefish *Coregonus sp.* (Wedekind *et al.* 2001), and moor frog *Rana arvalis* (Sheldon

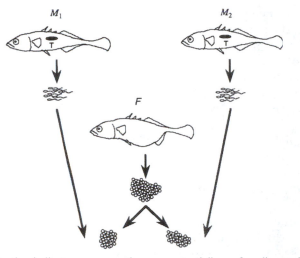

Figure 15-2 In testing indicator processes there are potentially confounding variables such as environmental variation, maternal investment depending on the quality of her mate, paternal material contributions to offspring, and mate compatibility effects. Some of these variables can be controlled by experiments such as suitably replicated maternal half-sib designs combined with *in vitro* fertilisation followed by standardised raising of offspring. Groups of maternal half-siblings from the same breeding event have different fathers. If offspring fitness increases with father's ornament size in such tests, this may be strong evidence that the trait is an indicator of male overall genetic quality, as the three confounding effects mentioned can then be excluded (modified from Barber & Arnott 2000).

et al. 2003b). Similar results also come from a field study comparing offspring sired by social and extra-pair males for the same female in collared flycatcher *Ficedula albicollis* (Sheldon *et al.* 1997)

In animals with internal fertilisation, artificial insemination similarly permits control of female differential investment in offspring based on behavioural interaction with the male (Parker 2003). Using this technique, Evans and colleagues (2004) showed that the ability of newborn offspring to evade capture by a predator increases with sire colouration in guppy *Poecilia reticulata*. A potential complication in tests of this kind is that sire effects might sometimes occur via seminal fluids, possibly leading to differential maternal allocation.

What are Condition and Genetic Quality?

Indicator traits are condition-dependent and reflect genetic quality. These two concepts are discussed in two recent papers pointing the way to further exploration. Tomkins and colleagues (2004) note that little is known empirically about the genetic basis of condition, which can only be measured by its phenotypic expressions. Suitable measures involve not only the accumulated pool of resources, but also the ability to acquire resources. The most successful or dominant individuals may not carry the largest accumulated resources, but may be superior at acquiring additional resources when needed. Tomkins and colleagues (2004) suggested that the genetic basis of condition can be elucidated using mutational techniques to create variance in genetic quality (also see, e.g., Kondrashov 1988; Rice 1988; Burt 1995; Rowe & Houle 1996; Blanckenhorn & Hosken 2003; Brandt & Greenfield 2004; Radwan 2004).

Hunt and colleagues (2004b) suggested that the essence of genetic quality is contained in the breeding value of an individual for total fitness (the summed additive effects of an individual's genes on fitness; also see Kokko *et al.* 2003). Although difficult, it can sometimes be estimated via the mean total fitness of the individual's progeny. As discussed earlier, counting the number of grandoffspring is desirable and sometimes possible.

This review has focused on indicator processes where females receive only genes from males, which is perhaps the hardest case to understand. In many species females receive material resources, and models for such situations have been constructed for example by Hoelzer (1989), Heywood (1989), Grafen (1990a), Price and colleagues (1993), Schluter and Price (1993) and Iwasa and Pomiankowski (1999). These models show that an indicator process can then have similar outcomes as in the purely genetic case, leading to evolution of costly male ornaments and female preferences. There is also abundant empirical evidence for mate choice influenced by material resources offered by mates (reviewed, e.g., by Kirkpatrick & Ryan 1991; Andersson 1994; Hill 2002).

Conclusions

Since the first ideas about sexual selection by condition-dependent indicators began to grow and spread some 40 years ago, there has been much progress both in theoretical development and modelling and in empirical testing of the ideas. With the arrival of increasingly clarifying genetic models and empirical tests, indicator processes have gone from being viewed by many as impossible, or at least unlikely, to plausible. Their relative importance compared with Fisherian mating advantages, however, still remains debated. There is much scope for imaginative empirical work to estimate the various fitness consequences of mate choice and the relative strength of the different mechanisms in a variety of species. Assumptions and predictions from indicator processes have been corroborated in quite a few animals, but more well-controlled studies of genetic aspects are needed, based, for example, on designs, such as maternal half-sib analysis and *in vitro* or *in vivo* artificial fertilisation, if possible also measuring fitness and offspring production over more than one generation. Recent advances in molecular analyses of gene identity and expression also seem likely to greatly clarify mechanisms of sexual selection in the future.

This brief chapter has only touched on some of the important issues. I hope it may stimulate reading the original papers and also the thorough recent reviews of indicator traits and related aspects of mate choice (e.g., Tregenza and Wedell 2000; Kokko *et al.* 2003; Zeh and Zeh 2003; Hunt *et al.* 2004b; Mead and Arnold 2004; Tomkins *et al.* 2004; and Neff and Pitcher 2005). This field is still full of fascinating unsolved problems requiring all sorts of research, from theoretical or lab-based genetics to behavioural and ecological fieldwork on a variety of wonderful beasts.

Acknowledgments

I thank Staffan Andersson, Leigh Simmons, Joe Tomkins, and a referee for helpful suggestions on the manuscript; Leigh Simmons for invitation to write this chapter; Iain Barber and E. J. Brill Publishers for permission to use Figure 15-2; and Leigh Simmons and Dale Roberts for hospitality during my stay at the Department of Zoology, University of Western Australia. The visit was made possible by a stipend from the Swedish Foundation for International Cooperation in Research and Higher Education.

References

Ahtiainen, J. J., Alatalo, R. V., Kotiaho, J. S., Mappes, J., Parri, P. & Vertainen, L. 2001. Sexual selection in the drumming wolf spider *Hygrolycosa rubrofasciata*. In: *European Arachnology 2000* (Ed. by S. Toft & N. Scharff), pp. 129–137. Aarhus, Denmark: Aarhus University Press.

Andersson, M. 1982. Sexual selection, natural selection and quality advertisement. *Biological Journal of the Linnean Society,* **17,** 375–393.

Andersson, M. 1986. Evolution of condition-dependent sex ornaments and mating preferences: sexual selection based on viability differences. *Evolution,* **40,** 804–816.

Andersson, M. 1994. *Sexual Selection*. Princeton, New Jersey: Princeton University Press.

Barber, I. & Arnott, S. A. 2000. Split-clutch IVF: a technique to examine indirect fitness consequences of mate preference in sticklebacks. *Behaviour,* **137,** 1129–1140.

Barber, I., Arnott, S. A., Braithwaite, V. A., Andrew, J. & Huntingford, F. A. 2001. Indirect fitness consequences of mate choice in sticklebacks: offspring of brighter males grow slowly but resist parasitic infections. *Proceedings of the Royal Society of London, Series B,* **268,** 71–76.

Bell, G. 1978. The handicap principle in sexual selection. *Evolution,* **32,** 872–885.

Blanckenhorn, W. U. & Hosken, D. J. 2003. Heritability of three condition surrogates in the yellow dung fly. *Behavioral Ecology,* **14,** 612–618.

Borgia, G. 1979. Sexual selection and the evolution of mating systems. In: *Sexual Selection and Reproductive Competition in Insects* (Ed. by M. S. Blum & N. A. Blum), pp. 19–80. New York: Academic Press.

Brandt, L. S. E. & Greenfield, M. D. 2004. Condition-dependent traits and the capture of genetic variance in male advertisement song. *Journal of Evolutionary Biology*, **17**, 821–828.

Brooks, R. 2000. Negative genetic correlation between male sexual attractiveness and survival. *Nature*, **406**, 67–70.

Burt, A. 1995. Perspective: the evolution of fitness. *Evolution*, **49**, 1–8.

Cameron, E., Day, T. & Rowe, L. 2003. Sexual conflict and indirect benefits. *Journal of Evolutionary Biology*, **16**, 1055–1060.

Darwin, C. 1871. *The Descent of Man, and Selection in Relation to Sex*. London: Murray.

David, P., Bjorksten, T., Fowler, K. & Pomiankowski, A. 2000. Condition-dependent signaling of genetic variation in stalk-eyed flies. *Nature*, **406**, 186–188.

Davis, J. W. F. and O'Donald, P. 1975. Sexual selection for a handicap: a critical analysis of Zahavi's model. *Journal of Theoretical Biology*, **57**, 345–354.

Ditchkoff, S. S., Lochmiller, R. L., Masters, R. E., Hoofer, S. R. & van den Bussche, R. A. 2001. Major-histocompatibility-complex-associated variation in secondary sexual traits of white-tailed deer (*Odocoileus virginianus*): evidence for good-genes advertisement. *Evolution*, **55**, 616–625.

Doty, G. V. & Welch, A. M. 2001. Advertisement call duration indicates good genes for offspring feeding rate in gray tree frogs (*Hyla versicolor*). *Behavioral Ecology and Sociobiology*, **49**, 150–156.

Emlen, J. M. 1973. *Ecology: an Evolutionary Approach*. Reading, Massachusetts: Addison-Wesley.

Eshel, I., Volovik, I. & Sansone, E. 2000. On Fisher–Zahavi's handicapped sexy son. *Evolutionary Ecology Research*, **2**, 509–523.

Evans, J. P., Kelley, J. L., Bisazza, A., Finazzo, E. & Pilastro, A. 2004. Sire attractivenes influences offspring performance in guppies. *Proceedings of the Royal Society of London, Series B*, **271**, 2035–2042.

Fisher, R. A. 1915. The evolution of sexual preference. *The Eugenics Review*, **7**, 184–192.

Fisher, R. A. 1930. *The Genetical Theory of Natural Selection*. Oxford: Clarendon Press.

Forstmeier, W. & Leisler, B. 2004. Repertoire size, sexual selection, and offspring viability in the great reed warbler: changing patterns in space and time. *Behavioral Ecology*, **15**, 555–563.

Grafen, A. 1990a. Sexual selection unhandicapped by the Fisher process. *Journal of Theoretical Biology*, **144**, 473–516.

Grafen, A. 1990b. Biological signals as handicaps. *Journal of Theoretical Biology*, **144**, 517–546.

Grether, G. F. 2000. Carotenoid limitation and mate preference evolution: a test of the indicator hypothesis in guppies (Poecilia reticulata). *Evolution*, **54**, 1712–1724.

Hamilton, W. D. & Zuk, M. 1982. Heritable fitness and bright birds: a role for parasites? *Science*, **218**, 384–387.

Hansen, T. F. & Price, D. K. 1995. Good genes and old age: do old mates provide superior genes? *Journal of Evolutionary Biology*, **8**, 759–778.

Hasselquist, D., Bensch, S. & von Schantz, T. 1996. Correlation between male song repertoire, extra-pair paternity and offspring survival in the great reed warbler. *Nature*, **381**, 229–232.

Heywood, J. S. 1989. Sexual selection by the handicap mechanism. *Evolution*, **43**, 1387–1397.

Hill, G. E. 1991. Plumage coloration is a sexually selected indicator of male quality. *Nature*, **350**, 337–339.

Hill, G. E. 2002. *A Red Bird in a Brown Bag: the Function and Evolution of Colorful Plumage in the House Finch*. New York: Oxford University Press.

Hoelzer, G. A. 1989. The good parent process of sexual selection. *Animal Behaviour*, **38**, 1067–1078.

Höglund, J. & Sheldon, B. C. 1998. The cost of reproduction and sexual selection. *Oikos*, **83**, 478–483.

Houle, D. & Kondrashov, A. S. 2002. Coevolution of costly mate choice and condition-dependent display of good genes. *Proceedings of the Royal Society of London, Series B,* **269,** 97–104.

Hunt, J., Brooks, R., Jennions, M. D., Smith, M. J., Bentsen, C. L. & Bussière, L. F. 2004a. High-quality male field crickets invest heavily in sexual display but die young. *Nature,* **432,** 1024–1027.

Hunt, J., Bussière, L. F., Jennions, M. D. & Brooks, R. 2004b. What is genetic quality? *Trends in Ecology & Evolution,* **19,** 329–333.

Iwasa, Y. & Pomiankowski, A. 1994. The evolution of mate preferences for multiple sexual ornaments. *Evolution,* **48,** 853–867.

Iwasa, Y. & Pomiankowski, A. 1999. Good parent and good genes models of handicap evolution. *Journal of Theoretical Biology,* **200,** 97–109.

Iwasa, Y., Pomiankowski, A. & Nee, S. 1991. The evolution of costly mate preferences. II. The "handicap" principle. *Evolution,* **45,** 1431–1442.

Iyengar, V. K. & Eisner, T. 1999. Heritability of body mass, a sexually selected trait, in an arctiid moth (*Utetheisa ornatrix*). *Proceedings of the National Academy of Sciences of the USA,* **96,** 9169–9171.

Jensen, H., Saether, B.-E., Ringsby, T. H., Tufto, J., Griffith, S. C. & Ellegren, H. 2004. Lifetime reproductive success in relation to morphology in the house sparrow *Passer domesticus. Journal of Animal Ecology,* **73,** 599–611.

Kirkpatrick, M. 1985. Evolution of female choice and male parental investment in polygynous species: the demise of the "sexy son". *American Naturalist,* **125,** 788–810.

Kirkpatrick, M. 1986. The handicap mechanism of sexual selection does not work. *American Naturalist,* **127,** 222–240.

Kirkpatrick, M. 1996. Good genes and direct selection in the evolution of mating preferences. *Evolution,* **50,** 2125–2140.

Kirkpatrick, M. & Barton, N. H. 1997. The strength of indirect selection on female mating preferences. *Proceedings of the National Academy of Sciences of the USA,* **94,** 1282–1286.

Kirkpatrick, M. & Ryan, M. J. 1991. The evolution of mating preferences and the paradox of the lek. *Nature,* **350,** 33–38.

Kodric-Brown, A. & Brown, J. H. 1984. Truth in advertising: the kinds of traits favoured by sexual selection. *American Naturalist,* **124,** 309–323.

Kokko, H. 2001. Fisherian and "good genes" benefits of mate choice: how (not) to distinguish between them. *Ecology Letters,* **4,** 322–326.

Kokko, H., Brooks, R., Jennions, M.D. & Morley, J. 2003. The evolution of mate choice and mating biases. *Proceedings of the Royal Society of London, Series B,* **270,** 653–664.

Kokko, H., Brooks, R., McNamara, J. M. & Houston, A. I. 2002. The sexual selection continuum. *Proceedings of the Royal Society of London, Series B,* **269,** 1331–1340.

Kondrashov, A. S. 1988. Deleterious mutations as an evolutionary factor. III. Mating preference and some general remarks. *Journal of Theoretical Biology,* **131,** 487–496.

Kotiaho, J. S. 2001. Costs of sexual traits: a mismatch between theoretical considerations and empirical evidence. *Biological Review,* **76,** 365–376.

Kotiaho, J. S., Simmons, L. W., Hunt, J. & Tomkins, J. L. 2003. Males influence maternal effects that promote sexual selection: a quantitative genetic experiment with dung beetles *Onthophagus taurus. American Naturalist,* **161,** 852–859.

Kotiaho, J. S., Simmons, L.W. & Tomkins, J. L. 2001. Towards a resolution of the lek paradox. *Nature,* **410,** 684–686.

Kraak, S. B. M. & Bakker, T. C. M. 1998. Mutual mate choice in sticklebacks: attractive males choose big females, which lay big eggs. *Animal Behaviour,* **56,** 859–866.

Kruuk, L. E. B., Slate, J., Pemberton, J. M., Brotherstone, S., Guinness, F., Clutton-Brock, T. 2002. Antler size in red deer: heritability and selection but no evolution. *Evolution,* **56,** 1683–1695.

Lande, R. 1981. Models of speciation by sexual selection on polygenic traits. *Proceedings of the National Academy of Sciences of the USA,* **78,** 3721–3725.

Lorch, P. D., Proulx, S., Rowe, L. & Day, T. 2003. Condition-dependent sexual selection can accelerate adaptation. *Evolutionary Ecology Research,* **5,** 867–881.

Maynard Smith, J. 1976. Sexual selection and the handicap principle. *Journal of Theoretical Biology,* **57,** 239–242.

Maynard Smith, J. 1978. *The Evolution of Sex.* Cambridge: Cambridge University Press.

Mead, L. S. & Arnold, S. J. 2004. Quantitative genetic models of sexual selection. *Trends in Ecology & Evolution,* **19,** 264–271.

Møller, A. P. & Alatalo, R. V. 1999. Good-genes effects in sexual selection. *Proceedings of the Royal Society of London, Series B,* **266,** 85–91.

Neff, B. D. & Pitcher, T. E. 2005. Genetic quality and sexual selection: an integrated framework for good genes and compatible genes. *Molecular Ecology,* **14,** 19–38.

Nowicki, S., Hasselquist, D., Bensch, S. & Peters, S. 2000. Nestling growth and song repertoire size in great reed warblers: evidence for song learning as an indicator mechanism in mate choice. *Proceedings of the Royal Society of London, Series B,* **267,** 2419–2424.

Nur, N. & Hasson, O. 1984. Phenotypic plasticity and the handicap principle. *Journal of Theoretical Biology,* **110,** 275–297.

Parker, T. H. 2003. Genetic benefits of mate choice separated from differential maternal investment in red junglefowl (*Gallus gallus*). *Evolution,* **57,** 2157–2165.

Pomiankowski, A. 1987a. Sexual selection: the handicap principle does work—sometimes. *Proceedings of the Royal Society of London, Series B,* **231,** 123–145.

Pomiankowski, A. 1987b. The costs of choice in sexual selection. *Journal of Theoretical Biology,* **128,** 195–218.

Pomiankowski, A. & Iwasa, Y. 1998. Handicap signalling: loud and true? *Evolution,* **52,** 928–952.

Price, T. D., Schluter, D. & Heckman, N. E. 1993. Sexual selection when the female benefits directly. *Biological Journal of the Linnaean Society,* **48,** 187–211.

Radwan, J. 2004. Effectiveness of sexual selection in removing mutations induced with ionizing radiation. *Ecology Letters,* **7,** 1149–1154.

Rice, W. 1988. Heritable variation in fitness as a prerequisite for adaptive female choice: the effect of mutation-selection balance. *Evolution,* **42,** 817–820.

Roff, D. A. 2002. *Life History Evolution.* Sunderland, Massachusetts: Sinauer.

Rowe, L. & Houle, D. 1996. The lek paradox and the capture of genetic variance by condition-dependent traits. *Proceedings of the Royal Society of London, Series B,* **263,** 1415–1421.

Sandvik, M., Rosenqvist, G. & Berglund, A. 2000. Male and female mate choice affects offspring quality in a sex-role reversed pipefish. *Proceedings of the Royal Society of London, Series B,* **267,** 2151–2155.

Schluter, D. and Price, T. 1993. Honesty, perception and population divergence in sexually selected traits. *Proceedings of the Royal Society of London, Series B,* **253,** 117–122.

Sheldon, B. C., Merilä, J., Qvarnström, A., Gustafsson, L. & Ellegren, M. 1997. Paternal genetic contribution to offspring condition predicted by size of male secondary sexual character. *Proceedings of the Royal Society of London, Series B,* **264,** 297–302.

Sheldon, B. C., Kruuk, L. E. B. & Merilä, J. 2003a. Natural selection and inheritance of breeding time and clutch size in the collared flycatcher. *Evolution,* **57,** 406–420.

Sheldon, B. C., Arponen, H., Laurila, A., Crochet, P.-A. & Merilä, J. 2003b. Sire coloration influences offspring survival under predation risk in the moorfrog. *Journal of Evolutionary Biology,* **16,** 1288–1295.

Tomkins, J. L., Radwan, J., Kotiaho, J. S. & Tregenza, T. 2004. Genic capture and resolving the lek paradox. *Trends in Ecology & Evolution,* **19,** 323–328.

Tregenza, T. & Wedell, N. 2000. Genetic compatibility, mate choice and patterns of parentage. *Molecular Ecology,* **9,** 1013–1027.

Trivers, R. L. 1972. Parental investment and sexual selection. In: *Sexual Selection and the Descent of Man 1871–1971* (Ed. by B. Campbell), pp. 136–179. London: Heinemann.

Wedekind, C., Muller, R. & Spicher, H. 2001. Potential genetic benefits of mate selection in whitefish. *Journal of Evolutionary Biology,* **14,** 980–986.

Welch, A. M. 2003. Genetic benefits of a female mating preference in gray tree frogs are context-dependent. *Evolution,* **57,** 883–893.

Welch, A. M., Semlitsch, R. D. & Gerhardt, H. C. 1998. Call duration as an indicator of genetic quality in male gray tree frogs. *Science,* **280,** 1928–1930.

West-Eberhard, M. J. 1979. Sexual selection, social competition, and evolution. *Proceedings of the American Philosophy Society,* **123,** 222–234.

Williams, G. C. 1966. *Adaptation and Natural Selection.* Princeton, New Jersey: Princeton University Press.

Zahavi, A. 1975. Mate selection: a selection for a handicap. *Journal of Theoretical Biology,* **53,** 205–214.

Zahavi, A. 1977. The costs of honesty (further remarks on the handicap principle). *Journal of Theoretical Biology,* **67,** 603–605.

Zeh, J. A. & Zeh, D. A. 2003. Toward a new sexual selection paradigm: polyandry, conflict and incompatibility. *Ethology,* **109,** 929–950.

16

Indirect Selection and Individual Selection in Sociobiology: My Personal Views on Theories of Social Behaviour

Amotz Zahavi
Institute for Nature Conservation Research
Tel-Aviv University

Abstract

This is the story of my involvement in sociobiological studies. I first discuss group selection models, which were common in the 1950s. I then move on to kin selection and reciprocity models, which were developed to replace group selection models and are still being used by many sociobiologists, even though I argue that they contain the same weaknesses that led group selection to be rejected. As an alternative, I present the handicap principle, an essential component in all signalling. The handicap principle is useful in understanding many components of social systems, not the least of which is why individuals invest in the benefit of other members of a social system (altruism).

I have been watching birds since childhood. As a student of biology in the early 1950s, I was attracted by the great advances in cell biology and in biochemistry that took place at that time. But after spending several months cooped up in a laboratory, I could not resist the temptation to go out again into the field, looking for rare birds and watching birds display. For my master's degree, I decided to study the avifauna of the Huleh swamp, even though I was sure at the time that the intellectual challenges in biology were taking place in the laboratory rather than in finding nests and counting birds. It was Tinbergen's (1951) book, *The Study of Instinct,* that convinced me that animal behaviour was a respectable science, full of intellectual challenges, and that the study of it could fit in with birdwatching and field studies. I spent most of 1955 with Tinbergen's group at Oxford and at Ravenglass watching black-headed gulls.

In the 1950s, studies around the world dealt with many aspects of animal behaviour. Ethologists in Western Europe with whom I was acquainted studied mostly the social interactions of animals in the wild. Ethology, then a new branch of the study of animal behaviour, was at that time mostly a descriptive science, which studied sequences of social interactions. We spent most of our time observing the natural behaviour of wild animals and doing simple experiments. Tinbergen (1963) described the kind of questions asked at Oxford at the time: '(1) what is the survival value of the observed behaviour; (2) what is its causation; (3) how does it develop; and (4) how has it evolved?' Theories that were developed at that time to explain the adaptive significance of a particular behaviour did not necessarily seek an ultimate explanation of why that behaviour should function the way it did. We often considered proximate explanations satisfactory. For example, when animals neither threatened nor attacked, but instead did something that seemed irrelevant to the situation, the behaviour was called 'displacement activity' (Tinbergen 1951), the assumption being that the stimulated animal had to do something. When males attacked visiting females, it was supposedly because the males could not control their aggression. Behaviours that were correlated with the strength of the social bond were considered behaviours that strengthen the bond (Lorenz 1966).

In the 1950s, ethologists explained the adaptive significance of many social behaviours by the benefit they conferred on other individuals (Tinbergen 1951; Lorenz 1966). All of us used group selection arguments: for example, that 'communication is reliable because if many cheat the system will collapse'. We believed at the time that signals evolved 'for the benefit of the communicating parties, to make the information clearer to the receiver'. Threat signals were supposed to replace aggression 'because it benefits the conflicting parties', and we believed that individuals utter warning calls 'to save their fellow group members'. In general we believed that it was adaptive to help members of a group 'because a large, successful group benefits all its members'.

In the 1960s, a debate emerged about the importance of group selection in evolution. Wynne-Edwards (1962) suggested that animals often reduced their reproduction in the interests of the population, while Lack (1966) asserted that individuals reproduce as much as they can. Maynard Smith (1964) and Williams (1966) supported the point of view of individual selection. Most evolutionary biologists eventually became convinced that group selection was rarely effective in the real world. This happened not because group selection models were illogical, but because under ordinary circumstances such models can be exploited by social parasites (Maynard Smith 1964). However, rejecting group selection models created big problems for behavioural scientists. There was no obvious alternative model to explain many social adaptations. It was especially difficult to explain the evolution of signals and of altruism by individual selection. Evolutionary biologists attempted to offer new models to explain the social behaviour of individuals. Hamilton (1964) suggested a genetic reason for the investment of animals in their relatives, a theory that was later named kin selection by Maynard Smith. Trivers (1971) suggested that reciprocal altruistic relationships could form a stable model of altruism among nonrelatives. Maynard Smith (1976a, 1982) suggested the use of evolutionarily stable strategy models (ESS) to explain the evolution of threat signals. Altruism and the evolution of signals became central problems in sociobiology. These new theories had a great effect on students of social behaviour, and many attempted to test in the field models based on kin selection and on reciprocity.

From 1955 until 1970 I had only limited contact with the study of social behaviour and ethology. I was occupied with establishing the conservation movement in Israel. By the time I returned to the academic world and to science, ethology had matured and was interacting with evolutionary biology. I was lucky to be able to spend 1970 with David Lack at the Edward Grey Institute at Oxford. Lack convinced me never to compromise on trying to explain adaptations on the basis of pure individual selection. I also learned from him to use my common sense to interpret behaviours. Meeting with many ornithologists, and especially with Peter Ward, gave me the confidence that field workers can use their observations to suggest theories. One result was our suggestion that gatherings of birds serve as information centres (Ward & Zahavi 1973).

My next involvement with evolutionary theory came out of a remark by a student who pointed out a weakness in Fisher's model (Fisher 1958). To solve the problem I suggested the handicap principle as an alternative to Fisher for explaining the use of waste in mate choice. The handicap principle suggests that if an individual is of high quality and its quality is not known, it may benefit from investing a part of its advantage in advertising that quality, by taking on a handicap, in a way that inferior individuals would not be able to do, because for them the investment would be too high. I am grateful to Maynard Smith, who agreed to publish my paper on the handicap principle (Zahavi 1975), even though he did not believe in verbal models. I am also grateful to him for publishing his own paper rejecting the principle (Maynard Smith 1976b). By doing so he drew the attention of the scientific community to the controversy.

Right away, I found myself debating the logic of the handicap principle with mathematicians (Davis & O'Donald 1976; Kirkpatrick 1986). They could not prove the handicap principle with genetic models, and therefore rejected it, even though I explicitly discussed its use in phenotypic interactions, especially since 1977 (Zahavi 1977a, b). The simple argument of the handicap principle was considered by theoreticians to be 'intuitive'; they insisted on having mathematical models to show its operation in evolution. For some reason that I cannot understand, logical models expressed verbally are often rejected as being 'intuitive'.

In 1990 Grafen formulated a mathematical model for the handicap principle, and thus made it acceptable to mathematically minded evolutionary biologists and ethologists. However, Grafen also stated that the main biological conclusions of his papers were 'the same as those of Zahavi's original papers on the handicap principle' (Grafen 1990a, page 487) and that 'the handicap principle is a strategic principle, properly elucidated by game theory, but actually simple enough that no formal elucidation is really required' (Grafen 1990b, page 541). Still, for some reason, biologists remained unimpressed by the logic of the verbal model, and accepted the handicap principle only when expressed in a complex mathematical model, which I and probably many other ethologists do not understand.

Since 1990 the handicap principle has been generally accepted as a mechanism that could explain the evolution of the reliability of signals; even so, many still believe that in many cases signals do not require handicaps, either because there is no incentive to cheat when the communicating parties are related to each other (Grafen 1990; Maynard Smith 1991), or because the signal evolved to be reliable without any investment (Hasson 1991). But there is an inherent conflict among all social partners: mates (Williams 1966), parents and offspring (Trivers 1974), and members of any social group. For that reason, an individual can never be sure at a particular moment whether or not there is a conflict of interest between itself and any particular collaborator, related or not. To be on the safe side, all signals demand reliability.

I believe that the conclusive evidence to support my suggestion, that the handicap principle is of use in the evolution of all communication systems, including isogenic individuals, comes from chemical signals within the multicellular body, which are also loaded with handicaps. Many signalling chemicals within the body are complex or noxious (such as Dopa, CO, NO, etc.) or have adverse effects on ordinary cells (Zahavi 1993; Zahavi & Zahavi 1997). Why is it that signalling systems within the body do not use nonharmful chemicals that are easy to produce and handle? I suggested that the adaptive significance of complex or harmful chemicals as signals is to inhibit signalling by cell phenotypes that are not the types of cells that should emit the signal. Since all cells have the same genetic information, some of them, perhaps a few millions out of the billions of cells, could start signalling at the wrong time or transmit the wrong information. For the receiver cell, and for the whole organism, it is important to be sure that the information it receives is reliable. Hence cells that develop into the types that should signal also develop the ability to cope with the adverse effects caused by the production or use of the chemical signal. In other words, the noxiousness is a handicap. Between organisms, handicaps in signals evolve to prevent cheaters from benefiting from using the signal; in the multicellular body, signals evolve with handicaps to decrease the possibility of their use by the wrong phenotypes.

I would like to correct several common misunderstandings about the handicap principle. First, some still assume that a handicap, by definition, evolves to decrease fitness. This is not the case. The selective process by which individuals develop their handicap increases their fitness, rather than decreases it. If 'cost' is measured by a loss in fitness, then handicaps do not have a cost for honest signallers, since honest signallers increase their fitness by signalling. Only cheaters would decrease their fitness if they were to take on a handicap that does not match their qualities, hence the efficacy of the handicap in discouraging dishonest signalling. For this reason, I now prefer the term 'investment' to the term 'cost'. Second, the investment in a handicap need not be very high or very detrimental, as is often assumed. The investment is proportional to the potential gain to cheaters from giving the signal. If the potential gain is small, the investment is small as well. The investment need not necessarily be in energy, risk, or material. It may be in information or in social prestige (Zahavi & Zahavi 1997). It is not up to the signaller to decide how much to invest; it is the receiver of the signal who is forcing the signaller to invest in the signal.

My study of the Arabian babbler, *Turdoides squamiceps,* followed my study of flocking and territorial behaviour in wintering wagtails, *Motacilla alba,* in Israel (Zahavi 1971) in which I managed to convert flocking individual wagtails into territorial ones by manipulating their food dispersal. I was interested in the ecological conditions responsible for the formation of the group-territorial way of life among babblers, and intended to study whether it would be possible to manipulate their social behaviour. I never did.

I developed the idea of the handicap principle only a year after I began to observe the babblers. Watching these birds at Hazeva in Israel for over 30 years with the handicap principle in mind has been a very fruitful coincidence. Within a few years, I found that the handicap principle could explain many phenomena other than the use of waste in mate choice; why is it, for example, that the same signals that attract mates also deter rivals and predators? This is something that Fisher's model could not explain. I found the handicap principle useful in interpreting babbler vocalizations (including their so-called alarm calls), their colour patterns, and more. I found that the social bond between partners could be tested by placing a burden (a handicap) on the collaborator ('the testing of the bond'. Zahavi 1977c). Such testing is constantly evident in babbler's clumping, dancing, allopreening and play, and in many other facets of their social behaviour.

The handicap principle and the complementary idea of testing the social bond provide ultimate explanations for, among other things, the importance of displaying hesitation by displacement activities and the aggressiveness of a male towards its mate (Zahavi 1977c), as well as the reliability of signals (Zahavi 1977a). For me as a birdwatcher, perhaps the most satisfying outcome of the handicap principle was the conclusion that there must be a logical relation between the pattern of a signal and its message (Zahavi 1977a; Zahavi & Zahavi 1997). From that point on, recognizing a species' colour pattern or vocal call brought with it not only the satisfaction of identifying it, but also valuable clues to the message encoded in these signals.

The study of the Arabian babblers at Hazeva suggested that their altruism can be interpreted as a signal displaying their claim to social prestige (Zahavi 1977a, 1995). Observations suggested that the help babblers provide to their group, their altruism, is often not needed, and that babblers often reject help offered to them by their group members, are aggressive to the helpers, and compete over performing altruistic acts. I used the handicap principle to interpret their altruism as a 'showing off' of quality to support individuals' claims to social prestige. Social prestige is the respect accorded an individual by others as a result of their assessment of that individual's strength and ability as shown by its actions and physique. Social prestige can be acquired, for example, by aggression, or by a show of waste, or by investing in the benefit of others. We have used the idea of prestige to explain the success of some social parasites (such as cuckoos), as well as to understand why individuals invest in the social welfare of their mates and of other collaborators; we have also discussed the use of prestige as a means to deter rivals.

The handicap principle thus suggests that, even when the altruistic act benefits others, the altruist gains directly from investing in its altruistic behaviours. There is therefore no need for any indirect-selection model to explain altruism. This idea provided me with an alternative to the other theories that were developed to interpret altruism: group selection, kin selection, reciprocal altruism and the other variations of reciprocity models. Only then did I realize that kin selection and reciprocal altruism share the weakness of group selection and should be rejected for the same reasons (Zahavi 1981, 1995; Zahavi & Zahavi 1997). Both are unstable and may be exploited by social parasites.

In kin selection, for example, let us assume that two or more individuals of the same brood have a chance to gain fitness by investing in their kin. Whichever of them invests in its kin loses some of its own direct fitness. But whether or not they invest in their kin, they all gain equally in their inclusive fitness from the investment of those who invest. The total gain by the ones that did not invest is higher, because they gained in inclusive fitness without investing anything and thus without losing any of their direct fitness. In other words, kin selection is as open as group selection to social parasitism and is not a stable model.

Reciprocal altruism was suggested by Trivers (1971). He proposed that altruism works by reciprocity, and to ensure reciprocation he suggested a system of punishment, for example a grudge, against social parasites. But one who does not invest in the punishment or does not display a grudge gains as much as individuals that do invest. Social parasites will again gain without investing, that is, they will gain more than honest individuals, making reciprocal altruism as unstable as group selection. Trivers (1971) also stated that an individual that can exploit another and does not do so is an altruist. This statement suggests that in all social systems individuals should try to exploit their partners. However, observations suggest that more often than not partners do help each other.

On the other hand, my suggestion that altruism is an investment in advertisement by the individual altruist (that is, a handicap) shows how altruism can provide a direct benefit to the altruist. The individuals that accord prestige to the altruist do so not to encourage altruism, or because they benefit from the altruistic act. In fact, they may not benefit from it at all. Rather, they accord prestige because of the quality displayed by the altruist, quality that the altruistic acts demonstrate reliably. The recipients and the observers, both collaborators and rivals, benefit directly from the information advertised by the altruistic act in their own decision making. The idea that the altruist acts to demonstrate its quality and to gain prestige explains why beneficiaries are often aggressive towards the altruist, and why individuals often compete to act as altruists, even when that competition runs counter to the interest of the group (Zahavi & Zahavi 1997). It is important to note that none of the other theories can explain the observations that altruists compete to act as altruists and may show aggression towards the altruist, and why altruistic activities deter their competitors within the group.

Because social behaviour is a cooperative act, its interpretation can easily slide into group selection arguments. I have made that mistake with Peter Ward (Ward & Zahavi 1973) when we suggested that advertising flights at a roost were selected to attract more individuals to the roost. After all, flock members that do not participate in the display gain just as much from advertising the roost as those who do the advertising. I corrected my mistake of using a group selection argument later, when I was more experienced at identifying group selection arguments (Zahavi 1983).

I consider myself a sociobiologist; I believe that the evolution of social adaptations throughout the biological world adheres to the same general principles. Even social interactions between unicellular organisms are best explained by direct individual selection. Together with my students, I used the handicap principle to explain some of the details of mate choice in yeast (Nahon et al. 1995) and suggested a model based on individual selection that explains the apparently suicidal traits of the slime moulds (Atzmoni et al. 1997), traits that until then were assumed to exist for the sake of kin or of the group. I believe that in future years ethologists, sociologists and others trying to find the ultimate reasons for the workings of social systems and for the patterns and reliability of signals will benefit from taking into account the importance of the quest for and the effect of social prestige as a mechanism that explains much of what happens in social systems. I also predict that the handicap principle (or 'costly signalling', as some who do not wish to refer to the handicap principle prefer to call it) will be found to be an inherent component in all signals. It is based strictly on direct individual selection, the only stable selection model in evolution.

I have often wondered whether, if I were living in Oxford or any other centre of sociobiological research, I would have developed the handicap principle and its implications. A major disadvantage of a dominant theory that is accepted by everyone around you is that observers in the field have a strong tendency to overlook findings that do not fit in with the theory. Even if the theory is wrong, as I believe that kin selection and reciprocity are, researchers in the field tend not to believe that the exceptions they observe suggest that the theory is erroneous; these exceptions either go unreported, or, if reported, are not considered important in discussions of the findings. The same goes for new suggestions such as the handicap principle that all around you, all your colleagues, consider them wrong. Being on the periphery has its benefits: if I were dependent on my colleagues for the advancement of my scientific career or my social status, I would not have been able to continue developing the handicap principle over the many years in which it was nearly unanimously rejected. Luckily I was living in a corner of the world, and usually interacted with other sociobiologists only once a year, at conferences. At home, my social status and my scientific career were well secured because of my previous 'altruistic' work in conservation.

Acknowledgments

Avishag Zahavi has been a partner to the development of this paper. Naama Zahavi-Ely and Melvin Ely edited it and markedly improved the English presentation. Yoram Yom-Tov, Arnon Lotem and Roni Ostreicher have provided helpful comments. Finally thanks are due to Leigh W. Simmons who encouraged me to give my personal views on the development of sociobiological theories and commented, with the help of an anonymous referee, on the manuscript.

References

Atzmoni, D., Zahavi, A. & Nanjundiah, V. 1997. Altruistic behaviour in *Dictyostelium discoideum* explained on the basis of individual selection. *Current Science,* **72,** 142–145.
Davis, G. W. F. & O'Donald, P. 1976. Sexual selection for a handicap. A critical analysis of Zahavi's model. *Journal of Theoretical Biology,* **57,** 345–354.
Fisher, R. A. 1958. *The Genetical Theory of Natural Selection*. London: Clarendon Press.
Grafen, A. 1990a. Sexual selection unhandicapped by the Fisher process. *Journal of Theoretical Biology,* **144,** 473–516.
Grafen, A. 1990b. Biological signals as handicaps. *Journal of Theoretical Biology,* **144,** 517–546.
Hamilton, W. D. 1964. The genetical evolution of social behaviour. *Journal of Theoretical Biology,* **7,** 1–52.

Hasson, O. 1991. Sexual displays as amplifiers. Practical examples with an emphasis on feather decorations. *Behavioral Ecology,* **2,** 189–197.

Kirkpatrick, M. 1986. The handicap mechanism of sexual selection does not work. *American Naturalist,* **127,** 222–240.

Lack, D. 1966. *Population Studies of Birds.* Oxford: Clarendon Press.

Lorenz, K. 1966. *On Aggression.* Fakenham, Norfolk: Cox & Wyman.

Maynard Smith, J. 1964. Group selection and kin selection. *Nature,* **201,** 1145–1147.

Maynard Smith, J. 1976a. Evolution and the theory of games. *American Scientist,* **64,** 41–45.

Maynard Smith, J. 1976b. Sexual selection and the handicap principle. *Journal of Theoretical Biology,* **57,** 239–242.

Maynard Smith, J. 1982. *Evolution and the Theory of Games.* Cambridge: Cambridge University Press.

Maynard Smith, J. 1991. Must reliable signals always be costly? *Animal Behaviour,* **47,** 1115–1120.

Nahon, E., Atzmony, D., Zahavi, A. & Granot, D. 1995. Mate selection in Yeast: a reconsideration of signals and the message encoded in them. *Journal of Theoretical Biology,* **172,** 315–322.

Tinbergen, N. 1951. *The Study of Instinct.* London: Oxford University Press.

Tinbergen, N. 1963. The work of the animal behaviour research group in the department of Zoology, University of Oxford. *Animal Behaviour,* **11,** 206–209.

Trivers, R. L. 1971. The evolution of reciprocal altruism. *Quarterly Review of Biology,* **46,** 35–57.

Trivers, R. L. 1974. Parent–offspring conflict. *American Zoologist,* **14,** 249–264.

Trivers, R. L. 1985. *Social Evolution.* Menlo Park, California: Benjamin/Cummings.

Ward, P. & Zahavi, A. 1973. The importance of certain assemblages of birds as 'Information Centers' for food finding. *Ibis,* **115,** 517–534.

Williams, G. C. 1966. *Adaptation and Natural Selection. A Critique of Some Current Evolutionary Thought.* Princeton, New Jersey: Princeton University Press.

Wynne-Edwards, V. C. 1962. *Animal Dispersion in Relation to Social Behaviour.* Edinburgh: Oliver and Boyd.

Zahavi, A. 1971. The social behaviour of the white wagtail, *Motacilla alba,* wintering in Israel. *Ibis,* **113,** 203–211.

Zahavi, A. 1975. Mate selection: a selection for a handicap. *Journal of Theoretical Biology,* **53,** 205–214.

Zahavi, A. 1977a. Reliability in communication systems and the evolution of altruism. In: *Evolutionary Ecology* (Ed. by B. Stonehouse & C. M. Perrins), pp. 253–259. London: MacMillan.

Zahavi, A. 1977b. The cost of honesty. (Further remarks on the Handicap Principle.). *Journal of Theoretical Biology,* **67,** 603–605.

Zahavi, A. 1977c. The testing of a bond. *Animal Behaviour,* **25,** 246–247.

Zahavi, A. 1981. Some comments on sociobiology. *Auk,* **98,** 412–414.

Zahavi, A. 1983. This week's citation classic: the importance of certain assemblages of birds as 'information centers' for food finding. *Current Contents,* **15,** 26.

Zahavi, A. 1993. The fallacy of conventional signalling. *Philosophical Transactions of the Royal Society of London, Series B,* **338,** 227–230.

Zahavi, A. 1995. Altruism as a handicap: the limitations of kin selection and reciprocity. *Avian Biology,* **26,** 1–3.

Zahavi, A. & Zahavi, A. 1997. *The Handicap Principle.* New York: Oxford University Press.

17

Honesty and Deception in Animal Signals

Michael D. Greenfield
Department of Ecology and Evolutionary Biology
University of Kansas

Abstract

The potential for animals to "deceive" one another via "dishonest" signals has been a major question in behaviour for many years. Currently, a prevalent view is that an individual's signals are more or less reliable indications of its species identity, gender, developmental or physiological state, social category, "motivation," or acquired information. This view is based on the argument that receivers are selected to ignore signals that are habitually unreliable, which, in turn, would select against the production of such signals. Formal analyses support this generalisation but also predict modest amounts of unreliability, particularly in situations where signallers and receivers have conflicting objectives. As expected, limited amounts of signal unreliability are observed in various species. The plasticity of signal traits across environments poses a different problem for reliable communication, which biologists are only now beginning to recognise. Because genotypes may respond in different ways to environmental changes across space or time, a situation may arise in which a given genotype exhibits the "superior" signal in one environment but the "inferior" one in another. Thus, signals may not be reliable indications if the environment changes across generations or offspring disperse to locations with different environments. This conundrum does not necessarily challenge the primacy of signal reliability, but it suggests that those traits that do evolve signalling functions may be somewhat resistant to such genotype × environment interaction.

Beginnings and Current Developments

Signalling and communication have held a central position in animal behaviour study since the very beginning of the field. Signals, and to lesser extent responses to them, are often the most conspicuous performances of an animal, those behavioural features that we may observe first and most readily. Moreover, they serve to mediate the behavioural processes of pair formation, parent–offspring interaction, social exchange and hierarchy maintenance within groups, and aggression. We find descriptions of and explanations for animal signals in antiquity, as in Aristotle's account of the honeybee's "dance," and throughout the Renaissance and early modern period. And in the nineteenth century, animal signals and communication figured prominently in the writings of Darwin and Fabre. Thus, it is fitting that we review the development of recent thought, as well as the major problems, in this aspect of animal behaviour study.

What distinguishes contemporary inquiry in animal communication from that practised by our predecessors is largely: (1) use of available technology to specify the physical and chemical characteristics of signals, and how the response functions of receivers to signals relate to those characteristics; and (2) our preoccupation with evolutionary processes. Technological advances of the twentieth century have spurred two marked improvements in our understanding of the physical–chemical nature of animal communications. First, instrumentation allowed us to simulate signals and thereby measure and confirm experimentally what had been suspected earlier. Thus, playback of acoustic recordings (the initial experimentation actually made use of the telephone system in pre–World War I Vienna; Regen 1913) convincingly demonstrated the role of the male cricket's advertisement and courtship songs in female attraction and pair formation, and laboratory synthesis of compounds manufactured and released from abdominal glands in the female silkworm moth showed how exceptionally minute quantities of these (pheromonal) substances elicited attraction, via upwind movement, in males (Butenandt & Karlson 1954). Second, instrumentation also revealed how diverse animals use communication channels that the unaided human cannot perceive (Greenfield 2002). Thus, we were made aware of the use of ultrasound for echolocation (autocommunication) by bats (Griffin 1958) and for pair formation by moths (Spangler *et al.* 1984; Conner 1999), of very low-frequency (infra-) sound signals for group cohesion and intergroup interactions by elephants (Payne *et al.* 1986; Garstang 2004) and whales (Tyack 2000), of vibration and near-field sound as the several modalities by which honeybees interpret their dance "language" (Michelsen *et al.* 1986; Towne & Kirchner 1989; Rohrseitz & Tautz 1999; Nieh & Tautz 2000) and the use of ultraviolet wavelengths (Silberglied 1979) and the plane of polarisation of light (Cronin *et al.* 2003) in visual communication of various species.

Our preoccupation with the evolution of communication includes both phylogenetic analysis of the origin of signals and of perception and the nature of the interaction between signaller and receiver. This latter aspect has come to focus largely on determining the "reliability" or "honesty" of signals: Do signal features perceived and evaluated by a receiver indicate physical characteristics of a signaller, its physiological or developmental state or its level of available energy, its "motivation" or "intent," or its acquired information? Or might individuals that are inferior in these above traits retain the ability to generate a superior signal? And if not, what factors limit the broadcast of unreliable signals in natural populations? In the remainder of this chapter, I shall concentrate on these problems of signal reliability in animal communication. In so doing, I recognise that a full consideration of the problem demands attention to phylogenetic issues as well as the physical and chemical characterisation of signals and perception.

As a point of clarification, I shall follow an accepted practice of designating as "communication" exchanges of "information" between a "transmitter" (signaller) and "receiver" in which both parties may expect some net benefit from the interaction (Hauser 1996; Bradbury & Vehrencamp 1998). The exchanges take place via "signals," which are taken to be temporary modifications of the external physical or chemical environment induced by the signaller's specialised actions. Signalling represents behaviour that has experienced some evolutionary modification that enhances the benefits obtained from transmitting information to receivers. The information is perceived by, and possibly stored in, the receiver's nervous system, and it influences the receiver to respond in a manner such that it and the signaller mutually benefit. Thus, signals may be distinguished from "cues," information that is broadcast inadvertently (i.e., by default) and has not been modified evolutionarily in the above manner. Moreover, the generation and transmission of signals ordinarily entails a specific expenditure of energy over and above that incurred in normal maintenance activities, during which cues may be evident. For example, cuticular hydrocarbons that are just part of an arthropod's integument but elicit sexual responses would nonetheless be considered cues. The compounds become pheromonal signals when they are transmitted at particular times under the arthropod's control or have undergone chemical alterations over evolutionary time that facilitate pair formation in some way (Greenfield 2002; cf. Wyatt 2003). Signals are said to travel from the transmitter to receiver over a "channel"—either olfactory, acoustic, substrate vibration, visual, or electrostatic—implying that communication is a means by which one animal influences the behaviour of another at a distance, without the use of direct, coercive force. Although this criterion might not seem to apply to tactile signals, the critical point holds that the influence is achieved by the receiver's willing response to a vibration signal (for which the receiver's body serves directly as the substrate) and not by its acquiescence to the transmitter's overt force. The olfactory channel presents special problems in that an animal may transmit chemical substances that represent food to a receiver, as in various cases of courtship feeding in arthropods. Here, the substance may yet be deemed a signal if its chemical, and possibly physical, properties are detected and processed neurally when contacted and then elicit a rather sudden change in behaviour.

Signal Variation, Cheating, and the Reliability Problem

As late as the mid-1970s most treatment of animal communication focused in a straightforward, almost typological, manner on the physical–chemical characterisation of signals; their putative function as identifiers of species, gender, physiological or developmental state, intention, or acquired information; and how they may have originated from cues or from other actions via a ritualisation process. Even E. O. Wilson's 1975 compendium on social behaviour, *Sociobiology: The New Synthesis,* which devoted two chapters entirely to communication, was largely restricted to these fundamentals. The behavioural ecology revolution of the late 1970s, with its emphases on the behaviour in natural populations and its evolution (Krebs & Davies 1978), may have changed this approach irreversibly. Among the central features of this revolution was recognition that variation in behaviour within a population was not simply a nuisance to researchers, but rather an aspect of major biological importance. Legitimate attention could now be paid to deviations from the behavioural norm, and considerable effort was applied to accounting for such variation. Quantitative modelling, whether of the formal population genetics variety or a short-cut approach adapted from game theory (Maynard Smith 1982) (i.e., evolutionarily stable strategy [ESS] analysis), offered some measure of solution to many problems, particularly in the area of reproductive behaviour. Many biologists focused on the occurrence of "alternative reproductive strategies," such as "satellite" male behaviour, for which models based on frequency-dependence and (developmental or physiological) condition-dependence could explain certain cases (see review in Brockmann 2001). These studies aroused interest in the possibility that some animals, limited by their developmental or physiological condition, might "cheat" by forgoing the normal broadcast of signals and "attempting" to encounter mates surreptitiously, or by somehow managing to broadcast a powerful and effective signal despite their condition. For example, in many anurans, females prefer larger males and can evaluate a suitor's size from the carrier frequency of his call. Male Fowler's toads *Bufo woodhousei fowleri* were reported to remain in cooler locations in the habitat and thereby reduce their carrier frequency, which makes them more attractive than males of their size would normally be (Fairchild 1981; see Christian & Tracy 1983 and

Fairchild 1983 on questions concerning these data). But observations that smaller males are not more likely than larger ones to practise this thermoregulatory behaviour rendered it an unlikely candidate for cheating. This latter finding, in fact, concurred with another, more critical, expectation originating from "ESS analysis," that observed behaviours, which ought to be stable by virtue of their regular occurrence, should actually be resistant to cheating (Maynard Smith 1982). This "resistance to cheating" criterion has come to represent a standard question in assessing a trait's evolutionary stability. We return to this expectation shortly, following a brief excursion into sexual selection theory.

Sexual Selection and Signal Honesty: Handicaps and Indexes

At the time behavioural ecology and ESS analysis were initially developing, sexual selection by female choice was recovering from the century-long period of neglect that followed Darwin's 1871 treatise outlining the subject. The primary explanations offered in the 1970s for female choice were: (1) the opportunity to obtain superior direct benefits, (e.g., paternal care, nuptial gifts, territorial resources, from particular males); and (2) Fisherian selection, wherein chosen males merely bore aesthetic features that could be inherited by their male offspring. It was variously proposed that female preferences for aesthetic features arose arbitrarily, originated from pressure to avoid interspecific mating, or had initially represented some sort of "perceptual bias" in a nonsexual context. In 1975, Amotz Zahavi added a rather different explanation for those sexual preferences based solely on aesthetics. Gaining certain insights from intensive observations of social interactions in group-living songbirds, Arabian babblers *Turdoides squamiceps,* at a field site in the Negev Desert of southern Israel, Zahavi proposed that aesthetic features were actually "handicaps" that potentially reduced the survival of males and that they, therefore, offered females a means to test a suitor's "quality": only males of superior "constitution" are capable of bearing or exhibiting such features (e.g., an elaborate courtship dance demanding a high expenditure of energy or that could be readily perceived by natural enemies) and avoiding an early demise (e.g., mortality from an inability to obtain the requisite energy or to escape predation). As intriguing as this proposal—which became known as the "handicap principle"—appeared, it also did not seem quite right to many (see Dawkins 1976, p. 172, for an amusing anecdote). Within a year it was analysed algebraically and pronounced unlikely (Maynard Smith 1976). A chosen male's daughters, as well as his sons, may inherit the handicap while obtaining no advantage in the mating arena. Moreover, the analysis suggested that handicaps were no more likely to be borne by superior males than by other individuals. Although Zahavi (1977a, 1977b) responded to these criticisms by refocusing his theory more generally on signal honesty and pointing out how the costs incurred by bearing handicaps protected sexual communication from cheating, most biologists remained sceptical (e.g., Dawkins & Krebs 1978; Kirkpatrick 1986)—for a while.

This sceptical attitude generally remained until several workers returned to the problem in the late 1980s and utilised formal models, which relied in part on a game theory approach, to analyse sexual selection for handicap features. The work of Andrew Pomiankowski (1987a, 1987b, 1988) and Alan Grafen (1990a, 1990b) convincingly vindicated Zahavi's basic idea by showing that handicaps will be selected for, provided that the cost imposed on the male signaller, measured in the currency of fitness reduction, is greater for low-quality rather than high-quality individuals. It was this differential cost that was missing from Maynard Smith's (1976) earlier formulation and analysis. Thus, a female receiver could reliably assess male quality because low-quality males would simply be incapable of displaying the handicap (see Maynard Smith 1991a; also see Cotton *et al.* 2004, who question the empirical support for this hypothesis). Alternatively, handicaps that do not impose a cost may be selected for if they reveal a male's quality in a reliable fashion. Because the notion of a "cost-free handicap" may appear oxymoronic, one tendency nowadays is to view these latter features as "indexes" rather than handicaps (Maynard Smith & Harper 2003). In either case, male sexual signals that bear certain features are favoured because they are honest indicators of quality. These indicator features cannot be faked by low-quality individuals, and females generally will not mate with males who do not display them.

Once these versions of the handicap principle were confirmed theoretically, several workers began exploring the general implications for animal communication of the expectation that signals are reliable indicators. Whereas the handicap principle had originally been devised to explicate courtship, sexual advertisements, and aggressive signals, it was recognised that reliability might be expected of all animal signalling. For example, the characteristics of begging signals given in parent–offspring and other solicitation interactions ought to indicate the solicitor's actual need for assistance (see Maynard Smith 1991b; also see the initial suggestion by Zahavi 1977b). These extensions of the reliability expectation to diverse signals led to the development of a more general theory with several main tenets. First, communications in which the signaller and receiver have similar interests (i.e., they both rank possible outcomes of the interaction in the same order) were distinguished from those where they differ. Signals are always expected to be honest (i.e., reliable) indicators of signaller quality or state, but where the signaller and receiver have divergent interests, some production cost for the signal is required to ensure that honesty. Most mating and (offspring) food solicitation signals would fall in the latter category, as males and females, and parents and offspring, seldom have identical objectives. On the other hand, where the signaller and receiver are genetically identical (as may occur in colonial invertebrates) or they are members of a social grouping in which all members rank outcomes similarly, as, for example, in responses to alarm calls signalling danger from predators, a special cost is unnecessary to ensure honesty. In this case, signals may effectively be "whispers," messages whose intensity is sufficient for reliable transmission to the receiver but no more (but see Johnstone 1998a, 1998b). Second, where the interests of signallers and receivers do not exactly coincide (i.e., they rank outcomes differently), the stipulation that signalling be costly can be expressed operationally in terms of the individual's cost–benefit ratio in signal production: this ratio must be relatively lower in signallers that are of high quality or in a state of greater need. It is this reduced (cost) value that allows only high-quality individuals or those with great need to produce an intense signal, thereby ensuring evolutionary stability. That is, low-quality or low-need individuals do not signal with intensity because it is too costly, relative to the benefits they might obtain, for them to do so. Various corollaries of these main economic tenets are found in Maynard Smith (1994); Johnstone (1995a, 1996, 1998a, 1998b, 1999); Krakauer and Johnstone (1995); Reeve (1997); and reviewed in Maynard Smith and Harper (2003).

At this point, we can summarise the fundamental expectations of honesty in animal communication by considering the selection pressures acting on receivers and signallers. Receivers will not be expected to attend to signals that do not reliably indicate critical information: the species identity, gender, developmental or physiological state, social category, motivation, or acquired information of the signaller. Attention and responses to such signals would not enhance the receiver's fitness, and, therefore, should not be favoured by selection. As a consequence of inattention by receivers, selection pressure on signallers to generate and transmit these broadcasts would no longer be maintained. At the very least, signalling demands energy and time and may exact further costs in exposure to natural enemies, and it should not be continued in the absence of receiver responses. These expectations placed on signallers should not be construed as implying that all transmissions in animal communication are completely honest (i.e., entirely devoid of "bluffing"), misrepresentation, and other forms of cheating. Rather, the expectations are that, on average, signalling is reliable and receiver responses enhance the fitness of both parties (see Hasson 1994, 1997 for additional perspectives from other models). Similarly, receivers are not necessarily expected to evaluate the magnitude of graded signals with accuracy over their entire range of broadcast intensity. "Environmental noise" and physiological constraints on perception may often render such receiver accuracy impossible, in which case high-quality signallers may simply be selected to transmit a signal of standard intensity, which is of a discrete level receivers can recognise as exceeding a threshold despite their impairments in perception, while others forgo transmission altogether (Johnstone & Grafen 1992; Grafen & Johnstone 1993;

Johnstone 1994). These principles, which do not differ appreciably from Zahavi's (1975, 1977a, 1977b) original conception of signal reliability, may apply to human as well as nonhuman communication. Whereas some biologists may hold to the notion that human communication is distinguished by its relatively high incidence of deception, others, including Zahavi (1997), maintain that the regular elements of human communication are essentially reliable. For example, cosmetic enhancement, such as the application of lipstick by women in many societies, may not be a means of concealing physical deficiencies but rather a way to exaggerate attributes expressed during vocal and facial communication—analogous to the thermoregulatory behaviour reported in male Fowler's toads.

Deception in Natural Populations

Because signal reliability has come to be viewed as a fundamental truth in animal communication, cases of apparently dishonest or unreliable signals draw much interest among biologists. Such exceptions may help us to probe and refine the basic principles outlined earlier. Perhaps the most obvious exceptions are those visual signals known as "badges of status," predominantly found in, but not restricted to, birds. Badges are typically small splotches of conspicuous colouration, such as the "bib" markings on sparrows, which signify dominance ranking within a social group (Dawkins & Krebs 1978; Krebs & Dawkins 1984; also see Wyatt 2003 on the occurrence of pheromonal badges in chemical signalling). Badges have posed a long-standing problem for the expectations of signal reliability because they seem to be produced and maintained rather cheaply, but nonetheless are generally attended to. Individuals of low rank who display badges of reduced development will normally defer to higher ranking individuals whose badges are commensurate with that rank. Two main explanations have been given for the respect that receivers accord status badges. First, the pigmentation substances that comprise badges might actually be expensive to form. However, recent analyses indicate that badge pigmentation is often based on melanins (e.g., McGraw *et al*. 2002) or other easily produced compounds, as opposed to substances such as carotenoids that would demand specialised dietary acquisition, making this explanation unlikely. Second, individuals might pay a continual cost for bearing a status badge, an expense that is incurred at all times rather than only during interactions (Johnstone & Norris 1993). Thus, low-ranking individuals that sport badges indicative of high rank may be "punished" in regular attacks by other members of the social group. A recent study, not in birds but in paper wasps, has found some support for this punishment explanation (Tibbetts & Dale 2004; also see Strassmann 2004 for remaining questions and controversy).

Other than status badges, most of the apparent exceptions to honest signalling reported among animals have involved bluffing during encounters over resource ownership and social rank, individuals misrepresenting the direct or indirect benefits they can offer to potential mates, withholding information, or providing false information (see Cheney & Seyfarth 1990). Bluffing is claimed to occur in various crustaceans that signal via appendage posturing or movements that ordinarily indicate physical ability in a reliable way, but would not be reliable shortly after a moult or in animals whose appendages had been lost and then regenerated. In the stomatopod *Gonodactylus bredini,* males extend the armoured second maxillipeds in a "meral display" that can signal the ability to attack an opponent successfully, and this signal is given both by intermoult individuals, who can attack effectively, and by recently moulted individuals, who cannot (Steger & Caldwell 1983). Curiously, receivers appear to attend to all meral displays regardless of the moulting state of the signaller. In the fiddler crab *Uca annulipes,* males signal aggression with movement of their enlarged claw, the mass of which indicates fighting prowess. Following accidental loss of this appendage, its regenerated form is longer but of greatly reduced mass (leptochely), and the animal's aggressive ability is thereby reduced (Backwell *et al.* 2000). Again, males do not appear to distinguish opponents bearing intact claws, who could fight effectively, from those with regenerated, leptochelous claws, who most likely could not. In *G. bredini,* the typical frequency with which newly moulted individuals are encountered, in conjunction with potential constraints on perceptual accuracy and a relatively low cost that a strong individual incurs if it misjudges a weak one (see Adams & Mesterton-Gibbons 1995), may allow a limited incidence of bluffing to occur in natural populations. A similar conclusion was reached from analyses of encounters and deceptions in the snapping shrimp *Alphaeus heterochaelis,* where the "open chela display" is largely honest, but some individuals present displays that indicate a body size and competitive ability that are larger than actually exist (Hughes 2000). These individuals tend to use the open chela display more often, a tendency which may reflect the relatively low cost–benefit ratio they experience while effecting this slight deception. In *U. annulipes,* however, the frequency of males with regenerated, leptochelous claws may be as high as 44% of the population. But regeneration typically occurs in older (and larger) individuals, among whom aggression is reduced (Backwell *et al.* 2000). These males may normally use claw movement for advertising to females, and courtship movements are more readily effected with a lighter appendage. Thus, the actual frequency of male–male bluffing in *U. annulipes* may likewise be low, despite a high incidence of regenerated, leptochelous claws. Nonetheless, this explanation does not account for female acceptance of males whose signalling is unhandicapped by a heavy claw.

In various anurans, males modify their advertisement calls at the beginning of encounters with other males, presumably to enhance the size and competitive ability that a rival would perceive (Gerhardt & Huber 2002). In green frogs *Rana clamitans,* modifications are most evident in small males who encounter the calls of larger individuals. Here, small males lower their call frequency, which seemingly exaggerates their apparent size (Bee *et al.* 2000).

Deception may also operate in female signallers. Funk and Tallamy (2000) reported that female long-tailed dance flies *Rhamphomyia longicauda* swallow air prior to courtship, which makes them appear larger—and more fecund. Male dance flies donate considerable parental investment (nuptial gifts, in the form of insect prey), and they prefer to mate with larger females who are ready to oviposit (but see LeBas *et al.* 2003, who report that female ornamentation—pinnate leg scales—honestly signals their fecundity). In all of these cases, the deception may not eliminate the relationship between the signal and the signaller's size (or competitive ability or fecundity), which would allow receivers to obtain, on average, a greater benefit by attending to the signal than by ignoring it (see also Wiley 1994; Bradbury & Vehrencamp 2001 on economic models of signalling).

The examples of potential cheating presented here suggest that signals need not be considered as entirely honest or entirely deceptive (see Hughes 2000). They also invite more dynamic analyses of the evolution of signalling and perception. That is, signalling and receiving functions may often coevolve, and the outcome or state of coevolution that we observe at present can assume several forms. In one scenario a coevolutionary "arms race" may have led signallers, particularly those of inferior status, to exhibit slight misrepresentations of their actual quality or condition via "propaganda" that is not always evaluated correctly by receivers (Dawkins & Krebs 1978; Krebs & Dawkins 1984). On the other hand, receivers may have evolved the ability to evaluate every aspect of a signaller's message and correctly predict actual quality. Where effective "mind reading" as such occurs, we might observe an apparent equilibrium between signalling and perception, although this state of affairs could be temporary: new forms of signalling propaganda that receivers may not fully interpret can always evolve in the future (cf. van Baalen & Jansen 2003).

But signalling and receiving functions do not necessarily coevolve, and the possibility of unreliability and deception may be higher where coevolution is absent or minimal. For example, male mating signals may evolve via "exploitation" of preexisting sensory abilities that receivers, both male and female, have for perceiving food, habitat, and other nonsexual features (Ryan *et al.* 1990). Where such ancestral "sensory bias" has played a role in the origin of male signals, females might not possess the ability to evaluate nuances of signalling that could reveal misrepresentation of signaller quality (Johnstone & Norris 1993). However, signallers may not be expected to retain this advantage on a permanent basis because signals that originate via the sensory bias mechanism are always vulnerable to subsequent coevolution with the receiving function (see Macias Garcia & Ramirez 2005 for an example of the evolution of honest signals from a sensory bias origin; see also Rodriguez & Snedden 2004 for general discussion). Thus, the ability of receivers is bound to catch up with signalling propaganda eventually.

Phenotypic Plasticity, Genotype × Environment Interaction, and a Conundrum

In addition to bluffing and the misrepresentation of benefits for mates and of information for social partners, there exists another category of unreliability in animal signalling that may be far more pervasive but has largely escaped the interest of biologists until quite recently (Qvarnström 2001; Greenfield & Rodriguez 2004). This category is the unreliability generated by complications from the plasticity of signal traits that often accompanies environmental change over space or time. It has passed unrecognised because evolutionary biologists who study plasticity have for the most part devoted little attention to behavioural traits, and behavioural biologists have often been more comfortable, even after several decades of research on alternative reproductive strategies, with treating an individual's behavioural repertoire as a more or less fixed entity (but see Sih *et al.* 2004 for an overview of behavioural variation in variable environments). This susceptibility to typology is readily seen in the basic sexual selection models, where the relative development of a male trait, such as a mating signal, is generally viewed as a given expression of his genotype. Consequently, male signals are considered as potentially conveying reliable information about the "indirect" fitness benefits that a female can expect from mating with the signaller: signals that are heritable indicate the expected attractiveness of her future sons (Fisherian, or arbitrary, model) or the expected viability of her sons and daughters as well as the attractiveness of her sons ("good genes" model; see Kokko *et al.* 2002 on the unity of Fisherian and good genes models).

A full treatment of the plasticity of signal traits, however, reveals just how tenuous the previously mentioned reliability might be. Consider a genotype whose mean phenotypic expression for a sexually-selected male signal trait differs markedly along an environmental gradient (Fig. 17-1b). This signal trait is said to exhibit "phenotypic plasticity," and the line connecting the genotype's signal expression in two environments is termed its "reaction norm." When two genotypes both exhibit phenotypic plasticity for the signal trait but each reacts differently to the several environments, a "genotype × environment (G × E) interaction" occurs and the reaction norms of the genotypes are not parallel (Fig. 17-2a; e.g., see David *et al.* 2000). If these reactions of the genotypes

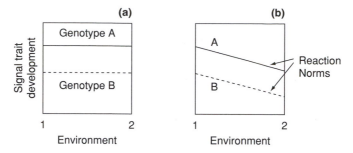

Figure 17-1 Variation in signal trait development among genotypes and environments. (a) Lack of phenotypic plasticity: Genotypes A and B express different levels of trait development, but neither shows plasticity across environments. (b) Phenotypic plasticity: Genotypes A and B express different levels of trait development, and both show a higher level in environment 1 than 2. Reaction norms are parallel, and genotype × environment interaction is not present.

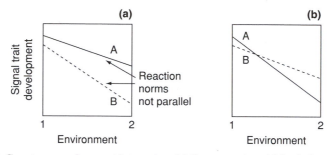

Figure 17-2 Genotype × environment interaction. (a) Genotypes A and B both show a reduction in signal trait development in environment 2, but the reduction is greater for genotype B than for A; reaction norms of genotypes A and B are not parallel. (b) Genotypes A and B both show a reduction in signal trait development in environment 2, but the reduction is greater for genotype A than for B and the two reaction norms intersect; neither genotype exhibits the superior trait development in both environments.

to environments are particularly different from each other such that neither genotype exhibits the superior signal development over the entire gradient, the G × E interaction is then termed "crossover" (see Roff 1997); this designation is used because the reaction norms of the two genotypes intersect (Fig. 17-2b). To visualise this situation with a supposed, but relevant, example: let genotype A males produce an advertisement song that is loud, delivered with a fast repetition rate, and features that are aesthetically attractive to females, if the males' immature development occurred under a favourable environment (regime 1; e.g., low population density and abundant food), but have the males' signalling performance decline markedly if their development occurred under an adverse environment (regime 2). Next, introduce a second genotype, B, wherein males produce signals that are inferior to genotype A under the favourable environment (regime 1), but who are better able to cope with an adverse environment (regime 2), and are actually the more attractive genetic variant if they developed there. Such crossover can upset the expectation of mating signal reliability because a female mating with an attractive male (genotype A) is no longer ensured that her offspring will be attractive should the environment change (from regime 1 to 2) or the offspring migrate (from 1 to 2). For a signal trait of given heritability, the occurrence and severity of this problem will increase with the magnitude of crossover, the incidence and extent of environmental change and dispersal, and an overall population genetic structure that includes diverse genotypes with very different—and nonparallel—reaction norms (Fig. 17-3). Additional factors that may influence unreliability include the variation (Jennions & Petrie 1997) and plasticity of female preference traits (e.g., Rodriguez & Greenfield 2003; the earlier example assumed that

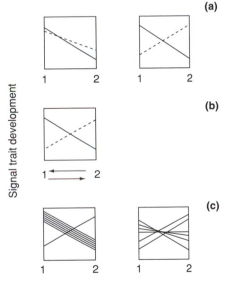

Figure 17-3 Reliability of signal traits. (a) Magnitude of crossover interactions between reaction norms of genotypes (solid and dashed lines); for a given pair of environments (1 and 2), traits for which crossover magnitude is small (left) will be more reliable signals than traits for which crossover magnitude is large (right). (b) Incidence of environmental change and dispersal; for a given signal trait and pair of environments (1 and 2) that can generate crossover between the reaction norms of genotypes (solid and dashed line), signals will be more reliable when the incidence of environmental change or dispersal is small rather than large. (c) Diversity of reaction norm variants; traits for which the diversity of reaction norms (thin solid lines) among genotypes is low (left) will be more reliable signals than traits for which reaction norm diversity—and genotype × environment interaction—is high (right).

female preference did not differ between environmental regimes 1 and 2) and the mode of inheritance of signalling traits. Finally, I have focused on male advertisement signals and female preference to illustrate the unreliability resulting from G × E crossover interactions, but the problem is conceivably more extensive and may occur wherever signal traits are plastic across environments.

Unreliability generated by G × E crossover interactions is a very different, and potentially more insidious, problem than bluffing and other forms of misrepresentation and false information. Unlike the deception created by animals whose signals indicate abilities or resources greater than they possess, the unreliability that G × E crossover interactions generate cannot be considered "intentional" or "dishonest," because the misrepresentation of future fitness benefits did not arise via selection specifically favouring signaller fitness. Rather, it arises from the circumstances of a population's genetic structure, environmental heterogeneity across space or time, and chance. Thus, unreliability generated by G × E crossover interactions may simply be an "emergent property." Nonetheless, this category of unreliability may pose severe constraints on signalling and communication that the various forms of deception and environmental (channel) noise do not. Whereas receiver function may coevolve with signaller deception or channel noise, culminating in sharpened perceptual ability (see Krebs & Dawkins 1984) or a simple acceptance threshold (see Johnstone 1994), the options for receiver adaptation to signal unreliability generated by G × E crossover interactions and environmental change may be limited. How could females in the population depicted in Figure 17-2b cope with a shift from environmental regime 1 to 2 over the course of a generation? Would it be realistic to expect a female preference strategy to incorporate the ability to predict a future environmental regime and choose mates accordingly (but see Lesna & Sabelis 1999, who report on diet-dependent female choice in soil mites, and Qvarnström et al. 2000, who report on seasonally dependent female choice in collared flycatchers)? Ignoring considerations of reality, could such preference shifts help when environmental regimes change unpredictably? Alternatively, could dispersed male offspring of the various genotypes be expected to settle in specific habitats whose environments are most conducive to development of their signal trait?

What does the unreliability potentially generated by G × E crossover interactions and environmental variability over space and time portend for animal signals and communication? The possible occurrence of this problem has become apparent through current studies of the genetic variation of male signal and female preference traits (Jia & Greenfield 1997; Qvarnström 1999; Jia et al. 2000; Rodriguez & Greenfield 2003; Welch 2003; Greenfield & Rodriguez 2004; Hunt et al. 2004), and it is too early to determine its overall extent. We would need far more information than is presently available for any species on the genetic variation and plasticity of signalling and receiving functions and the frequencies with which environmental changes that could affect crossover are experienced. I can, however, make the tentative prediction that traits that do serve as mating signals in natural populations should tend to be "canalised" (see Fig. 17-1a; see Kawecki 2000), or at least not subject to excessive G × E crossover interactions (see Fig. 17-3a). The latter specification is achieved if all genotypes show parallel reaction norms (see Fig. 17-1b), or if those environmental changes that might generate crossover seldom occur between localities among which dispersal takes place or over consecutive generations (see Fig. 17-3b). Traits that are poorly canalised would often misrepresent future fitness benefits, and receiver attention towards them would not be favoured by selection. Moreover, female preferences for such traits would switch between different genotypes over successive generations, which would disrupt linkage disequilibrium between preference and signal traits repeatedly and thereby prevent signal exaggeration via the Fisherian process. Mating signals are often quite exaggerated, however, and it is difficult to reconcile such development with the disruption of linkage disequilibrium that would inevitably follow from G × E crossover interactions. These several complications make it clear that studies of the reliability problem in communication cannot afford to ignore the evolutionary genetics of signal and receiver traits and the conundrum that genetic variation and phenotypic plasticity of these traits may pose.

Prognosis

Despite observations of bluffing, misrepresentation, and the havoc that environmental (channel) noise and G × E crossover interactions can create for receiver functions, animal signals are more or less reliable messages. Our appreciation and understanding of this general feature has taken a circuitous path over the past 30 years. But cases of pronounced and habitual deception that have arisen from selection on signaller function have yet to be demonstrated in natural populations. Is this absence of robust deception simply a tautology arising from the way in which we have defined signalling in animal behaviour? Probably not, based on reported observations (but see Johnstone 1995b on the potential for publication bias) and the evolutionary logic that regular attention paid to misinformation will eventually be selected against.

In closing, it is instructive to compare our current revelation with what must have been painfully obvious to our Palaeolithic and Neolithic predecessors pursuing the perfection of hunter-gatherer techniques and the domestication of agricultural and other animals. These pursuits generally demand an ability to interpret the signals and communication of nonhuman animals in a reliable fashion. Domestication often imposes the added demand that we actually participate in reliable communication with nonhuman animals (see Isack & Reyer 1989 on such participation during hunter-gatherer activities, honey gathering by the Boran people of northern Kenya, who rely on a vocal dialogue with the black-throated honeyguide (*Indicator indicator*), a member of the Old World bird family Indicatoridae, to localise honeybee colonies). This cross-species communication may essentially represent the subversion of nonhuman animal signalling and perception for human purposes. (One might also consider the reverse subversion, as those species that have entered into domestication have certainly proliferated far more than their relatives.) That we can intercede in these communications at all reliably implies that the messages that nonhuman animals send among themselves may too be largely reliable. Thus, we may have come full circle with our ancestors in recognising that when nonhuman animals communicate with one another, they are for the most part sending honest messages that are relatively free of deception. Perhaps, the wisdom to be gleaned from this historical perspective is that our field stands to gain much from reflection upon these ancestral traditions.

Acknowledgments

Much of this chapter was developed from presentations and discussions in the graduate seminar "Topics in Animal Communication," held at the University of Kansas in the spring of 2005. I thank Jeff Cole, Jeff Lucas, Ginger Miller, and Rafa Rodriguez for valuable suggestions to the text.

References

Adams, E. S. & Mesterton-Gibbons, M. 1995. The cost of threat displays and the stability of deceptive communication. *Journal of Theoretical Biology,* **175,** 405–421.

Backwell, P. R. Y., Christy, J. H., Telford, S. R., Jennions, M. D. & Passmore, N. I. 2000. Dishonest signalling in a fiddler crab. *Proceedings of the Royal Society of London, Series B,* **267,** 719–724.

Bee, M. A., Perrill, S. A. & Owen, P. C. 2000. Male green frogs lower the pitch of acoustic signals in defense of territories: a possible dishonest signal of size? *Behavioral Ecology,* **11,** 169–177.

Bradbury, J. W. & Vehrencamp, S. L. 1998. *Principles of Animal Communication.* Sunderland, Massachusetts: Sinauer.

Bradbury, J. W. & Vehrencamp, S. L. 2001. Economic models of animal communication. *Animal Behaviour,* **59,** 259–268.

Brockmann, H. J. 2001. The evolution of alternative strategies and tactics. *Advances in the Study of Behavior,* **30,** 1–51.

Butenandt, A. & Karlson, P. 1954. Uber die Isolierung eines Metamorphose-Hormons der Insekten in kristallisierter Form. *Zeitschrift für Naturforschung,* **9b,** 389–391.

Cheney, D. L. & Seyfarth, R. M. 1990. *How Monkeys See the World.* Chicago: University of Chicago Press.

Christian, K. A. & Tracy, C. R. 1983. Thermoregulation and mate-selection in Fowler's toads? *Science,* **219,** 518–519.

Conner, W. E. 1999. "Un chant d'appel amoureux": acoustic communication in moths. *Journal of Experimental Biology*, **202**, 1711–1723.

Cotton, S., Fowler, K. & Pomiankowski, A. 2004. Do sexual ornaments demonstrate heightened condition-dependent expression as predicted by the handicap hypothesis? *Proceedings of the Royal Society of London, Series B*, **271**, 771783.

Cronin, T. W., Shashar, N., Caldwell, R. L., Marshall, J., Cheroske, A. G. & Chiou, T. H. 2003. Polarization vision and its role in biological signaling. *Integrative and Comparative Biology*, **43**, 549–558.

Darwin, C. 1871. *The Descent of Man and Selection in Relation to Sex*, 2nd edn., 1874, London: John Murray.

David, P., Bjorksten, T., Fowler, K. & Pomiankowski, A. 2000. Condition-dependent signalling of genetic variation in stalk-eyed flies. *Nature*, **406**, 186–188.

Dawkins, R. 1976. *The Selfish Gene*. Oxford: Oxford University Press.

Dawkins, R. & Krebs, J. R. 1978. Animal signals: information or manipulation? In: *Behavioural Ecology: An Evolutionary Approach*. 1st edn. (Ed. by J. R. Krebs and N. B. Davies), pp. 282–309. Sunderland, Massachusetts: Sinauer.

Fairchild, L. 1981. Mate selection and behavioural thermoregulation in Fowler's toads. *Science*, **212**, 950–952.

Fairchild, L. 1983. Reply. *Science*, **219**, 519.

Funk, D. H. & Tallamy, D. W. 2000. Courtship role reversal and deceptive signals in the long-tailed dance fly, *Rhamphomyia longicauda*. *Animal Behaviour*, **59**, 411–421.

Garstang, M. 2004. Long-distance, low-frequency elephant communication. *Journal of Comparative Physiology, A*, **190**, 791–805.

Gerhardt, H. C. & Huber, F. 2002. *Acoustic Communication in Insects and Anurans: Common Problems and Diverse Solutions*. Chicago: University of Chicago Press.

Grafen, A. 1990a. Biological signals as handicaps. *Journal of Theoretical Biology*, **144**, 517–546.

Grafen, A. 1990b. Sexual selection unhandicapped by the Fisher process. *Journal of Theoretical Biology*, **144**, 475–518.

Grafen, A. & Johnstone, R. A. 1993. Why we need ESS signaling theory. *Philosophical Transactions of the Royal Society of London, Series B*, **340**, 245–250.

Greenfield, M. D. 2002. *Signalers and Receivers: Mechanisms and Evolution of Arthropod Communication*. Oxford: Oxford University Press.

Greenfield, M. D. & Rodriguez, R. L. 2004. Genotype-environment interaction and the reliability of mating signals. *Animal Behaviour*, **68**, 1461–1468.

Griffin, D. R. 1958. *Listening in the Dark: the Acoustic Orientation of Bats and Men*. New Haven, Connecticut: Yale University Press.

Hasson, O. 1994. Cheating signals. *Journal of Theoretical Biology*, **167**, 223–238.

Hasson, O. 1997. Towards a general theory of biological signaling. *Journal of Theoretical Biology*, **185**, 139–156.

Hauser, M. D. 1996. *The Evolution of Communication*. Cambridge, Massachusetts: MIT Press.

Hughes, M. 2000. Deception with honest signals: signal residuals and signal function in snapping shrimp. *Behavioral Ecology*, **6**, 614–623.

Hunt, J., Bussière, L. F., Jennions, M. D. & Brooks, R. 2004. What is genetic quality? *Trends in Ecology & Evolution*, **19**, 329–333.

Isack, H. A. & Reyer, H-U. 1989. Honey guides and honey-gatherers: interspecific communication in a symbiotic relationship. *Science*, **243**, 1343–1346.

Jennions, M. D. & Petrie, M. 1997. Variation in mate choice and mating preferences: a review of causes and consequences. *Biological Reviews of the Cambridge Philosophical Society*, **72**, 283–327.

Jia, F-Y. & Greenfield, M. D. 1997. When are good genes good? Variable outcomes of female choice in wax moths. *Proceedings of the Royal Society of London, Series B*, **264**, 1057–1063.

Jia, F-Y., Greenfield, M. D. & Collins, R. D. 2000. Genetic variance of sexually selected traits in waxmoths: Maintenance by genotype × environment interaction. *Evolution*, **54**, 953–967.

Johnstone, R. A. 1994. Honest signalling, perceptual error and the evolution of "all-or-nothing" displays. *Proceedings of the Royal Society of London, Series B*, **256**, 169–175.

Johnstone, R. A. 1995a. Honest advertisement of multiple qualities using multiple signals. *Journal of Theoretical Biology*, **177**, 87–94.

Johnstone, R. A. 1995b. Sexual selection, honest advertisement and the handicap principle: reviewing the evidence. *Biological Reviews of the Cambridge Philosophical Society*, **70**, 1–65.

Johnstone, R. A. 1996. Begging signals and parent-offspring conflict: do parents always win? *Proceedings of the Royal Society of London, Series B*, **263**, 1677–1681.

Johnstone, R. A. 1998a. Efficacy and honesty in communication between relatives. *American Naturalist*, **152**, 45–58.

Johnstone, R. A. 1998b. Conspiratorial whispers and conspicuous displays: games of signal detection. *Evolution*, **52**, 1554–1563.

Johnstone, R. A. 1999. Signaling of need, sibling competition, and the cost of honesty. *Proceedings of the National Academy of Sciences USA*, **96**, 12644–12649.

Johnstone, R. A. & Grafen, A. 1992. Error-prone signaling. *Proceedings of the Royal Society of London, Series B*, **248**, 229–233.

Johnstone, R. A. & Norris, K. 1993. Badges of status and the cost of aggression. *Behavioral Ecology and Sociobiology*, **32**, 127–134.

Kawecki, T. J. 2000. The evolution of genetic canalization under fluctuating selection. *Evolution*, **54**, 1–12.

Kirkpatrick, M. 1986. The handicap mechanism of sexual selection does not work. *American Naturalist*, **127**, 222–240.

Kokko, H., Brooks, R., McNamara, J. M. & Houston, A. I. 2002. The sexual selection continuum. *Proceedings of the Royal Society of London, Series B*, **269**, 1331–1340.

Krakauer, D. C. & Johnstone, R. A. 1995. The evolution of exploitation and honesty in animal communication: a model using artificial neural networks. *Philosophical Transactions of the Royal Society of London, Series B*, **348**, 355–361.

Krebs, J. R. & Davies, N. B. 1978. *Behavioural Ecology: an Evolutionary Approach*, 1st edn. Sunderland, Massachusetts: Sinauer.

Krebs, J. R. & Dawkins, R. 1984. Animal signals: mind-reading and manipulation. In: *Behavioural Ecology: an Evolutionary Approach*, 2nd edn., pp. 380–402 (Ed. by J. R. Krebs and N. B. Davies). Sunderland, Massachusetts: Sinauer.

LeBas, N. R., Hockham, L. R. & Ritchie, M. G. 2003. Nonlinear and correlated sexual selection on "honest" female ornamentation. *Proceedings of the Royal Society of London, Series B*, **270**, 2159–2165.

Lesna, I. & Sabelis, M. W. 1999. Diet-dependent female choice for males with "good genes" in a soil predatory mite. *Nature*, **401**, 581–584.

Macias Garcia, C. & Ramirez, E. 2005. Evidence that sensory traps can evolve into honest signals. *Nature*, **434**, 501–505.

Maynard Smith, J. 1976. Sexual selection and the handicap principle. *Journal of Theoretical Biology*, **57**, 239–242.

Maynard Smith, J. 1982. *Evolution and the Theory of Games*. Cambridge: Cambridge University Press.

Maynard Smith, J. 1991a. Theories of sexual selection. *Trends in Ecology & Evolution*, **6**, 146–151.

Maynard Smith , J. 1991b. Honest signalling: the Philip Sidney game. *Animal Behaviour*, **42**, 1034–1035.

Maynard Smith, J. 1994. Must reliable signals always be costly? *Animal Behaviour*, **47**, 1115–1120.

Maynard Smith, J. & Harper, D. 2003. *Animal Signals.* Oxford: Oxford University Press.

McGraw, K. J., Dale, J. & Mackillop, E. A. 2002. Social environment during molt and the expression of melanin-based pigmentation in male house sparrows (*Passer domesticus*). *Behavioral Ecology & Sociobiology,* **53,** 116–122.

Michelsen, A., Kirchner, W. H. & Lindauer, M. 1986. Sound and vibrational signals in the dance language of the honeybee, *Apis mellifera. Behavioral Ecology and Sociobiology,* **18,** 207–212.

Nieh, J. C. & Tautz, J. 2000. Behaviour-locked signal analysis reveals weak 200–300 Hz comb vibrations during the honeybee waggle dance. *Journal of Experimental Biology,* **203,** 1573–1579.

Payne, K. G., Langbauer, W. R. & Thomas, E. M. 1986. Infrasonic calls of the Asian elephant (*Elephas maximus*). *Behavioral Ecology and Sociobiology,* **18,** 297–301.

Pomiankowski, A. 1987a. Sexual selection: the handicap principle does work sometimes. *Proceedings of the Royal Society of London, Series B,* **231,** 123–145.

Pomiankowski, A. 1987b. The handicap principle works without Fisher. *Trends in Ecology & Evolution,* **2,** 2–3.

Pomiankowski, A. 1988. The evolution of female mate preferences for male genetic quality. *Oxford Surveys in Evolutionary Biology,* **5,** 136–184.

Qvarnström, A. 1999. Genotype-by-environment interactions in the determination of the size of a secondary sexual character in the collared flycatcher (*Ficedula albicollis*). *Evolution,* **53,** 1564–1572.

Qvarnström, A. 2001. Context-dependent genetic benefits from mate choice. *Trends in Ecology & Evolution,* **16,** 5–7.

Qvarnström, A., Part, T. & Sheldon, B. C. 2000. Adaptive plasticity in mate preference linked to differences in reproductive effort. *Nature,* **405,** 344–347.

Reeve, H. K. 1997. Evolutionarily stable communication between kin: a general model. *Proceedings of the Royal Society of London, Series B,* **264,** 1037–1040.

Regen, J. 1913. Über die Anlockung des Weibchens von *Gryllus campestris* L. durch telephonisch übertragene der Stridulationslaute des Männchens. *Pflügers Archiv für die Gesamte Physiologie des Menschen und der Tiere,* **155,** 193–200.

Rodriguez, R. L. & Greenfield, M. D. 2003. Genetic variance and phenotypic plasticity in a component of female mate choice in an ultrasonic moth. *Evolution,* **57,** 1304–1313.

Rodriguez, R. L. & Snedden, W. A. 2004. On the functional design of mate preferences and receiver biases. *Animal Behaviour,* **68,** 427–432.

Roff, D. A. 1997. *Evolutionary Quantitative Genetics.* New York: Chapman & Hall.

Rohrseitz, K. & Tautz, J. 1999. Honey bee dance communication: waggle run direction coded in antennal contacts? *Journal of Comparative Physiology, A,* **184,** 463–470.

Ryan, M. J., Fox, J., Wilczynski, W. & Rand, A. S. 1990. Sexual selection for sensory exploitation in the frog. *Physalaemus pustulosus. Nature,* **343,** 66–67.

Sih, A., Bell, A. M., Johnson, J. C. & Ziemba, R. E. 2004. Behavioral syndromes: an integrative overview. *Quarterly Review of Biology,* **79,** 241–277.

Silberglied, R. E. 1979. Communication in the ultraviolet. *Annual Review of Ecology and Systematics,* **10,** 373–398.

Spangler, H. G., M. D. Greenfield & Takessian, A. 1984. Ultrasonic mate calling in the lesser waxmoth. *Physiological Entomology,* **9,** 87–95.

Steger, R. & Caldwell, R. L. 1983. Intraspecific deception by bluffing: a defense strategy of newly molted stomatopods (Arthropoda: Crustacea). *Science,* **221,** 558–560.

Strassmann, J. E. 2004. Rank crime and punishment. *Nature,* **432,** 160–162.

Tibbetts, E. A. & Dale, J. 2004. A socially enforced signal of quality in a paper wasp. *Nature,* **432,** 218–222.

Towne, W. F. & Kirchner, W. H. 1989. Hearing in honey bees: detection of air particle oscillations. *Science,* **244,** 686–688.

Tyack, P. L. 2000. Functional aspects of cetacean communication. In: *Cetacean Societies: Field Studies of Dolphins and Whales* (Ed. by J. Mann, R. C. Connor, P. L. Tyack, and H. Whitehead) pp. 270–307. Chicago: University of Chicago Press.

van Baalen, M. & Jansen, V. A. A. 2003. Common language or Tower of Babel? On the evolutionary dynamics of signals and their meanings. *Proceedings of the Royal Society of London, Series B,* **270,** 69–76.

Welch, A. M. 2003. Genetic benefits of a female mating preference in gray tree frogs are context-dependent. *Evolution,* **57,** 883–893.

Wiley, R. H. 1994. Errors, exaggeration, and deception in animal communication. In: *Behavioral Mechanisms in Evolutionary Ecology* (Ed. by L. A. Real), pp. 157–189. Chicago: University of Chicago Press.

Wilson, E. O. 1975. *Sociobiology: the New Synthesis.* Cambridge, Massachusetts: Harvard University Press.

Wyatt, T. D. 2003. *Pheromones and Animal Behaviour: Communication by Smell and Taste.* Cambridge: Cambridge University Press.

Zahavi, A. 1975. Mate selection: a selection for a handicap. *Journal of Theoretical Biology,* **53,** 205–214.

Zahavi, A. 1977a. The cost of honesty (further remarks on the handicap principle). *Journal of Theoretical Biology,* **67,** 603–605.

Zahavi, A. 1977b. Reliability in communication systems and the evolution of altruism. In: *Evolutionary Ecology* (Ed. by B. Stonehouse and C. Perrins), pp. 253–259. London: MacMillan Press.

Zahavi, A. 1997. *The Handicap Principle: a Missing Piece of Darwin's Puzzle.* Oxford: Oxford University Press.

18

Fifty Years of Bird Song Research: A Case Study in Animal Behaviour

P. J. B. Slater
School of Biology
University of St. Andrews

Abstract

The growth of bird song research over the past half century has been cata-lysed by both technical and theoretical advances. The study of mechanisms has largely moved to the neurobiological level, where work on bird song has blossomed. At the behavioural level, development and function have been the prime foci of attention, and I briefly review the advances in these two areas. But, looking forwards, the well is far from dry: I suggest a few topics on which I expect that papers will appear in the journal in the next few decades.

Looking at the first few volumes of the *British Journal of Animal Behaviour,* as it was called when it first appeared in 1953, makes quite a con-trast with the last few. Most of the early articles in the journal were descrip-tive rather than experimental, those that did ask questions were largely about mechanisms, and such theoretical discussion as there was concerned instinct and the first rumblings of discontent about Lorenz's theories. There was lit-tle about communication in general or bird song in particular, an abstract on chaffinch song by a very young Peter Marler being an exception. The President of ASAB, W. H. Thorpe, wrote the Editorial to Volume 1. He was then best known for his work on learning in insects; the first of his seminal papers on song learning in birds would not appear until the following year.

Work described in recent volumes is almost entirely experimental, underpinned by the rich body of theory that has been developed in the intervening decades. This, and I would argue most notably the concept of inclusive fitness (Hamilton 1964) and the ramifications extending from it, have led to much of the research described now being either at the functional end of the spectrum, or at least placed firmly in a functional and evolutionary context. Many of the papers concern communication, powered especially by the current interest in sexual selection and mate choice; some 25 contributions in the last three volumes (over 5%) deal with bird song.

In this essay I would like first to consider some of the advances that have led this area of research to prosper as it has. Then I shall look at some of the achievements of the past 50 years, focusing on development and function as the two areas of greatest impact. Finally, I shall discuss a few topics where I feel that the fruit is ripening and will be picked in the years ahead.

Tools for the Trade

Bird song is a wonderful topic for attacking a wide variety of questions in animal behaviour and that realization, together with changes in theory over the past few decades, had undoubtedly boosted studies in this area. But technical advances, even more than theoretical, have been responsible for opening up new possibilities in the study of song. The introduction of the sound spectrograph, originally used by Thorpe (1958) in his study of chaffinch, *Fringilla coelebs,* song development, undoubtedly gave huge impetus to the field. This equipment made it possible to describe and measure sounds, and its successors have enabled the manipulation of them, in a degree of detail hard to achieve for other aspects of behaviour. Thorpe's classic study led the field to blossom. Similarly, the study by Nottebohm *et al.* (1976), which first applied neurobiological techniques to the mechanisms underlying song and its development, was another seed that has germinated to produce a huge tree. I would argue that the two main paradigm shifts in bird song research have stemmed from these papers. But paradigm shifts are not single-handed affairs (my bird song database includes over 2000 references): Thorpe's torch has been carried on, most notably by Marler and his colleagues on several small-repertoire species (see Marler 1997 for a recent review) and by Todt and his group on the nightingale, *Luscinia megarhynchos,* with its large repertoire of song types (see Todt & Hultsch 1996). Similarly, the neurobiological revolution that Nottebohm instituted, and has continued to lead, has been joined by many others whose findings have built up an impressive edifice (see, for example, the recent review by Brainard & Doupe 2000).

It would be easy to list many other technical advances that have spurred on the field. To me some of the most impressive have been the innovative techniques recently applied to understanding how the syrinx (the bird's sound-producing organ) works. It seemed remarkable enough that a bird would sing with a thermistor in each of its bronchii (Suthers *et al.* 1994), but subsequent papers have been based on endoscopic pictures of the syrinx in action (e.g. Larsen & Goller 1999, 2002). Such technical feats have shown that birds do not produce sounds in a way that the study of their cold anatomy had suggested: while the system is complex and many issues are unresolved, sound generation seems to depend more on vibration of the labia and lateral tympaniform membranes than on the medial tympaniform membranes as thought earlier.

At a less complex level, the simple facts that male birds will respond to playback of song by approaching the loudspeaker, calling and singing (Brooks & Falls 1975), and that females (especially with an oestrogen boost) will often respond with a copulation solicitation display (King & West 1977), have led to a spate of studies on responses to song. A large number of such experiments have now been conducted, demonstrating clearly the differences in response that birds have to different stimuli, for example to the songs of neighbours and of strangers. The design of many such experiments was criticized by Kroodsma (1986, 1989), to considerable controversy (see McGregor 1992). While some of his aspirations for experimental design were more exacting than is realistic, Kroodsma was certainly right to highlight the dangers of pseudoreplication, and this message has been largely taken on board. But the assumption that bird song playback experiments were in some way uniquely bedevilled by this problem is incorrect and harmful: tests of a drug using samples from a single production batch do not necessarily generalize to any other batches either. The self-criticism of bird song research in this respect could well be emulated by many others.

Song Development

Thorpe was not the first to study song learning. Barrington (1773) showed clearly that cross-fostering could lead birds to learn the song of the wrong species, a linnet, *Acanthis cannabina,* that of a skylark, *Alauda arvensis,* for example. But only the precision of the sound spectrograph has permitted experiments to reveal the full subtlety of the interactions involved in the development of song. While song is learnt, typically the breadth of that learning is limited so that young birds end up producing only the song of their own species. It is one of the most impressive examples of how nature and nurture interact during development.

Early models of song development saw young birds hatching with a rough idea (or crude template, to put it more correctly) of what their own species' song was like (e.g. Konishi & Nottebohm 1969; Marler 1970). Other songs failed to match this and were not learnt but, when the birds heard their own species' song, the template was honed to an exact one which they then attempted to match with their output when they began to sing themselves. In several of the species first studied, the process of song memorization was limited to a sensitive phase early in life, in some cases ending a good period before the bird began to sing itself.

Subsequent work has shown the need to amend this model in various ways as more detailed studies of song development have been carried out (see, for example, the recent description of how song emerges from subsong in zebra finches, *Taeniopygia guttata,* by Tchernichovski *et al.* 2001). The sensitive phase varies considerably between species, being completed before their first winter in some (e.g. marsh wren, *Cistothorus palustris:* Kroodsma 1978), but extending into adulthood in others (e.g. indigo bunting, *Passerina cyanea:* Margoliash *et al.* 1994). Its duration and timing may depend on the young bird's precise experience (e.g. Jones *et al.* 1996), although the extent to which it is modified by social interaction, as argued for example by Baptista & Petrinovich (1984), is a matter of some controversy (Nelson 1997). In addition to the role of other birds as sources of learnt material, it has been found that they may influence selection of the material used when the young bird starts to sing. In many species young birds learn a wide variety of song elements which they produce in subsong (e.g. swamp sparrow, *Melospiza georgiana:* Marler & Peters 1982). However, their full song is based on a more limited range: they may reject songs that fail to match those of neighbours with whom they interact (e.g. field sparrow, *Spizella pusilla,* Nelson 1992), or they may preferentially retain those that females find attractive (brown-headed cowbird, *Molothrus ater:* West & King 1988). This procedure has been called 'action-based learning' by Marler & Nelson (1993).

Despite these findings it is not the case that tutoring is simply a matter of getting conditions right and a young bird will master whatever song it is exposed to. Particular species may be limited in the range of sounds that they produce, and may be incapable of copying ones outside that range (e.g. swamp sparrow: Marler & Pickert 1984; see also Podos 1997). Young birds may also be especially prone to focusing on and learning the sounds of their own species. For example, fledgling white-crowned sparrows, *Zonotrichia leucophrys,* chirp more in response to playback of white-crown song than to that of other species, suggesting that it is, even at this early stage, a more salient stimulus to them and thus one that attracts their attention (Nelson & Marler 1993); they even show a preference for their own subspecies over others (Nelson 2000). The presence of the introductory whistles of white-crown song also serves as a cue for vocal learning: provided these whistles are present young birds learn alien sounds that follow and would normally be rejected (Soha & Marler 2000). Birds trained with isolated phrases will also reassemble them into the species-specific sequence, again implying some constraint on the form of song (Soha & Marler 2001).

Song learning remains a topic of particular interest because of the interplay between nature and nurture that it reveals. It is also a prime case of imitation.

While there have been occasional attempts to argue this away (see Whiten & Ham 1992), on the grounds that vocal learning is an easier skill than visual imitation, the discovery that some birds are at least as good as many primates in copying motor skills (Heyes & Ray 2000), may set this argument on its head. Perhaps the generic skills that vocal learning has given birds equip them well for other forms of imitation (see Moore 1992).

The Functions of Song

E. O. Wilson (1975), in his 'dumb-bell model', predicted that animal behaviour would be swallowed up by neurobiology at one end and sociobiology at the other. As far as song is concerned he has been largely right but only if, as sociobiologists are prone to do, one ignores development. The neurobiology of song would take an article in itself (and a different author!). But an immense amount of energy has also gone into understanding the functions of song.

The impetus for this study has come from theoretical considerations. In the 1950s it is probably true to say that most ethologists thought that 'good of the species' and 'good of the individual' arguments were alternative ways of expressing much the same thing. Wynne-Edwards (1962) did a service by challenging that view, and papers by Hamilton (1964) and others led to recognition of the importance of kin selection and the primacy of inclusive fitness. For communication it became clear, as put most strongly by Krebs & Dawkins (1984), that animals would signal only if it was to their own advantage. It was not primarily about cooperation and helping others, but about influencing them for the individual's own ends.

On the face of it, generating a large number of decibels from an exposed perch on the top of a tree is not the most obvious way of enhancing one's inclusive fitness. The energy costs of song do not appear to be great (Oberweger & Goller 2001), but time is expended, and predation risks must also weigh against the behaviour unless there are substantial gains to pit against them. These gains appear to be two-fold. Song repels rivals, as shown most elegantly by Krebs (1977a) on great tits, *Parus major,* in what has become the classic paper on bird song function. Song also attracts females (e.g. flycatchers, *Ficedula* sp.: Eriksson & Wallin 1986) and stimulates them (e.g. canaries, *Serinus canaria:* Kroodsma 1976). The balance between the two functions of rival repulsion and mate attraction probably differs between species, and this may account for some of the diversity of singing styles they show (Slater 1981).

The form of song, the rate of singing and many of its other features, may also convey more subtle information, for example on how good a parent a male will be (Greig-Smith 1982). Songs may also indicate male quality in several other ways (see review by Searcy & Yasukawa 1996). Females have sometimes been found to prefer some phrases to others (e.g. Vallet & Kreutzer 1995; Forstmeier *et al.* 2002); these may be ones that are difficult to produce so that only males of high quality can master them. Nowicki *et al.* (2002) have also recently shown a preference in female song sparrows, *Melospiza melodia,* for songs that have been accurately copied, which may be another cue to male quality. Repertoires have been a particularly challenging topic. There now seems little doubt that large ones, which may include hundreds or even thousands of song types, have arisen through sexual selection by female choice (MacDougall-Shackleton 1997). In various species larger repertoires are more attractive and stimulating to females (e.g. sedge warbler, *Acrocephalus schoenobaenus:* Catchpole *et al.* 1984; Buchanan & Catchpole 1997). Evidence as to why it benefits females to respond in this way is also coming forward. The most frequent suggestions have been that only high-quality males can afford large repertoires because the necessary brain space is costly (Gil & Gahr 2002), or because parasites (Buchanan *et al.* 1999) or developmental stress (Nowicki *et al.* 2000) affect the capacity to produce a variety of songs.

It has sometimes been suggested that variations in song may provide a marker of kinship, an attractive idea given the importance that kin recognition may play in various aspects of behaviour. For example, if males learn their songs from their fathers, then females could use them as a cue to avoid mating with close relatives. This may indeed be the case in Darwin's finches, *Geospiza* sp., in which males do learn their songs from their fathers, and females avoid mates who sing like their fathers, although not in their first breeding year when they breed late and have limited choice (Grant & Grant 1996). However, in this respect, Darwin's finches appear something of an exception: in most other species that have been studied song learning occurs primarily after independence from the parents and is thus unlikely to provide a cue to kinship (Slater & Mann 1990).

Key Questions for the Future

There are few areas of animal behaviour that the study of bird song has not illuminated in the last 50 years and, albeit very selectively, I hope I have illustrated some of these. I would like to finish by considering some current trends and future prospects to show that the cornucopia is not yet empty.

Females and Song

Song by females and the effects of male song on females have been two of the main growth areas of study in the past few years. The former has been a comparatively neglected topic because much of song research, indeed much of most research, is carried out in temperate regions of the world where female song is, at least relatively, rare (Morton 1996). On the other hand, females often sing in the tropics, and may also join in with males in more or less sophisticated duets (e.g. Levin 1996; Hall 2000). Even in temperate regions it is probably commoner than often assumed, and certainly deserves more study (Langmore 1998). The reasons why females sing, and the significance of duetting, remain matters of debate.

The response of females to the songs of males was for long neglected because of the difficulty of studying it in the field. While males interact with each other repeatedly throughout the season, the attraction of a mate may be the work of an instant. Radiotracking female great reed warblers, *Acrocephalus arundinaceus,* has, however, suggested how they sample among males before making their choice (Bensch & Hasselquist 1992); once mated they obtain extrapair fertilizations from neighbouring males with larger repertoire sizes than their own mate, and this appears beneficial as postfledging offspring survival correlates with paternal repertoire size (Hasselquist *et al.* 1996). In the laboratory, work on female preferences using copulation solicitation has been supplemented by the use of operant techniques (e.g. Riebel *et al.* 2002), which are a tool of great potential. Just how the songs of males are adapted to attract and stimulate females is a rich seam that is only just starting to be mined. Similarly, while we know much about song learning in males, with some exceptions (e.g. Clayton 1990), we still know little about how female preferences develop.

The Neurobiology of Repertoires

Studies of the behavioural mechanisms underlying song, once a major issue, have tended to decline as the neurobiological study of bird song has expanded. The neurobiologists have answered some fundamental questions about the brain mechanisms concerned with song learning, storage and production, but these questions would not even have been asked without the basic behavioural information in the first place. The complexity of song organization and sequencing has been well described for many species. Songs are often very much equivalent 'alternative motor patterns' (Hinde 1958), with the choice between them following clear rules (Slater 1983). Behavioural data such as these provide a challenge to neurobiological explanation. How birds select between songs may yield secrets on the broader issue of how animals decide what to do and when to do it.

Why do Songbirds Learn their Songs?

On present evidence, vocal learning has a surprisingly discontinuous distribution (Janik & Slater 1997), although within the groups of birds that show it (parrots, hummingbirds and oscine passerines) it appears to be universal.

The questions of why vocal learning is advantageous, and why it occurs in some groups and not others, remain to be satisfactorily answered. Given that it has been found throughout those groups that do show it, perhaps the question of why it occurs is best split in two. First, there is the historical question of why it arose in the first place, which it may have done before the evolution of anything that we would call 'song'. Second, once it evolved, why did it persist, despite the highly varied roles that song plays in the lives of different species? In view of the great differences in song between species, one functional theory (e.g. learning matches to neighbours or learning matches to transmission characteristics of habitat) seems unlikely to account for all (Slater 1989). For this reason, the possibility that, once learning had evolved, species showing it got caught in a 'cultural trap' does seem an attractive one (Lachlan & Slater 1999). But this question continues to be a challenging one and, again, one of likely significance beyond the world of bird song. Social learning has recently become an active field of study (e.g. Heyes & Galef 1996): bird song is a prime example of this phenomenon and one that may shed light on the advantage to animals of learning from others in other contexts as well.

The Rôle of Small Repertoires

Small repertoires of just a few song types are less easy to understand than large ones which, as discussed above, are likely to have evolved through sexual selection by female choice. By contrast small repertoires are often thought to have evolved primarily in a male–male context. Various theories of their function have been put forward. These range from the idea that they stop the listener from habituating (antimonotony, Hartshorne 1956), to the notion that they simulate the presence of more than one individual (Beau Geste, Krebs 1977b), to the suggestion that they avoid muscular fatigue (antiexhaustion, Lambrechts & Dhondt 1988). None of these ideas has received unqualified support, and the fact that many such species sing with 'eventual variety', singing each song type a number of times before singing the next, suggests that it pays the individual to get each message across before moving on to the next (Slater 1981). But why? Perhaps the most plausible hypothesis is that repertoires allow birds to match, or not do so, when countersinging with neighbours (e.g. Beecher et al. 2000); this is less likely where the level of sharing is low, although birds may still 'match' with similar songs (Burt et al. 2002). Interactive playback has been an important recent technical advance which is helping us to understand just how individuals use their songs in relation to one another (e.g. Vehrencamp 2001). It helps to simulate the dynamic interchange between two birds which is a far cry from the stereotyped repetition of a single unvarying song type that traditional playbacks involved. It may give us the key to understanding why one song type is the norm in many species, whereas in others individuals usually have three or four (see data in Read & Weary 1992).

Species Differences in Singing Behaviour

One of the striking things about bird song is its remarkable variation between species. Repertoire size that ranges from one simple song type to several thousand complex ones is but a single example. But it also varies in many other ways: in whether one or both sexes sing, in seasonal and daily cycles, in the relation between song and the breeding cycle, in whether variety is immediate or eventual, and so on. Many species have now been studied and it is becoming increasingly feasible to use the comparative method to see how these features of singing link with other features of way of life. From the first efforts in this direction, the answer does not seem to be simple (Read & Weary 1992). A great deal of judgement is also needed in deciding how species should be categorized and how the data should be framed. On repertoires, for example, should a species with a limited number of elements that are recombined to give a very large number of song types (e.g. willow warbler, *Phylloscopus trochilus*: Gil & Slater 2000) be scored at the element or song type level? It is certainly not satisfactory to look at some species at one level and others at another (Møller *et al*. 2000). But, these technical difficulties apart, with the increasing sophistication of the comparative method, and our rapidly growing knowledge of the lifestyles and singing patterns of different species, I would anticipate a spate of such studies. It is a topic of which the surface has barely been scratched.

Song and Interactions

As mentioned above, interactive playback is allowing a much more realistic approach to the relations between two males singing on adjacent territories. It is becoming apparent that the challenge males provide to each other is not just in what they sing, how much and how loudly, but in the way in which songs relate in time to each other, alternating or overlapping (e.g. Todt & Naguib 2000).

In various ways, even looking at interactions is an oversimplification. As shown with the alarm calls of chickens (Marler *et al*. 1986), birds may behave differently depending on whether or not they have an audience, and on the nature of that audience. Even where singing interactions are not involved, a male may use his songs differently in the presence of another male, a female and when on his own. This is most obvious in the growing number of species that appear to have songs that they use in different contexts, but it may also be an important, largely unexplored, issue in species where this is not the case.

A separate question is whether the influence of song spreads beyond pairs of interactants. The active space of song will often encompass many other individuals, and singing interactions may themselves involve more than two individuals, in relationships more akin to a network (McGregor & Dabelsteen 1996). Even where only two birds are singing, the form of their interaction may provide others with information about them. Evidence is beginning to accumulate that this 'eavesdropping' may indeed provide information to third parties (e.g. Peake *et al.* 2002).

Conclusion

In this short essay I have had to be very selective, and have obviously placed stress on subjects that interest me and ignored ones others may feel of prime importance. It is part of the richness of our subject that many different perspectives are possible. What I hope I have illustrated, however, is not only that the study of bird song has proved a particularly illuminating one over the past five decades, but that it will certainly also keep us busy in the next half century as well.

Acknowledgments

I am very grateful to Diego Gil, Vincent Janik, Katharina Riebel and Sally Ward for helpful comments on the manuscript.

References

Baptista, L. F. & Petrinovich, L. 1984. Social interaction, sensitive phases and the song template hypothesis in the white-crowned sparrow. *Animal Behaviour, 32,* 172–181.

Barrington, D. 1773. Experiments and observations on the singing of birds. *Philosophical Transactions of the Royal Society of London, 63,* 249–291.

Beecher, M. D., Campbell, S. E., Burt, J. M., Hill, C. E. & Nordby, J. C. 2000. Song-type matching between neighbouring song sparrows. *Animal Behaviour, 59,* 21–27.

Bensch, S. & Hasselquist, D. 1992. Evidence for female choice in a polygynous warbler. *Animal Behaviour, 44,* 301–311.

Brainard, M. S. & Doupe, A. J. 2000. What songbirds teach us about learning. *Nature, 417,* 351–358.

Brooks, R. J. & Falls, J. B. 1975. Individual recognition by song in white-throated sparrows. I: Discrimination of songs of neighbors and strangers. *Canadian Journal of Zoology, 53,* 879–888.

Buchanan, K. L. & Catchpole, C. K. 1997. Female choice in the sedge warbler, *Acrocephalus schoenobaenus*: multiple cues from song and territory quality. *Proceedings of the Royal Society of London, Series B, 264,* 521–526.

Buchanan, K. L., Catchpole, C. K., Lewis, J. W. & Lodge, A. 1999. Song as an indicator of parasitism in the sedge warbler. *Animal Behaviour, 57,* 307–314.

Burt, J. M., Bard, S. C., Campbell, S. E. & Beecher, M. D. 2002. Alternative forms of song matching in song sparrows. *Animal Behaviour*, **63**, 1143–1151.

Catchpole, C. K., Dittami, J. & Leisler, B. 1984. Differential responses to male song repertoires in female songbirds implanted with oestradiol. *Nature*, **312**, 563–564.

Clayton, N. S. 1990. Subspecies recognition and song learning in zebra finches. *Animal Behaviour*, **40**, 1009–1017.

Eriksson, D. & Wallin, L. 1986. Male bird song attracts females: a field experiment. *Behavioral Ecology and Sociobiology*, **19**, 297–299.

Forstmeier, W., Kempenaers, B., Meyer, A. & Leisler, B. 2002. A novel song parameter correlates with extra-pair paternity and reflects male longevity. *Proceedings of the Royal Society of London, Series B*, **269**, 1479–1485.

Gil, D. & Gahr, M. 2002. The honesty of bird song: multiple constraints for multiple traits. *Trends in Ecology and Evolution*, **17**, 133–141.

Gil, D. & Slater, P. J. B. 2000. Song organisation and singing patterns of the willow warbler, *Phylloscopus trochilus. Behaviour*, **137**, 759–782.

Grant, B. R. & Grant, P. R. 1996. Cultural inheritance of song and its role in the evolution of Darwin's finches. *Evolution*, **50**, 2471–2487.

Greig-Smith, P. W. 1982. Song rates and parental care by individual male stonechats *Saxicola torquata. Animal Behaviour*, **30**, 245–252.

Hall, M. L. 2000. The function of duetting in magpie larks: conflict, cooperation or commitment. *Animal Behaviour*, **60**, 667–677.

Hamilton, W. D. 1964. The genetical evolution of social behaviour. *Journal of Theoretical Biology*, **7**, 1–52.

Hartshorne, C. 1956. The monotony threshold in singing birds. *Auk*, **83**, 176–192.

Hasselquist, D., Bensch, S. & von Schantz, T. 1996. Correlation between male song repertoire, extra-pair patrenity and offspring survival in the great reed warbler. *Nature*, **381**, 229–232.

Heyes, C. M. & Galef, B. G. 1996. *Social Learning in Animals: The Roots of Culture.* San Diego: Academic Press.

Heyes, C. M. & Ray, E. D. 2000. What is the significance of imitation in animals? *Advances in the Study of Behavior*, **29**, 215–245.

Hinde, R. A. 1958. Alternative motor patterns in chaffinch song. *Animal Behaviour*, **6**, 211–218.

Janik, V. M. & Slater, P. J. B. 1997. Vocal learning in mammals. *Advances in the Study of Behavior*, **26**, 59–99.

Jones, A. E., Ten Cate, C. & Slater, P. J. B. 1996. Early experience and plasticity of song in adult male zebra finches (*Taeniopygia guttata*). *Journal of Comparative Psychology*, **110**, 354–369.

King, A. P. & West, M. J. 1977. Species identification in the North American cowbird: appropriate responses to abnormal song. *Science*, **195**, 1002–1004.

Konishi, M. & Nottebohm, F. 1969. Experimental studies in the ontogeny of avian vocalizations. In: *Bird Vocalizations* (Ed. by R. A. Hinde), pp. 29–48. Cambridge: Cambridge University Press.

Krebs, J. R. 1977a. Song and territory in the great tit, *Parus major.* In: *Evolutionary Ecology* (Ed. by B. Stonehouse & C. Perrins), pp. 47–62. London: Macmillan.

Krebs, J. R. 1977b. The significance of song repertoires: the Beau Geste hypothesis. *Animal Behaviour*, **25**, 475–478.

Krebs, J. R. & Dawkins, R. 1984. Animal signals: mind-reading and manipulation. In: *Behavioural Ecology: An Evolutionary Approach* (Ed. by J. R. Krebs & N. B. Davies), pp. 380–402. Oxford: Blackwell Scientific.

Kroodsma, D. E. 1976. Reproductive development in a female songbird: differential stimulation by quality of male song. *Science*, **192**, 574–575.

Kroodsma, D. E. 1978. Aspects of learning in the ontogeny of birdsong. In: *The Development of Behavior: Comparative and Evolutionary Aspects* (Ed. by G. M. Burghardt & M. Bekoff), pp. 215–230. New York: Garland STPM Press.

Kroodsma, D. E. 1986. Design of song playback experiments. *Auk*, **103**, 640–642.

Kroodsma, D. E. 1989. Suggested experimental designs for song playbacks. *Animal Behaviour,* **37,** 600–609.

Lachlan, R. F. & Slater, P. J. B. 1999. The maintenance of vocal learning by gene–culture interaction: the cultural trap hypothesis. *Proceedings of the Royal Society of London, Series B,* **266,** 701–706.

Lambrechts, M. & Dhondt, A. A. 1988. The anti-exhaustion hypothesis: a new hypothesis to explain song performance and song switching in the great tit. *Animal Behaviour,* **36,** 327–334.

Langmore, N. E. 1998. Functions of duet and solo songs of female birds. *Trends in Ecology and Evolution,* **13,** 136–140.

Larsen, O. N. & Goller, F. 1999. Role of syringeal vibrations in bird vocalizations. *Proceedings of the Royal Society of London, Series B,* **266,** 1609–1615.

Larsen, O. N. & Goller, F. 2002. Direct observation of syringeal muscle function in songbirds and a parrot. *Journal of Experimental Biology,* **205,** 25–35.

Levin, R. N. 1996. Song behaviour and reproductive strategies in a duetting wren, *Thryothorus nigricapillus.* 1. Removal experiments. *Animal Behaviour,* **52,** 1093–1106.

MacDougall-Shackleton, S. A. 1997. Sexual selection and the evolution of song repertoires. *Current Ornithology,* **14,** 81–125.

McGregor, P. K. (Ed.) 1992. *Playback and Studies of Animal Communication.* New York: Plenum.

McGregor, P. K. & Dabelsteen, T. 1996. Communication networks. In: *Ecology and Evolution of Acoustic Communication in Birds* (Ed. by D. E. Kroodsma & E. H. Miller), pp. 409–425. Ithaca, New York: Comstock.

Margoliash, D., Staicer, C. & Inoue, S. A. 1994. The process of syllable acquisition in adult indigo buntings (*Passerina cyanea*). *Behaviour,* **131,** 39–64.

Marler, P. 1970. A comparative approach to vocal learning: song development in white-crowned sparrows. *Journal of Comparative and Physiological Psychology,* **71**(Suppl), 1–25.

Marler, P. 1997. Three models of song learning: evidence from behavior. *Journal of Neurobiology,* **33,** 501–516.

Marler, P. & Nelson, D. A. 1993. Action-based learning: a new form of developmental plasticity in bird song. *Netherlands Journal of Zoology,* **43,** 91–103.

Marler, P. & Peters, S. 1982. Developmental overproduction and selective attrition: new processes in the epigenesis of bird song. *Developmental Psychobiology,* **15,** 369–378.

Marler, P. & Pickert, R. 1984. Species-universal microstructure in a learned birdsong: the swamp sparrow (*Melospiza georgiana*). *Animal Behaviour,* **32,** 673–689.

Marler, P., Dufty, A. & Pickert, R. 1986. Vocal communication in the domestic chicken. II is a sender sensitive to the presence and nature of a receiver? *Animal Behaviour,* **34,** 194–198.

Møller, A. P., Henry, P. Y. & Erritzoe, J. 2000. The evolution of song repertoires and immune defence in birds. *Proceedings of the Royal Society of London, Series B,* **267,** 165–169.

Moore, B. R. 1992. Avian movement imitation and a new form of mimicry: tracing the evolution of a complex form of learning. *Behaviour,* **122,** 230–263.

Morton, E. S. 1996. A comparison of vocal behavior among tropical and temperate passerine birds. In: *Ecology and Evolution of Acoustic Communication in Birds* (Ed. by D. E. Kroodsma & E. H. Miller), pp. 258–268. Ithaca, New York: Comstock.

Nelson, D. A. 1992. Song overproduction and selective attrition lead to song sharing in the field sparrow (*Spizella pusilla*). *Behavioral Ecology and Sociobiology,* **30,** 415–424.

Nelson, D. A. 1997. Social interaction and sensitive phases for song learning: a critical review. In: *Social Influences on Vocal Development* (Ed. by C. T. Snowdon & M. Hausberger), pp. 7–22. Cambridge: Cambridge University Press.

Nelson, D. A. 2000. A preference for own sub-species' song guides vocal learning in a song bird. *Proceedings of the National Academy of Sciences, U.S.A.,* **97,** 13348–13353.

Nelson, D. A. & Marler, P. 1993. Innate recognition of song in white-crowned sparrows: a role in selective vocal learning? *Animal Behaviour,* **46,** 806–808.

Nottebohm, F., Stokes, T. M. & Leonard, C. M. 1976. Central control of song in the canary. *Journal of Comparative Neurology,* **165,** 457–486.

Nowicki, S., Hasselquist, D., Bensch, S. & Peters, S. 2000. Nestling growth and song repertoire size in great reed warblers: evidence for song learning as an indicator mechanism in mate choice. *Proceedings of the Royal Society of London, Series B,* **267,** 2419–2424.

Nowicki, S., Searcy, W. A. & Peters, S. 2002. Quality of song learning affects female response to male bird song. *Proceedings of the Royal Society of London, Series B,* **269,** 1949–1954.

Oberweger, K. & Goller, F. 2001. The metabolic cost of birdsong production. *Journal of Experimental Biology,* **204,** 3379–3385.

Peake, T. M., Terry, A. M. R., McGregor, P. K. & Dabelsteen, T. 2002. Do great tits assess rivals by combining direct experience with information gathered by eavesdropping? *Proceedings of the Royal Society of London, Series B,* **269,** 1925–1929.

Podos, J. 1997. A performance constraint on the evolution of trilled vocalizations in a songbird family (Passeriformes: Emberizidae). *Evolution,* **51,** 537–551.

Read, A. F. & Weary, D. M. 1992. The evolution of bird song; comparative analyses. *Philosophical Transactions of the Royal Society of London, Series B,* **338,** 165–187.

Riebel, K., Smallegange, I. M., Terpstra, N. J. & Bolhuis, J. J. 2002. Sexual equality in zebra finch song preference: evidence for a dissociation between song recognition and production learning. *Proceedings of the Royal Society of London, Series B,* **269,** 729–733.

Searcy, W. A. & Yasukawa, K. 1996. Song and female choice. In: *Ecology and Evolution of Acoustic Communication in Birds* (Ed. by D. E. Kroodsma & E. H. Miller), pp. 454–473. Ithaca, New York: Comstock.

Slater, P. J. B. 1981. Chaffinch song repertoires: observations, experiments and a discussion of their significance. *Zeitschrift für Tierpsychologie,* **56,** 1–24.

Slater, P. J. B. 1983. Sequences of song in chaffinches. *Animal Behaviour,* **31,** 272–281.

Slater, P. J. B. 1989. Bird song learning: causes and consequences. *Ethology, Ecology and Evolution,* **1,** 19–46.

Slater, P. J. B. & Mann, N. I. 1990. Do male zebra finches learn their fathers' songs? *Trends in Ecology and Evolution,* **5,** 415–417.

Soha, J. A. & Marler, P. 2000. A species-specific acoustic cue for selective song learning in the white-crowned sparrow. *Animal Behaviour,* **60,** 297–306.

Soha, J. A. & Marler, P. 2001. Vocal syntax development in the white-crowned sparrow (*Zonotrichia leucophrys*). *Journal of Comparative Psychology,* **115,** 172–180.

Suthers, R. A., Goller, F. & Hartley, R. S. 1994. Motor dynamics of sound production in mimic thrushes. *Journal of Neurobiology,* **25,** 917–936.

Tchernichovski, O., Mitra, P. P., Lints, T. & Nottebohm, F. 2001. Dynamics of the vocal imitation process: how a zebra finch learns its song. *Science,* **291,** 2564–2569.

Thorpe, W. H. 1958. The learning of song patterns by birds, with especial reference to the song of the chaffinch *Fringilla coelebs. Ibis,* **100,** 535–570.

Todt, D. & Hultsch, H. 1996. Acquisition and performance of song repertoires: ways of coping with diversity and versatility. In: *Ecology and Evolution of Acoustic Communication in Birds* (Ed. by D. E. Kroodsma & E. H. Miller), pp. 79–96. Ithaca, New York: Comstock.

Todt, D. & Naguib, M. 2000. Vocal interactions in birds: the use of song as a model in communication. *Advances in the Study of Behavior,* **29,** 247–296.

Vallet, E. & Kreutzer, M. 1995. Female canaries are sexually responsive to special song phrases. *Animal Behaviour,* **49,** 1603–1619.

Vehrencamp, S. L. 2001. Is song-type matching a conventional signal of aggressive intentions? *Proceedings of the Royal Society of London, Series B,* **268,** 1637–1642.

West, M. J. & King, A. P. 1988. Female visual displays affect the development of male song in the cowbird. *Nature,* **334,** 244–246.

Whiten, A. & Ham, R. 1992. On the nature and evolution of imitation in the animal kingdom: reappraisal of a century of research. *Advances in the Study of Behavior,* **21,** 239–283.

Wilson, E. O. 1975. *Sociobiology: The New Synthesis.* Cambridge, Massachusetts: Belknap Press.

Wynne-Edwards, V. C. 1962. *Animal Dispersion in Relation to Social Behaviour.* Edinburgh: Oliver & Boyd.

19

Avian Navigation: From Historical to Modern Concepts

Roswitha Wiltschko
Wolfgang Wiltschko
Fachbereich Biologie und Informatik der J. W. Goethe-Universität
Frankfurt am Main, Zoologie

Abstract

Studies on avian navigation began at the end of the 19th century with testing various hypotheses, followed by large-scale displacement experiments to assess the capacity of the birds' navigational abilities. In the 1950s, the first theoretical concepts were published. Kramer proposed his 'Map-and-Compass' model, assuming that birds establish the direction to a distant goal with the help of an external reference, a compass. The model describes homing as a two-step process, with the first step determining the direction to the goal as a compass course and the second step locating this course with the help of a compass. This model was widely accepted when numerous experiments with clock-shifted pigeons demonstrated the use of the sun compass, and thus a general involvement of compass orientation, in homing. The 'map' step is assumed to use local site-specific information, which led to the idea of a 'grid map' based on environmental gradients. Kramer's model still forms the basis of our present concept on avian homing, yet route integration with the help of an external reference provides an alternative strategy to determine the home course, and the magnetic compass is a second compass mechanism available to birds. These mechanisms are interrelated by ontogenetic learning processes. A two-step process, with the first step providing the compass course and the second step locating this course with the help of a compass, appears to be a common feature of avian navigation tasks, yet the origin of the compass courses differs between tasks according to their nature, with courses acquired by experience for flights within the home range, courses based on navigational processes for returning home, and courses derived from genetically coded information in first-time migrants. Compass orientation thus forms the backbone of the avian navigational system.

In this paper we outline the changing views in bird orientation research and their role in the growing understanding of avian orientation and navigation. Our emphasis is on the theoretical concepts that form the basis of our present view of avian navigation, that is, on strategies and general mechanisms, without going into details about the factors used. We focus on homing of carrier pigeons, *Columba livia* f. *domestica,* because most of the findings forming our present concepts were obtained with this species; the few data available on wild birds indicate that their navigational system is based on the same principles (reviewed in R. Wiltschko 1992). Orientation during migration, which for first-time migrants means reaching a yet unknown goal, will be considered at the end when we discuss common features and differences between migration and homing.

Traditional Knowledge

Humans have long been aware of the excellent navigational abilities of birds. Descendants of wild rock doves, *C. livia,* were domesticated in ancient Egypt more than 4000 years ago and used to carry urgent messages, because they were faster than human couriers. The use of carrier pigeons as messengers spread through the Mediterranean countries, and finally reached central and northern Europe. European settlers, in turn, introduced carrier pigeons to other continents so that today carrier pigeons are found in both Americas, Africa, Australia and Oceania. Although modern communication techniques make the use of pigeons as couriers obsolete, releasing them in competitive races is still a popular pasttime in all parts of the world.

The ancient knowledge about the pigeons' ability to home and the long tradition in their use as messengers contrast sharply with an apparent lack of interest in the question of how they are able to find their way. The same is true for the orientation mechanisms of migratory birds. Only near the end of the 19th century did avian navigation become a topic of scientific interest.

Early Experiments

The first attempts to explain birds' mysterious navigational abilities approached the question in two ways: one began from theoretical considerations, the other from an inventory of the birds' abilities.

First Hypotheses Tested

The earliest authors used a deductive approach, discussing various theoretical possibilities, usually in connection with specific types of stimuli. A first hypothesis by Viguier (1882) was inspired by the familiar navigational charts and their graduation; it suggested that birds might use the spatial distribution of magnetic variables such as total intensity and inclination to determine their position relative to home. An alternative hypothesis, already mentioned by Darwin (1873), proposed that pigeons might somehow trace the route of their outward journey and derive their homeward route from this information (Exner 1883; Reynaud 1898). Attempts to test either hypothesis involved subjecting carrier pigeons to manipulations of the sensory input discussed; the results were largely inconclusive (e.g. Exner 1883; Reynaud 1898; Casamajor 1927).

In retrospect, however, it is interesting that these two first navigation hypotheses were based on opposite assumptions about the origin of navigational information: Viguier (1882) suggested the use of local, site-specific information obtained at the starting point of the homing flight, but Exner (1883) and Reynaud (1898) assumed the use of route-based information obtained during the outward journey. These two principal alternatives are still discussed today; meanwhile, both are supported by experimental evidence, as we discuss later.

An Inventory of Birds' Homing Abilities

The continuing discussion soon revealed that the general knowledge about birds' homing abilities was insufficient for a meaningful evaluation of the theoretical possibilities and potential stimuli. This led to an inductive approach. Large-scale displacement experiments with unmanipulated birds were initiated to find out from what distances birds were able to home, and how various conditions would affect their performance.

Watson (1908) and Watson & Lashley (1915) displaced terns, *Anous stolidus* and *Sterna fuscata,* from a Caribbean island to different sites, among them Cape Hatteras, far north of the natural distribution range of their test species. Birds were able to return home over the sea from these distant, unfamiliar sites (Fig. 19-1). This pioneering work was followed by other large-scale displacement experiments with wild birds, predominantly species of seabirds, starlings and swallows (e.g. *Sterna paradisea:* Dircksen 1932; *Hirundo rustica, Delichon urbica:* Rüppell 1934; *Sturnus vulgaris:* Rüppell 1935; *H. rustica, D. urbica:* Wojtusiak *et al.* 1937). The results again documented excellent homing abilities over considerable distances from totally unfamiliar sites; the homing mechanisms, however, remained mysterious. Lack & Lockley (1938), reporting successful homing of displaced petrels,

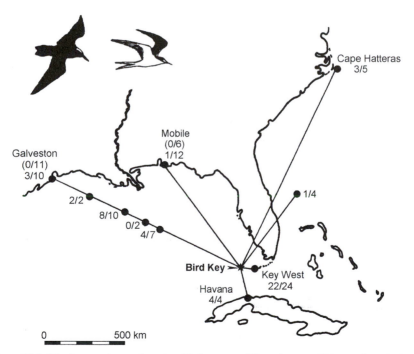

Figure 19-1 Displacement experiments with brown noddies, *Anous stolidus,* and sooty terns, *Sterna fuscata.* Birds from a breeding colony at Bird Key, Tortugas, were released at the points marked with black dots. Numbers indicate the relation between birds returned and birds released; data from releases where the birds had suffered from transport are placed in parentheses (plotted from data reported by Watson 1908 and Watson & Lashley 1915).

Hydrobates pelagicus, and shearwaters, *P. puffinus,* across the open ocean, showed that homing did not depend on the use of familiar landmarks.

Experiments with carrier pigeons, however, resulted in a different picture. An early study had revealed that pigeons displaced along twisted routes with extensive detours did not retrace the route of the outward journey, but returned by more or less direct flights (Claparède 1903). Others (e.g. Rivière 1923; Gundlach 1932; Heinroth & Heinroth 1941) observed a marked decrease in homing performance with increasing distance from the loft, which generally seemed to indicate poor homing abilities. Faster homing speeds and higher return rates from familiar sites, on the other hand, were interpreted as suggesting the use of familiar visual landmarks.

These contrasting findings led to an odd dichotomy in the views on the birds' navigation abilities: researchers working with wild birds attested to their birds' outstanding navigational abilities and claimed a 'sense of direction' and/or a 'sense of space', without being able to name the factors used, but researchers working with homing pigeons assumed limited abilities, questioned unusual 'senses' and considered random search and the use of familiar landmarks as a likely basis for any homing.

Even today, the poor performance of carrier pigeons in the early experiments is puzzling. Studies of displaced wild birds generally involved species that are fast and persevering flyers. Carrier pigeons, in contrast, perform well only when they are encouraged to fly by training releases or races. The early researchers might have grossly overestimated the spontaneous abilities of untrained pigeons. However, they were the first to emphasize the crucial role of experience in shaping the avian navigational system: it is not solely based on spontaneous abilities, but includes important learned components.

Research Handicaps

Until the middle of the 20th century, experimental research on avian navigation was handicapped in two ways. The first involved methods. In the early studies, the only criteria to assess navigational abilities were homing speed and return rate. In the 1950s, however, Matthews (1951) and Kramer & von Saint Paul (1952) realized that the directions in which pigeons vanished after release were closely related to the home direction. From then on, researchers have generally recorded vanishing bearings and included them in their considerations; they are taken to indicate what direction the pigeons at the release site assume to be their home direction.

The other handicap arose from a lack of theoretical framework. So far, findings had been mostly descriptive, documenting birds' homing abilities and limitations. The background for asking specific questions was vague. This, too, changed rapidly at the beginning of the 1950s, when two concepts on orientation behaviour were published. The early 1950s thus mark the beginning of modern orientation research.

Griffin's Three 'Types of Orientation'

When Griffin (1952a) classified orientation, he himself had had ample experience with releasing wild birds (e.g. *Oceanodroma leucorhoa:* Griffin 1940) and homing pigeons (e.g. Griffin 1952b) and had reviewed the existing literature on displacement experiments (Griffin 1944). He was also aware of pigeon breeders' practice of always releasing their birds in the same direction, which he considered crucial for successful homing.

Definitions of the Three 'Types'

Griffin (1952a, pp. 383–384) characterized the orientation processes according to their complexity:

'The first and simplest type of homing I shall call for convenience Type I; it is reliance on visual landmarks within familiar territory and the use of exploration or some form of undirected wandering when released in unfamiliar territory . . . Type II homing might then be designated as that by which birds are able to fly in a certain direction even when crossing unfamiliar territory . . . Type III homing ability goes one step further and allows the bird possessing it to choose approximately the correct direction of its home when it is carried into unfamiliar territory in a new and unaccustomed direction.'

Griffin's (1952a, 1955) classification reflects theoretical considerations as well as considerations on specific mechanisms. He suggested that most displaced birds would use Type I, 'piloting', and, when released in unfamiliar territory, would search until they by chance encountered familiar landmarks, which he regarded as the simplest possible navigational strategy. Type II, 'one directional orientation', as it was later called, was the next most complex behaviour. An example seemed to be provided by directionally trained racing pigeons flying in a fixed direction. Griffin (1952a) did not initially specify mechanisms for how this direction might be located and maintained; later, he suggested the sun compass as a possible mechanism (Griffin 1955). Type III represented the most advanced behaviour requiring sophisticated mechanisms, the nature of which remained open. Human seafaring served as a model, so this strategy has been called 'true navigation'.

Adler (1970) pointed out that Griffin's three Types of Orientation, in accordance with their increasing complexity, were based on an increasing number of references. Type I is independent of any external reference. Type II is based on one external factor as reference, the compass, and Type III, in agreement with the idea of bicoordinate navigation, makes use of (at least) two independent external factors.

Bellrose (1972) later expanded Griffin's scheme by associating the different Types of Orientation with the orientation mechanisms that had meanwhile been discovered and/or were being discussed, such as sun compass (Kramer 1950), sun navigation (Matthews 1953) and star compass (Emlen 1970).

Importance and Critique of Griffin's Classification

Griffin's classification was welcomed by the developing field of avian orientation research, because it allowed a first classification of orientation behaviour. Numerous review articles on avian navigation began by quoting Griffin's Types of Orientation (e.g. Schmidt-Koenig 1965; Keeton 1974; Able 1980). Descriptions of the orientation capacities of other animals such as salmon also used Griffin's classification (e.g. Groot 1982).

In the long run, however, Griffin's Types of Orientation proved insufficient and became subject to criticism (e.g. Keeton 1974). Type I, random search and piloting by familiar landmarks, fails to describe the strategies of homing birds adequately. Cases of seemingly random behaviour of wild birds cannot be interpreted simply as disorientation or random search, because they might represent stress responses to, for example, being captured, handled and displaced, and released in an unfamiliar habitat. The need to feed might also cause displaced wild birds to postpone the start of their homing flight in favour of foraging (reviewed by R. Wiltschko 1992). Type II, mostly discussed in connection with bird migration, would be an inadequate strategy for homing after displacement, because in homing, the birds must be able to determine the varying home course that depends on their present position with respect to home. Thus, all homeward-oriented behaviour at unfamiliar sites and all successful homing had to be subsumed under Type III orientation (Keeton 1974). This 'true navigation', however, could be defined only in a negative way by delimiting it from other concepts: it was more complex than compass orientation, and it was not based on direct cues related to the goal or on familiar landmarks. In short, the term 'true navigation' was used to summarize all the orientation processes that remained enigmatic.

Griffin's Concept of Landmark Use

One aspect of Griffin's Type I orientation, piloting or the orientation by landmarks alone, needs to be discussed in more detail. This idea was first proposed in the 1920s and 1930s (e.g. Rivière 1923; Gundlach 1932) and has occasionally been propagated ever since. The concept is derived from considerations of how we humans are believed to solve spatial problems. Piloting could certainly not be a simple strategy, because it requires birds to remember an enormous number of landmarks and the spatial relationships between them. It is by far more demanding than the use of landmarks together with a compass, as later proposed in the concept of a 'mosaic map' (Graue 1963; Wallraff 1974; W. Wiltschko & Wiltschko 1982, see below). An experimental approach is not easy, mainly because it is generally not possible to obtain positive evidence that homing birds in a given situation use landmarks as navigational cues; the use of other cues can never be excluded.

First attempts to assess the role of landmarks involved releasing homing pigeons with frosted lenses, which deprived them of object vision. On departure, the birds oriented homeward, and many even reached the immediate vicinity of their loft without view of landmarks (e.g. Schlichte 1973; Schmidt-Koenig & Walcott 1978). This was also true when olfactory cues were excluded to force the birds to rely on landmarks (Benvenuti & Fiaschi 1983). These findings indicate that landmarks are redundant for successful navigation, but do not necessarily mean that landmarks are not used when available. However, even at sites where pigeons are very familiar with the local landmarks, they do not follow sequences of landmarks. Instead they use a compass, as has been demonstrated by numerous clock-shift experiments (e.g. Graue 1963; Keeton 1974; Füller et al. 1983; Luschi & Dall'Antonia 1993). Together, these findings do not support a navigational strategy based solely on familiar landmarks.

Recently, the possible role of landmarks and landscape features as orientation cues at familiar sites has met revived attention, and concepts similar to Griffin's Type I orientation have been discussed again (e.g. Wallraff et al. 1999; Kamil & Cheng 2001). This renewed interest was inspired by experiments analysing the role of landmarks in 'small-scale navigation' using closed rooms or aviaries where birds (*Poecile atricapilla, Garrulus glandarius, Nucifraga columbiana, C. livia domestica*) were to search for hidden seed at specific sites (e.g. Cheng & Sherry 1992; Bennett 1993; Chapell & Guilford 1995; Kamil & Jones 1997; Duff et al. 1998). The respective experiments took place within a few square metres, that is, in a limited space that birds can easily scan directly, and the task to pinpoint a certain place within this limited space was fundamentally different from the one that birds are facing in homing experiments, where they have to determine the route to a distant goal outside the direct range of their senses. Hence, any conclusion drawn from these findings regarding navigational strategies (e.g. Kamil & Cheng 2001) would seem problematic.

New homing studies designed to demonstrate navigation by landmarks alone again involved manipulations of the sun compass (Bonadona et al. 2000; Holland et al. 2001). The results do not allow a final conclusion on the role of landmarks; since the flexibility of the sun compass and the role of the magnetic compass were not taken into account, their interpretation remains ambiguous (R. Wiltschko & Wiltschko 2001). Another approach used the technique of releasing birds from boxes that limited their view to the surrounding landscape (e.g. Braithwaite 1993; Burt *et al.* 1997; Biro *et al.* 2001), but it is unclear whether the observed effects indeed reflect an interference with navigational cues. In summary, piloting in the sense of following sequences of familiar landmarks has frequently been discussed as a theoretical possibility, but the evidence cited to support this strategy is not clearcut and also open to other interpretations.

Kramer's 'Map-and-Compass' Model

When Kramer (1953, 1957, 1961) proposed his Map-and-Compass model, he had already described the sun compass (Kramer 1950), the only orientation mechanism known at that time. So it is not surprising that this mechanism became a key element of his model. The model was developed during the controversy about the sun navigation hypothesis proposed by Matthews (1953), in an attempt to clarify the specific role of the sun in the navigational process.

Goal Orientation as a Two-Step Process

Kramer (1957, page 224) described avian homing, or goal orientation, as he termed it, as:
'composed of two fundamentally different steps, one establishing the position of the release place, the other determining the direction of flight. Both steps find their parallel in human orientation, the first being represented by the procedure of studying the map, the latter by consulting the compass'.

In a later review, he formulated this more explicitly (Kramer 1961, pp. 356–357):
'The first (step) would consist of establishing the geographic position of the release site relative to the home site, including the 'theoretical' homing direction. The latter is an immediate deduction from the first: both, therefore, are considered as one step and are called the "map" constituent. The second step would consist of ascertaining the deduced homing direction in the field. This in the analogous human performance, is usually done by means of a compass; it is therefore called the "compass" step.'

This led to the Map-and-Compass model as it is usually given today: in the first step, the displaced bird determines its home direction as a compass course, which corresponds to Kramer's (1961) 'theoretical' direction; in the second step, it uses a compass to locate this course. In other words: the first step produces a specification equivalent to 'south' or 'west' in human terms; in the second step, this course is converted with help of a compass into a direction of flight, that is into a specification of the type 'this way' or 'go there' (Fig. 19-2). Compass orientation had thus been recognized as an integral component of goal orientation.

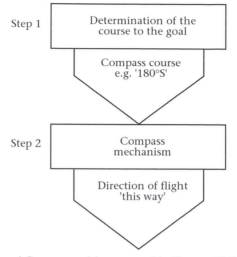

Figure 19-2 The Map-and-Compass model as proposed by Kramer (1953, 1957, 1961) showing homing as a two-step process.

Experimental Evidence for Sun Compass Use

To test the validity of Kramer's model, it was crucial to demonstrate the involvement of compass orientation in navigation. This was done by clock-shift experiments (Schmidt-Koenig 1958): since the sun's progress in the course of the day must be compensated, sun compass use can be demonstrated easily by manipulating the birds' internal clock. For this, pigeons are confined for at least 5 days to a light-sealed room and subjected to a photoperiod that is phase shifted with respect to the natural day. When birds are displaced and released after this treatment, the determination of the home course is unimpaired; when they locate this course with the help of their sun compass, however, their false subjective time results in their misjudging the sun's azimuth. This, in turn, leads to a characteristic, predictable deflection of their vanishing bearings (Fig. 19-3).

Clock-shift experiments widely confirmed the Map-and-Compass model. The deflections induced by clock shifting were found to depend solely on the amount and the direction of the shift, but not on direction and distance of the release site (Fig. 19-3; Kramer 1961; Schmidt-Koenig 1965; Keeton 1974 and many others), indicating that this manipulation indeed affected the compass step only. Clock-shift experiments produced the typical deflections at distances ranging from less than 1.5 km to more than 165 km, with the only exception when pigeons had direct view of their loft (Schmidt-Koenig 1965; Keeton 1974). This means that avian navigation follows the Map-and-Compass model within the entire range studied so far, including areas where local land-marks are familiar to the birds, such as the vicinity of the loft

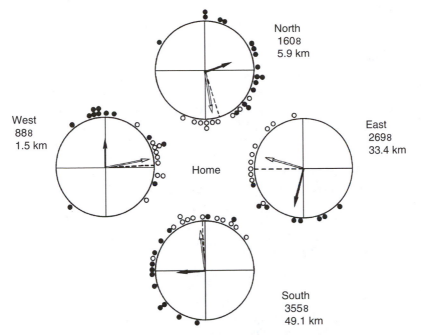

Figure 19-3 Sun compass orientation in pigeons, *Columba livia* f. *domestica*: effects of a 6-h fast shift in the four main compass directions at distances ranging from 1.4 to 50 km. The home direction is indicated by a dashed radius; the symbols at the periphery of the circle mark the vanishing bearings of individual pigeons (○: untreated controls; ●: 6-h fast-shifted pigeons), arrows represent the mean vectors of the respective groups (after Keeton 1979).

(Graue 1963; Keeton 1974; Schmidt-Koenig 1979) or sites from which the pigeons have homed more than 60 times before (e.g. Füller *et al.* 1983). The sun compass seems to be preferred even when alternative cues are available. This evidence emphasizes the crucial role of the sun compass, and thus compass orientation, in avian navigation and homing.

Importance of Kramer's Model

By stating that displaced birds establish their relation to a distant goal with the help of an external reference, Kramer's Map-and-Compass model identifies a fundamental aspect of avian navigation. The model provided a solid theoretical framework for the analysis of navigational processes in birds and other animals. It won wide acceptance, and most researchers studying pigeon homing have discussed their findings in terms of whether an experimental manipulation affects the map step or the compass step of homing.

One implication of the Map-and-Compass model is of crucial importance. When the key element, the involvement of an external reference, was confirmed in numerous clock-shift experiments, these findings excluded certain navigational strategies that had been discussed before, namely all those that do not involve a compass. We have already mentioned piloting based solely on sequences of familiar landmarks, Griffin's Type I orientation. Another navigational strategy excluded is inertial navigation as proposed by Barlow (1964), which corresponds to path integration based entirely on internal signals. Because it would generate the home direction with respect to the bird's own body position, it would not be affected by clock shifting. The experimental confirmation of the Map-and-Compass Model thus restricted considerations to those navigational strategies that indicate the home direction as a compass course.

Expanding Kramer's Model

Kramer (1953, 1957, 1961) did not provide a complete model for homing, however (see Keeton 1974). He named the sun compass as a mechanism for the compass step, but made no statements on possible mechanisms used to determine the home course. The map step remained entirely open.

Considerations on the 'Map'

Wallraff (1974) undertook a theoretical analysis of the map step, discussing the type of factors that might be used and how they might be processed. Starting out from Viguier's (1882) idea of a 'grid map', he suggested a 'map' based on (at least) two environmental gradients, that is, factors whose values continuously change in space. These gradients should intersect at an angle that is not too acute. Birds were assumed to be able to derive their home course from a comparison of the local scalar values at their present site with those remembered from home. Wallraff (1974) discussed in detail how such a 'map' may be used: it is a directionally oriented mental representation of the distribution of the gradients. Birds know their home values and are familiar with the gradient directions, and this allows them to interpret the local gradient values at distant sites. Figure 19-4 illustrates the basic aspects of the model, with the gradient values given relative to the home values. Gradient A increases to the east and gradient B to the south; at site P_1, where both gradients have lower values than at home, a bird 'knows' that it is north and west of home, and that consequently a southeastern course will lead homeward (Wallraff 1974; W. Wiltschko & Wiltschko 1998).

By postulating environmental gradients as components of the 'map', the model provides an explanation for the ability of birds to head homeward when released at distant, unfamiliar sites, because gradients might be extrapolated beyond the range of immediate experience. In the example given in Figure 19-4: if a bird encounters local values of gradient A that are higher than any it has experienced before, it 'knows' that it is further east than ever before and hence has to fly west. The concept of a 'grid map' of gradients can also explain the common observation at pigeon releases that displaced birds rarely head into the true home direction. The observed deviations are typical for a given site. Keeton (1973) coined the term 'release site bias' for this phenomenon when he analysed the behaviour at a site where his pigeons showed a marked clockwise deviation from the home direction in the range of 60°–90°. This 'bias' was not restricted to pigeons, but affected bank swallows, *Riparia riparia,* from a colony near his lofts in the same way (Fig. 19-5). This observation caused Keeton (1973) to attribute release site biases to irregularities of the 'map' (see P_2, P_3 and P_4 in Fig. 19-4).

In the vicinity of the home site, where the local gradient values can no longer be distinguished from the home values, birds must turn to other cues.

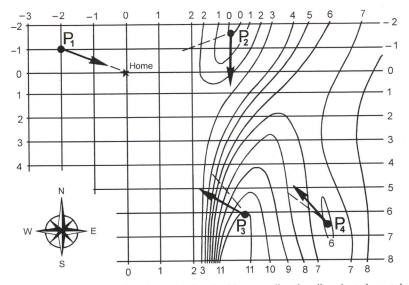

Figure 19-4 Diagram illustrating the navigational grid map, a directionally oriented mental representation of the distribution of environmental gradients. The isolines of two gradients are given in relative units with respect to the home values. Left side: regular course of gradients; right side: irregularities in the course of one gradient lead to initial errors and cause deviations from home. The star labelled 'Home' marks the positon of the home loft, P_1 to P_4 indicate different release sites, with the dashed line representing the true home courses and the arrows representing the home course as derived from the local combination of gradients, leading to release site biases at the sites P_2, P_3 and P_4 (after W. Wiltschko & Wiltschko 1982).

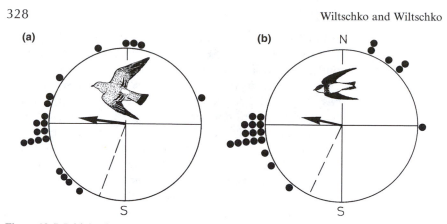

Figure 19-5 Initial orientation of pigeons and bank swallows, *Riparia riparia*, from a nearby colony at Castor Hill, a site 130 km north of the Ithaca loft; both species show the same type of clockwise release site bias. ●: Vanishing bearings of untreated birds; other symbols as in Figure 19-3 (data from Keeton 1973).

Familiar landmarks are the obvious choice. However, because pigeons normally use the sun compass even within a few kilometres of the home loft (Graue 1963; Keeton 1974; Schmidt-Koenig 1979), they do not simply follow sequences of familiar landmarks (see above). Graue (1963) proposed a different way of landmark use, suggesting that familiar landmarks mark positions from which the home course is known. This led to the model of the 'mosaic map' (Wallraff 1974), where landmarks are used in combination with a compass. The mosaic map is assumed to be a directionally oriented mental representation of the distribution of relevant landmarks within the home area (see also W. Wiltschko & Wiltschko 1982, 1998), complementing the grid map of gradients in the vicinity of home. Analogous to the grid map, the mosaic map indicates the home direction as a compass course.

An Alternative Compass Mechanism

Kramer's (1953, 1961) emphasis on the sun compass left open the question of homing under overcast skies. In general, orientation appeared to deteriorate under heavy cloud cover. Yet Keeton (1969) who, unlike other experimenters, also trained his pigeons on cloudy days, reported well-oriented flights under overcast skies. This finding indicated that homing was possible without the sun compass, and, at the first glance, seemed to contradict Kramer's model (Keeton 1974).

An alternative compass mechanism based on the geomagnetic field was first described for European robins, *Erithacus rubecula,* a migrant species

(W. Wiltschko 1968). This magnetic compass is also available to homing pigeons, as indicated by the observation that strong bar magnets on the birds' backs interfered with orientation under overcast skies, but not under sun (Keeton 1971; Ioalè 1984). Walcott & Green (1974) and Visalberghi & Alleva (1979) could make pigeons reverse their direction of flight under overcast skies by changing the magnetic field appropriately with battery-operated coils around the head. Obviously, pigeons rely on the magnetic field for finding directions when the sun is not visible. Because the magnetic compass provides birds with essentially the same type of directional information as the sun compass does, it may replace the sun compass in the second navigational step without violating Kramer's model.

An Alternative Strategy for Determining the Home Course

Similarly, the use of a grid map or a mosaic map as described by Wallraff (1974) is not the only way to determine the home course. Schmidt-Koenig (1965) pointed out that birds could use two fundamentally different strategies, which he termed 'reverse displacement navigation' or 'route reversal' (Schmidt-Koenig 1975) and 'bicoordinate navigation'. The latter relies on site-specific information obtained at the release site and corresponds to the use of a grid map as described by Wallraff (1974), whereas route reversal is based on routebased information obtained during the outward journey. Analogous to a navigational strategy described for desert ants, *Cataglyphis bicolor,* by Wehner (1972), birds were assumed to use a compass as an external reference for path integration.

Navigation based on outward journey information had been discussed as a theoretical possibility before, but its existence was usually discounted (e.g. Wallraff 1974), because in earlier experiments, different means of preventing birds from collecting information during the outward journey had failed to affect their orientation (e.g. Exner 1883; Reynaud 1900; Griffin 1940; Matthews 1951). However, this conclusion is true only for adult, experienced birds. Very young, inexperienced pigeons responded with disorientation when they were transported to the release site without access to the geomagnetic field (Fig. 19-6), indicating that they require magnetic information collected during the outward journey to determine their home course (R. Wiltschko & Wiltschko 1978, 1985a). These birds seem to record the direction of the outward journey using the magnetic field as an external reference, integrating detours, if necessary. This strategy would give them the net course of the outward journey, and, reversing this course, the home direction as a compass course (R. Wiltschko & Wiltschko 1985a, 2000). Using this type of route-specific information is thus in agreement with Kramer's model.

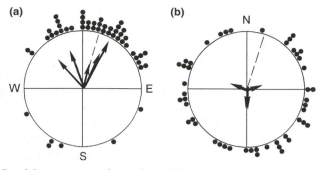

Figure 19-6 Depriving very young, inexperienced pigeons of magnetic information during displacement leads to disorientation. (a) Normally transported control birds, (b) birds deprived of magnetic information. Symbols as in Figure 19-5; the data of five releases at the same site are pooled with arrows representing the five mean vectors (after R. Wiltschko & Wiltschko 1985a).

Our Present Concept of Avian Homing

For the map step as well as for the compass step, birds have more than one option. Hence, our present concept of avian homing, although still based on Kramer's Map-and-Compass model, allows alternative mechanisms for both steps. The two compass mechanisms as well as the two mechanisms determining the home course are not independent, but interrelated through ontogenetic processes.

Ontogenetic Development

When young birds begin to fly, they have only one orientation mechanism, a magnetic compass provided by their innate ability to perceive the direction of the field lines of the geomagnetic field. This compass mechanism seems to form the backbone of their navigational system, because it provides a first means for navigation and homing (Keeton 1971; R. Wiltschko & Wiltschko 1978) and, at the same time, may serve as the directional reference for the learning processes that establish the other components of the fully developed navigational system (W. Wiltschko *et al.* 1983). The respective learning processes apparently take place as soon as the young birds begin to fly, during a sensitive phase where the birds are prepared to pick up the respective information and store it in the required way (R. Wiltschko & Wiltschko 1990).

The sun's arc varies with geographical latitude. To ensure that the bird's compensation mechanisms are closely tuned to the local sun's arc in its home region, the sun compass is based on experience. Young pigeons establish their sun compass by observing the sun's arc at various times of the day (R. Wiltschko & Wiltschko 1980, 1981; R. Wiltschko *et al.* 1981). Associating the sun azimuth with time of day provided by the internal clock and geographical direction provided by the magnetic compass (W. Wiltschko *et al.* 1983), they form an internal representation of the sun curve that provides the basis for the mechanisms compensating for the sun's progress (reviewed by W. Wiltschko & Wiltschko 1998). Similar processes may continue to adapt the compensation mechanisms to seasonal changes (see R. Wiltschko *et al.* 2000).

With the map step, the situation is similar. In the beginning, the young pigeons do not yet have the knowledge required to interpret site-specific factors at the release site. Instead, they seem to rely on information collected during the outward journey, recording the direction of the outward leg of their active flights with the help of their magnetic compass as described earlier for passive displacement (R. Wiltschko & Wiltschko 1978). The birds then apparently use the resulting net course of the outward journey in two ways. First, by reversing the course, they obtain their home course, a strategy that ensures homing during this early phase (R. Wiltschko & Wiltschko 1985a). Second, by associating it with local site-specific information, they can form mental representations of the distribution of local navigation cues, resulting in the mosaic map of landmarks in the vicinity of their home and the grid map of gradients later used to determine the home course at distant sites (see W. Wiltschko & Wiltschko 1998; R. Wiltschko & Wiltschko 2000).

Figure 19-7 illustrates the proposed ontogenetic relations between these mechanisms and strategies. For both steps of the navigational process, first mechanisms based on the magnetic compass, an innate mechanism, seem to be used to establish, by learning, rather complex, experience-based mechanisms that are perfectly tuned to the situation in the bird's home region.

The Mature Navigational System

With the magnetic compass and the sun compass, adult birds have two compass mechanisms. This raises questions about their relative importance. For a long time, the magnetic compass was considered a mere backup system for overcast days. The observation that shifting the pigeons' internal clock results in characteristic deflections (Fig. 19-3), although the magnetic compass provides pigeons with correct directional information, seemed to indicate that compass information from the sun dominates that from the geomagnetic field. The latter is not ignored, however. A quantitative analysis of the deflections induced by clock shifting (R. Wiltschko *et al.* 1994) and recent experiments with clock-shifted pigeons carrying magnets (R. Wiltschko & Wiltschko 2001) indicate that both systems are normally used together, with both contributing to deciding in which direction to fly.

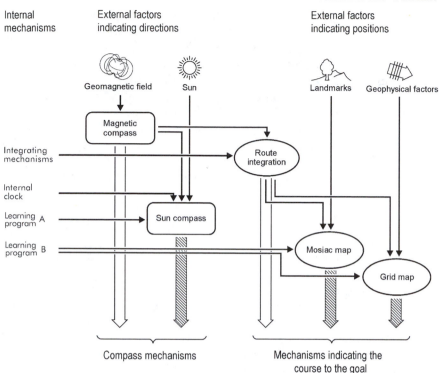

Figure 19-7 Proposed model of ontogenetic development of the avian navigational system based on the innate magnetic compass, route integration mechanisms, internal clock and learning programs. Wide open arrows: mechanisms based solely on innate components; wide hatched arrows: learned mechanisms.

Experienced birds also have two possible strategies for determining their home course. The numerous unsuccessful attempts to affect initial orientation and homing success by depriving pigeons of outward journey information (e.g. Exner 1883; Griffin 1940; Wallraff 1980 and others) appear to suggest that this type of navigational information is of little importance to adult birds; they normally rely on site-specific information obtained at the release site, using their 'maps' to determine the home course. The reasons for this change in strategy from route-based to site-specific information are obvious: a home course derived from route-based information depends entirely on the accuracy of recording and processing that information; it leaves the birds without any possibility to correct mistakes. Birds using their 'maps', in contrast, can redetermine their home course as often as necessary; initial mistakes are of little importance, because they can easily be corrected (R. Wiltschko & Wiltschko 1985a).

One frequently observed initial 'mistake' involves release site biases, which cause birds to depart in directions that are different from the true home direction.

Release site biases have mostly been attributed to local irregularities in the distribution of the map factors that indicate a course different from the true home course (e.g. Keeton 1973; see P_2, P_3 and P_4 in Fig. 19-4). Because very young pigeons normally do not show biases, the occurrence of release site biases has been taken as an indication for 'map' use (e.g. W. Wiltschko & Wiltschko 1982). An alternative interpretation (Wallraff 1978, 1986) attributed release site biases to a tendency to fly in a 'preferred compass direction', which, together with the home course, would determine the departure direction after release. This hypothesis led to the prediction that sites with similar home directions would have similar biases. The biases observed at such sites, however, often differ markedly (R. Wiltschko & Wiltschko 1985b). Because, in nature, environmental gradients cannot be expected to be perfectly regularly distributed, local irregularities of the grid map still offer the simplest explanation for the observed deviations from home (R. Wiltschko 1993). For the birds, the initial deviations might mean a certain detour, but because their 'map' allows them to check and correct their course frequently during the return trip, this is only a small disadvantage compared with the increase in security provided by the use of the 'map'.

Although adult pigeons can successfully navigate without outward journey information, it is not clear to what extent this type of information is used when it is available. The use of route-based navigational information is hard to demonstrate since, in most cases, route-specific and site-specific information must be expected to be in fairly good agreement. However, Wallraff *et al.* (1980) reported that the vanishing bearings of pigeons in Italy were slightly less well homeward-oriented when they had no access to outward journey information. A study in Germany indicated a similar phenomenon: although a second-order statistic did not reveal a significant difference in orientation between the adult pigeons transported with and without outward journey information, there were a few releases where the experimental birds showed markedly larger deviations from the home course than did the control birds (R. Wiltschko & Wiltschko 1985a). These observations may suggest that although adult birds mainly rely on their 'map', outward journey information may continue to minimize to some extent the effects of local irregularities in the distribution of map factors.

The 'Compass Principle'

Kramer originally advanced his Map-and-Compass model to describe the navigational processes of homing. However, its key element, the idea that the relation to a distant goal is established with the help of an external reference, applies to other avian navigation tasks as well.

Owing to their ability to fly, birds are highly motile and can cover long distances quickly; they range much further than do other animals of comparable size. As a result, birds intending to visit a certain site rarely have direct contact with their goal. This means that they cannot be guided by cues from the goal itself, but have to establish contact with the goal indirectly with the help of cues that are accessible at their present location as well as at the goal site. The geomagnetic field and celestial cues possess the required characteristic, and both are used as references for compass mechanisms. The crucial question concerns the mechanisms that provide the respective course leading to the desired goal.

Navigation within the Home Range

Every bird has to master the navigational tasks within its home area in a fast and efficient way to minimize energy expenditure and exposure to predators. However, spontaneous flights cannot be experimentally analysed. All we know about the homing mechanisms of birds is inferred from displacement experiments, which represent an unnatural interference. But the magnetic compass, the sun compass, the grid map and the mosaic map indicated by these experiments must have evolved to solve the navigation problems that birds face daily under natural conditions. This conclusion implies that birds make use of these mechanisms for return when roaming around their home range.

During the outward journey, birds will use similar mechanisms. Often, they may just fly about and look around where crucial resources are available at the moment. However, having found a rich food source, a convenient water hole or a source of suitable nesting material, they may remember the position of that site. How they do this is not completely known. The observation that pigeons normally use their sun compass even in the vicinity of their loft (Graue 1963; Keeton 1974; Schmidt-Koenig 1979) suggests that a compass might be involved. Experiments with corvids (*Aphelocoma californica, Gymnorhinus cyanocephalus, Nucifraga columbiana*) that cached and recovered seeds also indicate that compass orientation is a component of spatial memory (W. Wiltschko *et al.* 2000). Birds might store the compass course leading from home to a site of interest in memory to have it available when they want to visit the site again.

Birds thus might be expected to 'know' by experience a set of courses leading to relevant points within their home range, and probably also the courses between those points. This conclusion means that the mental representation of a bird's home range includes not only courses leading from prominent sites back to a 'home' or nest, as expressed by the concept of the mosaic map, but also the reversed courses to be used when birds leave home and go foraging, etc. Normal movements within the home range, if the birds are not searching at random, may thus represent flying compass directions, with the courses for the outward journey stored in memory, and those for the return trip provided by homing mechanisms, where the use of the 'maps' is, of course, a way to use memorized information.

Navigation during Migration

Migration means leaving the home area and moving to a distant region on earth, where a new home area will be established. The navigational task not only involves different spatial dimensions, but young first-time migrants have to reach an unfamiliar goal area, the population-specific winter quarters. Large-scale displacements with migrants during autumn migration (e.g. *Accipiter nisus*: Drost 1938; *Sturnus vulgaris, Fringilla coelebs*: Perdeck 1958) revealed an important difference between adult and juvenile migrants: adult birds compensated for the displacement and many of them reached their traditional winter quarters, but the first-time migrants continued in their migratory directions, ending up in a new wintering area that was shifted from the traditional one by the amount of the displacement (Fig. 19-8). In spring, however, the displaced young starlings, *S. vulgaris*, returned to their traditional breeding area (Perdeck 1958, 1983), as did young migrants displaced during spring migration (Perdeck 1974). Obviously, migrants en route towards a familiar goal can head towards it directly and change their course accordingly, but first-time migrants not yet familiar with the goal area cannot do so and maintain their normal migratory direction (see also Mouritsen & Larsen 1998). This evidence of fundamentally different strategies in first-time and experienced migrants is an interesting parallel to homing, where very young, inexperienced pigeons also use a strategy and mechanisms that are different from those used by older, experienced birds.

Numerous cage experiments, mostly with passerines migrating at night, have shown that both inexperienced and experienced migrants use the magnetic compass, a star compass and sunset-related cues at dusk for locating directions; the latter two mechanisms are a special development of nocturnal migrants (reviewed in W. Wiltschko *et al.* 1998). The sun compass is ill-suited for large-scale movements across geographical longitudes and latitudes because of its dependence on geographical postion and does not seem to be important (Munro & Wiltschko 1993); an exception may be in shorebirds in the high Arctic (Alerstam *et al.* 2001). Thus, the compass mechanisms appear to be the same in first-time migrants and older migrants; the crucial difference seems to lie in how the respective compass course is provided.

The displacement experiments mentioned above as well as cage studies with hand-reared migrants (e.g. *Passerina cyanea*: Emlen 1970; *Ficedula hypoleuca*: Beck & Wiltschko 1982) show that inexperienced migrants rely on innate information to reach their still unknown goal. An endogenous migration

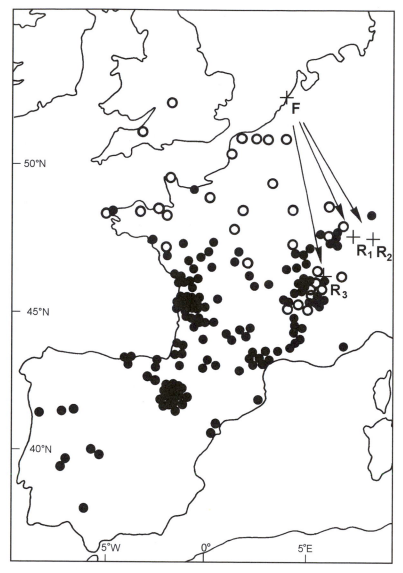

Figure 19-8 Displacement experiments with starlings, *Sturnus vulgaris,* during autumn migration. Birds of Baltic origin were migrating on a southwesterly course to their winter quarters in northern France and southern England, when they were caught as transmigrants at site F near Den Haag, Holland, and displaced to Switzerland, where they were released at the sites R_1, R_2 and R_3. Circles mark the sites of ringing recoveries during autumn and winter following displacement (o: adult migrants; •: juvenile first-time migrants; data from Perdeck 1958).

program (e.g. Berthold 1988 for European warblers, genus *Sylvia*) indicates the position of wintering area with respect to birthplace in polar coordinates, as a direction (or sequence of directions) and a distance to be travelled, the latter defined by a time program that controls the amount and duration of migratory activity (e.g. Gwinner 1986; Berthold 1991). A recently developed model based on these assumptions was found to be in agreement with ringing recoveries (Mouritsen 1998). Information on direction and distance are both passed genetically from one generation to the next (Berthold & Querner 1981; Helbig 1992).

The information on direction must be converted into a compass course. The processes providing this course take place during the premigratory period so that the migratory course is available when the young birds are ready to start migration (reviewed by W. Wiltschko *et al.* 1998). Two reference systems are involved, the geomagnetic field indicating magnetic North (e.g. Beck & Wiltschko 1982; Bletz *et al.* 1996) and celestial rotation indicating geographical North, indicated by the rotating stars at night (e.g. Emlen 1970; Able & Able 1990) and by the rotating pattern of polarized light during daytime (Able & Able 1993; Weindler *et al.* 1998). The conversion of the innate information on the migratory direction into the population-specific migration course in passerines normally requires both reference systems (Weindler *et al.* 1996). The complex interactions between celestial rotation, providing geographical South as a reference direction, and the magnetic field indicating the population-specific deviation from this reference, have been described in detail (W. Wiltschko *et al.* 1998). Here, migrants appear to have found solutions that are perfectly tuned to their needs. Routes taken by Arctic shore-birds led Alerstam *et al.* (2001) to suggest a different mechanism specifically adapted to the situation in the high Arctic. Once the migration course is established, young migrants can locate it with the help of their compass mechanisms. Thus, formally, migratory orientation in first-time migrants also seems to be a two-step process, with the first step converting innate information to provide the compass course, and the second step turning this course into an actual direction to fly with the help of a compass.

On their return trip and all later migrations, the situation for migrants has entirely changed: any migration after the first means homing to a familiar goal. Because migrants have stayed before at their goal areas (the birth place or former breeding site in spring, a former site that allowed successful wintering in autumn), these regions are well known to the birds. They would be familiar with the local navigational factors and have a navigational 'map' of their goal area. The 'map' of migrants may also include the terrain of the migration route crossed during previous migrations, because migrants must be expected to familiarize themselves with the distribution of navigational factors encountered en route. This means that, from their second migration onwards, migrants no longer have to rely solely on inherited information. Cage studies suggest that aninnate course is still available during later migrations (e.g. Helbig 1991); but displacement experiments during migration (e.g. Drost 1938; Perdeck 1958, 1974, 1983) show that experienced migrants modify this course if necessary to head directly towards the now-familiar goal (Fig. 19-8). The course for the second and later migrations thus appears to be provided mainly by navigational processes.

The navigational mechanisms used by experienced migrants, which allow individual birds to return to the same tree for breeding year after year after having completed a journey of up to several thousand kilometres, have not been experimentally analysed. It is reasonable to assume, however, that migrants rely on the same mechanisms that displaced homing pigeons use to return. We must expect, however, that the 'map' of migratory birds is adapted to the greater spatial dimensions and the specific requirements of migration. The 'map' would thus be considerably larger, reflecting the birds' extended spatial experience, and may also include cues that are helpful when distances of more than a thousand kilometres have to be covered. Nevertheless, the 'map' appears to meet limitations when birds are displaced far from their normal migration routes (e.g. Perdeck 1967). As in homing, using map information makes reaching the goal area more secure and minimizes the effect of unavoidable interferences such as winddrift and delay because of adverse weather. This may be why in migratory orientation, as in homing, there is a change in strategy as migrants gain experience: first-time migrants have to rely on innate information, but experienced migrants can use their experience in navigational processes.

Common Traits in Avian Navigation

The idea that birds establish contact with a distant goal with the help of an external reference allows us to suggest analogous structures in different orientation processes. The model of a two-step process originally described for homing can be applied to navigation tasks within the home range and to migration as well (Fig. 19-9). The first step that provides the course to the goal involves a variety of mechanisms according to the specific nature of the task: memory, navigation processes and genetic coding (e.g. R. Wiltschko & Wiltschko 1995). For the second step, the magnetic compass and celestial compass mechanisms are available.

Another common characteristic of homing and migratory orientation is the change in strategy with increasing experience, which mainly concerns the mechanisms providing the compass course (e.g. Perdeck 1958; R. Wiltschko & Wiltschko 1985a). Navigation by young, inexperienced birds must be based on innate mechanisms, because other mechanisms are not yet available. In homing, very young, inexperienced birds use path integration with the magnetic compass as an external reference (e.g. R. Wiltschko & Wiltschko 1978, 2000); in migration, the first-time migrants are guided by the inherited migration

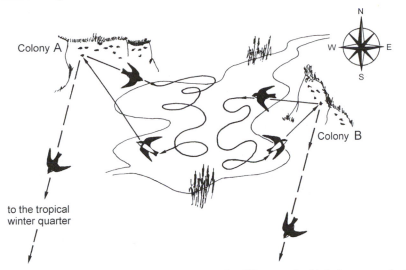

Colony A

to the tropical
winter quarter

Colony B

Figure 19-9 Bank swallows use compass orientation for different tasks: birds from two colonies fly different courses acquired by experience to reach a nearby lake: an easterly course from colony A and a westerly course from colony B. Their return courses depend on where they decide to head home and is determined by navigational processes. For autumn migration, birds from both colonies head southward towards their tropical winter quarters (dashed line); in this case, their course is first determined by genetically coded information, on later migrations also by navigational processes (from R. Wiltschko & Wiltschko 1995).

program (e.g. Berthold 1988), using the geomagnetic field and celestial rotation as reference (e.g. W. Wiltschko *et al.* 1998). These innate mechanisms would ensure that inexperienced birds reach their goal areas, at the same time giving them an opportunity to obtain the information needed to form the complex, experience-based mechanism preferentially used by experienced birds. These 'maps' allow birds to use site-specific information and thus offer more precision and security in reaching the desired goal in homing as well as in migration.

Outlook

Focusing on the key feature of Kramer's (1953, 1961) model, the 'compass principle' emphasizes the common structure of avian navigational processes: regardless of the specific mechanisms used, birds always establish the direction to distant goals with the help of an external reference as a compass course, a procedure that appears to reflect a general characteristic of the birds' way to code and memorize spatial information (W. Wiltschko & Wiltschko 1998). This principle provides a solid theoretical background for analysing navigational processes and asking specific questions about the different cues used in orientation and navigation.

Although the general structure of the avian navigational system is largely understood, the corresponding terminology is not always clear. Attempts to introduce specific names for particular strategies have led to a surplus of terms that often causes confusion rather than clarity. When classifying types of spatial orientation, it seems crucial to distinguish between cases where birds (and other animals) have direct contact with their goal on the one hand, and cases where birds establish contact with their goal indirectly with the help of an external reference on the other hand. That is, we must distinguish between direct responses to cues from the goal or 'beaconing' (Holland et al. 2001), and 'navigation', where the direction to the goal is obtained as a compass course. We use the term navigation here in this broad, general sense to characterize the typical way that birds proceed in distance orientation.

The most important problems in avian navigation, however, do not concern theoretical questions, but rather the environmental cues used as navigational factors. In the compass step, the factors are largely clear; the geomagnetic field and celestial cues such as the sun and, in migrants, the stars and the pattern of polarized light, are used to locate compass courses. Even the interactions between the different types of compass information are fairly well understood, although the number of bird species studied is still limited. The same is true for the factors providing the reference system for the innate migratory direction of young migrants. What is still largely unknown, however, is the nature of the factors allowing birds to determine their home course from distant, unfamiliar sites: the components of the grid map of gradients. Speculations about these factors date back to the 19th century, when Viguier (1882) suggested that parameters of the geomagnetic field may be such components. In the middle of the 20th century, Yeagley (1951) proposed a navigation model based on the Coriolis force, which originates in the rotation of the earth, and magnetic vertical intensity, and Matthews (1953) advanced the sun navigation hypothesis. Neither hypothesis has been supported by experimental evidence and both are considered refuted. More recently, Papi (1982) proposed navigation by specific distributions of odours and Walker (1998) again suggested magnetic parameters as navigational factors. All these models have in common that they attempt to explain avian navigation by attributing it to only one or two specific types of factors. Other researchers, assuming a multifactorial 'map', tried to identify at least one component of the 'map' and discussed environmental factors such as total intensity of the geomagnetic field (e.g. Walcott 1980), intensity of gravity (Lednor & Walcott 1984), as well as the changing visual appearance of landscape features (Baker 1984) or infrasound (Schöps & Wiltschko 1994; Hagstrum 2001). The evidence leaves open many questions and does not yet form a consistent picture. The lasting debate on the role of different cues, in particular magnetic parameters and odours, has been detailed extensively (e.g. Papi 1986; Wallraff 1999, 2001; R. Wiltschko & Wiltschko 1995; Able 1996; R. Wiltschko 1996); the discussion is still controversial. The identification of the map factors is indeed one of the most urgent problems in avian navigation.

Other questions concern the neurobiological basis of navigation. They begin with the mechanisms of magnetoreception (e.g. Ritz *et al.* 2000; W. Wiltschko & Wiltschko 2002) and the perception of polarized light (e.g. Able 1982; Able & Able 1993), which are not yet known in detail. The sun compass is probably based on visual input of the eyes, but it is still unclear where this input is combined with the internal clock to derive directions. In general, little is known about the parts of the brain involved in processing navigational information, which requires combining multimodal input. First attempts to clarify the potential role of some brain regions, in particular the hippocampal formation, in pigeon homing have been summarized by Bingman *et al.* (1998). However, in this field of research, the analysis is still at the very beginning and will require considerable research efforts in the future to understand fully how navigational information is obtained and processed.

Acknowledgments

We thank Robert C. Beason, University of Louisiana at Monroe, and Ariane Etienne, Université de Genève, for their help in obtaining older literature, all our friends and colleagues who helped us with many valuable discussions, and Klaus Schmidt-Koenig, Universität Tübingen, and two anonymous referees for critically reading the manuscript. We also thank Cambridge University Press for permission to include the quote from Griffin (1952a).

References

Able, K. P. 1980. Mechanisms of orientation, navigation and homing. In: *Animal Migration, Orientation and Navigation* (Ed. by S. A. Gauthreaux), pp. 283–373. New York: Academic Press.

Able, K. P. 1982. Skylight polarization patterns at dusk influence migratory orientation in birds. *Nature,* **299,** 550–551.

Able, K. P. 1996. The debate over olfactory navigation by homing pigeons. *Journal of Experimental Biology,* **199,** 121–124.

Able, K. P. & Able, M. A. 1990. Calibration of the magnetic compass of a migratory bird by celestial rotation. *Nature,* **347,** 378–380.

Able, K. P. & Able, M. A. 1993. Daytime calibration of magnetic orientation in a migratory bird requires a view of skylight polarization. *Nature,* **364,** 523–525.

Adler, H. E. 1970. Ontogeny and phylogeny of orientation. In: *Development and Evolution of Behavior: Essays in Memory of T. C. Schneirla* (Ed. by R. Aronson, E. Tobach, D. S. Lehrmann & J. S. Rosenblatt), pp. 303–336. San Francisco: W. H. Freeman.

Alerstam, T., Gudmundson, G. A., Green, M. & Hedenström, A. 2001. Migration along ortho-dromic sun compass routes by Arctic birds. *Science,* **291,** 300–303.

Baker, R. R. 1984. *Bird Navigation: The Solution of a Mystery?* London: Hodder & Stoughton.

Barlow, J. S. 1964. Inertial navigation as a basis for animal navigation. *Journal of Theoretical Biology,* **6,** 76–117.

Beck, W. & Wiltschko, W. 1982. The magnetic field as reference system for the genetically encoded migratory direction in pied flycatchers, *Ficedula hypoleuca. Zeitschrift für Tierpsychologie,* **60,** 41–46.

Bellrose, F. C. 1972. Possible steps in the evolutionary development of bird navigation. In: *Animal Orientation and Navigation, NASA SP-262* (Ed. by S. R. Galler, K. Schmidt-Koenig, G. J. Jacobs & R. E. Belleville), pp. 223–258. Washington, D.C.: U.S. Government Printing Office.

Bennett, A. T. D. 1993. Spatial memory in a food storing corvid: near tall landmarks are prima-rily used. *Journal of Comparative Physiology A,* **173,** 193–207.

Benvenuti, S. & Fiaschi, V. 1983. Pigeon homing: combined effect of olfactory deprivation and visual impairment. *Comparative Biochemistry and Physiology A,* **76,** 719–725.

Berthold, P. 1988. The control of migration in European warblers. In: *Acta XIX Congressus Internationalis Ornithologici* (Ed. by H. Ouellet), pp. 215–249. Ottawa: University of Ottawa Press.

Berthold, P. 1991. Spatiotemporal programmes and genetics of orientation. In: *Orientation in Birds* (Ed. by P. Berthold), pp. 86–105. Basel: Birkhäuser Verlag.

Berthold, P. & Querner, U. 1981. Genetic basis of migratory behavior in European warblers. *Science,* **212,** 77–79.

Bingman, V. P., Riters, L. V., Strasser, R. & Gargliardo, A. 1998. Neuroethology of avian navi-gation. In: *Animal Cognition in Nature* (Ed. by R. P. Balda, I. M. Pepperberg & A. C. Kamil), pp. 201–222. San Diego: Academic Press.

Biro, D., Guilford, T. & Dawkins, M. 2001. Visually-mediated site recognition by the homing pigeon may rely on a snapshot-like mechanism. In: *Orientation and Navigation: Birds, Humans and other Animals.* Paper 14. Oxford: Royal Institute of Navigation.

Bletz, H., Weindler, P., Wiltschko, R., Wiltschko, W. & Berthold, P. 1996. The magnetic field as reference for the innate migratory direction in blackcaps, *Sylvia atricapilla. Naturwissenschaften,* **83,** 430–432.

Bonadona, F., Holland, R., Dall'Antonia, L., Guilford, T. & Benvenuti, S. 2000. Tracking clock-shifted homing pigeons from familiar release sites. *Journal of Experimental Biology,* **203,** 207–212.

Braithwaite, V. A. 1993. When does previewing the landscape affect pigeon homing? *Ethology,* **95,** 141–151.

Burt, T., Holland, R. & Guilford, T. 1997. Further evidence for visual landmark involvement in the pigeons's familiar area map. *Animal Behaviour,* **53,** 1203–1209.

Casamajor, J. 1927. Le mystérieux 'sens de l'espace'. *Revue Scientifique,* **65,** 554–565.

Chapell, J. & Guilford, T. 1995. Homing pigeons primarily use the sun compass rather than fixed directional cues in an open-field arena food-searching task. *Proceedings of the Royal Society London, Series B,* **260,** 59–63.

Cheng, K. & Sherry, D. F. 1992. Landmark-based spatial memory in birds (*Parus atricapillus* and *Columba livia*): the use of edges and distances to represent spatial positions. *Journal of Comparative Psychology,* **106,** 331–341.

Claparède, E. 1903. La faculté d'orientation lointaine. *Archives de Psychologie (Genève),* **2,** 133–180.

Darwin, C. 1873. Origin of certain instincts. *Nature,* **7,** 417–418.

Dircksen, R. 1932. Die Biologie des Austernfischers, der Brandseeschwalbe und der Küstenseeschwalbe. *Journal für Ornithologie,* **80,** 427–521.

Drost, R. 1938. Über den Einfluß von Verfrachtungen zur Herbstzugzeit auf den Sperber, Accipiter nisus (L.). In: *Comprerendu IXe Congrès Ornithologique International* (Ed. by J. Delacour), pp. 503–521. Rouen.

Duff, S. J., Brownlie, L. A., Sherry, D. F. & Sangster, M. 1998. Sun compass and landmark orientation by black-capped chickadees (*Parus atricapillus*). *Journal of Experimental Psychology: Animal Behaviour Processes,* **24,** 243–253.

Emlen, S. T. 1970. Celestial rotation: its importance in the development of migratory orientation. *Science,* **170,** 1198–1201.

Exner, S. 1883. Negative Versuchsergebnisse über das Orientierungsvermügen der Brieftauben. *Sitzungsberichte der Akademie der Wissenchaften zu Wien, Mathematisch-Naturwissenschaftliche Klasse III,* **102,** 318–331.

Füller, E., Kowalski, U. & Wiltschko, R. 1983. Orientation of homing pigeons: compass orientation vs. piloting by familiar landmarks. *Journal of Comparative Physiology,* **153,** 55–58.

Graue, L. C. 1963. The effect of phase shifts in the day-night cycle on pigeon homing at distances of less than one mile. *Ohio Journal of Science,* **63,** 214–217.

Griffin, D. R. 1940. Homing experiments with Leach's petrels. *Auk,* **57,** 61–74.

Griffin, D. R. 1944. The sensory basis of bird navigation. *Quarterly Review of Biology,* **19,** 15–31.

Griffin, D. R. 1952a. Bird navigation. *Biological Reviews of the Cambridge Philosophical Society,* **27,** 359–400.

Griffin, D. R. 1952b. Airplane observations of homing pigeons. *Bulletin of the Museum of Comparative Zoology,* **107,** 411–440.

Griffin, D. R. 1955. Bird navigation. In: *Recent Studies in Avian Biology* (Ed. by A. Wolfson), pp. 154–197. Urbana, Illinois: University of Illinois Press.

Groot, C. 1982. Modification on a theme: a perspective on migratory behavior of Pacific salmon. In: *Proceedings of the Salmon and Trout Migratory Behavior Symposium* (Ed. by E. L. Brannon & E. O. Salo), pp. 1–21. Seattle: University of Washington Press.

Gundlach, R. H. 1932. A field study of homing in pigeons. *Journal of Comparative Psychology,* **13,** 397–402.

Gwinner, E. 1986. Circannual rhythm in the control of avian migration. *Advances in the Study of Behaviour,* **16,** 191–228.

Hagstrum, J. T. 2001. Infrasound and the avian navigational map. In: *Orientation and Navigation: Birds, Humans and other Animals.* Paper 43. Oxford: Royal Institute of Navigation.

Heinroth, O. & Heinroth, K. 1941. Das Heimfindevermögen der Brieftauben. *Journal für Ornithologie,* **89,** 213–256.

Helbig, A. J. 1991. Inheritance of migratory direction in a bird species: a cross breeding experiment with SE- and SW-migrating blackcaps (*Sylvia atricapilla*). *Behavioral Ecology and Sociobiology,* **28,** 9–12.

Helbig, A. J. 1992. Ontogenetic stability of inherited directions in a nocturnal bird migrant: comparison between the first and second year of life. *Ethology, Ecology and Evolution,* **4,** 375–388.

Holland, R., Bonadona, F., Dall'Antonia, L., Benvenuti, S., Burt de Perera, T. & Guilford, T. 2001. Short distance phase shifts revisited: tracking clock-shifted homing pigeons (rock dove *Columba livia*) close to the loft. *Ibis,* **142,** 111–118.

Ioalè, P. 1984. Magnets and pigeon orientation. *Monitore Zoologico Italiano (N.S.),* **18,** 347–358.

Kamil, A. C. & Cheng, K. 2001. Way-finding and landmarks: the multiple-bearing hypothesis. *Journal of Experimental Biology,* **204,** 103–113.

Kamil, A. C. & Jones, J. E. 1997. The seed-storing corvid Clark's nutcracker learns geometric relationships among landmarks. *Nature,* **390,** 276–279.

Keeton, W. T. 1969. Orientation by pigeons: is the sun necessary? *Science,* **165,** 922–928.

Keeton, W. T. 1971. Magnets interfere with pigeon homing. *Proceedings of the National Academy of Sciences, U.S.A.,* **68,** 102–106.

Keeton, W. T. 1973. Release-site bias as a possible guide to the 'map' component in pigeon homing. *Journal of Comparative Physiology,* **86,** 1–16.

Keeton, W. T. 1974. The orientational and navigational basis of homing in birds. *Advances in the Study of Behavior,* **5,** 47–132.

Keeton, W. T. 1979. Pigeon navigation. In: *Neural Mechanisms of Behavior in the Pigeons* (Ed. by A. M. Granda & J. H. Maxwell), pp. 5–20. New York: Plenum.

Kramer, G. 1950. Weitere Analyse der Faktoren, welche die Zugaktivität des gekäfigten Vogels orientieren. *Naturwissen-schaften,* **37,** 377–378.

Kramer, G. 1953. Wird die Sonnenhöhe bei der Heimfindeorientierung verwertet? *Journal für Ornithologie,* **94,** 201–219.

Kramer, G. 1957. Experiments in bird orientation and their interpretation. *Ibis,* **99,** 196–227.

Kramer, G. 1961. Long-distance orientation. In: *Biology and Comparative Physiology of Birds* (Ed. by A. J. Marshall), pp. 341–371. London: Academic Press.

Kramer, G. & von Saint Paul, U. 1952. Heimkehrleistungen von Brieftauben ohne Richtungsdressur. *Verhandlungen der Deutschen Zoologischen Gesellschaft in Wilhelmshaven,* **1951,** 172–178.

Lack, D. & Lockley, R. M. 1938. Skokholm bird homing experiments. I. 1936–37: puffins, storm-petrels and manx shearwater. *British Birds,* **31,** 242–248.

Lednor, A. J. & Walcott, C. 1984. The orientation of pigeons at gravity anomalies. *Journal of Experimental Biology,* **111,** 259–265.

Luschi, P. & Dall'Antonia, P. 1993. Anosmic pigeons orient from familiar sites by relying on the map and compass mechanism. *Animal Behaviour,* **46,** 1195–1203.

Matthews, G. V. T. 1951. The experimental investigation in homing pigeons. *Journal of Experimental Biology,* **28,** 508–536.

Matthews, G. V. T. 1953. Sun navigation in homing pigeons. *Journal of Experimental Biology,* **30,** 243–267.

Mouritsen, H. 1998. Modelling migration: the clock-and-compass model can explain the distribution of ringing recoveries. *Animal Behaviour,* **56,** 899–907.

Mouritsen, H. & Larsen, O. N. 1998. Migrating young pied flycatchers, *Ficedula hypoleuca,* do not compensate for geographic displacement. *Journal of Experimental Biology,* **201,** 2927–2934.

Munro, U. & Wiltschko, R. 1993. Clock-shift experiments with migratory Yellow-faced Honeyeaters, *Lichenostomus chrysops* (Meliphagidae), an Australian day-migrating bird. *Journal of Experimental Biology,* **181,** 233–244.

Papi, F. 1982. Olfaction and homing in pigeons: ten years of experiments. In: *Avian Navigation* (Ed. by F. Papi & H. G. Wallraff), pp. 149–159. Berlin: Springer Verlag.

Papi, F. 1986. Pigeon navigation: solved problems and open questions. *Monitore Zoologico Italiano,* **20,** 471–517.

Perdeck, A. C. 1958. Two types of orientation in migrating *Sturnus vulgaris and Fringilla coelebs* as revealed by displacement experiments. *Ardea,* **46,** 1–37.

Perdeck, A. C. 1967. Orientation of starlings after displacement to Spain. *Ardea,* **55,** 194–202.

Perdeck, A. C. 1974. An experiment on the orientation of juvenile starlings during spring migration. *Ardea,* **62,** 190–195.

Perdeck, A. C. 1983. An experiment on the orientation of juvenile starlings during spring migration: an addendum. *Ardea,* **71,** 255.

Reynaud, G. 1898. The laws of orientation among animals. *Revue des Deux Mondes (Paris),* **146,** 380–402.

Reynaud, G. 1900. The orientation of birds. *Bird-Lore,* **2,** 141–147.

Ritz, T., Adem, S. & Schulten, K. 2000. A model for vision-based magnetoreception in birds. *Biophysical Journal,* **78,** 707–718.

Rivière, B. B. 1923. Homing pigeons and pigeon racing. *British Birds,* **17,** 118–138.

Rüppell, W. 1934. Versuche zur Ortstreue und Fernorientierung der Vögel. III. Heimfindeversuche mit Rauchschwalben (*Hirundo rustica*) und Mehlschwalben (*Delichon urbica*) von H. Warnat (Berlin-Charlottenburg). *Vogelzug,* **5,** 161–166.

Rüppell, W. 1935. Heimfindeversuche mit Staren 1934. *Journal für Ornithologie,* **83,** 462–524.

Schlichte, H. J. 1973. Untersuchungen über die Bedeutung optischer Parameter für das Heimkehrverhalten der Brieftauben. *Zeitschrift für Tierpsychologie,* **32,** 257–280.

Schmidt-Koenig, K. 1958. Experimentelle Einflußnahme auf die 24-Stunden-Periodik bei Brieftauben und deren Auswirkung unter besonderer Berücksichtigung des Heimfindevermögens. *Zeitschrift für Tierpsychologie*, **15**, 301–331.

Schmidt-Koenig, K. 1965. Current problems in bird orientation. *Advances in the Study of Behavior*, **1**, 217–276.

Schmidt-Koenig, K. 1975. *Migration and Homing in Animals*. Berlin: Springer-Verlag.

Schmidt-Koenig, K. 1979. *Avian Orientation and Navigation*. London: Academic Press.

Schmidt-Koenig, K. & Walcott, C. 1978. Tracks of pigeons with frosted lenses. *Animal Behaviour*, **26**, 480–486.

Schöps, M. & Wiltschko, W. 1994. Orientation of homing pigeons deprived of infrasound. *Journal für Ornithologie*, **135**, 415.

Viguier, C. 1882. Le sens de l'orientation et ses organes chez les animaux et chez l'homme. *Revue Philosophique de la France et de l'Étranger*, **14**, 1–36.

Visalberghi, E. & Alleva, E. 1979. Magnetic influences on pigeon homing. *Biologica Bulletino*, **125**, 246–256.

Walcott, C. 1980. Magnetic orientation in homing pigeons. *IEEE Transactions on Magnetics*, **Mag-16**, 1008–1013.

Walcott, C. & Green, R. P. 1974. Orientation of homing pigeons altered by a change in the direction of the applied magnetic field. *Science*, **184**, 180–182.

Walker, M. M. 1998. On a wing and a vector: a model for magnetic navigation in birds. *Journal of Theoretical Biology*, **192**, 341–349.

Wallraff, H. G. 1974. *Das Navigationssystem der Vögel. Ein theoretischer Beitrag zur Analyse ungeklärter Orientierungsleistungen*. Schriftenreihe 'Kybernetik'. München, Wien: R. Oldenbourg Verlag.

Wallraff, H. G. 1978. Preferred compass direction in initial orientation of homing pigeons. In: *Avian Migration, Navigation, and Homing* (Ed. by K. Schmidt-Koenig & W. T. Keeton), pp. 171–183. Berlin: Springer Verlag.

Wallraff, H. G. 1980. Does pigeon homing depend on stimuli perceived during displacement? I. Experiments in Germany. *Journal of Comparative Physiology*, **139**, 193–201.

Wallraff, H. G. 1986. Directional components derived from initial-orientation data of inexperienced homing pigeons. *Journal of Comparative Physiology*, **159**, 143–159.

Wallraff, H. G. 1999. The magnetic map of homing pigeons: an evergreen phantom. *Journal of Theoretical Biology*, **197**, 265–269.

Wallraff, H. G. 2001. Navigation by homing pigeons: updated perspectives. *Ethology, Ecology and Evolution*, **13**, 1–48.

Wallraff, H. G., Chappell, J. & Guilford, T. 1999. The roles of the sun and the landscape in pigeon homing. *Journal of Experimental Biology*, **202**, 2121–2126.

Wallraff, H. G., Foà, A. & Ioalè, P. 1980. Does pigeon homing depend on stimuli perceived during displacement? II. Experiments in Italy. *Journal of Comparative Physiology*, **139**, 203–208.

Watson, J. B. 1908. The behavior of noddy and sooty terns. *Papers from the Tortugas Laboratory of the Carnegie Institution of Washington*, **2**, 187–255.

Watson, J. B. & Lashley, K. S. 1915. A historical and experimental study of homing. *Papers from the Department of Marine Biology of the Carnegie Institution of Washington*, **7**, 9–60.

Wehner, R. 1972. Visual orientation performances of desert ants (*Cataglyphis bicolor*) toward astromenotactic directions and horizon landmarks. In: *Animal Orientation and Navigation*. NASA SP-262 (Ed. by S. R. Galler, K. Schmidt-Koenig, G. J. Jacobs & R. E. Belleville), pp. 421–436. Washington, D.C.: U.S. Government Printing Office.

Weindler, P., Böhme, F., Liepa, V. & Wiltschko, W. 1998. The role of daytime cues in the development of magnetic orientation in a night-migrating bird. *Behavioral Ecology and Sociobiology*, **42**, 289–294.

Weindler, P., Wiltschko, R. & Wiltschko, W. 1996. Magnetic information affects the stellar orientation of young bird migrants. *Nature*, **383**, 158–160.

Wiltschko, R. 1992. Das Verhalten verfrachteter Vögel. *Vogelwarte*, **36**, 249–310.

Wiltschko, R. 1993. Pigeon homing: release site biases and their interpretation. In: *Orientation and Navigation: Birds, Humans and other Animals*. Paper 15. Oxford: Royal Institute of Navigation.

Wiltschko, R. 1996. The function of olfactory input in pigeon orientation: does it provide navigational information or play another role? *Journal of Experimental Biology*, **199**, 113–119.

Wiltschko, R., Kumpfmüller, R., Muth, R., & Wiltschko, W. 1994. Pigeon homing: the effect of a clock-shift is often smaller than predicted. *Behavioral Ecology and Sociobiology*, **35**, 63–73.

Wiltschko, R., Nohr, D. & Wiltschko, W. 1981. Pigeons with a deficient sun compass use the magnetic compass. *Science*, **214**, 343–345.

Wiltschko, R., Walker, M. & Wiltschko, W. 2000. Sun-compass orientation in homing pigeons: compensation for different rates of change in azimuth. *Journal of Experimental Biology*, **203**, 889–894.

Wiltschko, R. & Wiltschko, W. 1978. Evidence for the use of magnetic outward-journey information in homing pigeons. *Naturwissenschaften*, **65**, 112.

Wiltschko, R. & Wiltschko, W. 1980. The process of learning sun compass orientation in young homing pigeons. *Naturwissenschaften*, **67**, 512–514.

Wiltschko, R. & Wiltschko, W. 1981. The development of sun compass orientation in young homing pigeons. *Behavioral Ecology and Sociobiology*, **9**, 135–141.

Wiltschko, R. & Wiltschko, W. 1985a. Pigeon homing: change in navigational strategy during ontogeny. *Animal Behaviour*, **33**, 583–590.

Wiltschko, R. & Wiltschko, W. 1985b. Pigeon homing: can release site biases be explained by a 'preferred compass direction'? *Monitore Zoologico Italiano (N.S.)*, **19**, 197–206.

Wiltschko, R. & Wiltschko, W. 1990. Zur Entwicklung des Sonnenkompaß bei jungen Brieftauben. *Journal für Ornithologie*, **131**, 1–20.

Wiltschko, R. & Wiltschko, W. 1995. *Magnetic Orientation in Animals*. Berlin: Springer Verlag.

Wiltschko, R. & Wiltschko, W. 2000. A strategy for beginners! Reply to Wallraff (2000). *Animal Behaviour*, **60**, F37–F43. http://www.academicpress.com/anbehav and http://www.idealibrary.com.

Wiltschko, R. & Wiltschko, W. 2001. Clock-shift experiments with homing pigeons: a compromise between solar and magnetic information? *Behavioral Ecology and Sociobiology*, **49**, 393–400. Doi:10.1007/s002650000313.

Wiltschko, W. 1968. Über den Einflu-2 statischer Magnetfelder auf die Zugorientierung der Rotkehlchen (*Erithacus rubecula*). *Zeitschrift für Tierpsychologie*, **25**, 536–558.

Wiltschko, W., Weindler, P. & Wiltschko, R. 1998. Interaction of magnetic and celestial cues in the migratory orientation of passerines. *Journal of Avian Biology*, **29**, 606–617.

Wiltschko, W., Balda, R. P., Jahnel, M. & Wiltschko, R. 2000. Sun compass orientation in seed-caching corvids: its role in spatial memory. *Animal Cognition*, **2**, 215–221.

Wiltschko, W. & Wiltschko, R. 1982. The role of outward journey information in the orientation of homing pigeons. In: *Avian Navigation* (Ed. by F. Papi & H. G. Wallraff), pp. 239–252. Berlin: Springer Verlag.

Wiltschko, W. & Wiltschko, R. 1998. The navigation system of birds and its development. In: *Animal Cognition in Nature* (Ed. by R. P. Balda, I. M. Pepperberg & A. C. Kamil), pp. 155–199. San Diego: Academic Press.

Wiltschko, W. & Wiltschko, R. 2002. Magnetic compass orientation in birds and its physiological basis. *Naturwissenschaften*, **89**, 445–452. Doi:10.1007/s00114-002-0356-5.

Wiltschko, W., Wiltschko, R., Keeton, W. T. & Maddon, R. 1983. Growing up in an altered magnetic field affects the initial orientation of young homing pigeons. *Behavioral Ecology and Sociobiology*, **12**, 135–142.

Wojtusiak, R. L., Wodzicki, K. & Ferens, B. 1937. Untersuchungen über die Orientation und die Geschwindigkeit des Fluges der Vögel. II. Weitere Untersuchungen an Schwalben: Beeinflussung durch Nachtzeit und Gebirge. *Acta Ornithologica Musei Zoologici Polonici, Werk 2*, **4**, 39–61.

Yeagley, H. L. 1951. A preliminary study of a physical basis of bird navigation. *Journal of Applied Physics*, **18**, 1035–1063.

20

Animal Welfare

Marian Stamp Dawkins
Department of Zoology
University of Oxford

Abstract

For many years, animal welfare had an uneasy relationship with mainstream ethology because talk of suffering, feelings, and mental state was not regarded as scientific. The cognitive revolution, however, together with a reawakening of interest in questions of causation and development, has now brought the two together. Behaviour plays an increasingly important part in the scientific study of animal welfare, from the measurement of animal motivation to the recognition of signs of stress. It is increasingly used by veterinary surgeons to reveal signs of disease that may not be otherwise apparent. Above all, it gives us insight into the animals' "point of view" and enables us to give objective answers to questions about what the animals themselves want or find aversive in what we do to them.

Overview

Animal welfare had a bad start with ethology. Niko Tinbergen (for all the right reasons) was adamantly opposed to using any subjective terms in the explanation of behaviour. "Whether or not one can deduce anything useful about the subjective phenomena going on inside an animal," he wrote in a letter to Julian Huxley in 1965, "here we shall never agree. My conviction remains that our inclination to try and feel and say anything about these things is one of the most serious obstacles to progress."

Animal welfare, on the other hand, is unashamedly about what animals feel (Dawkins 1990; Duncan 1993; Broom 1998). It has two components: an animal's physical health, which can be judged reasonably objectively; and its mental health—whether, for example, it is fearful, bored, frustrated, hungry, thirsty, or satisfied with its lot—which is subjective and much more difficult

to judge. These emotional states may have behavioural or physiological manifestations that allow us to make what we may like to think of as objective,
public assessments of when they are present, but it is the presumed subjective
accompaniments to these outward signs that give animal welfare its problems
with the behavioural sciences. Many people believe that nonhuman animals
do have an inner subjective life in which pain actually hurts, and hunger is
actually experienced as profoundly unpleasant. A science of animal welfare
has, therefore, to do what behaviourists such as Tinbergen (1951) and
Kennedy (1992) have argued it is not scientifically respectable to do. It has
somehow to include the possible subjective experiences of animals within its
remit, while at the same time acknowledging that we can never actually know
what, if anything, they are experiencing. It is important to emphasise what a
dilemma this is for those of us who study animal welfare. Not for us the lux-
ury of being able to put the problems of animal consciousness to one side, as
many other people who study animal behaviour are able to do. Animal consciousness is no intriguing philosophical hobby for us. It's the day job.
Without it, our science is incomplete. With it, it is in danger of not being a
science at all.

As an ex-student of Tinbergen's, I have not totally abandoned my ethological roots. In fact, as I indicated in the second sentence of this chapter, I think
that Tinbergen was absolutely right to say that subjective terms should not be
used as *explanations* of behaviour. To say that an animal hunts for prey
because it is hungry gets us precisely nowhere (Tinbergen 1951). It tells us
nothing about mechanism, although it may confuse us by appearing to do so.
But believing that causal explanations of behaviour should proceed without
reference to subjective experience is quite compatible with the view that the
mechanisms we uncover by objective scientific means may be *accompanied* by
subjective experiences, for reasons that so far elude us. Tinbergen's problem
was with subjective experience being seen to stick its fingers into mechanistic
explanations of behaviour and become part of the causal chain. He thought
it was important to separate the issue of how behaviour is controlled, from
the issue of whether the control mechanisms are or are not accompanied by
subjective experiences, a view more reminiscent of T. H. than Julian Huxley.
T. H. Huxley believed that consciousness was an "epiphenomenon"—something that just happened when certain types of brain processes took place,
rather like, as he put it, a steam whistle on a locomotive, which is definitely
there but has nothing to do with making the train move. Thus, epiphenome-
nalism, or some version of it, allows us to park the problem of animal consciousness in a convenient place rather than banishing it altogether. We don't
have to solve the really difficult problem of how lumps of grey matter can
give rise to subjective experience before we can have a science of animal welfare. We can acknowledge the potential existence and importance of nonhuman consciousness, as well as its profoundly mysterious nature, but at the

same time we can heed the behaviourist warnings about the dangers of using it as a cause of behaviour, provided we exert a little self-discipline in how we "explain" behaviour.

In 1965, 14 years after the warnings given by Tinbergen in *The Study of Instinct* (1951), it looked as though ethology was set to make major contributions to animal welfare. That year saw the publication in the United Kingdom of a government report on the welfare of farm animals, prompted by increasing public concern over what was called "factory farming." Ruth Harrison, who was to animal welfare what Rachel Carson was to conservation, had published a book *Animal Machines* (1964), in which she claimed that modern farming methods were causing suffering in millions of animals. The U.K. government set up a special committee to look into such claims, and the resulting report contained a notable appendix entitled "The Assessment of Pain and Distress in Animals" by W. H. Thorpe of Cambridge University (1965). Thorpe outlined the great importance of understanding the behaviour of animals to assess the extent to which they suffered. Reading his words after 40 years, it is striking that he emphasised not just the contribution that ethology could make at the time, through its existing knowledge of species in their natural environments, but that he also outlined a whole programme of research for what it might do in the future. For example, he argued that an important field of study was going to be to "examine the incidence of those expressive movements that are known to be associated with damaging situations to assess whether animals brought up with a certain degree of deprivation 'suffer' from deprivation and stress in adulthood." He also argued that,

> *Whilst accepting the need for much restriction, we must draw the line at conditions which completely suppress all or nearly all the natural instinctive urges and behaviour patterns characteristic of actions appropriate to the high degree of social organisation as found in ancestral wild species and which have been little, if at all, bred out in the process of domestication.*

Here, surely, was a major role for ethology. Research into natural behaviour patterns, instincts, and the role of early experience in the development of behaviour was the very stuff of ethology. Thorpe was identifying the birth of the scientific study of animal welfare and even beginning to outline its agenda, or so it seemed.

But something else had happened in 1964 than just the publication of Ruth Harrison's book. The world of animal behaviour was about to be shaken to its foundations by a series of papers starting with W. D. Hamilton's (1964) explanation of altruism towards relatives. Ethologists began to call themselves behavioural ecologists and sociobiologists, emphasising one of Tinbergen's four questions (the one about survival value and adaptation) at the expense of all the others. The study of adaptation took a new lease of life with ideas about kin selection and reciprocal altruism, as well as a mathematical framework from game theory. It held out the promise of an evolutionary view of behaviour that was universally applicable just at the time when it was becoming clear that the Grand Theory of the Lorenz-Tinbergen model (Lorenz 1950) was singularly failing to give a universal account of animal motivation (Hinde 1960). How much more attractive (and modern) to be a behavioural ecologist applying mathematical ideas to widespread phenomena about the evolution of behaviour than an old-fashioned ethologist glumly concluding that the control of behaviour might be highly species-specific and much more complex than it seemed at first.

An unfortunate result of this emphasis on adaptation was that the questions of most relevance to animal welfare—those to do with mechanism and development—were being neglected by ethologists just at the time when their importance was beginning to be realised by people outside the field. For example, in assessing how much an animal suffers in a zoo cage or on a farm where it cannot perform many of its natural behaviour patterns, people wanted to know how motivated the animal is to perform the behaviour, and what happens if it is prevented from carrying out a behaviour it is highly motivated to perform—all standard questions in traditional ethology—but suddenly of no interest to the new behavioural ecology. Studies of development, too, were recognised as having a direct impact on animal welfare, because what animals experience when young may influence what they do (and potentially how much they suffer) as adults. The question of whether an animal can miss what it has never had, for example, has important implications for assessing the welfare of adult animals, but mainstream behaviour studies were no longer concerned with such conundrums. Ethology turned its back on the very research areas that were needed to found a true science of animal welfare. Therefore, that task was left to a group of people who came from rather different traditions—largely, agricultural science and veterinary medicine—rather than from a background of animal behaviour.

The ideal, of course, would have been an interdisciplinary mix of the practical experience of vets and farmers with the diverse contributions from agricultural and behavioural sciences, but as it turned out, "applied ethology" soon began to diverge from "pure" ethology, with its own conferences, its own journals (the first issue of *Applied Animal Ethology,* now *Applied Animal Behavior Science* appeared in 1974), and, more seriously, its own terminology and research agenda. Many people who called themselves applied ethologists were unfamiliar with (or at least unconvinced by) Hinde's (1960) swingeing criticisms of drive and energy models. They continued to use Lorenz's psychohydraulic model (1950) as an explanation for behaviour long after "pure" ethology had abandoned it in fright (e.g., Vestergaard 1980; Sambraus 1984; Vestergaard *et al.* 1999). Terms such as "ethological needs" (Fölsch 1980) were common currency and indeed still appear in European legislation on animal welfare to this day. But to describe animals as having "needs" to do a behaviour, or to rely on a model that says that drive to do all behaviour builds up if the animal cannot perform it, immediately implies that there will be drastic consequences if an animal is deprived of the means to carry out its entire ethogram. It is then a short step to saying that animals suffer if they cannot perform all of their natural behaviour patterns, a view that has been taken up widely outside ethology. The Farm Animal Welfare Council (1992), for example, said that all animals should be given the "freedom to carry out most natural patterns of behaviour."

My point is not that this is wrong. It may well be right. My point is that whether there are drastic consequences of an animal's being prevented from doing a specific behaviour should be a matter of empirical investigation that may have different results depending on the exact species, the exact behaviour, and the exact circumstances. It should not be left to intuition and anthropomorphism or to an outdated and far-from-general model of the causation of behaviour to define when animals are suffering. And the reason why we are still in this position of ignorance, rather than being able to base our decisions on empirical evidence, is precisely because the ethological tradition of trying to understand motivation from behaviour that flourished in the early 1960s (e.g., Rowell 1961; Sevenster 1961; Nelson 1964; Heiligenberg 1965) was discontinued when sociobiology came along and the questions about causal mechanisms of behaviour that could have given an empirical base to applied ethology were left unanswered (Dawkins 1989).

Of course, there were some notable exceptions, ethologists who managed to keep a foot in both pure and applied ethology (David Wood-Gush, Ian Duncan, Klaus Vestergaard, Jerry Hogan and Glen Mcbride, amongst others), but the split was there and ethology's new passion for sociobiology left a yawning gap where the study of mechanism and development had once been. Fortunately, there were new areas of behavioural studies that bridged the gap and not only kept the split from widening too far, but also indirectly gave animal welfare and the questions it was asking the respectability that behaviourism had always tried to deny it. One of those bridges was cognitive ethology.

Donald Griffin's book *The Question of Animal Awareness* was published in 1976. (For those of us lucky enough to hear him speak at the 1975 International Ethological Conference in Parma, Italy, liberation came a year earlier.) Griffin argued with great force that the previous reluctance of the scientific community to address the issue of the subjective experiences of animals was old-fashioned, short-sighted, and unnecessary. He argued that thought and feeling were biological phenomena, and that there was increasing evidence that should be acknowledged for highly developed cognitive abilities in animals. Griffin, coming as he did from the "hard" end of ethology (bat echolocation and bird navigation) could not be accused of woolly or undisciplined thinking. His standing within the biological sciences ensured that animal consciousness was here to stay as a scientific subject. Although cognitive ethology was primarily concerned with animal thought rather than with animal emotions, Griffin broke a barrier, a taboo. Clever, thinking animals demand our respect and make people more likely to treat them well. And if it was now scientifically respectable to talk about animal thought and animal awareness, this surely opened the door to the scientific study of animal emotions too. Animal cognition, therefore, directly feeds in to animal welfare, and the more information we have about the inner lives of animals—their thinking and feeling—the more likely we are to be able to assess their ability to suffer.

So, 40 years on from Thorpe's vision of an ethology of animal welfare, where does the science of animal welfare stand, and what role does behaviour play in it? What follows is a highly personal (and inevitably biased) view of animal welfare science, which is now one of the most comprehensive and interdisciplinary of all the biological sciences: it uses techniques and ideas from veterinary medicine, physiology, biochemistry, genetics, psychology, economics, and other disciplines, as well as animal behaviour. It is particularly concerned with questions about mechanism and development, but also asks questions about adaptation and the evolutionary significance of behaviour because domestic animals have a legacy from their evolutionary past that often intrudes into the lives we force them to lead now. In other words, the multiquestion approach of traditional ethology is alive and well in animal welfare (Duncan 1995), possibly more alive and in better shape than in other parts of biology.

The first question that most people ask about animal welfare is "What *is* animal welfare?" quickly followed by a supplementary, "And how on earth do you measure it?" There must be about as many different answers to these questions as there are people who have thought about them, but there is a consensus on one thing: there is no single measure of welfare (Dawkins 1980; Mason & Mendl 1993; Broom & Johnson 1993). Desirable though it might be, there is no such thing as the equivalent of a litmus test—something that goes red if an animal's welfare is poor and blue if it is good. We have to take a variety of measures, including the animal's disease state; physiologic measures, such as levels of corticosteroid hormones; and, of course, its behaviour. The division of opinion comes when we start to try to put all these different measures together to form a picture of how we might assess and then improve an animal's welfare. For example, laying hens show by their behaviour that they prefer an enriched environment with litter to scratch in to one that is just a bare wire floor, but their corticosteroid levels (often taken to measure "stress") are actually higher in birds given access to the preferred environment (Dawkins *et al.* 2004a). Increased levels of corticosteroids are also associated with experiences that humans find pleasurable, such as sex and the anticipation of food (Toates 1995), and are therefore difficult to interpret in welfare terms (Barnett & Hemsworth 1990; Rushen 1991). Deer that have been chased by dogs show a number of physiological differences from deer that have been shot by rifles, including higher levels of serum creatine kinase, aspartate aminotransferase, lactate dehydrogenase, plasma glucose, lactate, sodium, cortisol, and endorphins (Bateson & Bradshaw 1997). Although this clearly shows that there are differences between deer that have been running and those that have not, it is more difficult to interpret these differences in welfare terms because they may be primarily the physiological consequences of exercise. The problem is that many of the physiological indicators of "welfare" currently in use are in fact autonomic responses that indicate activity or arousal rather than being specific to poor welfare, and many vary naturally with time of day, temperature, or breeding condition.

Behavioural measures of welfare also run into problems of interpretation if taken in isolation. An increase in activity or in a specific behaviour in one environment over another could either mean that the animal's welfare is improved (more exercise), or reduced (it's trying to escape). Even the classic comparison with wild or free-ranging animals has its problems. Many wild animals spend considerable periods of time fleeing from predators or hiding from them in a state of fear, but it does not follow that their welfare in captivity is reduced because they show much less antipredator behaviour. Stereotypies are repetitive, invariant behaviours with no obvious goal or function (Mason 1991; Lawrence & Rushen 1993) and have been used as behavioural indicators of reduced welfare (Broom & Johnson 1993). Where actual physical injury results, as in repetitive bar-biting when a sow rubs her mouth on the bars of her crate repeatedly so that her mouth bleeds, then it is clear that welfare is reduced, but other stereotypies are much more difficult to interpret in welfare terms. Some repeated behaviours may even be beneficial to the animal doing them (Mason & Latham 2004). For example, non-nutritive sucking in calves (repeatedly sucking on an empty teat) has been found to have beneficial effects on digestion (de Passillé et al. 1993). And it's also something we encourage our own children to do to calm them down!

Far from having too few measures of animal welfare, then, our problem is that there are now so many—biochemical, physiological, and behavioural— and they often give contradictory answers or at least are often poorly correlated with each other.

What we need is a framework for encompassing all the different measures of welfare we now have available and resolving some of the problems of linking them up together. In my (very personal) view, the most serviceable and practical framework can be constructed out of just two sturdy pillars. These are what makes animals healthy and what animals want, or, to put it more succinctly, animal welfare is about physical health and mental health. As this probably sounds over-simplistic and even trite, I will now expand.

Physical health is the cornerstone, the basement, the first floor, the primary pillar of animal welfare. Injury, disease, and deformity are major sources of poor welfare and conditions that compromise animal health or that put them at high risk of dying, or both, are uncontroversially bad for animal welfare. That is why animal welfare science needs strong links with veterinary science, with immunology, with epidemiology, and other animal health disciplines. Good health is not contentious as a requirement for good animal welfare, but neither is it sufficient. Good welfare, for scientists and lay people alike, is more than just not dying of injury or disease. That is why we need to take into account the mental health of animals as well.

Mental health is the second pillar of animal welfare, the one that makes the study of animal welfare so difficult and so challenging. To say that an animal is mentally healthy implies that it is "content" with its life and that it is neither desperately trying to escape from something, nor desperately searching for something it does not have. Poor mental health or suffering occur when the animal is in a negative emotional state such as fear, frustration, extreme hunger, or thirst, or pain (Dawkins 1990). In fact, we use the single word "suffering" to cover a huge range of these negative emotional states, so it is hardly surprising that there is no single measure of poor welfare. The outward and visible signs we ourselves might show if we were suffering from thirst, for example, are quite different (as would the experience) from those we would show if we were suffering from loneliness or bereavement. Rather than dwell on how different the various sorts of suffering are, we need to ask what all these different states of suffering have in common, and the answer is surprisingly simple. They are all states that are unpleasant, often extremely so, and ones that we would rather not be in if we could get out of them. If we are hungry, what we want is to modify our negative emotional state by finding food. If we are frustrated, what we want is to get at something we cannot have, and so on. What we want or don't want is the key to whether we are in a positive or a negative emotional state (Cabanac 1992). By using only a small analogy with humans of what other animals want or don't want could also be the key to their emotional states.

There are three major advantages of expressing absence of suffering (presence of good mental health) in terms of whether animals have what they want. First, as I will discuss more fully later, we now have well-established ways of effectively asking animals whether they have what they want through choice tests, operant conditioning, consumer demand approaches, and so on. Second, even people who know very little about animals can readily understand what it means to say that an animal has what it wants. It fits in with what they already mean by "good welfare" and makes what animal welfare scientists do readily accessible and comprehensible to people outside the field. Third, it enables us to make sense of all the other measures of animal welfare in terms of whether they are associated with positive or negative emotional states. As we have seen, many of the physiological measures of "welfare," such as increased heart rate, are in fact autonomic responses indicating little more than that the animal is aroused or activated. A predator in a positive state of chasing its prey and the prey in a fearful state of running away from the predator will probably both have similar elevations of heart rate, adrenaline, body temperature, and so on. In humans, autonomic responses are a very unreliable guide to what people say they are feeling (Wagner 1989; Cacioppo *et al.* 1993; Oatley & Jenkins 1996) and it is difficult to distinguish from autonomic responses alone whether someone is aroused and angry or aroused and ecstatic. A favourite example of mine is the physiological state of two people who have just been on a roller-coaster ride at a fun fair. Both have been scared. Both have screamed and both have shown white knuckles and racing hearts. But one of them thought it was great fun and can't wait to do it again, whereas the other thought it was awful and vowed that was the last time they ever went through such an experience. A physiologist (without access to the state of their brains) might be hard pressed to tell the difference, but someone interested in behaviour could simply note whether they did or did not repeat the experience. Therefore, understanding what is positively and negatively reinforcing to people and other animals is to tap into the fundamental mechanisms of the way their brains work and tells us whether they are in positive or negative emotional states (Rolls 1999). One day, we may have a window into the physiology of emotional states of animals through brain scans (Bekoff & Sherman 2004) and other means of tapping into brain activity, but in the meantime, the best indicator we have for whether their emotions are pleasant or unpleasant (which is the essence of good welfare) is looking at what animals want and how much they want it.

Of course, what is best for animal health and what the animals themselves want may not always give the same answer (Dawkins 1990), because animals (like people) do not always choose what is best for them. But just as decisions about human health have to balance, say, our liking for too much fat and sugar against what is best for our health in the long run, so do decisions about animal welfare have to balance what the animals *tell* us they want against what *we know* is best for their health. In both the assessment of animal health and the assessment of what the animals want, knowledge of the animal's behaviour is increasingly recognised as crucial.

More and more veterinary surgeons have now realised that how an animal behaves can be extremely useful in diagnosing disease, both as a clinical symptom in its own right and also as giving early warning signs of health problems, before other symptoms become apparent. A good example of the use of behaviour in health assessment is the use of gait scoring or walking ability in broiler chickens (Kestin *et al.* 1992; Garner *et al.* 2002). The causes and pathological symptoms of lameness in broiler chickens are very varied (Bradshaw *et al.* 2002), but the welfare issue is whether the birds find it difficult to walk. Observing individual birds and scoring how well they can walk on a six-point score is a much easier way of assessing the leg health of large numbers of birds than screening them for the details of their leg pathology. The disturbances of normal walking behaviour correlate well with leg health and biomechanical damage (Corr *et al.* 1998) but are much easier to assess quickly and in large numbers on farms. Furthermore, the degree of lameness as assessed on this behavioural score correlates with self-selection of a pain-relieving drug. Danbury *et al.* (2000) showed that broiler chickens assessed as lame behaviourally would learn to choose coloured food containing Carprofen, which is a nonsteroidal anti-inflammatory drug, whereas healthy birds with good walking scores did not show such a preference. The behaviour here is helping diagnosis leg problems and providing evidence that the birds want pain relief.

And it is here—finding out what animals want—where behaviour really comes in to its own. We now have a range of techniques for finding out not just what animals want, but how much they want it. Laboratory rats, for example, do not just choose to be with other rats when given the choice, they will work hard (press a lever many times) to gain access to companion rats, much harder, in fact, than they will work to gain access to a larger cage or a cage with novel objects (Patterson-Kane *et al.* 2002). Mink (*Mustela vison*) will push very heavy doors to gain access to water they can swim in (Mason *et al.* 2001), and the rise in urinary cortisol that occurs when they are locked out of their swimming bath is only slightly lower than that which occurs when they are locked out of their food compartment. The application of consumer demand theory to animal choice experiments enables us to ask not only what they want, but how much they want it. Behavioural studies have asked what happens when animals are forced to pay an increasing price (such as increasing number of key presses or increasing physical barriers) to get what they want (e.g., Arey 1992; McAdie *et al.* 1993; Mathews & Ladewig 1994; Cooper & Appleby 1996; Gunnarsson *et al.* 2000; Olsson *et al.* 2002). Such quantitative assessments of the relative prices that animals will pay for different commodities gives us a measure of what matters to them that has immediate appeal for both scientists and lay people alike.

An illustration of the power of a relatively simple behavioural experiment to indicate what an animal wants (or in this case, what it doesn't want) is a study on sheep by Rushen (1986a, b). By all obvious criteria, sheep find being sheared of their wool a cause of at least a temporary reduction in welfare. They struggle and run away if they can. Rushen used an aversion-learning technique to find out the answer to a seemingly impossible question: w*hich* parts of the shearing process did the sheep dislike most? He made sheep run individually down a corridor at the far end of which they were treated in one of three ways: they were allowed to run unhindered back to the flock; they were restrained for a few minutes in a sheep handling machine; or they were put into the machine and subjected to simulated shearing (clippers run backwards and forwards without removing wool). The sheep were subjected to these procedures for seven trials and on each occasion, their speed of running down the corridor was recorded. Sheep that were not handled continued to run down the corridor without hesitation and without needing to be pushed. Sheep that were restrained, however, showed great reluctance and, by the fourth trial, sheep that had experienced both restraint and shearing had to be pushed continuously. Rushen also used the same technique to show that commercial electroimmobilisation of sheep (which reduced struggling) was even more aversive than mechanical restraint, and the reluctance of the sheep to move down the corridor was directly proportional to the amount of current applied. Interestingly, physiological measures such as corticosteroid and b-endorphin levels showed no differential response to shearing, physical restraint, or electroimmobilisation. Behaviour was the more sensitive measure of what the animal did not want to happen again.

Rushen's experiment was carried out in standard farm conditions, so the results are directly applicable to "real" sheep, but it has been pointed out that many other tests of what animals want are less easy to interpret (Fraser & Matthews 1997) because many factors including the animal's developmental history, the precise choices they are offered, and even how stressed they are when making the choice (Mendl 1999) will affect what they choose and what they appear to want. Mink, for example, appear to value resources differently depending on whether they can see what they are working for (Mason & Warburton 2003). Apart from making the obvious point that physiologic and other measures used in the assessment of welfare are as likely, if not even more so, to vary in the face of the same factors, an exciting new research area in animal welfare is the development of what can be called *in situ* measures of what animals want. These are measures that can be applied *in the place* where there is concern for their welfare such as on commercial farms or in zoos. By discovering as nonintrusively and noninvasively as we can what a commercially farmed chicken or cow wants or does not want in the environment in which it is normally kept, we ensure that it has the commercially relevant developmental history, the commercially relevant experience, and can be offered choices that a commercial farmer is able to offer. All of these factors may be important, but at least they enable conclusions to be drawn about commercially farmed animals in a way that is often difficult with small-scale studies on animals in research laboratories or in small pens on experimental farms. We may not have the ability to vary all the factors that might affect what animals want, but at least we can focus our research on the settings of those that affect real farm animals. For example, by looking at the ways animals distribute themselves in space, we can learn a great deal about how close they want to be to each other (Stricklin *et al.* 1979; Keeling & Duncan 1991) and to features in their environments (e.g., Dawkins *et al.* 2003). Consumer demand approaches can be adapted to on-farm choices such as titrating the need to lie down and the need to feed in cattle (Matthews, in press). Weary and Fraser (1995) have come closer than anyone to Thorpe's vision of understanding the distress signals of animals by relating the sounds that piglets make to their degree of food deprivation. Such measures can then be looked for on farms to assess the state of the animals there.

Behavioural studies have made major contributions to the science of animal welfare and are set to increase in importance as new technology (e.g., automatic tracking) becomes available and we can quantify large amounts of behavioural data *in situ*. The view that physiological measurements provide objective hard evidence and behaviour is subjective and difficult to measure has given way to the realisation that physiological measures may often be difficult to interpret and that behaviour—particularly what animals want—can be a means of making sense of them by giving them valence (showing whether the animal is in a positive or negative emotional state). Knowing what animals want is also a way of making sense of the confusing plethora of "welfare" measures now available. We have not solved the issue of whether animals have subjective feelings because choices and preferences, even weighted choices, can be carried out without the necessity for conscious experiences (Dawkins 2001), but they do bring us a little closer. For example, it is difficult (though not impossible) to argue that an animal would learn to choose painkillers if it did not feel real pain.

At the same time, I feel I could look Niko in the eye and say, yes, he was right that we should be cautious about the subjective states of animals, and no, they should not form part of our causal explanations of behaviour, but we now have tools for going a little further than he felt comfortable going in talking about the emotional states of animals. And I would also tell him that, paradoxically, some of the greatest strengths of the growing science of animal welfare are its use of animal behaviour and its powerful roots in the multiquestion, multidisciplinary science of ethology.

References

Arey, D. S. 1992. Straw and food as reinforcers for prepartal sows. *Applied Animal Behaviour Science,* **33,** 217–226.

Barnett, J. L. & Hemsworth, P. H. 1990. The validity of physiological and behavioural measures of animal welfare. *Applied Animal Behaviour Science,* **25,** 177–187.

Bateson, P. & Bradshaw, E. L. 1997. Physiological effects of hunting red deer (*Cervus elephus*). *Proceedings of the Royal Society of London, Series B,* **264,** 1707–1714.

Bekoff, M. & Sherman, P. W. 2004. Reflections on animal selves. *Trends in Ecology & Evolution,* **19**(4), 176–180.

Bradshaw, R. H., Kirkden, R. D. & Broom, D. M. 2002. A review of the aetiology and pathology of leg weakness in broilers in relation to welfare. *Avian and Poultry Biology Reviews,* **13,** 45–103.

Broom, D. M. 1998. Welfare, stress and the evolution of feelings. *Advances in the Study of Behavior,* **27,** 317–403.

Broom, D. M. & Johnson, K. G. 1993. *Stress and Animal Welfare*. London: Chapman & Hall.

Cabanac, M. 1992. Pleasure: the common currency. *Journal of Theoretical Biology,* **155,** 173–200.

Cacioppo, J. T., Klein, D. J., Berntson, G. C. & Hatfield, J. M. 1993. The psychophysiology of emotion In: *Handbook of Emotions* (Ed. by M. Lewis & J. M. Hatfield), pp. 119–142. New York: Guilford,

Cooper, J. J. & Appleby, M. C. 1996. Demand for nest boxes in laying hens. *Behavioural Processes,* **36,** 171–182.

Corr, S. A., Gentle, M. J., McCorquodale, C. C. & Bennett, D. 1998. The effect of morphology on the musculoskeletal system of the modern broiler. *Animal Welfare,* **12,** 145–147.

Danbury, T. C., Weeks, C. A., Chambers, J. P., Waterman-Pearson, A. E. & Kestin, S. C. 2000. Self-selection of the analgesic drug Carprofen by lame broiler chickens. *The Veterinary Record,* **146,** 307–311.

Dawkins, M. S. 1980. *Animal Suffering: the Science of Animal Welfare*. London: Chapman & Hall.

Dawkins, M. S. 1989. The future of ethology: how many legs are we standing on? In: *Perspectives in Ethology, Vol. 8, Whither Ethology?* (Ed. by P. P. G. Bateson & P. H. Klopfer), pp. 47–54. New York: Plenum Press.

Dawkins, M. S. 1990. From an animal's point of view: motivation, fitness and animal welfare. *Behavioral and Brain Sciences,* **13,** 1–9.

Dawkins, M. S. 2001. Who needs consciousness? *Animal Welfare,* **10,** 319–329.

Dawkins, M. S., Edmond, A., Lord, A., Solomon, S. & Bain, M. 2004a. Time course of changes in egg-shell quality, faecal corticosteroids and behaviour as welfare measures in laying hens. *Animal Welfare,* **13,** 321–332.

Dawkins, M. S., Cook, P. A., Whiltingham, M. J., Mansell, K. A. & Harper A. E. 2003. What makes free-range broilers range? In situ measurement of habitat preference. *Animal Behaviour,* **66,** 151–160.

Dawkins, M. S., Donnelly, C. A. & Jones, T. A. 2004a. Chicken welfare is influenced more by housing conditions than by stocking density. *Nature,* **427,** 342–344.

Dawkins, M. S., Donnelly, C. A. & Jones, T. A. 2004b. Chicken welfare is influenced by housing than by stocking density. *Nature,* **427,** 342–344.

De Passillé, A. M. B., Christopherson, R. & Rushen, J. 1993. Non-nutritive sucking by the calf and postprandial secretion of insulin, CCK and gastrin. *Physiology & Behavior,* **54,** 1069–1073.

Duncan, I. J. H. 1993. Welfare is what animals feel. *Journal of Agricultural and Environmental Ethics,* **6,** Suppl 2, 8–14.

Duncan, I. J H. 1995. D. G. M. Wood-Gush Memorial Lecture: an applied ethologist looks at the question "Why?" *Applied Animal Behavior Science,* **44,** 205–217.

Farm Animal Welfare Council. 1992. *Report on the Welfare of Broiler Chickens*. Surbiton, Surrey: Ministry of Agriculture, Fisheries and Food.

Fölsch, D. W. 1980. Essential behavioural needs. In: *The Laying Hen and Its Environment,* (Ed. by R. Moss), pp. 121–132. The Hague: Martinus Nijhoff.

Fraser, D. & Matthews, L. R. 1997. Preference and motivation testing in animal welfare assessment. In: *Animal Welfare* (Ed. by M. C. Appleby & B. O. Hughes), pp. 59–173. Wallingford: CAB International.

Garner, J. P., Falcone, C., Wakenell, P., Martin, M. & Mench, J. A. 2002. Reliability and validity of a modified gait scoring system and its use in assessing tibial dyschondorplasia in broilers. *British Poultry Science,* **43(3),** 355–363.

Griffin, D. R. 1976. *The Question of Animal Awareness: Evolutionary Continuity of Mental Experience*. New York: Rockefeller University Press.

Gunnarsson, S., Matthews, L. R., Foster, T. M. & Temple, W. 2000. The demand of straw and feathers as litter substrates by laying hens. *Applied Animal Behavior Science,* **65,** 321–330.

Hamilton, W. D. 1964. The genetical theory of social behaviour. I, II. *Journal of Theoretical Biology*, **7**, 1–52.

Harrison, R. 1964. *Animal Machines*. London: Vincent Stuart.

Heiligenberg, W. 1965. A quantitative analysis of digging movements and their relationship to aggressive behaviour in cichlids. *Animal Behaviour*, **13**, 163–170.

Hinde, R. A. 1960. Energy models of motivation. **14**, *Symposia of the Society for Experimental Biology*, 199–218.

Keeling, L. J. & Duncan, I. J. H. 1991. Social spacing domestic fowl under semi-natural conditions. The effect of behavioural activity and behavioural transitions. *Applied Animal Behavior Science*, **32**, 205–217.

Kennedy, J. S. 1992. *The New Anthropomorphism*. Cambridge: Cambridge University Press.

Kestin, S. C., Knowles, T. G., Tinch, A. E. & Gregory, N. G. 1992. Prevalence of leg weakness in broiler chickens and its relationship with genotype. *The Veterinary Record*, **131**, 190–194.

Ladewig, J. & Matthews, L. R. 1996. The role of operant conditioning in animal welfare research. *Acta agriculturae Scandinavica. Section A, Animal Science*, **S27**, 64–68.

Lawrence, A. & Rushen, J. 1993. *Stereotypic Animal Behaviour: Fundamentals and Applications to Welfare*. Wallingford: CAB International.

Lorenz, K. 1950. The comparative method in studying innate behaviour patterns. *Symposia of the Society for Experimental Biology*, **4**, 221–268.

Mason, G. 1991. Stereotypies: a critical review. *Animal Behaviour*, **41**, 1015–1037.

Mason, G. & Mendl, M. 1993. Why is there no simple way of measuring animal welfare? *Animal Welfare*, **2**, 301–319.

Mason, G. J., Cooper, J. & Clarebrough, C. 2001. Frustrations of fur-farmed mink. *Nature*, **410**, 35–36.

Mason, G. J. & Latham, N. R. 2004. Can't stop, won't stop: is stereotypy a reliable animal welfare indicator? *Animal Welfare*, **13**, S57–S69.

Mason, G. J. & Warburton, H. 2003. Is out of sight out of mind? The effects of resource cues on motivation in mink, *Mustela vison*. *Animal Behaviour*, **65**, 755–762.

Matthews, L. R. & Ladewig, J. 1994. Environmental requirements of pigs measured by behavioral demand functions. *Animal Behaviour*, **47**, 713–719.

McAdie, T. M., Foster, T. M. & Temple, W. 1993. Concurrent schedules: quantifying the aversiveness of noise. *Journal of the Experimental Analysis of Behavior*, **65**, 37–55.

Mendl, M. 1999. Performing under pressure: stress and cognitive function. *Applied Animal Behavior Science*, **65**, 221–224.

Nelson, K. 1964. The temporal patterning of courtship behaviour in the glandulocaudine fishes (*Ostariophysi Charadae*). *Behaviour*, **24**, 90–146.

Oatley, K. & Jenkins, J. M. 1996. *Understanding Emotions*. Oxford: Blackwell.

Olsson, I. A. S., Keeling, L. J. & McAdie, T. M. 2002. The push-door method for measuring motivation in hens: An adaptation and critical discussion of the method. *Animal Welfare*, **11**(1), 1–10.

Patterson-Kane, E. G., Hunt, M. & Harper, D. 2002. Rats demand social contact. *Animal Welfare*, **11**, 327–332.

Rolls, E. T. 1999. *The Brain and Emotion*. Oxford: Oxford University Press.

Rowell, C. H. F. 1961. Displacement grooming in the chaffinch. *Animal Behaviour*, **9**, 38–63.

Rushen, J. 1986a. Aversion of sheep to electroimmobilization and mechanicam restraint. *Applied Animal Behavior, Science*, **16**, 315–324.

Rushen, J. 1986b. The validity of behavioural measures of aversion: a review. *Applied Animal Behavior Science*, **15**, 315–324.

Rushen, J. 1991. Problems associated with the interpretation of physiological data in the assessment of animal welfare. *Applied Animal Behavior Science*, **28**, 381–386.

Sambraus, H. H. 1984. Accumulation of action-specific energy in the eating behaviour of rabbits. In: *Proceedings of the International Congress on the Applied Ethology of Farm Animals, Kiel* (Ed. by J. Unselm, G. van Putten & K. Zeeb), pp. 335–338. Kuratorium für Technikund Bauwesen in der Landwirtschaft, Darmstadt.

Sevenster, P. 1961. A causal analysis of displacement activity (Fanning in Gasterosteus aculeatus L.). *Behaviour,* **9**, Suppl, 1–170.

Sørensen, D. B., Ladewig, J. Ersbøll, A. K. & Matthews, L. 2004. Using the cross-point of demand functions to assess animal priorities. *Animal Behaviour,* **68**, 949–955.

Stricklin, W. R., Graves, H. B. & Wilson, L. L. 1979. Some theoretical and observational relationships of fixed and protable spacing behavior of animals. *Applied Animal Ethology,* **5**, 201–214.

Tinbergen, N. 1951. *The Study of Instinct.* Oxford: Clarendon Press.

Tinbergen, N. 1963. On aims and methods of ethology. *Zeitschrift für Tierpsychologie,* **20**, 410–433

Thorpe, W. H. 1965. Brambell, F. W. R. (Chairman, 1965) *Report of the Technical Committee to Enquire into the Welfare of Animals Kept under Intensive Livestock Husbandry Systems.* London: Her Majesty's Stationery Office.

Toates, F. 1995. *Stress: Conceptual and Biological Aspects.* New York: Wiley.

Vestergaard, K. 1980. The regulation of dustbathing and other behaviour patterns in the laying hen: a Lorenzian approach. In: *The Laying Hen and Its Environment* (Ed. by R. Moss), pp. 101–113. The Hague: Martinus Nijhoff.

Vestergaard, K. S., Damm, B. L., Abbot, U. K. & Bildsøe, M. 1999. Regulation of dustbathing in feathered and featherless domestic chicks: the Lorenzian model revisisted. *Animal Behaviour,* **58**, 1017–1025.

Wagner, H. 1989. The peripheral physiology and differentiation of emotions. In: *Handbook of Psychophysiology* (Ed. by H. Wagner & A. Mainstead), pp. 78–98. New York: Wiley.

Weary, D. & Fraser, D. 1995. Calling by domestic piglets: reliable signals of need? *Animal Behaviour,* **50**, 1047–1055.

Index